The Blackwell Guide to Mill's *Utilitari*

Blackwell Guides to Great Works

A proper understanding of philosophy requires engagement with the foundational texts that have shaped the development of the discipline and which have an abiding relevance to contemporary discussions. Each volume in this series provides guidance to those coming to the great works of the philosophical canon, whether for the first time or to gain new insight. Comprising specially commissioned contributions from the finest scholars, each book offers a clear and authoritative account of the context, arguments, and impact of the work at hand. Where possible the original text is reproduced alongside the essays.

Published
1. The Blackwell Guide to Plato's *Republic*, edited by Gerasimos Santas
2. The Blackwell Guide to Descartes' *Meditations*, edited by Stephen Gaukroger
3. The Blackwell Guide to Mill's *Utilitarianism*, edited by Henry R. West
4. The Blackwell Guide to Aristotle's *Nicomachean Ethics*, edited by Richard Kraut
5. The Blackwell Guide to Hume's *Treatise*, edited by Saul Traiger

Forthcoming
The Blackwell Guide to Kant's Ethics, edited by Thomas E. Hill, Jr.
The Blackwell Guide to Hegel's *Phenomenology of Spirit*, edited by Kenneth Westphal
The Blackwell Guide to Heidegger's *Being and Time*, edited by Robert Scharff

THE BLACKWELL GUIDE TO

MILL'S
Utilitarianism

EDITED BY HENRY R. WEST

BLACKWELL PUBLISHING
350 Main Street, Malden, MA 02148-5020, USA
9600 Garsington Road, Oxford OX4 2DQ, UK
550 Swanston Street, Carlton, Victoria 3053, Australia

First published 2006 by Blackwell Publishing Ltd

1 2006

Library of Congress Cataloging-in-Publication Data

The Blackwell guide to Mill's *Utilitarianism* / edited by Henry R. West.
p. cm. – (Blackwell guides to great works)
Includes bibliographical references and index.
ISBN-13: 978-1-4051-1948-1 (hardcover : alk. paper)
ISBN-10: 1-4051-1948-9 (hardcover : alk. paper)
ISBN-13: 978-1-4051-1949-8 (pbk. : alk. paper)
ISBN-10: 1-4051-1949-7 (pbk. : alk. paper)   1. Mill, John Stuart, 1806–1873.   Utilitarianism.
2. Utilitarianism.   I. West, Henry R., 1933–   II. Series.

B1603.U873B74 2005
171′.5 – dc22
2005009841

A catalogue record for this title is available from the British Library.

Set in 10 on 13 pt Galliard
by SNP Best-set Typesetter Ltd, Hong Kong
Printed and bound in the United Kingdom
by TJ International, Padstow, Cornwall

The publisher's policy is to use permanent paper from mills that operate a sustainable forestry
policy, and which has been manufactured from pulp processed using acid-free and elementary
chlorine-free practices. Furthermore, the publisher ensures that the text paper and cover board used
have met acceptable environmental accreditation standards.

For further information on
Blackwell Publishing, visit our website:
www.blackwellpublishing.com

Contents

Notes on Contributors

Susan Leigh Anderson is Professor of Philosophy at the University of Connecticut. She is the author of three books in the Wadsworth Philosophers series – *On Mill*, *On Kierkegaard*, and *On Dostoevsky* – and numerous articles on the Self, applied ethics, and nineteenth-century philosophy. Her most recent book, inspired in part by her examination of Mill's attempt to combine the philosophies of Individualism and Collectivism, is titled *Equal Opportunity Individualism: An Interpretation of the American Dream*.

Wendy Donner is Professor of Philosophy at Carleton University, Ottawa, Canada. She is the author of *The Liberal Self: John Stuart Mill's Moral and Political Philosophy* (1991) and of articles and chapters of books on Mill, including "John Stuart Mill's liberal feminism," *Philosophical Studies* (1993), "Mill's Utilitarianism" in *The Cambridge Companion to Mill* (1997), and (with Richard Fumerton) "John Stuart Mill" in *The Blackwell Guide to Modern Philosophers* (2001). She has also written on environmental ethics, feminist ethics, Buddhist ethics, and nationalism.

Alan E. Fuchs is Professor of Philosophy and former chair of the Philosophy Department at the College of William and Mary. He specializes in ethics, social and political philosophy, and the philosophy of law.

Bart Gruzalski is Director of the Pacific Center for Sustainable Living, and before that was Associate Professor of Philosophy at Northeastern University. He is a nationwide lecturer on nonviolence and environmental issues. He has written articles on utilitarianism, medical ethics, environmental ethics, and Asian philosophy. Recent books are *Value Conflicts in Health Care Delivery* (1982), *On the Buddha* (2000), and *On Gandhi* (2001).

Brad Hooker is Professor of Moral Philosophy at the University of Reading, in England. He has written extensively on moral philosophy and especially on rule-utilitarianism. A recent book is *Ideal Code, Real World: A Rule-Consequentialist Theory of Morality* (2000).

Dale E. Miller is Associate Professor of Philosophy at Old Dominion University. He has written several articles on different aspects of Mill's thought, including "Internal sanctions in Mill's moral psychology," *Utilitas* (1998); "John Stuart Mill's civic liberalism," *History of Political Thought* (2000), and "Sympathy versus spontaneity: a tension in Mill's conception of human perfection," *The International Journal of Politics and Ethics* (2003). He has also written on other aspects of utilitarianism of social-political philosophy.

Alastair Norcross is Associate Professor of Philosophy at Rice University. His articles on ethics and applied ethics have appeared in the *Philosophical Review*, the *Journal of Philosophy*, and *Philosophy and Public Affairs*. He is co-editor (with Bonnie Steinbock) of *Killing and Letting Die* (1994).

Gerald J. Postema is Cary C. Boshamer Professor of Philosophy and Professor of Law at the University of North Carolina at Chapel Hill. He is the author of *Bentham and the Common Law Tradition* (1986), and, more recently, the editor of *Jeremy Bentham: Political and Legal Philosophy*, 2 vols. (2002).

William H. Shaw is Professor of Philosophy at San Jose State University, where he was chair of the Philosophy Department for eleven years. In addition to essays in a variety of professional journals, he has edited or co-edited five books and is the author of *Marx's Theory of History* (1978), *Moore on Right and Wrong: The Normative Ethics of G. E. Moore* (1995), *Contemporary Ethics: Taking Account of Utilitarianism* (Blackwell, 1999), *Business Ethics* (5th edn., 2005), and (with Vincent Barry) *Moral Issues in Business* (9th edn., 2004).

John Skorupski is Professor of Moral Philosophy at the University of St Andrews, Scotland. He is the author of *John Stuart Mill* (1989), *English-Language Philosophy 1750–1945* (1993), and the editor of *The Cambridge Companion to John Stuart Mill* (1998). Some of his essays have been published as *Ethical Explorations* (1999).

L. W. Sumner is University Professor in the Department of Philosophy at the University of Toronto. His research interests are in ethical theory, applied ethics, political philosophy, and philosophy of law. He is the author of *Abortion and Moral Theory* (1981), *The Moral Foundation of Rights* (1987), *Welfare, Ethics, and Happiness* (1996), and *The Hateful and the Obscene: Studies in the Limits of Free Expression* (2004).

Henry R. West is Professor of Philosophy at Macalester College. He is the author of *Mill's Utilitarian Ethics* (2004) and (with Joel Feinberg) co-author/editor of *Moral Philosophy: Classic Texts and Contemporary Problems* (1977). He has contributed to philosophical periodicals and written encyclopedia articles including "Utilitarianism," in *Encyclopaedia Britannica*, and "Mill, John Stuart," in *Encyclopedia of Ethics*.

Introduction

John Stuart Mill was the foremost British philosopher of the nineteenth century. His *System of Logic* and his *Principles of Political Economy* established his reputation as a philosopher and an economist, and they were adopted by British universities as authoritative textbooks in those fields. But it is his two shorter essays, *On Liberty* and *Utilitarianism*, that are most widely read today. Utilitarianism continues to be one of the most prominent ethical theories of the twentieth and twenty-first centuries, and Mill's *Utilitarianism* is the classic work defining and defending that theory.

Utilitarianism is the theory that actions, laws, policies, and institutions are to be evaluated by their utility, that is, by the degree to which they have better consequences than alternatives. Such a theory then requires an answer to the question what consequences are good and what are bad. For Mill, the answer is happiness and unhappiness, pleasure and pain. In his words,

> actions are right in proportion as they tend to promote happiness, wrong as they tend to produce the reverse of happiness. By happiness is intended pleasure, and the absence of pain; by unhappiness, pain, and the privation of pleasure. (Mill 1861, reprinted as Part II of this volume, Ch. II, para. 2. Subsequent citations of this work will simply be by roman numeral for chapter, and arabic numeral for paragraph.)

By "pleasure" and "pain" Mill does not mean only "bodily" pleasure and pain. He includes "higher" pleasures such as those "of the intellect, the feelings and imagination, and of the moral sentiments" (II, 4). And there would be corresponding psychological pains, such as boredom, grief, shame, and so on.

Utilitarianism is thus a *hedonistic* theory (from the Greek word for "pleasure"), but its hedonism is to be understood in this broad sense to include all mental or psychological pleasures and pains, not just those of the bodily senses. It is also a specific form of *consequentialism*, in that there might be a theory that evaluated actions, laws, and so on, by their consequences, but included other values as ends beyond pleasure and pain. Some consequentialists regard such things as knowledge, beauty, love, friendship, and justice as values good in themselves and not just from their contribution to pleasure and the avoidance of pain.

In Britain in the nineteenth century, utilitarianism was not just a philosophy. It was also the creed of a political movement, the "philosophical radicals," who published journals and elected members to Parliament. James Mill, John Stuart's father, was one of the leaders of this movement, and the young John Stuart was a participant. They looked back to Jeremy Bentham as the founder of the movement, and we can look back to Bentham as the originator of modern utilitarianism.

John Stuart Mill's life was an interesting one. He was tutored by his father, learning Greek at the age of 3. And he fell in love with Harriet Taylor, a married woman with whom he had a "Platonic" relationship until her husband died and they were able to be married. He was never associated with an academic institution, employed full time, until his retirement, by the East India Company. But he led an active life of writing (his *Collected Works* run to 33 volumes) and he served one term in Parliament, where he introduced, although it was defeated, a bill to give women the right to vote. The details of Mill's life are recounted in this volume by Susan Leigh Anderson in Chapter 1, "Mill's Life." Bentham's philosophy, so far as it relates to Mill's, is summarized in this volume by Gerald J. Postema in Chapter 2, "Bentham's Utilitarianism." In Chapter 3, John Skorupski reports Mill's "naturalistic" epistemology and metaphysics and his "political liberalism" to give some sense of "The Place of *Utilitarianism* in Mill's Philosophy."

Part II of this volume contains the complete text of *Utilitarianism*. There are five chapters, the first of which, entitled "General Remarks," might be regarded as a preface. The second chapter, "What Utilitarianism Is," presents a succinct formulation of the utilitarian "creed" and then attempts to answer objections to it, objections supposedly based on mistaken interpretations of its meaning. Chapter III, "Of the Ultimate Sanction of the Principle of Utility," is a discussion of the sources of motivation for conformity to a morality based on the general happiness. Chapter IV is Mill's presentation "Of What Sort of Proof the Principle of Utility is Susceptible." The final and longest chapter, which Mill had begun writing as a separate essay, is "On the Connection between Justice and Utility." This last chapter is in the form of an answer to another objection to utilitarianism, but in this case the objection could be better described as due to an inadequate and incomplete analysis of the idea and sentiment of justice, rather than a mistaken interpretation of utility. Mill's project in the chapter is to show that, when properly understood, justice is consistent with, subordinate to, and an important branch of utility, rather than opposed to it.

In Chapter I, Mill contrasts his own tradition, which he calls the "inductive," with the "intuitive" school. According to his opponents, we have a natural faculty, or sense or instinct, informing us of right and wrong. According to the inductive school, right and wrong, as well as truth and falsehood, are questions of observation and experience.

In Chapter II, Mill attempts to answer several objections. One is that to suppose that life has no higher end than pleasure is a doctrine worthy only of swine. It is in reply to this objection that Mill argues for pleasures of high "quality": those of the intellect, the feelings and imagination, and moral sentiments. And the procedure for determining what are higher pleasures is to see what pleasures are preferred by those who are competent judges because of their experience of both kinds. In Chapter 4 of this volume, "Mill's Theory of Value," Wendy Donner addresses this distinction between pleasures and pains based on quality as well as quantity, as well as the question of who is a competent judge of the difference. She emphasizes the importance of personal development and self-development in becoming a competent judge.

A second objection is that happiness is unattainable. To this Mill replies that he does not mean a life of rapture, but moments of such, with few and transitory pains, and many and various pleasures. Another objection is that people can do without pleasure and that it is noble to do so. Mill agrees that it is noble when self-sacrifice increases the amount of happiness or decreases the amount of unhappiness in the world, but self-sacrifice is not good in itself. Another objection is that it is expecting too much to require that people always act from the motive of promoting the general happiness. To this Mill replies that utilitarianism is a standard of right and wrong action, but ninety-nine hundredths of our actions can be done from other motives so long as they are in accordance with the utilitarian standard. It is in this context that Mill says:

> In the case of abstinences indeed – of things which people forbear to do, from moral considerations, though the consequences in the particular case might be beneficial – it would be unworthy of an intelligent agent not to be consciously aware that the action is of a class which, if practiced generally, would be generally injurious, and that this is the ground of the obligation to abstain from it. (II, 19)

This passage has been cited to support the claim that Mill is a *rule-utilitarian* rather than an *act-utilitarian*. According to act-utilitarianism, the right act in any situation is that which can be expected to have best consequences in that particular situation. According to rule-utilitarianism, it is necessary to set up a moral code with rules governing some types of situations, and in those situations, one is to act in accordance with the useful rule, not make a case-by-case analysis of consequences. In Chapter 5 of this volume, "Mill's Theory of Morally Correct Action," Alan Fuchs interprets Mill as a rule-utilitarian. On the other hand, in Chapter 8, "Mill's Theory of Rights," L. W. Sumner interprets Mill as an act-utilitarian so far as what acts are objectively right and wrong, but he thinks that Mill advocates an indirect procedure for deciding how to act in many circumstances. Where there is a useful rule in place, one should decide how to act by following the rule, thereby doing the right thing more often than if one tried to decide case by case. As you can see, this is a controversial point in Mill scholarship. In Chapter 5, Fuchs also places Mill's theory of morally correct action within the context of what Mill calls the "Art of Life," which includes other areas of life besides morality.

Some other objections that Mill takes up in Chapter II are: that utilitarianism renders people cold and unsympathizing, to which Mill replies that it need not do so; that it is a godless doctrine, to which Mill replies that if one believes that God desires the happiness of creation, then utilitarianism can be regarded as profoundly religious; that utilitarianism permits expediency to override principle, to which Mill replies that the expedient – in the sense of what is in the interest of the agent or for some temporary purpose but not for the general interest or in the long run – is not what utilitarianism advocates.

Another objection is that there is not time, previous to action, for calculating the effects of choices on general happiness. To this Mill replies that throughout all of human history humans have been learning by experience the tendencies of actions, and these beliefs have come down as the rules of morality for the multitude "and for the philosopher until he has succeeded in finding better" (II, 24).

In Chapter III, Mill is addressing what motives there are to be act in accordance with a utilitarian standard. His claim is that all the motives that now lead people to obey customary morality can lead them to obey utilitarian morality. In Chapter 6 of this volume, "Mill's Theory of Sanctions," Dale E. Miller explores the "external" and "internal" sanctions that enforce moral behavior, especially the role of sympathetic feelings in Mill's philosophy.

In Chapter IV, Mill gives a psychological argument for his theory that happiness and unhappiness are the ends of all conduct and therefore of morality as a part of all conduct. In Chapter 7 of this volume, "Mill's 'Proof' of the Principle of Utility," Henry R. West discusses the validity and soundness of Mill's argument.

Chapter V, the longest of *Utilitarianism*, is a discussion of the objection that justice is independent of utility and often takes precedence over it. Mill recognizes that the subjective mental feeling (which he calls the "sentiment") of justice is different from that which commonly attaches to expediency or the general promotion of happiness. (In Chapter V, Mill uses the term "expediency" differently from the way that he used it in Chapter II, where it means something self-interested or of temporary benefit. In Chapter V, he uses it to refer to general utility in contrast to the more limited demands of duty or justice.) He admits that the sentiment of justice does not arise from the idea of utility. But in the course of the chapter he argues that what is moral in the sentiment does depend upon utility: that justice is a particular kind or branch of general utility and that there is even a utilitarian basis for distinguishing justice from other moral obligations and making its requirement more demanding. After analyzing the concept of justice, Mill concludes that the idea of penal sanction, as the essence of law, is the generating idea of the notion of justice, but it does not distinguish justice from moral obligation in general. To explain the difference between justice and other branches of morality, Mill appeals to the distinction between those duties in which a correlative *right* resides in some person or persons and those moral obligations that do not give birth to any right.

> Justice implies something which it is not only right to do, and wrong not to do, but which some individual person can claim from us as his [or her] moral right. No one has a moral right to our generosity or beneficence, because we are not bound to practice those virtues towards any given individual. (V, 15)

In Chapter 8 of this volume, L. W. Sumner analyzes "Mill's Theory of Rights." When asked why society ought to recognize such rights, Mill says that he can give no other reason than general utility. It is an extraordinarily important and impressive kind of utility that is concerned: that of security – security is something no human being can possibly do without. On it we depend for all immunity from evil and the whole value of every good beyond the passing moment (V, 25).

Having analyzed the concept of justice, Mill argues against the notion that justice is independent of utility by showing that there is great controversy about what policies, in punishment, wages, and taxation, are just and unjust. He says that if justice is something that the mind can recognize by simple introspection, it is hard to understand why that internal oracle is so ambiguous. For instance, some argue against deterrent punishment, saying that it is unjust to punish anyone for the sake of example to others; that punishment is just only when intended for the reform of the criminal. Others maintain the extreme reverse, that to punish persons for their own benefit is unjust, violating their right to choose their own lives, but they may be justly punished to prevent evil to others. And there are conflicting conceptions of the just amount of punishment. Likewise there are conflicting conceptions of just wages and just taxes. Mill says that one cannot settle these disputes by appeal to justice itself. They each have utilitarian arguments in their favor, and appeal to utility is the only way to adjudicate the conflicting claims.

Mill's *Utilitarianism* is a classic source of utilitarian ethical theory, and there have been different interpretations and different criticisms and defenses of the position taken in that work. The chapters in Part III of this volume, "Essays on the Text," are primarily concerned with interpretation and critical discussion of Mill's theory. But utilitarianism as an ethical theory has had a life beyond Mill. In Part IV a few of these controversies are presented. In Chapter 9, "Contemporary Criticisms of Utilitarianism: A Response," William H. Shaw addresses and replies to some of the most prominent criticisms of utilitarianism in the twentieth and twenty-first centuries. In Chapter 10, "The Scalar Approach to Utilitarianism," Alastair Norcross makes the radical suggestion that right and wrong, duty and obligation, are not the most fundamental concepts for a utilitarian ethics. He claims that relatively good and relatively bad consequences give moral reasons for action which are on a scale of better and worse, not a sharp line between right and wrong, wrong and permissible. In contrast, in Chapter 11, "Right, Wrong, and Rule-Consequentialism," Brad Hooker defends a rule-based consequentialist ethics as the one which is most in accord with our considered moral judgments, and he claims that Norcross's scalar approach would not stand up to that test. Finally, utilitarianism has applications to practical ethics. Utilitarian arguments have been made to support mercy-killing and many other difficult decisions in bio-medical ethics; to support animal rights; women's liberation; the preservation of the environment; and positions on many other issues. In Chapter 12, "Some Implications of Utilitarianism for Practical Ethics: The Case Against the Military Response to Terrorism," Bart Gruzalski makes a case study of what consequences could be foreseen before the United States invaded Afghanistan and also before it invaded Iraq as responses to the terrorist attacks upon the World Trade Center and other targets. He considers first the consequences for American interests, a perspective that he calls "chauvinistic consequentialism." Then he considers the consequences from an impartial utilitarian perspective. From either perspective, he thinks that the consequences could be foreseen to be bad.

The chapters of this volume are intended to be understood by the general reader who is not a professional philosopher. Explanation in advance of a few philo-sophical terms may be helpful. *Utility, utilitarianism, hedonism,* and *consequen-tialism* were explained at the beginning of this Introduction. *Act-utilitarianism* and *rule-utilitarianism* have also been defined.

An alternative to utilitarianism or, more generally, to consequentialism, is a *deontological* theory. That would be a theory that has *duty* as the most funda-mental ethical concept. For example, a deontological theory might regard the telling of the truth (or prohibition from lying), the keeping of promises, the helping of others in distress (and prohibition from murder, assault, rape, false imprisonment, or enslavement) as duties in themselves. They do not derive their obligatoriness from good or bad consequences. Sometimes these duties are called *prima facie* duties, which means duties at "first face": they are obligatory if not in conflict with some other duty. In case of conflict between duties, one *prima facie* duty must give way to another and thus is not a duty, all things considered.

Other alternatives to utilitarianism are *virtue ethics* and *rights based ethics.* Virtue ethics makes the virtues – honesty, loyalty, compassion, fairness, and so on – the fundamental concepts of ethics. These are character traits, and actions take their ethical worth from the character traits from which they flow. Utilitarianism recognizes valuable character traits, but, at least in Mill's system, acts can be right or wrong independent of the character traits from which they flow, and character traits are desirable or undesirable according to whether they tend to produce acts with good or bad consequences. Utilitarianism also recognizes rights, but they are not fundamental: they derive their authority from their utility. A rights based ethics makes rights fundamental: they are not based on their utility, although they may have utility.

Another concept that will appear in some of the chapters is that of *supereroga-tion.* An act is supererogatory if it "goes beyond the call of duty." It is praise-worthy, but failure to perform it is not blameworthy. A *maximizing* form of utilitarianism leaves no room for supererogatory acts. It is one's duty to do the best one can. A *satisficing* form of utilitarianism would leave room for supererogation: it would require acts that meet a certain level of good consequences but not require that one make the sacrifices necessary to produce the very best consequences that could be achieved.

The appeal of utilitarianism is that happiness is at least one of the good things in life, desired as an end, not just as a means to other values. The appeal of consequentialism enlarges this to include additional intrinsic values. A second appeal of both is that they provide a foundation for duties, virtues, and rights. If one asks why ought one to do certain kinds of actions, or why one ought to develop certain character traits, or why one ought to respect certain rights, the utilitarian has an answer. A duty, virtue, or right derives its value from its contribution to general happiness. This also provides a basis for critical evaluation of the duties, virtues, and rights that are recognized in a society or that ought to be recognized. John Stuart Mill's *Utilitarianism* is a powerful statement of this utilitarian theory.

References

Mill, John Stuart (1861) *Utilitarianism*, in J. M. Robson (ed.) *Collected Works of John Stuart Mill*, Vol. X: *Essays on Ethics, Religion, and Society* (pp. 203–59). Toronto: University of Toronto Press, 1969. (Reprinted as Part II of this volume; citations are to chapter by roman numeral and to paragraph by arabic numeral.)

Part I
The Background of
Mill's Utilitarianism

Part I

The Background of Mill's *Utilitarianism*

Chapter 1

Mill's Life

Susan Leigh Anderson

John Stuart Mill was born in London on May 20, 1806, the eldest son of James and Harriet Burrow Mill. James Mill (1773–1836) – philosopher, historian, economist, and psychologist – was the most influential person in Mill's life during his formative years. It is, therefore, appropriate to begin the story of John Stuart Mill's life with some background on his father.

James Mill was the son of a Scottish country shoemaker. But his proud mother, who had known better days, was determined that her first-born son should be brought up as a gentleman. With the help of the local minister and Sir John and Lady Jane Stuart of Fettercairn, who were impressed with the young man, James was able to attend Montrose Academy and then sent to study for the ministry at the University of Edinburgh.

At the age of 17, James was hired to tutor Sir John and Lady Jane's only daughter, Wilhelmina, who was then 14. He taught her for four years, at Edinburgh during the school year, where the Stuarts spent their winters, and at Fettercairn during the summers. He fell in love with her; but having an "iron will," he was able to control his feelings. We do not know what Wilhelmina thought of her handsome, young, blue-eyed tutor, but she ended up marrying the son of the banker Sir William Forbes and later inspired a romantic passion in Sir Walter Scott. Some biographers maintain that Wilhelmina was the love of James Mill's life.

While at Edinburgh, James discovered Plato. He would later pass on his tremendous admiration for this philosopher to his son. James also read a number of skeptics – including Rousseau, Voltaire, and Hume – with the result that he ended up not following the profession for which he was trained.

After Edinburgh, James supported himself by tutoring for several years. In 1802, at the age of 29, James Mill left Scotland for London in the company of Sir John Stuart. He soon had a small income from writing for periodicals and editing, and in 1805 he married pretty Harriet Burrow who was about ten years younger than he was and the eldest daughter of a widow who ran a private lunatic asylum. They moved into a small house in Pentonville owned by Mrs Burrow.

John Stuart Mill, named after the squire of Fettercairn, was born the next year. Harriet soon resented the family's modest circumstances; and the impatient, sarcastic James, who perhaps missed the responsive intelligence he had found in Wilhelmina, began treating his wife more and more like a *hausfrau*. Although they produced nine children, there was very little affection in the relationship between James and his wife. Perhaps John picked up on his father's dismissal of his mother as not being very important because, except for one brief indirect reference, her existence is entirely ignored in his *Autobiography*.

James Mill was an extremely disciplined and hard-working man. In the year of his eldest son's birth he began to write a history of British India. He expected the project to take three years and believed it would make his name. In the end it took ten years to write his *History of India*, which became the standard work on the subject. It was published, in three volumes, in 1817 and led to an appointment at the East India Company in 1819, which finally gave him and his family economic security.

Meanwhile, James spent a considerable part of almost every day on the education of his children, especially his eldest son. James had unlimited faith in the power of education, and he particularly stressed the early training of character. Besides perseverance, temperance and self-restraint were two of his most important virtues. He was extremely suspicious of strong emotion, perhaps because of his own romantic failures. Unfortunately, James Mill's control over his feelings affected his relationship with his children, at least the older ones. John received little affection from the father he tried so hard to please. He lived for the rare moments when his father seemed to approve of him.

In 1808 James Mill had met Jeremy Bentham, the patriarch of the English Utilitarians, who was then 60 years old. He became Bentham's "lieutenant," and Bentham did what he could to help the Mill family through the early period of financial difficulty. In 1810 he installed the Mills in a cottage where John Milton had once lived, on the grounds of his own house at no. 2 Queen Square Place; but they found it too dank to stay very long and soon moved to Newington Green. Four years later Bentham tried again. He leased a house, close to his own, at no. 1 Queen Square Place, and sublet it to the Mills for a nominal fee. This was John's home from his eighth to his twenty-fourth years. During the summers, Bentham took the entire family to his country retreats, first to Barrow Green House in the Surrey Hills, and later to Ford Abbey, a wonderful country estate where ornamental Tudor work alternated with Inigo Jones additions. John particularly enjoyed its spacious rooms and the opportunity to take long walks, exploring the rolling hills of rural England. He also liked listening to Bentham play the Abbey organ.

Although not the original thinker that Bentham was, James Mill, through his own personality, drew a small circle of active reformers around them both. This group became known as the "philosophical radicals" for advocating democracy and complete freedom of discussion. These men were the avant-garde of their time, just as the Fabians were seventy-five years later.

James Mill wrote numerous articles that applied Benthamite principles to such subjects as government, education, freedom of the press, colonies, jurisprudence, and prisons. He also wrote several books, the most notable of which, besides his *History of India*, were his *Elements of Political Economy* (1821) and his *Analysis of the Phenomena of the Human Mind* (1829).

Despite all these achievements, James Mill's greatest creation was his own son. As James Mill confided in Bentham, young John Stuart Mill had been selected to be "a successor worthy of both of us." In preparation for filling this role, John was given perhaps the most rigorous and ambitious education that anyone has ever received, an education later described in great detail in his *Autobiography*. At 3 years of age, John was given lessons in Greek and soon began reading in that language, beginning with *Æsop's Fables*. When he was 8, he began studying Latin and added works in that language. His days were taken up with studying and then teaching what he had learned to his younger siblings, which he hated doing, although he admitted later that it helped him to learn how to explain things to others. He had no toys or children's books, except for a few gifts given to him by relatives or acquaintances, most notably a treasured *Robinson Crusoe*. He had no friends to play with; his father limited his contact with other young boys because "he was earnestly bent upon [his] escaping not only the ordinary corrupting influence which boys exercise over boys, but the contagion of vulgar modes of thought and feeling" (Mill 1957: 24), and his only exercise consisted of taking long walks with his father, reciting and discussing what he'd learned that day.

By his twelfth year, in addition to having read the Greek classics, John had learned algebra, geometry, and differential calculus. He had also written a number of "histories" and done some reading on science. At age 12 he began studying logic, beginning with the Latin treatises on scholastic logic. John claimed that the "first intellectual operation in which I arrived at any proficiency, was dissecting a bad argument, and finding in what part the fallacy lay." Later he asserted that the study of logic was a good activity for young philosophy students. He thought they "may become capable of disentangling the intricacies of confused and self-contradictory thought, before their own thinking faculties are much advanced" and that the study of logic would "form exact thinkers, who attach a precise meaning to words and propositions" (1957: 14–15). Demonstrating his firm belief in utilitarian principles, James Mill emphasized the *utility* of the study of logic.

John continued reading in Latin and Greek as well, particularly the orations in those languages, and he also began reading the most important dialogues of Plato. About Plato's influence on both father and son, John said: "There is no author to whom my father thought himself more indebted for his own mental culture, than Plato . . . I can bear similar testimony in regard to myself" (pp. 15–16).

At the age of 13, James Mill gave John a complete course on political economy, giving him lectures which John had to clearly, precisely, and completely summarize, and then having him read Adam Smith as well as a book which had just been published by James's good friend David Ricardo, *Principles of Political Economy and Taxation*.

James Mill seemed to have expected too much from the young boy, for even though John had praise for his excellent education, maintaining that "in the main his method was right, and it succeeded," he complained that his father "was often, and much beyond reason, provoked by my failures in cases where success could not have been expected" (p. 20). Still, John was not very critical of his father on this account, since he was convinced that "a pupil from whom nothing is ever demanded which he cannot do, never does all he can" (p. 22).

At 14, John was invited to spend a year in France with Jeremy Bentham's brother, Sir Samuel, and his family. From this time on, although his studies continued under his father's general direction, there were no longer formal lessons.

Mill concluded, in his *Autobiography*, that as a result of the formal instruction which he received from his father, he started life "with an advantage of a quarter of a century over my contemporaries." However, John did not feel superior to others because of this:

> If I thought anything about myself, it was that I was rather backward in my studies, since I always found myself so, in comparison with what my father expected from me. (p. 23)

Mill believed that "any boy or girl of average capacity and healthy physical constitution" could have accomplished what he had, since he modestly believed he was "rather below than above par" in natural talent. What he thought was best about the education he received was that he was not "crammed with mere facts, and with the opinions or phrases of other people," using this as a substitution for forming opinions of one's own. Instead:

> My father never permitted anything which I learnt to degenerate into a mere exercise of memory. He strove to make the understanding not only go along with every step of the teaching, but, if possible, precede it. Anything which could be found out by thinking I never was told, until I had exhausted my efforts to find it out for myself. (p. 22)

One controversial aspect of John's upbringing was that he was raised without any religious beliefs. Not only did his father find "it impossible to believe that a world so full of evil was the work of an Author combining infinite power with perfect goodness and righteousness," but he looked upon religion "as the greatest enemy of morality." He complained that religion held up as the ideal of perfect goodness a Being who created Hell, that is, a Being:

> who would create the human race with the infallible foreknowledge, and therefore with the intention, that the great majority of them were to be consigned to horrible and everlasting torment. (p. 28)

Not only was this abhorrent, according to James Mill; but as long as people looked to religion for morality, "morality continues to be a matter of blind tradition, with no consistent principle, nor even any consistent feeling, to guide it."

The opinions on the subject of religion which James passed on to his son could have been a problem for young John, since others would have found these sentiments to be offensive. It was only his "limited intercourse with strangers, especially such as were likely to speak to [him] on religion" which prevented him from "being placed in the alternative of avowal [of atheism] or hypocrisy." John Stuart Mill continued, throughout his life, to be disturbed by the automatic connection most people make between the rejection of religion and "bad qualities of either mind or heart." As a result of this prejudice, atheists tend to keep silent about their beliefs. Mill suspected that:

> The world would be astonished if it knew how great a proportion of its brightest ornaments – of those most distinguished even in popular estimation for wisdom and virtue – are complete skeptics in religion . . . (p. 30)

John's year in France was a happy one. He enjoyed his first taste of freedom, "breath[ing] for a whole year, the free and genial atmosphere of Continental life" (p. 38). He spent most of the time continuing his studies, writing detailed accounts of the work he did to his father; but the Benthams insisted that he also learn to fence and ride, neither of which he enjoyed, and to dance, which to his great surprise, he loved. John also learned the French language and read classic French literature, and he spent much time in the company of the Benthams' oldest son George, who introduced him to the joys of plant collecting during their long walks together. This became a lifelong hobby for John.

The Benthams did not stay in one place during this year. John traveled with them from the Chateau of Pompignan to the Pyrenees, where he discovered a passion for the mountains, and then to an estate near Montpellier. John took university courses at the Faculté des Sciences during their six months in Montpellier.

John was particularly impressed with the competent and dignified Lady Bentham, the daughter of a celebrated chemist, who was the undisputed head of the Bentham household. To see the roles reversed from what they were in his own home showed him the potential to be found in women.

John returned to England to find his father just finishing his *Elements of Political Economy*. John was asked to summarize each paragraph, an exercise which Jeremy Bentham did with all of his writings, "to enable the writer more easily to judge of, and improve, the order of the ideas, and the general character of the exposition." Soon after, he began studying the French Revolution which, he recorded in his *Autobiography*, "took an immense hold of my feelings." He also "read Roman law" during the winter of 1821–2 with John Austin, who "had made Bentham's best ideas his own, and added much to them from other sources and from his own mind."

At the beginning of these studies, James gave John, whose entire education had prepared him for the acceptance of the "principle of utility," his first direct taste of Jeremy Bentham's ideas; he had him read Dumont's three-volume exposition and translation of some of Bentham's published and unpublished works, the *Traité de Législation Civile et Pénale*. The reading of this work he later said was "an epoch in my life, one of the turning points in my mental history." In his *Autobiography*, John wrote of the tremendous impact reading the *Traité* had on his life:

> When I laid down the last volume of the *Traité*, I had become a different being . . . I now had opinions; a creed, a doctrine, a philosophy; in one of the best senses of the word, a religion . . . And I had a grand conception laid before me of changes to be effected in the condition of mankind through that doctrine . . . the vista of improvement which [Bentham] did open was sufficiently large and brilliant to light up my life, as well as to give definite shape to my aspirations. (pp. 42–4)

John continued to read what he could of Bentham's work, in addition to advanced work in "analytic psychology," under his father's direction. He read Locke, Helvetius, Hartley, Berkeley, Hume, Reid and others, as well as a book, published under the pseudonym of Richard Beauchamp, titled *Analysis of the Influence of Natural Religion on the Temporal Happiness of Mankind*, which impressed him because it was critical of the usefulness of religious belief.

From the summer of 1822 on, when he wrote his first argumentative essay, John "began to carry on [his] intellectual cultivation by writing still more than by reading" (p. 46). At this point he could only manage to compose a "dry argument." He also conversed more with learned friends of his father's and began to feel "a man among men," rather than "a pupil under teachers."

In the winter of 1822–3, John formed a society composed of young men who accepted Utility "as their standard in ethics and politics." They met every two weeks for a period of three and a half years. John decided to call the group the "Utilitarian Society" and "the term ['Utilitarian'] made its way into the language from this humble source." John acknowledged that he'd taken the term from a novel he'd read:

> I did not invent the word, but found it in one of Galt's novels, the "Annals of the Parish," in which the Scotch clergyman, of whom the book is a supposed autobiography, is represented as warning his parishioners not to leave the Gospel and become utilitarians. With a boy's fondness for a name and a banner I seized on the word . . . (1957: 52)

In May 1823, James Mill obtained a position for John at the East India Company in the office of the Examiner of India Correspondence, initially working immediately under his father as a clerk and finally becoming an Examiner. James chose this occupation for his son because he thought it would allow him time to think and write. It would also give him practical experience in public affairs, which James thought would be of much value to him as a theoretician. The main draw-back of his job was being confined to London, with only a month of vacation time allowed each year. John's trip to France had given him a taste for country living and travel.

In the year he began working for the East India Company, John began writing for newspapers, starting with letters to the editor. Some of these letters, support-ing the publication of all opinions on religion, appeared in the *Morning Chroni-cle*, written under a pseudonym. The *Morning Chronicle*, edited by John Black, increasingly became "a vehicle of the opinions of the Utilitarian radicals." So did the *Westminster Review*, established by Bentham in 1823, which "made the so-called Bentham school in philosophy and politics fill a greater place in the public mind than it had held before, or has ever again held" (Mill 1957: 65). John was the most frequent contributor, eventually having thirteen articles published in the *Review*.

The "Utilitarian radicals" did not entirely agree with one another on their views. John commented, in his *Autobiography*, on a difference of opinion between his father and himself and his friends:

> [H]e maintains that women may consistently with good government, be excluded from the suffrage, because their interest is the same with that of men. From this doc-trine, I, and all those who formed my chosen associates, most positively dissented. (p. 67)

John was convinced that "every reason which exists for giving the suffrage to anybody, demands that it should not be withheld from women." He was pleased that Bentham agreed with him on this important matter.

At this time of his life, John maintained that he had become a Benthamite "reasoning machine." He had inherited his father's and Bentham's suspicion of feelings, the undervaluing of poetry – according to Bentham, "all poetry is misrepresentation" – and imagination in general.

About 1825, Bentham asked John to edit his five-volume work, *Rationale of Judicial Evidence*, which had been written much earlier. It took up his leisure time for about a year, but John thought it well worth doing, since it contained "very fully developed, a great proportion of all [Bentham's] best thoughts" and also:

> [I]t gave a great start to my powers of composition. Everything which I wrote sub-sequently to this editorial employment, was markedly superior to anything that I had written before it. (p. 75)

In addition to his editing assignment and writing for the *Westminster Review*, Mill continued his studies. He learned German and he formed a study group which took up political economy, then syllogistic logic, and finally analytic psychology.

The discussions of logic led to his forming the idea of eventually writing a book on logic. The study group, Mill believed, was very important to his development:

> I have always dated from these conversations my own real inauguration as an original and independent thinker. It was also through them that I acquired, or very much strengthened, a mental habit to which I attribute all that I have ever done, or shall ever do, in speculation; that of never accepting half-solutions of difficulties as complete . . . (pp. 79–80)

From 1825 to 1829, Mill did some public speaking. A debate with the Owenites led to the formation of a debating society, which took up so much of his time that he was relieved when the *Westminster Review* faltered. His last article, in the spring of 1828, concerned the French Revolution, which continued to interest him.

In the autumn of 1826, when he was just 20 years old, Mill fell into a state of depression. Since first reading Bentham in the winter of 1821, he had known what he wanted to do with his life: "to be a reformer of the world" (p. 86). His own happiness was entirely bound up in that goal. But then one day, in a mood when he found himself "unsusceptible to enjoyment or pleasurable excitement":

> In this frame of mind it occurred to me to put the question directly to myself: "Suppose that all your objects in life were realized; that all the changes in institutions and opinions which you are looking forward to, could be completely effected at this very instant: would this be a great joy and happiness to you?" And an irrepressible self-consciousness distinctly answered, "No!" At this my heart sank within me: the whole foundation on which my life was constructed fell down . . . I seemed to have nothing left to live for. (1957: 87)

Months went by and Mill's depression only deepened. He had no one to whom he felt he could turn, no one to whom he felt really close, which was part of the problem. It was clear that his upbringing, which had turned him into a veritable thinking machine, had harmed him by neglecting an important aspect of the human psyche: the emotions. "I now saw," he said later in his *Autobiography*, "that the habit of analysis has a tendency to wear away the feelings" (p. 89). Mill managed to continue with his "usual occupations," doing them "mechanically, by the mere force of habit;" but he didn't think he could go on living in this way for very long. Fortunately, after about six months, "a small ray of light broke in upon [his] gloom" when reading a passage of Marmontel's "Mémoires" reduced him to tears. He realized that feelings were not entirely dead within him, that his situation was "no longer hopeless."

After this experience, he began to find enjoyment again in nature, books, conversations, and public affairs; and, although there were some relapses, he was never again as miserable as he had been. Mill learned two things from what he had gone through. First, to be happy, you must focus on something else. Mill did not give up his conviction that "happiness is the test of all rules of conduct, and the end of life," but he had discovered the *hedonist paradox*, that the only way to find happiness is not to think about it. Second, "the cultivation of the feelings" is as important as the cultivation of other capacities: "The maintenance of a due balance among the faculties, now seemed to me of primary importance" (p. 93).

To put this into practice in his own life, Mill began reading poetry to supplement his long-standing love of music. He discovered Wordsworth, whose love of natural scenery, particularly the mountains, revived feelings already latent in Mill, and he found that the appreciation of the beauty of nature could coexist in a mind which had been scientifically trained:

> The intensest feeling of the beauty of a cloud lighted by the setting sun, is no hindrance to my knowing that the cloud is vapour of water, subject to all the laws of vapours in a state of suspension . . . (1957: 98)

With his awakened interest in poetry, Mill found new friends like the Coleridgeans John Sterling and Frederick Maurice.

It was not only in his realization of the importance of the emotions and a new-found interest in poetry that Mill started to break away, ideologically, from his father. By participating in the Debating Society, which he quit in 1829, Mill had come to realize, while trying to defend Bentham's and his father's views, some of the difficulties with their simplistic theory of government. He now saw that "identity of interest between the governing body and community at large is not . . . the only thing on which good government depends" (p. 102). By now Mill felt "at a great distance" from his father in many respects, but he believed that "no good . . . only pain to both of us" would come from discussing their differences.

Looking for new input, Mill became interested in the St Simonian School in France, particularly the views of Auguste Comte. What struck him about this school, which was at that time only in its earliest stages of speculation, besides "proclaiming the perfect equality of men and women," was the belief in "the natural order of human progress" and "their division of all history into organic periods and critical periods." Mill began to realize that his mission was to assist England, and perhaps the rest of the world as well, in making the transition from a critical period into a new organic period.

Despite his hopeful prognosis and a renewed sense of purpose in his life, Mill had occasional relapses of depression. During one of these, he fretted over determinism, or what was then called the doctrine of "Philosophical Necessity." He was concerned that "[his] character and that of all others had been formed for us by agencies beyond our control, and was wholly out of our own power" (p. 109). Gradually, however, he realized that determinism did not have to be viewed as something negative. Indeed, this doctrine allowed for the possibility that our will could causally affect our behavior, which would give us control over what happened to us, rather than deny us that control. This insight of Mill's, an early attempt at formulating the now popular position known as soft determinism or compatibilism, he eventually published in the chapter "Liberty and Necessity" in the concluding book of his *System of Logic.*

In addition to contributing to several newspapers, Mill wrote five essays – later published as *Essays on Some Unsettled Questions of Political Economy* – in 1830–1. Also in 1831, Mill attempted to state some of his new views on government, inspired in part by the French Revolution, in a series of articles titled *The Spirit of the Age.* Mill thought "the predominance of the aristocratic classes, the noble and the rich, in the English Constitution, an evil worth any struggle to get rid of" (1957: 110). It bothered him that "riches, and the signs of riches, were almost the only things really respected, and the life of the people was mainly devoted to the pursuit of them" (p. 110). He also hoped to convince those in power that "they had more to fear from the poor when uneducated, than when educated" (p. 111). His series impressed Thomas Carlyle enough for him to come out of seclusion in Scotland to meet Mill.

Mill returned again to questions of logic, puzzling over "the great paradox of the discovery of new truths by general reasoning," since he believed that "all reasoning is resolvable into syllogisms, and that in every syllogism the conclusion is actually contained and implied in the premises" (p. 116). He continued to read widely in logic, finding some inspiration in the work of Dugald Stewart. Finally, Mill began to put his own thoughts down on paper.

Meanwhile, by 1830, when he was 25 years old, Mill had met a woman who, he said, was by this time in the process of becoming "the honour and chief blessing of my existence, as well as the source of a great part of all that I attempted to do, or hope to effect hereafter, for human improvement" (p. 119). This woman was Harriet Hardy Taylor who, when they first met, was the 23-year-old wife of John Taylor, a wholesale druggist, and the mother of two children. Generally known as "a beauty and a wit, with an air of natural distinction," she had married her older husband at a very young age. Although she had been raised to think that a respectable marriage and family was all that a woman should aspire to, Harriet had come to discover the drawbacks of her marriage. The sexual part had come as an unpleasant shock to her and she found the role of "a businessman's household ornament" (August 1975: 48) to be unfulfilling. She was "shut out by the social disabilities of women from any adequate exercise of her highest faculties in action on the world without" (ibid.), but Mill had extremely high praise for her abilities and her character.

Not all agreed with Mill's assessment of Harriet Taylor. While Mill "worshipped Mrs. Taylor as an embodiment of all that was excellent in human nature" (L. Stephen 1950: 44), others saw her as "only a spoiled, would be bluestocking" (August 1975: 47). In any case, Harriet Taylor was not only the great love of John Stuart Mill's life, but also became Mill's collaborator on many of his greatest works. He claimed that he "acquired more from her teaching, than from all other sources taken together" (Mill 1957: 122) and that "all my published writings were as much [her] work as mine; her share in them constantly increasing as years advanced" (p. 157).

Harriet Taylor could neither part with her husband, nor forgo Mill's company. The three settled into "a thoroughly respectable version of a *ménage à trois*, with John Taylor conveniently dining out a lot and John Mill calling during specified hours" (August 1975: 48). John and Harriet's relationship was Platonic and her marriage apparently also became so after Helen Taylor's birth in 1831. Mill's family and friends disapproved of his relationship with Harriet, causing Mill to break with many of them as Harriet became the most important person in his life.

In 1834 Mill published abstracts of several of Plato's dialogues, together with introductory remarks, which he had written several years earlier. Also in the same year, he consented to become the editor of a new review, initially called the *London Review*, which was intended to take the place of the *Westminster Review*. This occupied much of his spare time between 1834 and 1840.

Mill's father's health declined during 1835 and he died in June of 1836 of "pulmonary consumption." While Mill acknowledged all that his father had done for him, he admitted that, upon his death, while

> deprived of my father's aid, I was also exempted from the restraints and reticences by which that aid had been purchased . . . I resolved henceforth to give full scope to my own opinions and modes of thought . . . (pp. 132–3).

After a five-year break, Mill resumed work on his *System of Logic* in 1837. He finished it in 1840; and the following year, as he did with each of his books, he rewrote it. During the rewriting of his *System of Logic*, Mill was able to incorporate material from Comte as well as present his ideas in the form of a rebuttal to Whewell's *Philosophy of the Inductive Sciences*, which had just come out.

Mill's *System of Logic* was published in 1843. It was an immediate success, being adopted as a text first at Oxford and then later at Cambridge, but also read by many outside the universities. *System of Logic* was Mill's first attempt at a comprehensive statement of his empiricist and utilitarian views and an attack on "intuitionism." With this book, Mill hoped to demonstrate that an empiricist position could lead to knowledge, and guide social planning and political action, and not just lead to skepticism as Hume had argued.

Harriet Taylor, who suffered from ill health, spent much of each year in the country with her young daughter, only occasionally visiting her husband in London. Mill saw her in both places and their relationship strengthened. In their discussions, they found themselves leaning more towards a socialist economy, while "repudiat[ing] with the greatest energy that tyranny of society over the individual which most socialist systems are supposed to involve" (p. 148):

> The social problem of the future we considered to be, how to unite the greatest individual liberty of action, with a common ownership in the raw material of the globe, and an equal participation of all in the benefits of combined labour. (Mill 1957: 149)

"Education, habit, and the cultivation of the sentiments" is what they thought was needed to change human beings from egoists into beings who are interested in the common good. They believed it could come about one day, but that the social conditions of their day tended to reinforce selfishness. This view was increasingly incorporated into the *Principles of Political Economy*, completed in 1847, as it went though several editions. Also included was Mill's new belief that a representative form of democracy was better than the pure form. The reading of Alexis de Tocqueville's *Democracy in America* had a hand in convincing him of this. As with his *Logic*, Mill's *Principles of Political Economy* was an immediate success, which he attributed to the fact that it was an applied work, not just theory, and that it treated the subject of political economy as a branch of the larger topic of social philosophy.

Harriet's husband died in July, 1849 and, after a suitable period of mourning, Harriet and John married in April of 1851. Two weeks before the wedding, Mill signed a document renouncing the "odious powers" that English law at that time gave husbands over wives and promising Harriet the freedom to act and dispose of her property, including a half-share in Mill's books. They had but seven and a half married years together; and although Mill claimed in his *Autobiography* that marriage added to "the partnership of thought, feeling, and writing which had long existed, a partnership of our entire existence" (p. 154), it is doubtful that their relationship was ever sexually consummated. Harriet had been an invalid for years and now Mill's own health began to deteriorate. He had his first attack of "the family disease," tuberculosis, which forced him to take a leave of absence from the India House for more than six months, during which time a journey to Italy and Greece helped him to regain his health.

In 1854, Mill began working on a short essay which, the next year, he decided to turn into the book eventually published under the title *On Liberty*. None of his other books was "so carefully composed" or "so sedulously corrected" as this one. In addition to his usual practice of writing it twice, he and Harriet continued to look at it, from time to time, "weighing and criticizing every sentence."

In 1856, Mill was promoted to the rank of Examiner of India Correspondence, second in rank only to the Secretary of the East India Company. He held this position for only two years and then Parliament decided to dissolve the company, despite Mill's fight to prevent it. The closing of the company turned out to be personally beneficial for him, however, since his newfound leisure afforded him more time for his writing and he was granted liberal retirement benefits.

Mill planned to do the final revision of *On Liberty* in France during the winter of 1858–9, the first after his retirement; but tragedy struck when Harriet died of "a sudden attack of pulmonary congestion" in Avignon. Mill bought a cottage as close as possible to the place where Harriet was buried and there he and Helen Taylor, Harriet's daughter, decided to live for most of each year. Mill dedicated the rest of his life to pursuing his and Harriet's common goals.

Mill returned to the task of finishing *On Liberty*, the book which he said "was more directly and literally [his and Harriet's] joint production than anything else which bears my name" and which he correctly anticipated "is likely to survive longer than anything else" he wrote. *On Liberty* was published in 1859 and had "an electrifying effect on the ardent men and women of the younger generation" (Borchand 1957: 128).

After *On Liberty*, the political circumstances of the time inspired Mill to complete and publish a pamphlet which he'd started a number of years before, *Thoughts on Parliamentary Reform*. One of his ideas for reform was to give more votes to those with "proved superiority of education," an idea which "found favor with nobody." Mill next published a selection, which he and Harriet had chosen together, of his minor writings, under the heading *Dissertations and Discussions*. After this, Mill turned to completing two works for publication, *Considerations on Representative Government* and *Utilitarianism*. The latter work was first published in *Fraser's Magazine* and afterwards printed as a book.

Mill also at this time wrote *The Subjection of Women*, at Helen Taylor's suggestion, but he delayed publishing it until "the time when it should seem likely to be most useful." In this work, Mill argued that every Victorian wife was, by law, a slave. Even if most women, in addition to all men, were satisfied with the arrangement, it was not consistent with "utility in the largest sense, grounded on the permanent interests of man as a progressive being," which he had argued, in *On Liberty*, is "the ultimate appeal on all ethical questions." Instead of the existing patriarchal arrangement, Mill advocated a "principle of perfect equality" in the relationship between the sexes. He argued that everyone would benefit from living within households based on equality and friendship, even the children who learn their first lessons about what is just in the home.

By the time Mill had finished *The Subjection of Women* the American Civil War had begun, and Mill believed that it "was destined to be a turning point, for good or evil, of the course of human affairs" (1957: 171). He wrote an essay for *Fraser's Magazine*, titled "The Contest in America," which appeared in January, 1862.

For the next two years Mill worked on *An Examination of Sir William Hamilton's Philosophy*. Hamilton was the leading defender of the philosophy of intuitionism and much admired. Mill felt if reform was ever to be possible, it was extremely important to refute:

> a philosophy which discourages the explanation of feelings and moral facts by circumstances and association, and prefers to treat them as ultimate elements of human nature; a philosophy which is addicted to holding up favourite doctrines as intuitive truths, and deems intuition to be the voice of Nature and of God, speaking with authority higher than that of our reason. (1957: 175)

Mill next decided to "undertake the task of sifting what is good from what is bad in M. Comte's speculations." Since he was responsible, more than anyone else, for making Comte known to English audiences, he thought he had a responsibility to do this. He wrote two essays, published first in the revived *Westminster Review*, and then as a book titled *Auguste Comte and Positivism*.

In 1865, Mill arranged to have cheap editions of some of his most accessible writings published, even though it cost him financially to do so. Also, in that same year, he received a proposal which, if he acted on it, would mark a great change in the purely literary life into which he had settled. He was asked to stand for election to become a member of the House of Commons. It was not the first such opportunity, but he hadn't been able to consider earlier offers, when he was employed at the East India House, since a conflict of interest might have arisen.

Mill had unusual views about candidates running for office. He would only consider running if he did not have to raise funds – which he thought to be "fundamentally wrong, because it amounts to buying his seat" – or use his own money. He further stipulated that if elected he would not spend time on "local interests": and, in answer to questions posed to him, he said frankly that he supported women's suffrage – which is said to have started the women's suffrage movement in England – and that he would not discuss his views on religion. His terms were accepted and he thought that his honesty was much appreciated.

Mill was elected and helped to pass the Reform Bill. There was little time for writing; he only had time during the recesses, but he did publish a few things during this period, including a pamphlet on Ireland and an essay on Plato. In 1868, the Parliament was dissolved and Mill was not re-elected. He was relieved to return to a private life spent mostly in France, near his wife's grave, with occasional visits to London.

The Subjection of Women was published in 1869, during a period of feminist activism following Mill's championing of women's rights while he was a Member of Parliament. The work was highly controversial at the time. The conservative Victorian moralist James Fitzjames Stephen called it "a work from which I dissent from the first sentence to the last"; but Elizabeth Cady Stanton's reaction was to say, "I lay the book down with a peace and joy I never felt before" (Lutz 1940: 171).

Mill died at Avignon, on May 8, 1873, after a sudden attack, "having three days before walked fifteen miles on a botanical excursion" (L. Stephen 1950: 68). His last words were: "You know that I have done my work" (Borchard 1957: 148). He was laid to rest beside Harriet, in the small St Véran Cemetery outside the ancient walled city of Avignon. Mill's *Autobiography*, which he had begun in 1853 and added to over the years, was published a few months after his death.

Summing up his life, Leslie Stephen said:

[Since] he was singularly candid, fair in argument, most willing to recognize merits in others, and a staunch enemy of oppression in every form, we may say that Mill possessed in an almost unsurpassable degree the virtues particularly appropriate to a philosopher . . . he was from his youth upwards devoted to the spread of principles which he held to be essential to human happiness. No philanthropist . . . could labour more energetically and unremittingly for the good of mankind . . . Whatever his limitations, he brought the whole energy of a singularly clear, comprehensive, and candid intellect to bear upon the greatest problems of his time . . . (1950: 69–74)

References

August, Eugene (1975) *John Stuart Mill: A Mind at Large.* New York: Charles Scribner's Sons.

Borchard, Ruth (1957) *John Stuart Mill, the Man.* London: Watts.

Lutz, Alma (1940) *Created Equal: A Biography of Elizabeth Cady Stanton, 1815–1902.* New York: John Day.

Mill, John Stuart (1957) [1873] *Autobiography.* New York: Library of Liberal Arts.

Stephen, James Fitzjames (1995) "Liberty, equality, fraternity," in Andrew Pyle (ed.) *The Subjection of Women, Contemporary Responses to John Stuart Mill.* Bristol: Thoemmes Press.

Stephen, Leslie (1950) *The English Utilitarians.* New York: Peter Smith.

Chapter 2

Bentham's Utilitarianism

Gerald J. Postema

The first encounter of John Stuart Mill (1806–73) with a volume entitled *Traité de Législation* had the intensity of a conversion experience. The book was a French translation of some of the most important early work of Jeremy Bentham (1748–1832), elaborating ideas first announced in his *Introduction to the Principles of Morals and Legislation* (1789). It was all the rage on the European Continent when Mill, a precocious 15-year-old, read it in London in 1821. Later, in his *Autobiography*, he wrote of its immediate impact on him.

> When I laid down the [book], I had become a different being. The 'principle of utility' understood as Bentham understood it . . . gave unity to my conceptions of things. I now had opinions; a creed, a doctrine, a philosophy; in one among the best senses of the word, a religion. (Mill 1989: 68)

The ideas contained in the text were not entirely new to the young Mill. His whole education up to this point at the feet of his domineering and humorless father had been "a course in Benthamism." James Mill, once a struggling itinerant preacher in Scotland, but by then a successful civil servant in the British East India Company, had met Bentham two years after John Stuart was born and soon had become a close associate, even disciple, of the eccentric and reclusive political philosopher and social critic. The Mills spent much time with Bentham, sharing holidays and even for a time living in a cottage that he owned and later in a house next door to him that he leased, in Queen's Square Place, London. Despite his indoctrination into Benthamism, the pages from *Traité* burst upon the young Mill "with all the force of novelty" (1989: 67).

In the *Introduction*, Bentham had outlined a bold new public philosophy that had caught the attention of the Earl of Shelburne, Secretary of State of Britain for a time in the 1760s and thereafter a powerful leader of the Whig opposition. While visiting the Earl's Wiltshire country estate, in 1791, two years after the publication of his *Introduction*, Bentham recorded a dream:

I dreamt t'other night that I was the founder of a sect . . . It was called the sect of *utilitarians* . . . [Later] as I was musing over [a] book there came to me a great man named Ld S and he said unto me what shall I do to save the nation? I said unto him – take up my book & follow me. (Bentham, n.d.)

Always a militant secularist, Bentham nevertheless thought of his utilitarian philosophy as a creed, not merely as a set of abstract theses and arguments. His blueprint to "rear the fabric of felicity by the hands of reason and of law" (1996: 11) called for a life commitment and he gladly devoted heart and mind to the cause. Forty years later the young Mill would embrace the same creed. Not long after reading the *Traité*, Mill drew together a group of young intellectuals into a debating society, a cadre for radical social reform, which he called "the Utilitarian Society." Bentham's dream had come true.

Since the 1770s, inspired by the principle of utility, Bentham worked tirelessly for fundamental legal, social, political, and ecclesiastical reforms. He wrote and published complex and detailed constitutional codes for Britain and many other countries, and he argued forcefully for representative government, universal suffrage (including women's), free markets, sexual liberation, decriminalization of sodomy, poor relief, prison reform, the abolition of capital punishment, and a host of other reforms. In the young Mill, his godson, Bentham found a worthy intellectual heir to carry on the tradition.

However, the fate of the utilitarian movement darkened in 1826, when the 20-year-old Mill plunged into a deep depression. Mill was overcome with apathy, utterly indifferent to the utilitarian program that, just a few months earlier, had driven his prodigious effort to edit Bentham's monumental *Rationale of Judicial Evidence* (Bentham 1838–43, vols. VI and VII). Bentham's vision of a human utopia suddenly appeared to him empty and lifeless, a condition barely human. It inspired nothing but a kind of loathing. Mill's "crisis" surely had complex psychological causes, but he experienced it as a deep crisis of faith, the loosening of the very moorings that had given his life structure and purpose.

Eventually Mill emerged from this depression with his commitment to the utilitarian project intact, but his understanding of it had subtly yet substantially changed. Mill was no mere disciple of Bentham. The utilitarian banner he carried into the second half of the nineteenth century was not a strictly Benthamite one, and the utilitarian doctrine that gained influence in the twentieth century moved even further from that of its founder. This may have been due in part to Mill's break with certain aspects of Bentham's creed, perhaps also to the increasing influence of economic thinking after Mill on the formulation of basic utilitarian ideas. But it was equally due to Bentham's own eccentricities, especially his inability to settle some of the most fundamental aspects of his doctrine and his reluctance to see his writing, the amount and scope of which is simply staggering, all the way to publication. Nevertheless, Mill's utilitarianism cannot fully be understood without a grasp of Bentham's path-breaking work. This chapter is focused exclusively on Bentham's special brand of utilitarianism. It will leave to others the task of tracing its influence on Mill and subsequent converts to the faith. The story told here is the story of a vision that nearly died with the old man.

Is and Ought

The principle of utility – or, as he later preferred to call it, the "greatest happiness principle" (1996: 11 n. a) – was the fundamental axiom of Bentham's moral and political philosophy. This "ruler and decider of all things" was to function as an evaluative principle and as a decision principle. As an *evaluative principle,* it set out the ultimate grounds of the rightness of action and offered the ultimate court of appeal for moral and political disputes. As a *decision principle,* it was meant to guide the deliberations and decisions of all moral agents, and yet Bentham's work focused almost exclusively on matters of public and institutional, rather than inter-personal, morality. This greatly shaped his understanding of the principle of utility. Bentham articulated a *public philosophy,* addressed primarily to legislators and con-stitution makers concerned with the design and construction of social, economic, and political institutions. Late in his life, he wrote a book addressed to matters of private, interpersonal morality. He entitled it *Deontology* (Bentham 1983) – a term he, the father of modern utilitarianism, invented! But even this book approaches morality in the spirit of his public philosophy, focusing largely on informal ways of getting people to do the right thing according to the utilitarian principle (Postema 2002: xxiii–xxiv; Dinwiddy 2004: 134–54).

Bentham's understanding of morality was born of two fundamental insights. The first he borrowed from Hume and never thought to question: that promot-ing the overall good of the community is the basic aim of morality. We might call this *universal consequentialism,* since the rightness of actions is said to be strictly a function of their consequences for everyone. His second insight was that plea-sure and pain alone are good or bad in themselves (1996: 88–9, 100). "*Good,*" Bentham wrote, just is "pleasure or exemption from pain: or a cause or instru-ment of either" and evil "is pain or loss of pleasure; or a cause or instrument of either" (1998: 256); and *moral good* is a matter of pleasure and pain *impartially considered,* insofar as they tend to be produced by *voluntary human action* (1989: 235, 1983: 89). (Bentham never questioned the ultimate intrinsic value of plea-sure, but we will see later that the role of pleasure and pain in his moral theory was more complex than this initial formulation suggests.) Joining this *impartial hedonism* with *universal consequentialism* yields the view that what moral agents *ought* to do, or what is *right* for them to do, is that which promotes the overall happiness of people impartially considered (1996: 11–13). To this Bentham adds that only when words such as "good," "evil," "right," and "wrong" are understood in this way do they "have a meaning," otherwise "they have none" (1996: 13, 1983: 89).

This is a very rough formulation of his principle and we shall see that Bentham refined it a good deal. But for a very long time critics have argued that we do not have to consider the view any further, because we can see already that it rests on an elemental confusion. To *define* "good" in terms of pleasure, and "moral ought" in terms of the tendencies of voluntary actions to promote it generally, they argue, is to confuse *value* with *fact* and *ought* with *is* – a confusion that Hume clearly identified forty years before Bentham began to write (Moore 1993: 69–72). Bentham's hedonistic utilitarianism, critics argue, rests on a fundamental mistake.

However, this is a trumped-up charge (Harrison 1984: 100–3, 109–10). For one thing, Bentham did not ignore, he *celebrated* Hume's "discovery" of the distinction between *is* and *ought* and relied heavily on it for his criticism of old fashioned natural law theories of morality and law (1838–43, VIII: 128n, 1954, III: 257). Like Hume, he took moral and evaluative judgments to be expressions of sentiment (Harrison 1984: 192–4). Something is good, he claimed, if the idea of it excites in the mind a sentiment of approval of it (Bentham 1989: 244). So, for me to say that Sheila ought to stand by her friend is for me to express my approval of her doing so (1838–43, VIII: 93, 1983: 149). If this is how Bentham understood moral judgments, the critic may ask whether it commits him to the view that moral judgments are merely disguised statements about one's state of mind. (Let's call this the *self-reference* view.) The answer is surely no, since we must distinguish someone's *saying that* one likes, hates, approves, or detests something and one's *expressing* that sentiment. Suppose I sincerely utter the sentence, "The moon is made of green cheese." What I have *stated* or *said* is something about the moon, not about what I believe, but what I have *expressed* (sincerely or perhaps insincerely) is my belief that the moon is cheesy. The critic, undeterred, may retort that this *expressivist* analysis does not get Bentham out of the wood, since it merely reduces moral judgments to expressions of subjective, arbitrary sentiments. So, Bentham can escape the confusion of is and ought only by denying the objectivity of moral judgments.

It is true that Bentham's grasp of the expressivist analysis of moral judgments was unsure. He found it difficult to give up the idea that, in addition to expressing sentiments or beliefs, our judgments are self-referential (1989: 229–30). But unlike modern subjectivists and some expressivists, Bentham rejected the idea that this feature of moral judgments forces us into moral skepticism. For one thing, he thought the analysis was appropriate for *all* judgments, factual as well as evaluative (1838–43, VIII: 321; Hart 1982: 13, 248–9); so he did not think it provided a basis to single out morality for skepticism, and he found universal skepticism unthinkable. Moreover, he thought the analysis provided him with the starting point for a knock-down argument for his principle of utility.

Public Justification and the Principle of Utility

Like many other eighteenth-century philosophers, Bentham regarded the principle of utility as a constituent of our psychologies – "an act of the mind" – rather than as a normative proposition existing apart from our experience. It is

> a sentiment of approbation . . . which, when applied to an action, approves of its utility, as that quality of it by which the measure of approbation or disapprobation bestowed upon it ought to be governed. (1996: 12 n. b)

Seen in this light, the principle takes as its primary object our sentiments of approval and disapproval. It judges our judgments. Two profound claims are embedded here. First, he implies that our approvings and disapprovings are themselves subject to rational assessment. Our sentiments are *world-directed*; they are about the world beyond them, not merely brute psychological facts. And they can be correct or mistaken, appropriate or inappropriate in light of facts about the world to which they are directed. So, Bentham assumes that meaningful moral judgments do not merely express, or state a fact about, the appraiser's state of mind; they point beyond subjective sentiments to something public and available to others. Second, he maintains that the principle of utility provides the resources for judging these judgments and the sentiments they express; indeed, the principle of utility is the *only* principle that can do this:

> No otherwise than by reference to the *greatest happiness* principle, can such epithets such as *good* and *evil*, or *good* and *bad*, be expressive of any quality in the *act* or other *object* to which they are applied. (1998: 256)

Let's connect this with Bentham's analysis of moral judgments. Moral judgments are expressions of approbation, he held, but not all expressions of approbation qualify as meaningful moral judgments, because moral judgments purport to be more than "mere averment[s] of [one's] own unfounded sentiments . . . what in another person [one] might be apt to call *caprice*" (1996: 14). They claim an authority for themselves that is rooted in reasons independent of the sentiment expressed and independent of the appraiser's *ipse dixit* ("because I said so"). A moral principle is "a standard of right and wrong, with respect to every other man" (ibid.). It must be neither "despotical" (imposing one's idiosyncratic sentiments on everyone else, without permitting them the same privilege) nor "anarchical" (allowing "as many different standards of right and wrong as there are men" (1996: 15)). Moral justification, as Bentham sees it, has an essential *public* dimension: it is justification "by a person addressing himself to the community" (1996: 28 n. d). Thus, reasons in support of moral judgments must be capable of being communicated to and appreciated by others.

Judgments of the utility of actions, and they alone, pass this stringent publicity test, Bentham argues (1996: 32–3). Pleasure and pain, and the actions that tend to produce them, "are the only clear sources of ideas in morals," because they are "matters of experience" for all of us and, hence, "[t]hese ideas may be rendered familiar to all the world" (1838–43, I: 163, 1983: 169). On the basis of this common experience, moral right and wrong can be "made known and demonstrated . . . [made a] matter of account" (1838–43, VI: 238). Bentham concluded that the principle of utility, although it expresses a sentiment of approbation, refers beyond itself to a publicly observable property of actions, namely their utility, and more specifically to the pleasure and pain they produce. This property provides a measure by which the sentiment expressed by moral judgments can be assessed as reasonable or not.

The publicity condition also explains and underwrites the requirement of impartiality at the heart of Bentham's utilitarian principle. Suppose one accepts that considerations of one's own happiness provide one with compelling reasons to act. Could a principle that gives singular weight to considerations of my happiness pass the publicity test? Surely not, Bentham insists, for moral judgments are put forward as binding on all moral agents, and no principle that privileges my point of view could hope to secure the agreement of other moral agents. Public argument in support of moral judgments is possible only if equal importance is given to the point of view of each agent: because the moral point of view is public it must be *impartial*. Viewed impartially, the happiness of one person is no more or less important than the happiness of any other person; so the fundamental moral principle must treat the happiness or interests of each person equally. The only version of a utility principle that fulfills this requirement, Bentham argued, is the Greatest Happiness Principle:

> In the eyes of every impartial arbiter, writing in the character of legislator, and having exactly the same regard for the happiness of every member of the community in question as for that of every other, the greatest happiness of the greatest number of the members of that same community can not but be recognized in the character of the right and proper, and sole right and proper, end of government. (1989: 235)

Pestilential Nonsense: Rights, Justice, and Utility

In 1792, Bentham was made an honorary citizen of France by its new revolutionary government. This did not dissuade him, however, from excoriating the historic *Declaration of the Rights of Man and of the Citizen* (Waldron 1987: 22–8). He dismissed the idea of *natural rights*, which lay at the center of the revolutionary *Declaration*, as "pestilential nonsense" and the idea of natural and *imprescriptible* rights as "nonsense upon stilts" (Bentham 1987: 53). His famous attack fits a pattern of Benthamic hostility to appeals to justice, natural law, natural rights, and related notions in legal and political discourse. He felt that all such appeals suffered from "*ipse dixitism*." We should not be surprised to find, then, that his critique of rights drew directly on the argument for the publicity of moral judgments that we just considered.

Natural rights are said to be moral rights that exist apart from law and are rooted in the nature of human beings; moreover, they are said to trump the claims of law and of general welfare. This notion of natural rights is either contradictory or empty, Bentham argued. His demonstration presupposes his analysis of the concept of a right. To claim a right, he argued, is to demand that someone do something else for one's benefit or refrain from interfering with one's liberty in some respect. If this claim is to amount to more than the expression of an idle wish, that is, if it is to be taken seriously as a *moral* claim, it must assert the existence of an *obligation* on the other party to provide that service or to refrain from certain actions. This moral judgment is credible, according to Bentham, only if it is underwritten by a public standard that imposes the obligation on the other party and supports it with a credible sanction. Positive law provides such standards, but "natural law" does not, precisely because it cuts itself off from the only possible sources of such public standards. Rights are real when the obligations they imply are sanctioned by positive law, but in the absence of positive law, rights are empty, self-contradictory fictions. A right is "the child of law," Bentham insisted, but "a natural right is a son that never had a father . . . a species of cold heat, a sort of dry moisture, a kind of resplendent darkness" (1987: 73).

Moreover, the idea of imprescriptible rights is practically incoherent and unworkable, in Bentham's view. To recognize Jean's right is to recognize John's correlative obligation, but that obligation restricts John's freedom and frustrates his interests. Doing so may be justified, but only if the competing interests of all the parties are clearly kept in view. Imprescriptible rights, however, focus our attention exclusively on the interests of the lucky person claiming the right, and blind us to the interests of all others.

Bentham's critique of natural rights, like his criticism of justice more generally, is at bottom a critique of the rhetoric of rights and justice. In his view, the problem with these important moral notions is that, in moral and political discourse, they are cut off from the one context in which they could be given rational content, namely, consideration of community happiness or well-being. In less polemical moods, rather than simply rejecting talk of justice and rights, Bentham tended to think of justice as a *species* of overall utility, concerned with certain especially important resources necessary for the protection and promotion of community welfare, for example, security of action and of the means of subsistence and well-being.

Late in his life he jotted down an intriguing idea in his commonplace book. "Justice is beneficence," he wrote,

> in cases in which the non-performance of it is considered as punished, or punishable by the force of one or other of the several sanctions: principally the political, including the legal, and the moral or popular. (1838–43, X: 511)

The idea seems to be that justice and moral rights are among the most important concerns of morality, so important to social welfare in fact that the substantial costs of enforcing them by law can be justified on utilitarian grounds. This is the kernel of the analysis of justice and moral rights which Mill later developed in Chapter V of *Utilitarianism*. Mill may have gotten his idea from Bentham, but it was never more than temporarily entertained by the senior utilitarian. Rather, he consistently maintained that rights are *real* just insofar as they *are actually enforced* by law, not merely that certain goods or opportunities *ought to be* enforced. In *Anarchical Fallacies*, he wrote, "a reason for wishing that a certain right were established, is not that right – want is not supply – hunger is not bread" (1987: 53).

However, Bentham's way of making his peace with the rhetoric of rights and justice, by assimilating them by treating them as species of utility, leaves Bentham's public philosophy vulnerable to a very common criticism. It has often been argued that utilitarianism fails to take rights, or individual persons, seriously (Rawls 1971; Dworkin 1978). The principle of utility, it is argued, requires that we sacrifice the happiness of individual human beings whenever a net increase of community welfare can be achieved. This sacrifice of the individual to the good of the larger community is not prevented by insuring that the good or happiness of all members of the community is considered impartially, it is argued, because good that can be done for the community as a whole, even if the good is only marginal, can utterly dwarf the sacrifice of the few.

Is this a fair criticism of Bentham's utilitarianism? It is, if (1) Bentham understands the welfare of a community at any point in time to be the simple sum of the pleasure enjoyed by its individual members minus the pains they experience, and (2) the greatest happiness principle requires that we maximize the happiness of the community understood in this way. However, there is evidence (although it is not conclusive) that he had a quite different, more complex and subtle, understanding of the utilitarian principle and especially the theory of value at its core. We would do well to take a closer look at Bentham's utilitarian theory of value.

The Calculus of Pleasure

Bentham opens his most widely read work with the following declamation:

> Nature has placed mankind under the governance of two sovereign masters, *pain* and *pleasure*. It is for them alone to point out what we ought to do, as well as to determine what we shall do. On the one hand, the standard of right and wrong, on the other the chain of causes and effects, are fastened to their throne. (1996: 11)

It is not surprising that many generations of readers have inferred from this passage that Bentham was committed to the view that the concept of pleasure (and pain) was fundamental both to his moral philosophy ("the standard of right and wrong") and his theory of human motivation ("chain of cause and effect" binding human action). But it is easy to overlook the fact that Bentham concludes this opening paragraph with the words, "But enough of metaphor and declamation: it is not by such means that moral science is to be improved" (ibid.). Bentham thought his metaphor had its value, but he warned that if taken too seriously it would obscure core features of morality. Bentham challenges us here to look carefully at the role that the concepts of pleasure and pain play in his moral theory.

Why was Bentham tempted to crown pleasure and pain sovereign masters of the moral life? We can answer this question by looking at an intuitive idea that decisively shaped his whole moral outlook. Promoting the good of the community as a whole (universal consequentialism) is the central aim of morality, as Bentham saw it, but the fundamental moral concern is the well-being or welfare of individuals (call this *individual welfarism*) (Bentham 1983: 125). Morality is focused not on the good of some abstract entity ("the community"), but rather on the good of human beings – in particular, on how well or badly their lives are going – and, as Bentham saw it, we assess this from the point of view of the individuals living those lives. The morally relevant good of a person is good *in that person's eyes*, something she cares about and takes an active interest in. Thus, whether a person's life is going well or badly must be measured by the extent to which she *experiences* it as satisfying or disappointing (Sumner 2002: 103). "Happiness" is an empty word, he often said, unless it is understood in terms of human feelings, subjective experience. "[T]he principle of utility . . . holds up to view, as the only sources and tests of right and wrong, human suffering and enjoyment" (1838–43, VI: 238). This intuitive notion even led Bentham to define the scope of his utilitarian moral theory very broadly to include the well-being of all sentient creatures. If the fundamental moral fact is *suffering*, then a creature deserves our moral attention just insofar as it is capable of suffering, he argued. "[T]he question is not, Can they *reason*? nor, Can they *talk*? but, Can they *suffer*?" (1996: 283 n. b).

Pleasure was a basic psychological concept in the British philosophical lexicon, at least since the seventeenth century, so it was natural for Bentham to associate subjective experience – suffering and enjoyment – with the simple and familiar concepts of pleasure and pain. First, he thought that to care about something just is to take pleasure in it. Moreover, like Hume, he thought that the immediate experience of pleasure and pain provided a unique point of sympathetic contact between sensitive beings. By nature we respond sympathetically to the suffering and joys of others; so, he thought, we can hope to move people to recognize the moral value of the sufferings and joys of others by reflecting on their conviction of the moral significance of their own experience. "Who is there, that is not susceptible of discomfort and comfort – of pain and pleasure?" he asks, and he assumes that we naturally join him in drawing the conclusion that the "happiness and unhappiness of any one member of the community . . . [is no] greater or less [a] part . . . of the universal happiness and unhappiness, than that of any other" and for that reason is due full respect (1838–43, III: 459). Also, as we have seen,

Bentham was inclined to think that pleasures and pains have a kind of empirical solidity and public reality that makes them especially appropriate as bases for public moral discourse.

With pleasures and pains as the basic units of value, and the ultimate goal the welfare of the community as a whole, it was tempting for someone like Bentham, who hated abstractions, to think of the welfare of the community as a grand composite of the pleasures and pains of individuals. Sometimes he suggests that on the basis of ethical hedonism it is possible to construct a powerful ethical deliberating machine capable of churning out precise, determinate, and publicly verifiable judgments and prescriptions for all moral occasions, both private and public. On this view, once we make a precise and determinate assessment of the quantities of pleasure and pain of all the creatures affected by some range of actions or policies open to us, we can calculate their relative welfare sums and choose the action or policy that comes out on top. But this notion of a calculus of pleasure assumes (1) that pleasure is a simple, discrete, and homogeneous felt quality that accompanies every enjoyable experience, (and that pain is the corresponding quality of experiences of suffering, frustration, and disappointment), (2) that they come in publicly measurable quantities (psychic packets, or *quale*, as it were), and (3) that the *quale* experienced by one person can be compared, at least with respect to their morally relevant quantities, with those experienced by all others affected and the quantities added together. A little reflection reveals, however, that these assumptions are highly implausible (see Sumner 2002). Bentham recognized this. Although at times (notably in chapter IV of *Introduction*) he seems to endorse the notion of a moral calculus of pleasure, there are good reasons to think he did not put much stock in the idea.

Problems about Pleasure

One problem with the pleasure calculus, as Bentham frankly acknowledged, is that there are grave limits on the possibility of measuring pleasures and pains. "Pleasure itself [is] not . . . ponderable or measurable," he wrote.

> Weight, extent, heat, light, – for quantities of all these articles, we have perceptible and expressible measures: unhappily or happily, for quantities of pleasure or pain, we have no such measures and the measures we might propose are likely to "vary according to the purpose." (1998: 251, 253)

The problem is not that an individual cannot assess his own pleasurable experiences, but that doing so meaningfully across persons is very difficult.

> To every man, by competent attention and observation the quality of his own sensibility may be made known: it may be known by the most impressive and infallible

of all direct evidence, the evidence of a man's own senses. To no man, can the quality of sensibility in the breast of any other man be made known by any thing like equally probative and unfallacious evidence. (1983: 130–1)

He suggests here that the problem is epistemic. (We shall see later that he also recognizes a deeper problem.) We do not have the necessary evidence to judge with any confidence the sensibility of others. Such matters are "out of the reach of direct observation" (1997: 146).

A second problem with the pleasure calculus is that *quale* conception of pleasure is implausible. Bentham also had his doubts about this conception. He frequently took great pains to point out the vast diversity of things in the world that people seem to take pleasure in (see Bentham 1996: chs 5–6), and he acknowledged that there may be no single, discrete felt quality common to all of them. Sometimes he embraced a very different conception of pleasure. In an unpublished manuscript he wrote,

I call pleasure every sensation that a man had rather feel at that instant than feel *none*. I call pain every sensation that a man had rather feel none than feel. (Dinwiddy 2004: 27)

Bentham suggests here that what is common to all pleasurable experiences is not some discrete, felt quality, but the fact that people like to have them and pains are experiences people would like to avoid. Pleasure, on this view, picks out an attitude of persons towards certain experiences they have – their wanting the experience, and wanting it to continue – rather than any particular discrete quality of the experience.

Which conception of pleasure and pain did Bentham endorse? Both, I think, but he put the attitude conception in the foreground of his moral theory. He made the respective roles of these two conceptions clear in an unusual discussion in his late work called *Deontology*. The discussion is noteworthy because in it Bentham relies on a distinction between the *quality* and the *quantity* of pleasure, which calls to mind Mill's famous discussion of the quality of pleasure (Mill 1861: ch. II).

Bentham's distinction, however, is very different from Mill's. Bentham often insisted that each person is the best judge – indeed, "the only proper judge" – of his or her own pleasure (1983: 150). But in this passage he qualifies this general claim: Each of us is the best judge of our *present* pleasure or pain, he argued, but not of our *future* ones. "*Like a third person* his future contingent individual pleasure and pain can not be judged of by him otherwise than from the *species it belongs to*" (1983: 195 n. 1, emphasis added). Bentham here astutely observes that we are not especially good at what recent social psychologists call "affective forecasting" (Gertner 2003; Wilson and Gilbert 2003; Pelham 2004). We systematically overestimate the emotional satisfaction or distress we will get from experiences we anticipate as great pleasures or horrible pains (e.g., owning a BMW or one's team losing the championship). We are better able to anticipate the value of these future experiences by looking at them from the outside, Bentham maintains. The resources we have for the purpose of predicting our future well-being are the resources available in the same way to third parties. Such predictions depend on our "general" sensibility to pleasures, not our *particular* sensibilities. And then he adds: "Quantity depends upon *general* sensibility [to pleasure and pain] . . . quality upon *particular* sensibility" (1983: 130). This distinction marks two important contrasts. First, "quality" is a matter of the *immediately felt* quality of a pleasurable experience. This is *strictly present*, immediate to the experiencer's mind (presumably). But once it is gone, or when it is considered in prospect or in the abstract, one's own access to it is no different from the access of any other person. The *quality – quale* – of an experience is not publicly available; it is not available to others or even to *oneself* at a different time. Beyond the present moment, our access even to our own experience is only indirect, by inference.

Secondly, the shift to the third-person perspective marks a shift from the *quale* conception to the attitude conception of pleasure. For when we shift to the third person, we are not only dependent on others to help us grasp the impact of contingent features of our world on the availability of pleasures, but we are also forced to look to sensibilities we tend to share with others. Experiences we know by participating with others in daily life are the kind that I and many others would like to have again. For these purposes, these pleasures are not adequately portrayed in terms of some single, homogeneous *quale* attached to them. The relevant conception of pleasure, for these purposes, is the attitude conception. Pleasure understood in this way is more likely to be publicly available. At the same time, it is no longer a matter of immediate experience; it is "inferential" rather than ontologically of the first order, as Bentham thinks of these things. This suggests an account of the respective roles of the two conceptions. Pleasure on the *quale* conception ultimately anchors pleasure on the attitude conception in immediate experience. Pleasure on the attitude conception, by the same token, is more closely tied to public features of the states of affairs, objects, or persons in which people take pleasure. Indeed, it is not the pleasure *qua quale* but the *taking pleasure in* that seems to be far more important for the ordinary business of moral and political deliberation. That is the kind of thing that we can track across time and across people, one that we can gather into kinds ("species") and attribute to the people in the community generally with greater or lesser confidence on the basis of experience. The things we talk about together as "pleasures" are the kind of things about which over time our judgments may even to some degree tend to converge.

Interests

This shift to a more public conception of pleasure is complemented by the increasing importance of the notion of interest, in Bentham's later work. In his work on matters of constitutional design, he typically formulated the principle of utility itself in terms of the "universal interest" rather than happiness or pleasure. Bentham always thought of the concepts of pleasure and interest as close kin. He referred to pleasure and pain as "interesting perceptions" (1996: 42), that is, as sensations that attract and hold our attention. An interest for Bentham is never merely a legally protected benefit abstractly conceived; rather, it is something that we *care about*, something in which we take an active interest. Moreover, he believed (implausibly, I think) that interests always have motivational force. "It is by his own particular interest," he wrote, "that on every occasion, be it what it may, a man's conduct will be governed" (1983: 192). He also thought that interests have a kind of self-referential character in the sense that one is thought to have a unique *stake in* the object of one's interest.

So Bentham seemed to think that the concept of interest can do much of the work in his theory of value that he wanted the public concept of pleasure to do. But it has the further advantage of allowing one to abstract from immediate felt experience and to focus on the object of one's interest. This makes it possible to think about how interests might fit together with others into more or less coherent packages. While rooted in the subjective experiences of persons and their stake in how their lives are going, interests have a kind of public dimension that allows us to think about shared or common interests and to assess the compatibility of some interests with others. Moreover, interests are tied to resources, opportunities, security, and capabilities, and these are the kinds of things that utilitarian legislators and policy-makers (the primary intended audience of his philosophy) can focus on. From the very beginning of his career, Bentham conceived of his utilitarian creed as a public philosophy – a rational guide for managing public affairs – and for this purpose the notion of interest proved especially useful. While he always insisted that pleasure and pain ultimately anchored all talk of interests, insuring that when we talk of interests we talk about something real and do not merely express an idle wish, nevertheless, he also insisted that the language of the ordinary business of utilitarian moral deliberation, policy-making, and law-making must be fully public, and for this the language of interests was best suited. We will consider further the significance of this emphasis shortly, but first we would do well to consider Bentham's notion of equality, because it will offer us further insights into his distinctive theory of value.

Equality

In Chapter V of *Utilitarianism,* Mill claimed that the principle of utility embodied an ideal of equality. He argued that the dictum, "everybody to count for one, nobody for more than one" is not something added to the principle of utility, but rather it is "involved in [its] very meaning . . . [and it] might be written under the principle of utility as an explanatory commentary" (Mill 1861, reprinted as Part

II of this volume, Ch. V, para. 36. . Further citations are simply to chapter by roman numeral and paragraph by arabic numeral.). It is likely that Mill came across this important dictum, while editing (at the age of 19!) Bentham's massive *Rationale of Judicial Evidence*. There Bentham wrote that the assumption of all his moral and political thinking is "every individual in the country tells for one; no individual for more than one" (1838–43, VII: 334). This precept was not merely a convenient rule of thumb; it was fundamental to the way he thought about utility, happiness, and social welfare. We saw earlier that Bentham argued that publicity, a necessary feature of all moral judgments, required that equality be involved in the very meaning of the principle of utility (1989: 235). Thus, he asked,

> The happiness or unhappiness of any one member of the community – high or low, rich or poor – what greater or less part is it of the universal happiness and unhappiness, than that of any other? (1838–43, III: 459)

This rhetorical question suggests a familiar principle of equality: the anti-discrimination principle, which demands that we ignore social status, wealth, gender, virtue, merit, and any of the other familiar bases for prejudicial discrimination when we assess the effects of our actions or policies on the community. Prince or pauper, male or female, straight or gay, Christian or Hindu, painter, plumber, or philosophy professor – nothing about persons, except their suffering and enjoyment, have any utilitarian moral significance (1838–43, IX: 107, 108, 1998: 250).

This has not impressed critics, however. They argue that although equality in this sense can be derived directly from the utilitarian principle, the ideal of equality born of this parentage lacks any real moral content. The principle of utility is still open to the objection we encountered before, that it is willing to sacrifice the welfare of individuals on the altar of the community's welfare. The anti-discrimination principle does not prevent this sacrifice; it merely instructs utilitarian agents and policy-makers to pay attention *only* to happiness, rather than to any features of the persons experiencing it, because happiness (or welfare or interests) is the only ultimate morally relevant consideration. Utilitarian theory is no respecter of persons; this sounds attractively egalitarian, but in fact it is the bright side of the dark fact that the utilitarian principle is *utterly indifferent* to the dignity or value of individual persons (Hart 1982: 51–2, 97–100). It "treats individuals as mere receptacles with no intrinsic value for the experiences of pleasure and pain" (Hart 1996: xci).

This is a most serious criticism, but I think Bentham's utilitarian principle, unlike modern versions, is not vulnerable to it. His concern for individual dignity is more deeply rooted than his critics acknowledge. To see this we need to distinguish two different conceptions of individual welfare. According to the *abstract happiness conception*, happiness alone has intrinsic value, and has it irrespective of who experiences it. Mill wrote, "equal amounts of happiness are equally desirable [i.e., valuable], whether felt by the same or different persons" (1861: V, 36n.).

Indeed, on this view they are equally valuable whether enjoyed by *one* person or *many* persons. The fact that someone in particular experiences happiness has absolutely no moral significance. It is only happiness, abstracted from the fact that someone experienced it, that has moral significance on this view. Contrast this with the *individualist conception* of happiness. On this view, the fact that happiness is the happiness *of someone* is of fundamental moral importance. Happiness is not a good considered apart from the people who experience it. Happiness is morally relevant just because people experience it and integrate the experiences meaningfully into their lives. The fundamental moral fact for the individualist utilitarian is the suffering of concrete individual people. It is *people* who suffer and flourish, *people* who take delight in or are distressed by the events of their lives. If these experiences are abstracted from the meaning they have within the lives of individual human beings they lose utterly their moral significance.

I believe Bentham's theory of value is best understood on the model of the individualist, rather than the abstract, conception. Some evidence for this can be seen in his diagnosis of the problems with the crude calculus of pleasure that we discussed earlier. "[O]ne man's happiness," he wrote, "will never be another man's happiness: a gain to one man is no gain to another: you might as well pretend to add 20 apples to 20 pears" (quoted in Dinwiddy 2004: p. 49). Each person's happiness remains distinct, not just epistemically, but *morally*. Considered in terms of their moral significance, the happiness of Jean and that of John cannot be added; morally speaking, that would mix apples and oranges.

Bentham's commitment to the individualist conception of happiness is also evident in his lifelong insistence that the principle of utility is fundamentally concerned with promoting the widest *distribution*, and not the maximal *quantity*, of happiness or welfare (1838–43, III: 211, 1989: 3, 234–5). He insisted, for example, that the equal consideration of all particular interests in a community ("each is to tell as one . . .") requires as he understands it that "with exceptions to as *small* extent as possible, [the] interest of *all* [is] to be *advanced*" (1838–43, III: 452). Late in his career, he wrote that the only proper end of government is "the greatest happiness of all" members of the community, "*an equal quantity of happiness for every one* of them" – "in so far as possible." Where this proves impossible, and the happiness of some must be sacrificed for the happiness of others, government must seek the greatest happiness of *the greatest number* of them (an 1831 pamphlet of Bentham's quoted in Dinwiddy 2004: 31, emphasis added).) This passage makes clear that Bentham's *basic principle*, which defines the target of utilitarian aspiration, is committed to the *greatest equal* happiness, not to maximizing total net (abstract) happiness. Only when this goal cannot be achieved and some sacrifice is inevitable does a *fallback principle* come into play. However, this principle does not require that *happiness* be maximized, but that the greatest and widest possible distribution of happiness be achieved.

Thus, while it appears that Bentham was willing to justify the sacrifice of the happiness of one individual for the good of others in some cases at least, nevertheless he took equal distribution of happiness as the starting point and bench-mark of utilitarian deliberation, and insisted that we keep our eye on that bench-mark even when we have to consider sacrifices. The concern for distribution was not, on his view, something *added to* the concern for promoting social welfare, it was strictly intrinsic to that end. This is, I think, because he embraced the indi-vidualist rather than abstract conception of utilitarian value. This concern for the distribution of happiness at the very center of his utilitarian principle is a distrac-tion on the abstract happiness conception, but makes good sense on the individ-ualist conception. The concern for distribution of happiness is rooted in the more fundamental thought, at the core of Bentham's understanding of value, that hap-piness is valuable just because and just insofar as it is experienced by individual human beings. What has moral value on this view is happiness integrated into the lives of human beings. It cannot pay attention just to the total amount of happi-ness that might be produced by competing public policies without losing its fun-damental focus on the good of human beings.

If this reading of Bentham's theory of welfare is correct, then his utilitarian phi-losophy looks very different from utilitarianism as it has been understood, prac-ticed, and criticized for the past one hundred years. In contrast with the latter view, Bentham thought it fundamentally important that the welfare of each indi-vidual be considered one-by-one. He did not accept the view, often attributed to him, that the good or welfare of an individual could be entirely subordinated to the welfare of the community as a whole. However, he clearly recognized that the utilitarian principle applied in a world in which conflicts of interest are pervasive and where sacrifices of the happiness of some for the happiness of others are unavoidable and not always unreasonable. There is an evident tension in these views and Bentham struggled with it over much of his long career. Yet he seemed to think that, for the domain of politics and public policy at least, this tension could be substantially relieved even if not entirely eliminated. One major way in which he dealt with this tension brings us back to his idea of interests and in par-ticular the idea of *the universal interest*.

The Universal Interest

Interests conflict and public policy decisions always involve trade-offs, sacrificing some interests for the sake of others. According to the standard utilitarian view (relying on the abstract happiness conception), such trade-offs are justified just in case the aggregate utility or happiness of members of the community taken as a whole is maximized. However, Bentham's individualist conception of happiness and his focus on interests rather than pleasure led him to a rather different view. The principle of utility, he argued, required that utilitarian policy-makers and deci-sion-makers promote the "universal interest" and avoid at all costs "the sinister sacrifice" (1989: 17f., 195, 235n.). By "universal interest" he meant "that interest which is common to [oneself] and every other member of the community." Opposed to the universal interest is "sinister" or private interest: "that interest which is particular and peculiar" to an individual or small group, and in conflict with the universal interest (1838–43, IX: 127, 1989: 192).

The universal interest is not the product of *aggregating* the interests of all the members of the community. It is, rather, the product of the *convergence* of the diverse interests of the community around certain goods and opportunities. Bentham's notion shares some features with what economists call "public goods". Providing these goods benefits (nearly) everyone in the community – everyone has a share – and it is possible to provide them to some only if they are available on the same basis for all. Bentham's favorite example of such a good is security: security from violent attack and dispossession and enjoyment of a reasonably predictable and non-hostile environment for ordinary daily social interaction.

The universal interest, then, is not the interest of some collective entity, neither is it the net sum of the (potentially conflicting) interests or happiness of individual members of the community. It is rather the intersection of their individual interests, the product of a kind of virtual negotiation among the members of a community. The universal interest consists of projects that one can reasonably hope to enlist others to pursue with one: "each separate and sinister interest finds a bar, and that an insuperable one, in every other separate and sinister interest," Bentham wrote, "but each man's share in the universal interest finds an ally and coadjutor in every other man's share in the universal interest" (1990: 266). Thus, Bentham thought of social welfare in terms of broadly converging interests of members of the community. This formulation of his notion of social welfare may have come relatively late in his career, but it explains why already in his early writings he trained his attention narrowly on four subordinate ends of utility: security, subsistence (resources people need to survive), abundance (material wealth beyond what is needed for survival), and equality (wide and equal distribution of these resources) (1838–43, I: 301–13, 1989: 16). These goods, in his view, met the condition of convergence and mutual benefit. They are ends immediately subordinate to the fundamental end of promoting the universal interest because they are the most important constituents of the universal interest, providing the infrastructure of social life and preconditions for seeking any other constituents. Thus, on this view, the utilitarian aim is not to promote all the interests of everyone (that would be impossible), nor the greatest net satisfaction of interests of everyone (for some of these interests are *private*), but rather that set of interests common in the community as a whole, the satisfaction of which benefits each more or less equally. Thus, Bentham wrote:

> in the instance of each individual such part of the whole mass of his happiness as is not adverse to the happiness of any other individual will be, in so far as depends upon the agency of the government, secured to him: the correspondent part of his interest will be provided for: the correspondent part of his desires, of his wishes, will

receive its gratification: while all such portions of happiness as he could not be made to enjoy without depriving others of happiness to greater amount will not be given to him: the correspondent part of his interest will be left unpromoted: the correspondent part of his desires, of his wishes, left ungratified. (1989: 135–6)

In this way, although some individuals' *private* interests may be sacrificed for the good of the community, these individuals are not. They are accorded proper moral attention not merely by taking their interests into account, counting them along with all the others, but also by ensuring that they have a significant share in the fulfillment of the universal interest, that they benefit on an equal basis with all the others in the community from the achievement of their common interests. In this way, Bentham thought, while individual private *interests* may be sacrificed, no *individual* is sacrificed to the insatiable Moloch of aggregate social welfare.

On this understanding, Bentham's utilitarian public philosophy is untidy and fraught with unresolved tensions. It is also, surely, open to many challenges. But it is more subtle and in many respects more attractive than the version that came to be identified as classical utilitarianism by the beginning of the twentieth century. Doubtless, Bentham's thought, and his person and intellect, had a profound impact on Mill. Yet, in the years after recovering from his "crisis," Mill found it necessary to forge his own understanding of the utilitarian creed, drawing inspiration from the same moral and philosophical insights as Bentham did. It is primarily Mill's, rather than Bentham's, version of the creed that has entered the modern philosophical canon. But there is still much to be learned from Bentham's struggles and the unorthodox views to which they led him.

References and further reading

Bentham, Jeremy (1838–43) *The Works of Jeremy Bentham*, 11 vols., ed. J. Bowring. Edinburgh: William Tait. Reproduced New York: Russell & Russell, 1962.

——(1954) *Jeremy Bentham's Economic Writings*, 3 vols., ed. W. Stark. London: George Allen & Unwin.

——(1983) *Deontology together with a Table of the Springs of Action and Article on Utilitarianism*, ed. A. Goldworth. Oxford: Clarendon Press.

——(1987) "Anarchical fallacies and supply without burden," in J. Waldron (ed.) *Nonsense upon Stilts*. London: Methuen.

——(1989) *First Principles Preparatory to a Constitutional Code*, ed. P. Schofield. Oxford: Clarendon Press.

——(1990) *Securities against Misrule and Other Constitutional Writings for Tripoli and Greece*, ed. P. Schofield. Oxford: Clarendon Press.

——(1996) *An Introduction to the Principles of Morals and Legislation*, ed. F. Rosen. Oxford: Clarendon Press (revised edition of J. H. Burns and H. L. A. Hart (eds.), London: Athlone Press, 1970).

——(1997) *De l'ontologie*, ed. P. Schofield, J.-P. Cléro, and C. Laval. Paris: Éditions du Seuil.

——(1998) *Legislator of the World: Writings on Codification, Law, and Education*, ed. P. Schofield and J. Harris. Oxford: Clarendon Press.

——(n. d.) Unpublished manuscript in the library of University College London, Box 169, folio 79.

Dinwiddy, J. (2004) *Bentham: Selected Writings of John Dinwiddy*, ed. W. Twining. Stanford: Stanford University Press.

Dworkin, R. (1978) *Taking Rights Seriously*. Cambridge, MA: Harvard University Press.

Gertner, J. (2003) "The futile pursuit of happiness," *New York Times Magazine*, September 7 (available at http://www.wjh.harvard.edu/~dtg/Futile_Pursuit.htm).

Harrison, R. (1984) *Bentham*. London: Routledge & Kegan Paul.

Hart, H. L. A. (1982) *Essays on Bentham*. Oxford: Clarendon Press.

——(1996) "Bentham's principle of utility and theory of penal law," introductory essay in *J. Bentham, An Introduction to the Principles of Morals and Legislation* (pp. lxxix–cxii), ed. F. Rosen. Oxford: Clarendon Press.

Mill, J. S. (1861) *Utilitarianism*, in J. M. Robson (ed.) *Collected Works of John Stuart Mill*, Vol. X: *Essays on Ethics, Religion, and Society* (pp. 203–59). Toronto: University of Toronto Press, 1969. (Reprinted as Part II of this volume; citations are to chapter in roman numerals and paragraph in arabic numerals.)

——(1989) *Autobiography*. New York: Penguin Books.

Moore, G. E. (1993) *Principia ethica*, rev. edn. Cambridge: Cambridge University Press.

Pelham, B. (2004) "Affective forecasting: the perils of predicting future feelings," APA On-line18: no. 4 (http://www.apa.org/science/psa/apr4pelhamprt.html).

Postema, G. J. (1986) *Bentham and the Common Law Tradition*. Oxford: Clarendon Press.

——(2002) Introduction, in G. J. Postema (ed.) *Jeremy Bentham: Moral, Political and Legal Philosophy*, Vol. 1 (pp. xi–xxxi). Aldershot: Dartmouth.

Rawls, J. (1971) *A Theory of Justice*. Cambridge, MA: Harvard University Press.

Sumner, L. W. (2002) "Welfare, happiness, and pleasure," in G. J. Postema (ed.) *Jeremy Bentham: Moral, Political and Legal Philosophy*, Vol. 1 (pp. 103–27). Aldershot: Dartmouth.

Waldron, J. (ed.) (1987) *Nonsense upon Stilts*. London: Methuen.

Wilson, T. D., and D. T. Gilbert (2003) "Affective forecasting," *Advances in Experimental Social Psychology* 35, pp. 345–411.

Chapter 3

The Place of Utilitarianism in Mill's Philosophy

John Skorupski

Three features shape Mill's philosophy. He is a naturalist and empiricist about human beings and what they can know. He is a liberal, and a liberal of a specifically philosophical, nineteenth-century kind. And, of course, he is a utilitarian.

These views are independent in the sense that you cannot force a path from any one or two of them to the third. Yet they constrain and influence each other. As a naturalist Mill thinks that human beings have no supernatural or otherwise non-natural aspect. They belong in the natural order that is studied by science. So he cannot base his liberal argument on any conception of human freedom that says our capacity to act from reasons is beyond scientific explanation – as Kant does with his conception of autonomy. Likewise, since he is a utilitarian, he must hold that the liberal political institutions he favors are those that produce the most happiness, at any rate in sufficiently developed societies. Moreover, Mill thinks that his empiricist account of knowledge has broadly progressive implications for ethics and politics and, even, that it in some way provides support for utilitarianism.

Which if any of these commitments is most fundamental for him, in the sense of mattering most to him personally – being closest to his heart? This is a matter of one's personal impression: my own impression is that Mill is by temperament both an Enlightenment naturalist and a romantic liberal. He thought the *System of Logic* and the essay *On Liberty* would turn out to be the works of his that would survive longest. Each of these is supported by other substantial works. Mill himself, in two great essays on Bentham and Coleridge, and in his *Autobiography*, describes his overall aim as being to show how the deeper views of human nature and human good developed in the nineteenth century could be defended on the sound philosophical foundations proposed by the Enlightenment.

In the context of his voluminous writings, the "little work" entitled *Utilitarianism*, as Mill referred to it, stands rather on its own. But it has become a classic, because it has the incisiveness and eloquence that mark out Mill as a moral philosopher. And although Mill's discussion of the basic questions that arise about this theory is often tantalizingly rudimentary, the questions are all there. Nonetheless, we should bear in mind that this little work, classic as it may be, was presented from a particular philosophical standpoint, to a particular audience. It is a kind of extended memo to his contemporaries, setting out for them Mill's personal understanding of utilitarianism. In particular, Mill was concerned to further the overall aim that I mentioned above. He wanted to defend utilitarianism within his naturalistic and empiricist framework. And – to him even more important – he wanted to give an account of happiness and morality that would make the utilitarian doctrine a foundation for his kind of liberalism, a liberalism which, like that of some other influential liberals of his century, was strongly founded on the notion of human self-development.

So we should review his naturalism and his liberalism, and consider how these illuminate his utilitarianism. The following section will sketch out Mill's naturalistic epistemology; the next will be concerned with its bearing on his utilitarianism. The last section will consider how Mill's liberal vision of human beings influences his understanding of happiness and character.

Naturalized Epistemology

Mill made an outstanding contribution to the development of radically naturalist philosophy. Naturalism holds that human beings are entirely a part of the natural order. That this is no triviality can be seen from Mill's struggles with it. One set of problems that it raised for him concerns the nature of mind and self. How do you fit minds into nature? What about the thinking and acting self? Is there an order of things independent of the mind? Mill's attempt to deal with these questions still seemed to end up leaving the mental in a strangely transcendental role, somehow not *within* nature, and the critics of naturalism, who in the nineteenth century were mainly idealists, were quick to seize on that.

Naturalism also has implications about the sources of our knowledge. It seems to rule out any knowledge that is not based on empirical evidence. How can there be such knowledge if thinking and information are just natural causal processes? If we have any knowledge at all it must come to us from the evidence of our own states of mind, our memory, and our perception. Mill follows this empiricist line of thought through to radical lengths. In the *System of Logic* he presents the first thoroughly naturalistic analysis of all deductive reasoning and he argues that not only mathematics but logic itself are empirical sciences.

So he is an epistemological radical. But he is not an epistemological skeptic: he did not think skepticism raised significant philosophical issues and never entered into battle with it. Studied avoidance of skeptical questions is part of his naturalized approach to epistemology. Another is rejection of Descartes's method of doubt in favor of starting from within what we already know. He dismisses "the well-meant but impracticable precept of Descartes" of "setting out from the supposition that nothing had been already ascertained" (Mill 1843: 318–19); epistemology itself, he thinks, is an empirical science:

> Principles of Evidence and Theories of Method are not to be constructed *a priori*. The laws of our rational faculty, like those of every other natural agency, are only learnt by seeing the agent at work . . . we should never have known by what process truth is to be ascertained, if we had not previously ascertained many truths . . . (1843: 833)

Critics of naturalism argue that such a view can lead only to the conclusion that knowledge is impossible. To avoid the challenge of skepticism, they hold, is merely to avert one's gaze from this unpalatable conclusion. Epistemology and ethics, they point out, are normative discourses, not empirical sciences. Seeing agents at work may tell us how they *do* think, but what can it show about how they should think? "The laws of our rational faculty" is an ambiguous phrase. Truths about how we *should* think, or come to that, what we *should* do, can only rest on *a priori* foundations.

They have a very good point. However my concern here is not to assess this fundamental philosophical debate, but to locate Mill within it. What did Mill think about this question of normativity? It is surprisingly difficult to say.

I think he accepted that epistemology and ethics are normative disciplines. Even this can be contested, but for the case of ethics at least various passages seem unambiguous. Thus he says that ethics is art not science, and that every art is "a joint result of laws of nature disclosed by science, and of the general principles of what has been called Teleology, or the Doctrine of Ends" (1843: 949). He takes the Doctrine of Ends to be normative and says that it has just one fundamental principle: the utility principle.

If he accepts that there are normative truths, does he think that normative truths simply reduce to empirical facts? That view has had subtle defenders in recent philosophy, but I don't think it is Mill's view. "Propositions of science," he says, "assert a matter of fact: an existence, a coexistence, a succession, or a resemblance." In contrast, propositions that "enjoin or recommend that something should be"

> are a class by themselves. A proposition of which the predicate is expressed by the words *ought* or *should be*, is generically different from one which is expressed by *is*, or *will be*. (1843: 949)

So in what way do we discover which basic propositions of this kind, about what ought or should be, are true? In line with his anti-Cartesianism, Mill thinks the only way is careful scrutiny of how we actually reason, and reflective analysis of which principles in this reasoning practice turn out to be treated by us as normatively basic: "seeing the agent at work." This is the only "evidence" that can be produced for the philosopher's normative claims. He follows this naturalistic method in the *System of Logic*, and it is also the method he is following in *Utilitarianism*, when he argues that happiness is the one and only desirable end:

> the sole evidence it is possible to produce that anything is desirable, is that people do actually desire it. If the end which the utilitarian doctrine proposes to itself were not, in theory and in practice, acknowledged to be an end, nothing could ever convince any person that it was so. (Mill 1861, reprinted as Part II of this volume, Ch. IV, para. 3. Future citations to this work will be simply by roman numeral for chapter and arabic numeral for paragraph.)

Mill is not saying that the desirable reduces to the desired, or that facts about the desired entail facts about the desirable. What he says is that facts about what is desired, "in theory and practice" are "evidence" for normative claims about what is desirable. Just as in the case of science – where he thinks that induction is the sole ultimate norm of reasoning – he supports this claim by a simple appeal to our reflectively considered practice.

This is "evidence" in a rather strained sense. Mill means, in the first place, that getting at the fundamental norms of people's thinking calls for a careful psychological and historical inquiry into how they think, including how they think they should think – what kind of normative attitudes they display in their actions and their reflection. But there is a little more to it. The naturalist can also examine whether some normative dispositions can be shown to originate from other such dispositions. And he can consider whether some are explicable in a way that subverts their authority. Suppose I can explain your low opinion of your brother's intelligence as the product of sibling rivalry, or just sheer envy and resentment. That will subvert the authority of this opinion: it may be true, but you don't have good grounds for thinking it is. Or an example Mill would have liked: normative views of what women's role should be may simply reflect unequal power relationships between men and women. That, if true, subverts these normative views.

The Epistemology of Mill's Utilitarianism

The discussion of the preceding section helps to explain why Mill considers a very strong dose of empiricism to be a healthy tonic for moral philosophers, and what, in his view, is the "evidence" such philosophers can legitimately appeal to. Mill was specially proud of his radically empiricist treatment of logic and mathematics in the *System of Logic*:

> The notion that truths external to the human mind may be known by intuition or consciousness, independently of observation and experience, is, I am persuaded, in these times, the great intellectual support of false doctrines and bad institutions. By the aid of this theory, every inveterate belief and every intense feeling, of which the

origin is not remembered, is enabled to dispense with the obligation of justifying itself by reason, and is erected into its own all-sufficient voucher and justification. There never was such an instrument devised for consecrating all deep-seated prejudices. And the chief strength of this false philosophy in morals, politics, and religion, lies in the appeal which it is accustomed to make to the evidence of mathematics and of the cognate branches of physical science. To expel it from these, is to drive it from its stronghold . . . (1873: 233–5)

He thought he had done so in the *System of Logic*, and that in doing so he had carried out a public service for ethics. The path had been cleared for a down-to-earth investigation of the origin of "inveterate beliefs and intense feelings." Many of the explanations such an investigation would provide might be subversive.

However, Mill also realized that following the naturalistic method could not secure utilitarianism in any simple and straightforward way. There were plenty of philosophers who would agree with him about his method, deny that they were appealing to "intuition or consciousness, independently of observation and experience," but still reject utilitarianism. As he explains in his 1833 essay, "Remarks on Bentham's philosophy," they would say

that by an inductive and analytical examination of the human mind, they had satisfied themselves, that what we call our moral sentiments . . . are as much part of the original constitution of man's nature as the desire of happiness and the fear of suffering: That those sentiments do not indeed attach themselves to the same actions under all circumstances, but neither do they, in attaching themselves to actions, follow the law of utility, but certain other general laws, which are the same in all mankind naturally; though education or external circumstances may counteract them, by creating artificial associations stronger than they. No proof can indeed be given that we ought to abide by these laws; but neither can any proof be given, that we ought to regulate our conduct by utility. All that can be said is, that the pursuit of happiness is natural to us; and so it is contended, is the reverence for, and the inclination to square our actions by, certain general laws of morality . . .

"These views of the origin of moral distinctions are *not*," Mill goes on,

what [Bentham] says all such views are, destitute of any precise and tangible meaning; nor chargeable with setting up as a standard the feelings of the particular person. They set up as a standard what are assumed (on grounds which are considered to be sufficient) to be the instincts of the species, or principles of our common nature as universal and inexplicable as instincts. (1833: 5–6)

Mill does not respond by dismissing all appeals to "principles of our common nature," or contrasts between them and "artificial associations," as irrelevant. Nor could he; his only possible reply, as a naturalist, is that an "inductive and analytical examination of the human mind" *in fact* reveals none of the irreducible principles to which critics of utilitarianism appeal.

So how can Mill establish the utility principle? He must argue (1) that the principle of utility is not an artificial construct but expresses natural ethical dispositions that are basic to our theory and practice and (2) that no other ethical disposition is in this way basic. All our other ethical dispositions – our dispositions to blame and condemn people who cheat, assault others, or show base ingratitude for example – can either be reduced to our natural and basic utilitarian disposition, or subversively explained away.

This is a tall order. In *Utilitarianism* his main attempt under (2) is his treatment of conscience in Chapter II and justice in Chapter V. He tries to show that conscience is not a non-natural faculty of moral knowledge but a disposition of the feelings that can naturally, and not merely artificially, become attached as a sanction to the utility principle itself. Similarly with the sentiment of justice: he tries to show that it is not *sui generis* (V, 3) but derivative, and that the "moral" part of it derives from our utilitarian disposition, our regard for impartially considered general good. One can look at III, 4–10, or V, 16–23, and ask how well he does. Take for example our ethical disposition to proportion punishments of wrongdoing. A naturalist who is not a utilitarian can argue that this stems from a "principle of our common nature," – the principle of desert – just as basic as whatever in our common nature supports the utility principle. Mill must either show that our ideas about desert are, in empirical fact, dependent on our ideas about utility, or he must subversively explain them away. Does he achieve that? (In effect, it seems to me, he combines the two approaches at V, 34.) And this is just one of the cases he would have to deal with in a full treatment. We have many other ethical values that seem to rest on affective dispositions which are neither reducible to others nor subversively explicable. There are things we naturally find admirable, for example, as well as things that we naturally find desirable. If this is right, then Mill's own method requires him to recognize the normative authority of these other values. The naturalistic moral philosophers who are pluralists about our ethical values will have been vindicated.

Mill could take a weaker line. He could argue that the utility principle plays the role of a master principle to which other ethical norms must give way, even when they have their own independent standing in our theory and practice. In this argument the emphasis would fall on the claim that the general happiness is the only final or ultimate good, together with the thought that even well-grounded ethical principles must give way if they turn out to be systematically incompatible with the final good. And of course he does argue that the general happiness is the only final good. Let's consider how he does.

This claim breaks down into a number of sub-claims. There is the question of what is good for human beings. There is the question of why the general good, the good of all, should be the ultimate criterion – rather than the good of the person who is deliberating about what to do. And even if the general good of all is the criterion, why should we represent the general good as the sum of the good of each? Mill is at his best in answering the first question, and quite perfunctory in answering the other two.

To ask what is ultimately good, he says, is to ask what ends are ultimately desirable, desirable in their own right. Now this could be challenged at the outset: perhaps, for example, to ask what is ultimately good is to ask what ways of acting are ultimately admirable. But suppose we waive that objection and accept Mill's first step. Then, according to Mill, an ultimately desirable end is happiness, understood as "pleasure, and freedom from pain" (II, 2). And the "evidence" for that normative claim is that happiness *is* ultimately desired.

The next question is whether happiness is the *only* ultimately desirable thing. Mill responds to this question at length. He has to show that happiness is the only thing ultimately desired. This, he thinks, is "a question of fact and experience" which "can only be determined by practised self-consciousness and self-observation, assisted by observation of others." On this basis he claims that when we want something for its own sake and with no further end in view we want it because we think of it as enjoyable, or of not having it as positively painful. He regards this as a psychological law about all desires.

It does not mean, however, that we desire all objects as *means* to our pleasure. The desire for an object is genuinely a desire for that *object*; it is not the desire for pleasure as such. Mill's way of marking this is to say that the object is desired as a "part" of one's happiness, not as a means to it. So the claim that happiness is the sole human end, put more carefully, is this:

> Whatever is desired otherwise than as a means to some end beyond itself, and ultimately to happiness, is desired as itself a part of happiness, and is not desired for itself until has become so. (IV, 8)

Note that this is a claim about *desire*. Mill thinks the distinction between will and desire is important. We will come back to it in the next section.

A pluralist about human ends who accepts Mill's naturalistic method must deny his psychological thesis that whatever we desire we desire under the idea of it as pleasant. He might say that desiring something always involves the idea of it as *worth doing or achieving*, but not always the idea that the doing or achieving will be *pleasant* (or pain-avoiding). This is a debate that can be pursued with subtlety. But I want to turn to the other two questions I mentioned above. Why should the general good, the good of all, be the ultimate criterion, rather than each particular person's good being the ultimate criterion for that particular person? And even if the general good of all is the criterion, why should we represent the general good as the sum of the good of each?

Mill never adequately examined these elements in the principle of utility. When he states the utilitarian doctrine before considering what kind of proof can be given of it, he states it thus: "happiness is desirable, and the only thing desirable, as an end, all other things being only desirable as means to that end" (IV, 2). He clearly thinks that the controversial part of his task is to show that this is true. All he has to say about the further move from this thesis to the utility principle is that if "each person's happiness is a good to that person" then "the general happiness" must be "a good to the aggregate of all persons." In a letter in which he explains this unclear remark, he says:

> I merely meant in this particular sentence to argue that since A's happiness is a good, B's a good, C's a good, etc, the sum of all these goods must be a good. (1972: 1414)

This remark makes two assumptions. The more obvious point is that an egoist may accept that Mill has shown that "each person's happiness is a good to that person," but deny that he has shown that happiness is a good. There's no such thing as the good *period*, the egoist says; there's only what's good *for you* or *for me*. Against the egoist Mill needs a postulate of impartiality, and a corresponding natural ethical disposition. We must be naturally disposed to hold that everyone's good is of legitimate concern to all of us and no one's well-being is more important than anyone else's.

The second assumption is more subtle. At the end of the last chapter of *Utilitarianism*, "On the Connection between Justice and Utility," Mill does explain that he takes "perfect impartiality between persons" to be part of the very meaning of the Greatest Happiness Principle:

> That principle is a mere form of words without rational signification, unless one person's happiness, supposed equal in degree (with the proper allowance made for kind), is counted for exactly as much as another's. (V, 36)

So here Mill supplies the required postulate of impartiality. However the concept of impartiality does not, on its own, yield utilitarianism's aggregative principle of distribution. Maximizing the *sum* of individuals' happiness, if it makes sense to talk in this way at all, is one way of being impartial. But a wide variety of non-equivalent distributive principles is impartial in the sense that they don't count anyone's happiness as more important than anyone else's. The most one could get from combining a postulate of impartiality with the principle that happiness is the only good is that the general good is a positive impartial function of the happiness of all individuals and of nothing else. Here again Mill should have argued that we are naturally disposed to take the sum of individuals' happiness rather than applying some other welfarist criterion. But as a psychological hypothesis, that might well be thought implausible.

We might speculate that Mill's most fundamental commitment in this area is simply that well-being is the ultimate standard of all conduct, everyone's well-being being taken into account in some impartial way. If so, he could retreat from the more specific theses that happiness (pleasure and the absence of pain) is all there is to well-being, and that the impartial pursuit of everyone's well-being must entail pursuing the simple sum of their well-being, while still holding to this fundamental commitment. We could go on to ask whether the naturalistic view of human beings somehow supports it. Perhaps something like the following could be said in reply. In the absence of divine guidance or *a priori* intuition, we must focus on what is found, by an empirical inquiry into our sentiments, to be what human beings in fact desire. Furthermore, when we look at human beings (or all sentient beings?) from a naturalistic perspective, we see no reason to hold that any one of them is more important than any other. And finally we find ourselves thinking that they all are important. This is perhaps the most debatable, in that you might think that once you adopt the naturalistic perspective *nothing* is "important." But this interesting debate cannot be pursued here.

Liberalism and Happiness

Mill's essay *On Liberty* puts forward a famous principle that is intended to safeguard the liberty of the individual. He spells it out and illustrates it extensively throughout the essay, which means that it resists neat summary. Its broad import however is that in sufficiently developed societies freedom of conduct should be constrained only on certain limited grounds: that the conduct in question is liable to cause harm to others, or that it constitutes a nuisance in a public place, or that it involves a failure to act that can justifiably be considered a violation of duty to others.

Mill defends this principle on utilitarian grounds. He forgoes "any advantage which could be derived to my argument from the idea of abstract right, as a thing independent of utility." Utility is "the ultimate appeal on all ethical questions." But, he adds, "it must be utility in the largest sense, grounded on the permanent interests of a man as a progressive being" (1859: 224).

Behind this interesting phrase lies a comprehensive ethical vision. Man has "permanent interests" as "a progressive being" both in world history and in personal life. Like many other thinkers of the nineteenth century, Mill thought of these interests as the fixed substratum of progressive realization of human potential towards freedom: in the history of social formations and, once liberty had arrived, in the many stories of individual lives.

Human beings, Mill believes, are capable of raising or lowering themselves by their own self-culture. He thinks, or fervently hopes, that that capacity is present in every human being. However, he also thinks that societies in which free self-culture becomes truly possible for all come about only through a long historical development. When they are reached, self-development becomes the proper task of human beings: development of oneself *by* oneself. People have to do their own work of self-development, because human potentialities are diverse and best known to the individual person, and because only when human beings work out their own plans of life do they develop moral freedom, a quality of character that is itself indispensable to a higher human nature. Furthermore, this self-development takes place in a dynamic historical setting which always contains possibilities of regression as well as progress. The liberty principle is meant to entrench the social conditions that allow free self-development to flourish and go on flourishing, without stagnating or regressing.

A main source of Mill's ideal lies in a certain vision of classical Greek life, re-imagined and rethought for the present day by the Romantic movement. It is the ideal of a balanced development of personal qualities – rational self-governance on the one hand and development and education of the feelings, "aesthetic education," on the other: "a Greek ideal of self-development, which the Platonic and Christian ideal of self-government blends with, but does not supersede" (1859: 226). Such an ideal of active and high-minded self-culture may seem hardly suited to the utilitarian tradition, with its tough-minded, somewhat low and passive-sounding insistence on "pleasure and the absence of pain." Mill did not agree. The liberal ideal of human self-culture, he thought, was perfectly compatible with the utilitarian ethical framework. For only through free self-culture, subject to the rules required by the interests of all, is the fullest self-development achieved; and only the fullest self-development gives access to the highest forms of human happiness. Mill's adherence to this, for him crucial, tenet helps us to understand three distinctions that feature in *Utilitarianism*: 1) between desire and will, 2) between quality and quantity of pleasure, and 3) between that which is morally obligatory and that which is simply a good thing to do. All stem from his liberal ideal and all are vital to it. Let us look at each of them in turn.

In his autobiography he dates two new convictions to a period of depression that assailed him in 1826–7 (when he was 20). After his period of depression he still thought that happiness alone is the true end of life. But he now adopted a "theory of life" according to which "this end was only to be attained by not making it the direct end" (1873: 145). And, secondly, he

> gave its proper place, among the prime necessities of human well-being, to the internal culture of the individual . . . The maintenance of a due balance among the faculties now seemed to me to be of primary importance. The cultivation of the feelings became one of the cardinal points in my ethical and philosophical creed. (1873: 147)

In the *System of Logic* he affirms "that the promotion of happiness is the ultimate principle of Teleology" (i.e. the doctrine of ends) but continues,

> I do not mean to suggest that the promotion of happiness should be itself the end of all actions, or even of all rules of action. It is the justification, and ought to be the controller, of all ends, but is not itself the sole end . . . I fully admit that . . . the cultivation of an ideal nobleness of will and conduct, should be to individual human beings an end, for which the specific pursuit either of their own happiness or of that of others (except so far as included in that idea) should, in any case of conflict, give

way. But I hold that the very question, what constitutes this elevation of character, is itself to be decided by a reference to happiness as the standard (1843: 952)

Cultivating the feelings meant educating them, not simply indulging them; and educating them was not a matter of disciplining them by a moral or religious standard external to them. It meant working from within their spontaneity, criticizing and strengthening them by their own internal standards. As to self-government, the moral capacity to take charge of one's own life, that involved a development of the will as well as an education of the feelings. Mill calls this developed will "moral freedom":

> A person feels morally free who feels that his habits or his temptations are not his masters, but he theirs: who even in yielding to them knows that he could resist . . . we must feel that our wish, if not strong enough to alter our character, is strong enough to conquer our character when the two are brought into conflict in any particular case of conduct. And hence it is said with truth, that none but a person of confirmed virtue is completely free. (1843: 841)

Like Kant, then, Mill identifies virtue with moral freedom. But he did not think that moral freedom was incompatible with the Enlightenment's naturalistic view of human beings – though this problem had indeed deeply worried him. In the *System of Logic* (bk 6, ch. 2, which Mill thought the best chapter in the whole work) he sought to show how they could be reconciled. What we do, he said, is always causally explicable by a motive, but that motive need not be a desire. As we saw in the preceding section, he thinks desire always involves anticipation of pleasure of pain. Yet

> When the will is said to be determined by motives, a motive does not mean always, or solely, the anticipation of a pleasure or of a pain . . . A habit of willing is commonly called a purpose; and among the causes of our volitions, and of the actions which flow from them, must be reckoned not only likings and aversions, but also purposes. (1843: 842)

Will evolves through the psychological differentiation of purposes from desires; when we have developed purposes we can will against mere likings or aversions. The distinction is essential to Mill's conception of character. It reappears in *Utilitarianism*, where we again find him insisting "positively and emphatically"

> that the will is a different thing from desire; that a person of confirmed virtue, or any other person whose purposes are fixed, carries out his purposes without any thought of the pleasure he has in contemplating them, or expects to derive from their fulfilment. (IV, 11)

That "virtuous will," however, is not for him an intrinsic good, as it is for Kant. It is a means to good, not intrinsically a good; and does not contradict the doctrine that nothing is good to human beings but in so far as it is either itself pleasurable, or a means of attaining pleasure or averting pain. (IV, 11)

It does not contradict the doctrine, because the criterion of what is good or desirable as a final end remains what we *desire*, not what we will. Happiness – pleasure and the absence of pain – remains the sole final end of life. True, we can come to desire virtue; Mill thinks it can in that way become a "part" of our happiness, and of course believes it a good thing that it should be so. But he also recognizes that we can and should cultivate a settled and habitual "will to do right" that is independent of our desires and feelings. Balanced self-development calls for strength of willing as well as strength of feeling.

Happiness always remains the sole final end of life. But in the *System of Logic* we find a surprising formulation:

> The character itself should be, to the individual, a paramount end, simply because the existence of this ideal nobleness of character, or of a near approach to it, in any abundance, would go further than all things else towards making human life happy; both in the comparatively humble sense, of pleasure and freedom from pain, and in the higher meaning, of rendering life, not what it now is almost universally, puerile and insignificant – but such as human beings with highly developed faculties can care to have. (1843: 952)

In this passage Mill makes happiness consist in whatever human beings with highly developed faculties can care to have. And he seems to give up on a hedonistic conception of happiness, in that "pleasure and freedom from pain" are regarded as just a part of, rather than constitutive of, happiness. "Happiness" covers anything that people of developed feeling find it worth caring about.

In *Utilitarianism*, however, Mill presents the same idea in a way that avoids this apparent rejection of hedonism (i. e. the view that happiness is the sole constituent of human good and consists in pleasure and freedom from pain). He does so by distinguishing between qualities of pleasure. In Chapter II he replies to those who think hedonism "a doctrine worthy only of swine"; his reply is that "the accusation supposes human beings to be capable of no pleasures except those of which swine are capable" (II, 3–4). And he adds,

> It is quite compatible with the principle of utility, to recognise the fact that some *kinds* of pleasure are more desirable and more valuable than others. It would be absurd that while, in estimating all other things, quality is considered as well as quantity, the estimation of pleasures should be supposed to depend on quantity alone. (II, 4)

These pleasures of higher quality are the pleasures of more fully developed human beings, the ones that "human beings with highly developed faculties can care to have."

Whether this falling into line with hedonism is more than formal is an interesting question. Presumably Mill wanted to maintain his psychological thesis connecting desire and anticipated pleasure; as we noted, it features importantly in his "proof" of the principle of utility. The charge has often been made that the supposed distinction between quality and quantity of pleasure is actually inconsistent with hedonism. But this is not obvious. There is no reason in logic why more than one characteristic of pleasures should not be relevant to estimating their value; though if we call those characteristics "quantity" and "quality," we need to maintain a careful distinction between the quantity and quality of a pleasure on the one hand and its degree of value on the other. Activity A can be more valuable pleasure-wise than activity B, because though it gives less pleasure the pleasure it gives is of higher quality. All that hedonism requires is that the only things that make a pleasure valuable are its characteristics as a *pleasure*.

How then do we know the qualities of pleasures? According to Mill, qualities, like quantities, are determined by "the feelings and judgments of the experienced" (II, 8). And how do we know that a higher-quality pleasure (other things equal) is more valuable? As a naturalist, Mill thinks the only criterion for this judgment, as with basic value judgments in general, is reflective practice: self-examination and discussion. What often raises readers' hackles here is Mill's elitism: he thinks that only some people are competent to judge the quality, as against the quantity, of pleasure. Yet this elitism is the direct consequence of the idea that feelings can be cultivated and developed. One gains access to higher qualities of pleasure by this cultivation; so cultivation is required if one is to be a competent judge. However, as I noted, Mill thinks that in principle all human beings can cultivate their feelings, though their affective sensibilities may point in different directions of development and give them different powers of enjoyment. (If I, unlike you, get nothing out of poetry, there is a higher pleasure that is lost to me but accessible to you. But perhaps the reverse holds with respect to the higher pleasure of chess.)

There is no inconsistency in Mill's position: but that is not to say it is true. Also, an impression lingers that he in fact appeals to intuitions which are not hedonistic. For example he remarks that a

> being of higher faculties requires more to make him happy, is capable probably of more acute suffering, and is certainly accessible to it at more points, than one of an inferior type; but in spite of these liabilities, he can never really wish to sink into what he feels to be a lower grade of existence. (II, 6)

And he suggests that this preference can be explained by a sense of dignity which all human being possess. It sounds then as though Mill thinks everyone has a desire for dignity, or self-respect, which is distinct from the desire for pleasure. In which case, by his own test, dignity is desirable as well as pleasure. Suppose that a being of higher faculties is faced with a choice: on the one hand a life of acute suffering, with no access to any of the higher pleasures which its faculties make it capable of appreciating; on the other, a cure which relieves its suffering but leaves it only with pleasures accessible by much simpler faculties (say pleasant tunes and good food). Is Mill saying that in *all* such cases the life of suffering should be preferred? He does not say so explicitly and if he does adhere to hedonism he should not. Cases must be possible in which life after the cure offers a stream of pleasures more valuable overall, taking quality as well as quantity into account, than the life of suffering in which one retains one's higher faculties but can *obtain* no higher pleasures. So if pleasure is all that matters then in these cases one should choose the cure. Only if a separate desire for dignity trumps the desire for pleasure could such a choice be wrong.

Let's finally consider how Mill's liberalism influences his account of moral duty. I noted that his principle of liberty allows prohibition or compulsion of conduct only on specific grounds. One such ground is that an action will harm others, another is that a failure to act can justifiably be considered a violation of duty to others. But what duties to others do we have? Do we not, according to the utilitarian, have a standing moral duty to do that which is best for all? Can we not therefore be compelled to carry out this duty, consistently with the liberty principle? Such a conclusion would collapse the principle, because a distinction between the moral significance of harming others on the one hand and failing to benefit them on the other is quite basic to its liberty-protecting force.

Mill does not think we have a standing duty to do that which is best for all. In fact he strenuously opposes that notion – for example in his critique of his French contemporary Auguste Comte, whom he thought a "morality-intoxicated man":

> There is a standard of altruism to which all should be required to come up, and a degree beyond which it is not obligatory, but meritorious. It is incumbent on every one to restrain the pursuit of his personal objects within the limits consistent with the essential interests of others. What those limits are, it is the province of ethical science to determine; and to keep all individuals and aggregates of individuals within them, is the proper office of punishment and of moral blame. If in addition to fulfilling this obligation, persons make the good of others a direct object of disinterested exertions, postponing or sacrificing to it even innocent personal indulgences, they deserve gratitude and honour, and are fit objects of moral praise. So long as they are in no way compelled to this conduct by any external pressure, there cannot be too much of it; but a necessary condition is its spontaneity; since the notion of a happiness for all, procured by the self-sacrifice of each, if the abnegation is really felt to be a sacrifice, is a contradiction. (1865: 337–8)

The theory of moral duty that Mill gives in Chapter V is fundamental to this liberal version of utilitarianism. There he defines a moral wrongdoing as an act for which the individual ought to be punished "if not by law, by the opinion of his fellow-creatures; if not by opinion, by the reproaches of his own conscience." "It is," he continues, a part of the notion of Duty in every one of its forms, that a person may rightfully be compelled to fulfill it. Duty is a thing which may be *exacted* from a person, as one exacts a debt. (V, 14)

Morality is concerned with that which an individual may be "compelled," and not merely "persuaded and exhorted," to do.

So in Mill's view morality and law are both disciplinary codes by which society exercises its sovereignty over individual behavior. This is not to deny that there are important questions about when society should exercise its sovereignty by means of moral punishment alone and when it should do so by positive legal sanction. Either way, however, Mill is concerned to ensure that society's sovereignty is kept within strict limits. His doctrine is that an action which breaches no other-regarding duty is never morally wrong, and his theory of moral duties is liberal, not rigorist. Nevertheless the justification for this liberal view, according to Mill, remains utilitarian. The basic case for liberalism is that human beings achieve the most valuable forms of happiness under liberal morality and liberal law.

References

Mill, John Stuart (1833) "Remarks on Bentham's philosophy," in J. M. Robson (ed.) *Collected Works of John Stuart Mill*, Vol. X: *Essays on Ethics, Religion, and Society* (pp. 3–18). Toronto: University of Toronto Press, 1969.

——(1843) *A System of Logic Ratiocinative and Inductive*, in J. M. Robson (ed.) *Collected Works of John Stuart Mill*, Vols. VII–VIII. Toronto: University of Toronto Press, 1973.

——(1859) *On Liberty*, in J. M. Robson (ed.) *Collected Works of John Stuart Mill*, Vols. XVIII–XIX: *Essays on Politics and Society* (pp. 213–310). Toronto: University of Toronto Press, 1977.

——(1865) *August Comte and Positivism*, in J. M. Robson (ed.) *Collected Works of John Stuart Mill*, Vol. X: *Essays on Ethics, Religion, and Society* (pp. 261–368). Toronto: University of Toronto Press, 1969.

——(1861) *Utilitarianism*, in J. M. Robson (ed.) *Collected Works of John Stuart Milli*, Vol. X: *Essays on Ethics, Religion, and Society* (pp. 203–59). Toronto: University of Toronto Press, 1969. (Reprinted as Part II of this volume; citations are by roman numeral to chapter and by arabic numeral to paragraph of this reprint.)

——(1873) *Autobiography*, in J. M. Robson and John Stillinger (eds.) *Collected Works of John Stuart Mill*, Vol. I: *Autobiography and Literary Essays* (pp. 1–290). Toronto: University of Toronto Press, 1981.

——(1972) Letters, in Francis E. Mineka and Dwight N. Lindley (eds.) *Collected Works of John Stuart Mill*, Vols. XIV–XVII: *The Later Letters of John Stuart Mill 1849–1873*. Toronto: University of Toronto Press.

Part II

The Complete Text of
John Stuart Mill's
Utilitarianism

Chapter I

General Remarks

THERE ARE few circumstances among those which make up the present condition of human knowledge, more unlike what might have been expected, or more significant of the backward state in which speculation on the most important subjects still lingers, than the little progress which has been made in the decision of the controversy respecting the criterion of right and wrong. From the dawn of philosophy, the question concerning the *summum bonum*, or, what is the same thing, concerning the foundation of morality, has been accounted the main problem in speculative thought, has occupied the most gifted intellects, and divided them into sects and schools, carrying on a vigorous warfare against one another. And after more than two thousand years the same discussions continue, philosophers are still ranged under the same contending banners, and neither thinkers nor mankind at large seem nearer to being unanimous on the subject, than when the youth Socrates listened to the old Protagoras, and asserted (if Plato's dialogue be grounded on a real conversation) the theory of utilitarianism against the popular morality of the so-called sophist.

[2]   It is true that similar confusion and uncertainty, and in some cases similar discordance, exist respecting the first principles of all the sciences, not excepting that which is deemed the most certain of them, mathematics; without much impairing, generally indeed without impairing at all, the trustworthiness of the conclusions of those sciences. An apparent anomaly, the explanation of which is, that the detailed doctrines of a science are not usually deduced from, nor depend for their evidence upon, what are called its first principles. Were it not so, there would be no science more precarious, or whose conclusions were more insufficiently made out, than algebra; which derives none of its certainty from what are commonly taught to learners as its elements, since these, as laid down by some of its most eminent teachers, are as full of fictions as English law, and of mysteries as theology. The truths which are ultimately accepted as the first principles of a science, are really the last results of metaphysical analysis, practised on the elementary notions with which the science is conversant; and their relation to the

science is not that of foundations to an edifice, but of roots to a tree, which may perform their office equally well though they be never dug down to and exposed to light. But though in science the particular truths precede the general theory, the contrary might be expected to be the case with a practical art, such as morals or legislation. All action is for the sake of some end, and rules of action, it seems natural to suppose, must take their whole character and colour from the end to which they are subservient. When we engage in a pursuit, a clear and precise conception of what we are pursuing would seem to be the first thing we need, instead of the last we are to look forward to. A test of right and wrong must be the means, one would think, of ascertaining what is right or wrong, and not a consequence of having already ascertained it.

[3] The difficulty is not avoided by having recourse to the popular theory of a natural faculty, a sense or instinct, informing us of right and wrong. For – besides that the existence of such a moral instinct is itself one of the matters in dispute – those believers in it who have any pretensions to philosophy, have been obliged to abandon the idea that it discerns what is right or wrong in the particular case in hand, as our other senses discern the sight or sound actually present. Our moral faculty, according to all those of its interpreters who are entitled to the name of thinkers, supplies us only with the general principles of moral judgments; it is a branch of our reason, not of our sensitive faculty; and must be looked to for the abstract doctrines of morality, not for perception of it in the concrete. The intuitive, no less than what may be termed the inductive, school of ethics, insists on the necessity of general laws. They both agree that the morality of an individual action is not a question of direct perception, but of the application of a law to an individual case. They recognise also, to a great extent, the same moral laws; but differ as to their evidence, and the source from which they derive their authority. According to the one opinion, the principles of morals are evident *a priori*, requiring nothing to command assent, except that the meaning of the terms be understood. According to the other doctrine, right and wrong, as well as truth and falsehood, are questions of observation and experience. But both hold equally that morality must be deduced from principles; and the intuitive school affirm as strongly as the inductive, that there is a science of morals. Yet they seldom attempt to make out a list of the *a priori* principles which are to serve as the premises of the science; still more rarely do they make any effort to reduce those various principles to one first principle, or common ground of obligation. They either assume the ordinary precepts of morals as of *a priori* authority, or they lay down as the common groundwork of those maxims, some generality much less obviously authoritative than the maxims themselves, and which has never succeeded in gaining popular acceptance. Yet to support their pretensions there ought either to be some one fundamental principle or law, at the root of all morality, or if there be several, there should be a determinate order of precedence among them; and the one principle, or the rule for deciding between the various principles when they conflict, ought to be self-evident.

[4]   To inquire how far the bad effects of this deficiency have been mitigated in practice, or to what extent the moral beliefs of mankind have been vitiated or made uncertain by the absence of any distinct recognition of an ultimate standard, would imply a complete survey and criticism, of past and present ethical doctrine. It would, however, be easy to show that whatever steadiness or consistency these moral beliefs have attained, has been mainly due to the tacit influence of a standard not recognised. Although the non-existence of an acknowledged first principle has made ethics not so much a guide as a consecration of men's actual sentiments, still, as men's sentiments, both of favour and of aversion, are greatly influenced by what they suppose to be the effects of things upon their happiness, the principle of utility, or as Bentham latterly called it, the greatest happiness principle, has had a large share in forming the moral doctrines even of those who most scornfully reject its authority. Nor is there any school of thought which refuses to admit that the influence of actions on happiness is a most material and even predominant consideration in many of the details of morals, however unwilling to acknowledge it as the fundamental principle of morality, and the source of moral obligation. I might go much further, and say that to all those *a priori* moralists who deem it necessary to argue at all, utilitarian arguments are indispensable. It is not my present purpose to criticise these thinkers; but I cannot help referring, for illustration, to a systematic treatise by one of the most illustrious of them, the *Metaphysics of Ethics*, by Kant. This remarkable man, whose system of thought will long remain one of the landmarks in the history of philosophical speculation, does, in the treatise in question, lay down a universal first principle as the origin and ground of moral obligation; it is this: "So act, that the rule on which thou actest would admit of being adopted as a law by all rational beings." But when he begins to deduce from this precept any of the actual duties of morality, he fails, almost grotesquely, to show that there would be any contradiction, any logical (not to say physical) impossibility, in the adoption by all rational beings of the most outrageously immoral rules of conduct. All he shows is that the consequences of their universal adoption would be such as no one would choose to incur.

[5]   On the present occasion, I shall, without further discussion of the other theories, attempt to contribute something towards the understanding and appreciation of the Utilitarian or Happiness theory, and towards such proof as it is susceptible of. It is evident that this cannot be proof in the ordinary and popular meaning of the term. Questions of ultimate ends are not amenable to direct proof. Whatever can be proved to be good, must be so by being shown to be a means to something admitted to be good without proof. The medical art is proved to be good by its conducing to health; but how is it possible to prove that health is good? The art of music is good, for the reason, among others, that it produces pleasure; but what proof is it possible to give that pleasure is good? If, then, it is asserted that there is a comprehensive formula, including all things which are in themselves good, and that whatever else is good, is not so as an end, but as a mean, the formula may be accepted or rejected, but is not a subject of what is

commonly understood by proof. We are not, however, to infer that its acceptance or rejection must depend on blind impulse, or arbitrary choice. There is a larger meaning of the word proof, in which this question is as amenable to it as any other of the disputed questions of philosophy. The subject is within the cognisance of the rational faculty; and neither does that faculty deal with it solely in the way of intuition. Considerations may be presented capable of determining the intellect either to give or withhold its assent to the doctrine; and this is equivalent to proof.

[6]   We shall examine presently of what nature are these considerations; in what manner they apply to the case, and what rational grounds, therefore, can be given for accepting or rejecting the utilitarian formula. But it is a preliminary condition of rational acceptance or rejection, that the formula should be correctly understood. I believe that the very imperfect notion ordinarily formed of its meaning, is the chief obstacle which impedes its reception; and that could it be cleared, even from only the grosser misconceptions, the question would be greatly simplified, and a large proportion of its difficulties removed. Before, therefore, I attempt to enter into the philosophical grounds which can be given for assenting to the utilitarian standard, I shall offer some illustrations of the doctrine itself; with the view of showing more clearly what it is, distinguishing it from what it is not, and disposing of such of the practical objections to it as either originate in, or are closely connected with, mistaken interpretations of its meaning. Having thus prepared the ground, I shall afterwards endeavour to throw such light as I can upon the question, considered as one of philosophical theory.

Chapter II

What Utilitarianism Is

A PASSING REMARK is all that needs be given to the ignorant blunder of supposing that those who stand up for utility as the test of right and wrong, use the term in that restricted and merely colloquial sense in which utility is opposed to pleasure. An apology is due to the philosophical opponents of utilitarianism, for even the momentary appearance of confounding them with any one capable of so absurd a misconception; which is the more extraordinary, inasmuch as the contrary accusation, of referring everything to pleasure, and that too in its grossest form, is another of the common charges against utilitarianism: and, as has been pointedly remarked by an able writer, the same sort of persons, and often the very same persons, denounce the theory "as impracticably dry when the word utility precedes the word pleasure, and as too practically voluptuous when the word pleasure precedes the word utility." Those who know anything about the matter are aware that every writer, from Epicurus to Bentham, who maintained the theory of utility, meant by it, not something to be contradistinguished from pleasure, but pleasure itself, together with exemption from pain; and instead of opposing the useful to the agreeable or the ornamental, have always declared that the useful means these, among other things. Yet the common herd, including the herd of writers, not only in newspapers and periodicals, but in books of weight and pretension, are perpetually falling into this shallow mistake. Having caught up the word utilitarian, while knowing nothing whatever about it but its sound, they habitually express by it the rejection, or the neglect, of pleasure in some of its forms; of beauty, of ornament, or of amusement. Nor is the term thus ignorantly misapplied solely in disparagement, but occasionally in compliment; as though it implied superiority to frivolity and the mere pleasures of the moment. And this perverted use is the only one in which the word is popularly known, and the one from which the new generation are acquiring their sole notion of its meaning. Those who introduced the word, but who had for many years discontinued it as a distinctive appellation, may well feel themselves called upon to resume it, if by doing so they can hope to contribute anything towards rescuing it from this utter degradation.*

[2]   The creed which accepts as the foundation of morals, Utility, or the Greatest Happiness Principle, holds that actions are right in proportion as they tend to promote happiness, wrong as they tend to produce the reverse of happiness. By happiness is intended pleasure, and the absence of pain; by unhappiness, pain, and the privation of pleasure. To give a clear view of the moral standard set up by the theory, much more requires to be said; in particular, what things it includes in the ideas of pain and pleasure; and to what extent this is left an open question. But these supplementary explanations do not affect the theory of life on which this theory of morality is grounded – namely, that pleasure, and freedom from pain, are the only things desirable as ends; and that all desirable things (which are as numerous in the utilitarian as in any other scheme) are desirable either for the pleasure inherent in themselves, or as means to the promotion of pleasure and the prevention of pain.

[3]   Now, such a theory of life excites in many minds, and among them in some of the most estimable in feeling and purpose, inveterate dislike. To suppose that life has (as they express it) no higher end than pleasure – no better and nobler object of desire and pursuit – they designate as utterly mean and grovelling; as a doctrine worthy only of swine, to whom the followers of Epicurus were, at a very early period, contemptuously likened; and modern holders of the doctrine are occasionally made the subject of equally polite comparisons by its German, French, and English assailants.

[4]   When thus attacked, the Epicureans have always answered, that it is not they, but their accusers, who represent human nature in a degrading light; since the accusation supposes human beings to be capable of no pleasures except those of which swine are capable. If this supposition were true, the charge could not be gainsaid, but would then be no longer an imputation; for if the sources of pleasure were precisely the same to human beings and to swine, the rule of life which is good enough for the one would be good enough for the other. The comparison of the Epicurean life to that of beasts is felt as degrading, precisely because a beast's pleasures do not satisfy a human being's conceptions of happiness. Human beings have faculties more elevated than the animal appetites, and when once made

---

* The author of this essay has reason for believing himself to be the first person who brought the word utilitarian into use. He did not invent it, but adopted it from a passing expression in Mr. Galt's *Annals of the Parish*. After using it as a designation for several years, he and others abandoned it from a growing dislike to anything resembling a badge or watchword of sectarian distinction. But as a name for one single opinion, not a set of opinions – to denote the recognition of utility as a standard, not any particular way of applying it – the term supplies a want in the language, and offers, in many cases, a convenient mode of avoiding tiresome circumlocution.

conscious of them, do not regard anything as happiness which does not include their gratification. I do not, indeed, consider the Epicureans to have been by any means faultless in drawing out their scheme of consequences from the utilitarian principle. To do this in any sufficient manner, many Stoic, as well as Christian elements require to be included. But there is no known Epicurean theory of life which does not assign to the pleasures of the intellect, of the feelings and imagination, and of the moral sentiments, a much higher value as pleasures than to those of mere sensation. It must be admitted, however, that utilitarian writers in general have placed the superiority of mental over bodily pleasures chiefly in the greater permanency, safety, uncostliness, etc., of the former – that is, in their circumstantial advantages rather than in their intrinsic nature. And on all these points utilitarians have fully proved their case; but they might have taken the other, and, as it may be called, higher ground, with entire consistency. It is quite compatible with the principle of utility to recognise the fact, that some *kinds* of pleasure are more desirable and more valuable than others. It would be absurd that while, in estimating all other things, quality is considered as well as quantity, the estimation of pleasures should be supposed to depend on quantity alone.

[5]   If I am asked, what I mean by difference of quality in pleasures, or what makes one pleasure more valuable than another, merely as a pleasure, except its being greater in amount, there is but one possible answer. Of two pleasures, if there be one to which all or almost all who have experience of both give a decided preference, irrespective of any feeling of moral obligation to prefer it, that is the more desirable pleasure. If one of the two is, by those who are competently acquainted with both, placed so far above the other that they prefer it, even though knowing it to be attended with a greater amount of discontent, and would not resign it for any quantity of the other pleasure which their nature is capable of, we are justified in ascribing to the preferred enjoyment a superiority in quality, so far outweighing quantity as to render it, in comparison, of small account.

[6]   Now it is an unquestionable fact that those who are equally acquainted with, and equally capable of appreciating and enjoying, both, do give a most marked preference to the manner of existence which employs their higher faculties. Few human creatures would consent to be changed into any of the lower animals, for a promise of the fullest allowance of a beast's pleasures; no intelligent human being would consent to be a fool, no instructed person would be an ignoramus, no person of feeling and conscience would be selfish and base, even though they should be persuaded that the fool, the dunce, or the rascal is better satisfied with his lot than they are with theirs. They would not resign what they possess more than he for the most complete satisfaction of all the desires which they have in common with him. If they ever fancy they would, it is only in cases of unhappiness so extreme, that to escape from it they would exchange their lot for almost any other, however undesirable in their own eyes. A being of higher faculties requires more to make him happy, is capable probably of more acute suffering, and is certainly accessible to it at more points, than one of an inferior type; but

in spite of these liabilities, he can never really wish to sink into what he feels to be a lower grade of existence. We may give what explanation we please of this unwillingness; we may attribute it to pride, a name which is given indiscriminately to some of the most and to some of the least estimable feelings of which mankind are capable: we may refer it to the love of liberty and personal independence, an appeal to which was with the Stoics one of the most effective means for the inculcation of it; to the love of power, or to the love of excitement, both of which do really enter into and contribute to it: but its most appropriate appellation is a sense of dignity, which all human beings possess in one form or other, and in some, though by no means in exact, proportion to their higher faculties, and which is so essential a part of the happiness of those in whom it is strong, that nothing which conflicts with it could be, otherwise than momentarily, an object of desire to them. Whoever supposes that this preference takes place at a sacrifice of happiness – that the superior being, in anything like equal circumstances, is not happier than the inferior- confounds the two very different ideas, of happiness, and content. It is indisputable that the being whose capacities of enjoyment are low, has the greatest chance of having them fully satisfied; and a highly endowed being will always feel that any happiness which he can look for, as the world is constituted, is imperfect. But he can learn to bear its imperfections, if they are at all bearable; and they will not make him envy the being who is indeed unconscious of the imperfections, but only because he feels not at all the good which those imperfections qualify. It is better to be a human being dissatisfied than a pig satisfied; better to be Socrates dissatisfied than a fool satisfied. And if the fool, or the pig, is a different opinion, it is because they only know their own side of the question. The other party to the comparison knows both sides.

[7]   It may be objected, that many who are capable of the higher pleasures, occasionally, under the influence of temptation, postpone them to the lower. But this is quite compatible with a full appreciation of the intrinsic superiority of the higher. Men often, from infirmity of character, make their election for the nearer good, though they know it to be the less valuable; and this no less when the choice is between two bodily pleasures, than when it is between bodily and mental. They pursue sensual indulgences to the injury of health, though perfectly aware that health is the greater good. It may be further objected, that many who begin with youthful enthusiasm for everything noble, as they advance in years sink into indolence and selfishness. But I do not believe that those who undergo this very common change, voluntarily choose the lower description of pleasures in preference to the higher. I believe that before they devote themselves exclusively to the one, they have already become incapable of the other. Capacity for the nobler feelings is in most natures a very tender plant, easily killed, not only by hostile influences, but by mere want of sustenance; and in the majority of young persons it speedily dies away if the occupations to which their position in life has devoted them, and the society into which it has thrown them, are not favourable to keeping that higher capacity in exercise. Men lose their high

aspirations as they lose their intellectual tastes, because they have not time or opportunity for indulging them; and they addict themselves to inferior pleasures, not because they deliberately prefer them, but because they are either the only ones to which they have access, or the only ones which they are any longer capable of enjoying. It may be questioned whether any one who has remained equally susceptible to both classes of pleasures, ever knowingly and calmly preferred the lower; though many, in all ages, have broken down in an ineffectual attempt to combine both.

[8]   From this verdict of the only competent judges, I apprehend there can be no appeal. On a question which is the best worth having of two pleasures, or which of two modes of existence is the most grateful to the feelings, apart from its moral attributes and from its consequences, the judgment of those who are qualified by knowledge of both, or, if they differ, that of the majority among them, must be admitted as final. And there needs be the less hesitation to accept this judgment respecting the quality of pleasures, since there is no other tribunal to be referred to even on the question of quantity. What means are there of determining which is the acutest of two pains, or the intensest of two pleasurable sensations, except the general suffrage of those who are familiar with both? Neither pains nor pleasures are homogeneous, and pain is always heterogeneous with pleasure. What is there to decide whether a particular pleasure is worth purchasing at the cost of a particular pain, except the feelings and judgment of the experienced? When, therefore, those feelings and judgment declare the pleasures derived from the higher faculties to be preferable *in kind*, apart from the question of intensity, to those of which the animal nature, disjoined from the higher faculties, is suspectible, they are entitled on this subject to the same regard.

[9]   I have dwelt on this point, as being a necessary part of a perfectly just conception of Utility or Happiness, considered as the directive rule of human conduct. But it is by no means an indispensable condition to the acceptance of the utilitarian standard; for that standard is not the agent's own greatest happiness, but the greatest amount of happiness altogether; and if it may possibly be doubted whether a noble character is always the happier for its nobleness, there can be no doubt that it makes other people happier, and that the world in general is immensely a gainer by it. Utilitarianism, therefore, could only attain its end by the general cultivation of nobleness of character, even if each individual were only benefited by the nobleness of others, and his own, so far as happiness is concerned, were a sheer deduction from the benefit. But the bare enunciation of such an absurdity as this last, renders refutation superfluous.

[10]   According to the Greatest Happiness Principle, as above explained, the ultimate end, with reference to and for the sake of which all other things are desirable (whether we are considering our own good or that of other people), is an existence exempt as far as possible from pain, and as rich as possible in enjoyments, both in point of quantity and quality; the test of quality, and the rule for

measuring it against quantity, being the preference felt by those who in their opportunities of experience, to which must be added their habits of self-consciousness and self-observation, are best furnished with the means of comparison. This, being, according to the utilitarian opinion, the end of human action, is necessarily also the standard of morality; which may accordingly be defined, the rules and precepts for human conduct, by the observance of which an existence such as has been described might be, to the greatest extent possible, secured to all mankind; and not to them only, but, so far as the nature of things admits, to the whole sentient creation.

[11]   Against this doctrine, however, arises another class of objectors, who say that happiness, in any form, cannot be the rational purpose of human life and action; because, in the first place, it is unattainable: and they contemptuously ask, what right hast thou to be happy? a question which Mr. Carlyle clenches by the addition, What right, a short time ago, hadst thou even *to be*? Next, they say, that men can do *without* happiness; that all noble human beings have felt this, and could not have become noble but by learning the lesson of Entsagen, or renunciation; which lesson, thoroughly learnt and submitted to, they affirm to be the beginning and necessary condition of all virtue.

[12]   The first of these objections would go to the root of the matter were it well founded; for if no happiness is to be had at all by human beings, the attainment of it cannot be the end of morality, or of any rational conduct. Though, even in that case, something might still be said for the utilitarian theory; since utility includes not solely the pursuit of happiness, but the prevention or mitigation of unhappiness; and if the former aim be chimerical, there will be all the greater scope and more imperative need for the latter, so long at least as mankind think fit to live, and do not take refuge in the simultaneous act of suicide recommended under certain conditions by Novalis. When, however, it is thus positively asserted to be impossible that human life should be happy, the assertion, if not something like a verbal quibble, is at least an exaggeration. If by happiness be meant a continuity of highly pleasurable excitement, it is evident enough that this is impossible. A state of exalted pleasure lasts only moments, or in some cases, and with some intermissions, hours or days, and is the occasional brilliant flash of enjoyment, not its permanent and steady flame. Of this the philosophers who have taught that happiness is the end of life were as fully aware as those who taunt them. The happiness which they meant was not a life of rapture; but moments of such, in an existence made up of few and transitory pains, many and various pleasures, with a decided predominance of the active over the passive, and having as the foundation of the whole, not to expect more from life than it is capable of bestowing. A life thus composed, to those who have been fortunate enough to obtain it, has always appeared worthy of the name of happiness. And such an existence is even now the lot of many, during some considerable portion of their lives. The present wretched education, and wretched social arrangements, are the only real hindrance to its being attainable by almost all.

[13]   The objectors perhaps may doubt whether human beings, if taught to consider happiness as the end of life, would be satisfied with such a moderate share of it. But great numbers of mankind have been satisfied with much less. The main constituents of a satisfied life appear to be two, either of which by itself is often found sufficient for the purpose: tranquillity, and excitement. With much tranquillity, many find that they can be content with very little pleasure: with much excitement, many can reconcile themselves to a considerable quantity of pain. There is assuredly no inherent impossibility in enabling even the mass of mankind to unite both; since the two are so far from being incompatible that they are in natural alliance, the prolongation of either being a preparation for, and exciting a wish for, the other. It is only those in whom indolence amounts to a vice, that do not desire excitement after an interval of repose: it is only those in whom the need of excitement is a disease, that feel the tranquillity which follows excitement dull and insipid, instead of pleasurable in direct proportion to the excitement which preceded it. When people who are tolerably fortunate in their outward lot do not find in life sufficient enjoyment to make it valuable to them, the cause generally is, caring for nobody but themselves. To those who have neither public nor private affections, the excitements of life are much curtailed, and in any case dwindle in value as the time approaches when all selfish interests must be terminated by death: while those who leave after them objects of personal affection, and especially those who have also cultivated a fellow-feeling with the collective interests of mankind, retain as lively an interest in life on the eve of death as in the vigour of youth and health. Next to selfishness, the principal cause which makes life unsatisfactory is want of mental cultivation. A cultivated mind – I do not mean that of a philosopher, but any mind to which the fountains of knowledge have been opened, and which has been taught, in any tolerable degree, to exercise its faculties – finds sources of inexhaustible interest in all that surrounds it; in the objects of nature, the achievements of art, the imaginations of poetry, the incidents of history, the ways of mankind, past and present, and their prospects in the future. It is possible, indeed, to become indifferent to all this, and that too without having exhausted a thousandth part of it; but only when one has had from the beginning no moral or human interest in these things, and has sought in them only the gratification of curiosity.

[14]   Now there is absolutely no reason in the nature of things why an amount of mental culture sufficient to give an intelligent interest in these objects of contemplation, should not be the inheritance of every one born in a civilised country. As little is there an inherent necessity that any human being should be a selfish egotist, devoid of every feeling or care but those which centre in his own miserable individuality. Something far superior to this is sufficiently common even now, to give ample earnest of what the human species may be made. Genuine private affections and a sincere interest in the public good, are possible, though in unequal degrees, to every rightly brought up human being. In a world in which there is so much to interest, so much to enjoy, and so much also to correct and

improve, every one who has this moderate amount of moral and intellectual requisites is capable of an existence which may be called enviable; and unless such a person, through bad laws, or subjection to the will of others, is denied the liberty to use the sources of happiness within his reach, he will not fail to find this enviable existence, if he escape the positive evils of life, the great sources of physical and mental suffering – such as indigence, disease, and the unkindness, worthlessness, or premature loss of objects of affection. The main stress of the problem lies, therefore, in the contest with these calamities, from which it is a rare good fortune entirely to escape; which, as things now are, cannot be obviated, and often cannot be in any material degree mitigated. Yet no one whose opinion deserves a moment's consideration can doubt that most of the great positive evils of the world are in themselves removable, and will, if human affairs continue to improve, be in the end reduced within narrow limits. Poverty, in any sense implying suffering, may be completely extinguished by the wisdom of society, combined with the good sense and providence of individuals. Even that most intractable of enemies, disease, may be indefinitely reduced in dimensions by good physical and moral education, and proper control of noxious influences; while the progress of science holds out a promise for the future of still more direct conquests over this detestable foe. And every advance in that direction relieves us from some, not only of the chances which cut short our own lives, but, what concerns us still more, which deprive us of those in whom our happiness is wrapt up. As for vicissitudes of fortune, and other disappointments connected with worldly circumstances, these are principally the effect either of gross imprudence, of ill-regulated desires, or of bad or imperfect social institutions. All the grand sources, in short, of human suffering are in a great degree, many of them almost entirely, conquerable by human care and effort; and though their removal is grievously slow – though a long succession of generations will perish in the breach before the conquest is completed, and this world becomes all that, if will and knowledge were not wanting, it might easily be made – yet every mind sufficiently intelligent and generous to bear a part, however small and unconspicuous, in the endeavour, will draw a noble enjoyment from the contest itself, which he would not for any bribe in the form of selfish indulgence consent to be without.

[15]   And this leads to the true estimation of what is said by the objectors concerning the possibility, and the obligation, of learning to do without happiness. Unquestionably it is possible to do without happiness; it is done involuntarily by nineteen-twentieths of mankind, even in those parts of our present world which are least deep in barbarism; and it often has to be done voluntarily by the hero or the martyr, for the sake of something which he prizes more than his individual happiness. But this something, what is it, unless the happiness of others or some of the requisites of happiness? It is noble to be capable of resigning entirely one's own portion of happiness, or chances of it: but, after all, this self-sacrifice must be for some end; it is not its own end; and if we are told that its end is not happiness, but virtue, which is better than happiness, I ask, would the sacrifice be

made if the hero or martyr did not believe that it would earn for others immunity from similar sacrifices? Would it be made if he thought that his renunciation of happiness for himself would produce no fruit for any of his fellow creatures, but to make their lot like his, and place them also in the condition of persons who have renounced happiness? All honour to those who can abnegate for themselves the personal enjoyment of life, when by such renunciation they contribute worthily to increase the amount of happiness in the world; but he who does it, or professes to do it, for any other purpose, is no more deserving of admiration than the ascetic mounted on his pillar. He may be an inspiriting proof of what men *can* do, but assuredly not an example of what they *should*.

[16]   Though it is only in a very imperfect state of the world's arrangements that any one can best serve the happiness of others by the absolute sacrifice of his own, yet so long as the world is in that imperfect state, I fully acknowledge that the readiness to make such a sacrifice is the highest virtue which can be found in man. I will add, that in this condition the world, paradoxical as the assertion may be, the conscious ability to do without happiness gives the best prospect of realising, such happiness as is attainable. For nothing except that consciousness can raise a person above the chances of life, by making him feel that, let fate and fortune do their worst, they have not power to subdue him: which, once felt, frees him from excess of anxiety concerning the evils of life, and enables him, like many a Stoic in the worst times of the Roman Empire, to cultivate in tranquillity the sources of satisfaction accessible to him, without concerning himself about the uncertainty of their duration, any more than about their inevitable end.

[17]   Meanwhile, let utilitarians never cease to claim the morality of self devotion as a possession which belongs by as good a right to them, as either to the Stoic or to the Transcendentalist. The utilitarian morality does recognise in human beings the power of sacrificing their own greatest good for the good of others. It only refuses to admit that the sacrifice is itself a good. A sacrifice which does not increase, or tend to increase, the sum total of happiness, it considers as wasted. The only self-renunciation which it applauds, is devotion to the happiness, or to some of the means of happiness, of others; either of mankind collectively, or of individuals within the limits imposed by the collective interests of mankind.

[18]   I must again repeat, what the assailants of utilitarianism seldom have the justice to acknowledge, that the happiness which forms the utilitarian standard of what is right in conduct, is not the agent's own happiness, but that of all concerned. As between his own happiness and that of others, utilitarianism requires him to be as strictly impartial as a disinterested and benevolent spectator. In the golden rule of Jesus of Nazareth, we read the complete spirit of the ethics of utility. To do as one would be done by, and to love one's neighbour as oneself, constitute the ideal perfection of utilitarian morality. As the means of making the nearest approach to this ideal, utility would enjoin, first, that laws and social arrangements should place the happiness, or (as speaking practically it may be called) the interest, of every individual, as nearly as possible in harmony with the interest of the

whole; and secondly, that education and opinion, which have so vast a power over human character, should so use that power as to establish in the mind of every individual an indissoluble association between his own happiness and the good of the whole; especially between his own happiness and the practice of such modes of conduct, negative and positive, as regard for the universal happiness prescribes; so that not only he may be unable to conceive the possibility of happiness to himself, consistently with conduct opposed to the general good, but also that a direct impulse to promote the general good may be in every individual one of the habitual motives of action, and the sentiments connected therewith may fill a large and prominent place in every human being's sentient existence. If the impugners of the utilitarian morality represented it to their own minds in this its true character, I know not what recommendation possessed by any other morality they could possibly affirm to be wanting to it; what more beautiful or more exalted developments of human nature any other ethical system can be supposed to foster, or what springs of action, not accessible to the utilitarian, such systems rely on for giving effect to their mandates.

[19]   The objectors to utilitarianism cannot always be charged with representing it in a discreditable light. On the contrary, those among them who entertain anything like a just idea of its disinterested character, sometimes find fault with its standard as being too high for humanity. They say it is exacting too much to require that people shall always act from the inducement of promoting the general interests of society. But this is to mistake the very meaning of a standard of morals, and to confound the rule of action with the motive of it. It is the business of ethics to tell us what are our duties, or by what test we may know them; but no system of ethics requires that the sole motive of all we do shall be a feeling of duty; on the contrary, ninety-nine hundredths of all our actions are done from other motives, and rightly so done, if the rule of duty does not condemn them. It is the more unjust to utilitarianism that this particular misapprehension should be made a ground of objection to it, inasmuch as utilitarian moralists have gone beyond almost all others in affirming that the motive has nothing to do with the morality of the action, though much with the worth of the agent. He who saves a fellow creature from drowning does what is morally right, whether his motive be duty, or the hope of being paid for his trouble; he who betrays the friend that trusts him, is guilty of a crime, even if his object be to serve another friend to whom he is under greater obligations.* But to speak only of actions done from

---

* An opponent, whose intellectual and moral fairness it is a pleasure to acknowledge (the Rev. J. Llewellyn Davies), has objected to this passage, saying "Surely the rightness or wrongness of saving a man from drowning does depend very much upon the motive with which it is done. Suppose that a tyrant, when his enemy jumped into the sea to escape from him, saved him from drowning simply in order that he might inflict upon him more exquisite tortures, would it tend to clearness to speak of that rescue as 'a morally right action?' Or suppose again, according to one of the stock illustrations of ethical inquiries, that a man

the motive of duty, and in direct obedience to principle: it is a misapprehension of the utilitarian mode of thought, to conceive it as implying that people should fix their minds upon so wide a generality as the world, or society at large. The great majority of good actions are intended not for the benefit of the world, but for that of individuals, of which the good of the world is made up; and the thoughts of the most virtuous man need not on these occasions travel beyond the particular persons concerned, except so far as is necessary to assure himself that in benefiting them he is not violating the rights, that is, the legitimate and autho-rised expectations, of any one else. The multiplication of happiness is, according to the utilitarian ethics, the object of virtue: the occasions on which any person (except one in a thousand) has it in his power to do this on an extended scale, in other words to be a public benefactor, are but exceptional; and on these occasions alone is he called on to consider public utility; in every other case, private utility, the interest or happiness of some few persons, is all he has to attend to. Those alone the influence of whose actions extends to society in general, need concern themselves habitually about large an object. In the case of abstinences indeed – of things which people forbear to do from moral considerations, though the conse-quences in the particular case might be beneficial – it would be unworthy of an intelligent agent not to be consciously aware that the action is of a class which, if practised generally, would be generally injurious, and that this is the ground of the obligation to abstain from it. The amount of regard for the public interest implied in this recognition, is no greater than is demanded by every system of morals, for they all enjoin to abstain from whatever is manifestly pernicious to society.

betrayed a trust received from a friend, because the discharge of it would fatally injure that friend himself or some one belonging to him, would utilitarianism compel one to call the betrayal 'a crime' as much as if it had been done from the meanest motive?"

I submit, that he who saves another from drowning in order to kill him be torture after-wards, does not differ only in motive from him who does the same thing from duty or benevolence; the act itself is different. The rescue of the man is, in the case supposed, only the necessary first step of an act far more atrocious than leaving him to drown would have been. Had Mr. Davies said, "The rightness or wrongness of saving a man from drowning does depend very much" – not upon the motive, but – "upon the *intention*," no utilitar-ian would have differed from him. Mr. Davies, by an oversight too common not to be quite venial, has in this case confounded the very different ideas of Motive and Intention. There is no point which utilitarian thinkers (and Bentham pre-eminently) have taken more pains to illustrate than this. The morality of the action depends entirely upon the intention – that is, upon what the agent *wills to do*. But the motive, that is, the feeling which makes him will so to do, when it makes no difference in the act, makes none in the morality; though it makes a great difference in our moral estimation of the agent, especially if it indicates a good or a bad habitual *disposition* – a bent of character from which useful, or from which hurtful actions are likely to arise. [Footnote added to edition of 1864].

[20]   The same considerations dispose of another reproach against the doctrine of utility, founded on a still grosser misconception of the purpose of a standard of morality, and of the very meaning of the words right and wrong. It is often affirmed that utilitarianism renders men cold and unsympathising; that it chills their moral feelings towards individuals; that it makes them regard only the dry and hard consideration of the consequences of actions, not taking into their moral estimate the qualities from which those actions emanate. If the assertion means that they do not allow their judgment respecting the rightness or wrongness of an action to be influenced by their opinion of the qualities of the person who does it, this is a complaint not against utilitarianism, but against having any standard of morality at all; for certainly no known ethical standard decides an action to be good or bad because it is done by a good or a bad man, still less because done by an amiable, a brave, or a benevolent man, or the contrary. These considerations are relevant, not to the estimation of actions, but of persons; and there is nothing in the utilitarian theory inconsistent with the fact that there are other things which interest us in persons besides the rightness and wrongness of their actions. The Stoics, indeed, with the paradoxical misuse of language which was part of their system, and by which they strove to raise themselves above all concern about anything but virtue, were fond of saying that he who has that has everything; that he, and only he, is rich, is beautiful, is a king. But no claim of this description is made for the virtuous man by the utilitarian doctrine. Utilitarians are quite aware that there are other desirable possessions and qualities besides virtue, and are perfectly willing to allow to all of them their full worth. They are also aware that a right action does not necessarily indicate a virtuous character, and that actions which are blamable, often proceed from qualities entitled to praise. When this is apparent in any particular case, it modifies their estimation, not certainly of the act, but of the agent. I grant that they are, notwithstanding, of opinion, that in the long run the best proof of a good character is good actions; and resolutely refuse to consider any mental disposition as good, of which the predominant tendency is to produce bad conduct. This makes them unpopular with many people; but it is an unpopularity which they must share with every one who regards the distinction between right and wrong in a serious light; and the reproach is not one which a conscientious utilitarian need be anxious to repel.

[21]   If no more be meant by the objection than that many utilitarians look on the morality of actions, as measured by the utilitarian standard, with too exclusive a regard, and do not lay sufficient stress upon the other beauties of character which go towards making a human being lovable or admirable, this may be admitted. Utilitarians who have cultivated their moral feelings, but not their sympathies nor their artistic perceptions, do fall into this mistake; and so do all other moralists under the same conditions. What can be said in excuse for other moralists is equally available for them, namely, that, if there is to be any error, it is better that it should be on that side. As a matter of fact, we may affirm that among utilitar-

ians as among adherents of other systems, there is every imaginable degree of rigidity and of laxity in the application of their standard: some are even puritanically rigorous, while others are as indulgent as can possibly be desired by sinner or by sentimentalist. But on the whole, a doctrine which brings prominently forward the interest that mankind have in the repression and prevention of conduct which violates the moral law, is likely to be inferior to no other in turning the sanctions of opinion again such violations. It is true, the question, What does violate the moral law? is one on which those who recognise different standards of morality are likely now and then to differ. But difference of opinion on moral questions was not first introduced into the world by utilitarianism, while that doctrine does supply, if not always an easy, at all events a tangible and intelligible mode of deciding such differences.

[22]   It may not be superfluous to notice a few more of the common misapprehensions of utilitarian ethics, even those which are so obvious and gross that it might appear impossible for any person of candour and intelligence to fall into them; since persons, even of considerable mental endowments, often give themselves so little trouble to understand the bearings of any opinion against which they entertain a prejudice, and men are in general so little conscious of this voluntary ignorance as a defect, that the vulgarest misunderstandings of ethical doctrines are continually met with in the deliberate writings of persons of the greatest pretensions both to high principle and to philosophy. We not uncommonly hear the doctrine of utility inveighed against as a godless doctrine. If it be necessary to say anything at all against so mere an assumption, we may say that the question depends upon what idea we have formed of the moral character of the Deity. If it be a true belief that God desires, above all things, the happiness of his creatures, and that this was his purpose in their creation, utility is not only not a godless doctrine, but more profoundly religious than any other. If it be meant that utilitarianism does not recognise the revealed will of God as the supreme law of morals, I answer, that a utilitarian who believes in the perfect goodness and wisdom of God, necessarily believes that whatever God has thought fit to reveal on the subject of morals, must fulfil the requirements of utility in a supreme degree. But others besides utilitarians have been of opinion that the Christian revelation was intended, and is fitted, to inform the hearts and minds of mankind with a spirit which should enable them to find for themselves what is right, and incline them to do it when found, rather than to tell them, except in a very general way, what it is; and that we need a doctrine of ethics, carefully followed out, to interpret to us the will God. Whether this opinion is correct or not, it is superfluous here to discuss; since whatever aid religion, either natural or revealed, can afford to ethical investigation, is as open to the utilitarian moralist as to any other. He can use it as the testimony of God to the usefulness or hurtfulness of any given course of action, by as good a right as others can use it for the indication of a transcendental law, having no connection with usefulness or with happiness.

[23]   Again, Utility is often summarily stigmatised as an immoral doctrine by giving it the name of Expediency, and taking advantage of the popular use of that term to contrast it with Principle. But the Expedient, in the sense in which it is opposed to the Right, generally means that which is expedient for the particular interest of the agent himself; as when a minister sacrifices the interest of his country to keep himself in place. When it means anything better than this, it means that which is expedient for some immediate object, some temporary purpose, but which violates a rule whose observance is expedient in a much higher degree. The Expedient, in this sense, instead of being the same thing with the useful, is a branch of the hurtful. Thus, it would often be expedient, for the purpose of getting over some momentary embarrassment, or attaining some object immediately useful to ourselves or others, to tell a lie. But inasmuch as the cultivation in ourselves of a sensitive feeling on the subject of veracity, is one of the most useful, and the enfeeblement of that feeling one of the most hurtful, things to which our conduct can be instrumental; and inasmuch as any, even unintentional, deviation from truth, does that much towards weakening the trustworthiness of human assertion, which is not only the principal support of all present social well-being, but the insufficiency of which does more than any one thing that can be named to keep back civilisation, virtue, everything on which human happiness on the largest scale depends; we feel that the violation, for a present advantage, of a rule of such transcendant expediency, is not expedient, and that he who, for the sake of a convenience to himself or to some other individual, does what depends on him to deprive mankind of the good, and inflict upon them the evil, involved in the greater or less reliance which they can place in each other's word, acts the part of one of their worst enemies. Yet that even this rule, sacred as it is, admits of possible exceptions, is acknowledged by all moralists; the chief of which is when the withholding of some fact (as of information from a malefactor, or of bad news from a person dangerously ill) would preserve some one (especially a person other than oneself) from great and unmerited evil, and when the withholding can only be effected by denial. But in order that the exception may not extend itself beyond the need, and may have the least possible effect in weakening reliance on veracity, it ought to be recognised, and, if possible, its limits defined; and if the principle of utility is good for anything, it must be good for weighing these conflicting utilities against one another, and marking out the region within which one or the other preponderates.

[24]   Again, defenders of utility often find themselves called upon to reply to such objections as this – that there is not time, previous to action, for calculating and weighing the effects of any line of conduct on the general happiness. This is exactly as if any one were to say that it is impossible to guide our conduct by Christianity, because there is not time, on every occasion on which anything has to be done, to read through the Old and New Testaments. The answer to the objection is, that there has been ample time, namely, the whole past duration of the human species. During all that time, mankind have been learning by experi-

ence the tendencies of actions; on which experience all the prudence, as well as all the morality of life, is dependent. People talk as if the commencement of this course of experience had hitherto been put off, and as if, at the moment when some man feels tempted to meddle with the property or life of another, he had to begin considering for the first time whether murder and theft are injurious to human happiness. Even then I do not think that he would find the question very puzzling; but, at all events, the matter is now done to his hand. It is truly a whimsical supposition that, if mankind were agreed in considering utility to be the test of morality, they would remain without any agreement as to what is useful, and would take no measures for having their notions on the subject taught to the young, and enforced by law and opinion. There is no difficulty in proving any ethical standard whatever to work ill, if we suppose universal idiocy to be conjoined with it; but on any hypothesis short of that, mankind must by this time have acquired positive beliefs as to the effects of some actions on their happiness; and the beliefs which have thus come down are the rules of morality for the multitude, and for the philosopher until he has succeeded in finding better. That philosophers might easily do this, even now, on many subjects; that the received code of ethics is by no means of divine right; and that mankind have still much to learn as to the effects of actions on the general happiness, I admit, or rather, earnestly maintain. The corollaries from the principle of utility, like the precepts of every practical art, admit of indefinite improvement, and, in a progressive state of the human mind, their improvement is perpetually going on. But to consider the rules of morality as improvable, is one thing; to pass over the intermediate generalisations entirely, and endeavour to test each individual action directly by the first principle, is another. It is a strange notion that the acknowledgment of a first principle is inconsistent with the admission of secondary ones. To inform a traveller respecting the place of his ultimate destination, is not to forbid the use of landmarks and direction-posts on the way. The proposition that happiness is the end and aim of morality, does not mean that no road ought to be laid down to that goal, or that persons going thither should not be advised to take one direction rather than another. Men really ought to leave off talking a kind of nonsense on this subject, which they would neither talk nor listen to on other matters of practical concernment. Nobody argues that the art of navigation is not founded on astronomy, because sailors cannot wait to calculate the Nautical Almanack. Being rational creatures, they go to sea with it ready calculated; and all rational creatures go out upon the sea of life with their minds made up on the common questions of right and wrong, as well as on many of the far more difficult questions of wise and foolish. And this, as long as foresight is a human quality, it is to be presumed they will continue to do. Whatever we adopt as the fundamental principle of morality, we require subordinate principles to apply it by; the impossibility of doing without them, being common to all systems, can afford no argument against any one in particular; but gravely to argue as if no such secondary principles could be had, and as if mankind had remained till now, and always must remain, without drawing any general conclusions from the experience of human life, is as high a pitch, I think, as absurdity has ever reached in philosophical controversy.

[25]   The remainder of the stock arguments against utilitarianism mostly consist in laying to its charge the common infirmities of human nature, and the general difficulties which embarrass conscientious persons in shaping their course through life. We are told that a utilitarian will be apt to make his own particular case an exception to moral rules, and, when under temptation, will see a utility in the breach of a rule, greater than he will see in its observance. But is utility the only creed which is able to furnish us with excuses for evil doing, and means of cheating our own conscience? They are afforded in abundance by all doctrines which recognise as a fact in morals the existence of conflicting considerations; which all doctrines do, that have been believed by sane persons. It is not the fault of any creed, but of the complicated nature of human affairs, that rules of conduct cannot be so framed as to require no exceptions, and that hardly any kind of action can safely be laid down as either always obligatory or always condemnable. There is no ethical creed which does not temper the rigidity of its laws, by giving a certain latitude, under the moral responsibility of the agent, for accommodation to peculiarities of circumstances; and under every creed, at the opening thus made, self-deception and dishonest casuistry get in. There exists no moral system under which there do not arise unequivocal cases of conflicting obligation. These are the real difficulties, the knotty points both in the theory of ethics, and in the conscientious guidance of personal conduct. They are overcome practically, with greater or with less success, according to the intellect and virtue of the individual; but it can hardly be pretended that any one will be the less qualified for dealing with them, from possessing an ultimate standard to which conflicting rights and duties can be referred. If utility is the ultimate source of moral obligations, utility may be invoked to decide between them when their demands are incompatible. Though the application of the standard may be difficult, it is better than none at all: while in other systems, the moral laws all claiming independent authority, there is no common umpire entitled to interfere between them; their claims to precedence one over another rest on little better than sophistry, and unless determined, as they generally are, by the unacknowledged influence of considerations of utility, afford a free scope for the action of personal desires and partialities. We must remember that only in these cases of conflict between secondary principles is it requisite that first principles should be appealed to. There is no case of moral obligation in which some secondary principle is not involved; and if only one, there can seldom be any real doubt which one it is, in the mind of any person by whom the principle itself is recognised.

Chapter III

Of the Ultimate Sanction
of the Principle of Utility

THE QUESTION is often asked, and properly so, in regard to any supposed moral standard – What is its sanction? what are the motives to obey
it? or more specifically, what is the source of its obligation? whence does
it derive its binding force? It is a necessary part of moral philosophy to provide
the answer to this question; which, though frequently assuming the shape of an
objection to the utilitarian morality, as if it had some special applicability to that
above others, really arises in regard to all standards. It arises, in fact, whenever a
person is called on to *adopt* a standard, or refer morality to any basis on which he
has not been accustomed to rest it. For the customary morality, that which education and opinion have consecrated, is the only one which presents itself to the
mind with the feeling of being *in itself* obligatory; and when a person is asked to
believe that this morality *derives* its obligation from some general principle round
which custom has not thrown the same halo, the assertion is to him a paradox;
the supposed corollaries seem to have a more binding force than the original
theorem; the superstructure seems to stand better without, than with, what is represented as its foundation. He says to himself, I feel that I am bound not to rob
or murder, betray or deceive; but why am I bound to promote the general happiness? If my own happiness lies in something else, why may I not give that the
preference?

[2]   If the view adopted by the utilitarian philosophy of the nature of the
moral sense be correct, this difficulty will always present itself, until the influences
which form moral character have taken the same hold of the principle which they
have taken of some of the consequences – until, by the improvement of education, the feeling of unity with our fellow-creatures shall be (what it cannot be
doubted that Christ intended it to be) as deeply rooted in our character, and to
our own consciousness as completely a part of our nature, as the horror of crime
is in an ordinarily well brought up young person. In the meantime, however, the
difficulty has no peculiar application to the doctrine of utility, but is inherent in
every attempt to analyse morality and reduce it to principles; which, unless the

principle is already in men's minds invested with as much sacredness as any of its applications, always seems to divest them of a part of their sanctity.

[3]   The principle of utility either has, or there is no reason why it might not have, all the sanctions which belong to any other system of morals. Those sanctions are either external or internal. Of the external sanctions it is not necessary to speak at any length. They are, the hope of favour and the fear of displeasure, from our fellow creatures or from the Ruler of the Universe, along with whatever we may have of sympathy or affection for them, or of love and awe of Him, inclining us to do his will independently of selfish consequences. There is evidently no reason why all these motives for observance should not attach themselves to the utilitarian morality, as completely and as powerfully as to any other. Indeed, those of them which refer to our fellow creatures are sure to do so, in proportion to the amount of general intelligence; for whether there be any other ground of moral obligation than the general happiness or not, men do desire happiness; and however imperfect may be their own practice, they desire and commend all conduct in others towards themselves, by which they think their happiness is promoted. With regard to the religious motive, if men believe, as most profess to do, in the goodness of God, those who think that conduciveness to the general happiness is the essence, or even only the criterion of good, must necessarily believe that it is also that which God approves. The whole force therefore of external reward and punishment, whether physical or moral, and whether proceeding from God or from our fellow men, together with all that the capacities of human nature admit of disinterested devotion to either, become available to enforce the utilitarian morality, in proportion as that morality is recognised; and the more powerfully, the more the appliances of education and general cultivation are bent to the purpose.

[4]   So far as to external sanctions. The internal sanction of duty, whatever our standard of duty may be, is one and the same – a feeling in our own mind; a pain, more or less intense, attendant on violation of duty, which in properly cultivated moral natures rises, in the more serious cases, into shrinking from it as an impossibility. This feeling, when disinterested, and connecting itself with the pure idea of duty, and not with some particular form of it, or with any of the merely accessory circumstances, is the essence of Conscience; though in that complex phenomenon as it actually exists, the simple fact is in general all encrusted over with collateral associations, derived from sympathy, from love, and still more from fear; from all the forms of religious feeling; from the recollections of childhood and of all our past life; from self-esteem, desire of the esteem of others, and occasionally even self-abasement. This extreme complication is, I apprehend, the origin of the sort of mystical character which, by a tendency of the human mind of which there are many other examples, is apt to be attributed to the idea of moral obligation, and which leads people to believe that the idea cannot possibly attach itself to any other objects than those which, by a supposed mysterious law, are found in our present experience to excite it. Its binding force, however, consists in the existence of a mass of feeling which must be broken through in order to do what violates

our standard of right, and which, if we do nevertheless violate that standard, will probably have to be encountered afterwards in the form of remorse. Whatever theory we have of the nature or origin of conscience, this is what essentially constitutes it.

[5]   The ultimate sanction, therefore, of all morality (external motives apart) being a subjective feeling in our own minds, I see nothing embarrassing to those whose standard is utility, in the question, what is the sanction of that particular standard? We may answer, the same as of all other moral standards – the conscientious feelings of mankind. Undoubtedly this sanction has no binding efficacy on those who do not possess the feelings it appeals to; but neither will these persons be more obedient to any other moral principle than to the utilitarian one. On them morality of any kind has no hold but through the external sanctions. Meanwhile the feelings exist, a fact in human nature, the reality of which, and the great power with which they are capable of acting on those in whom they have been duly cultivated, are proved by experience. No reason has ever been shown why they may not be cultivated to as great intensity in connection with the utilitarian, as with any other rule of morals.

[6]   There is, I am aware, a disposition to believe that a person who sees in moral obligation a transcendental fact, an objective reality belonging to the province of "Things in themselves," is likely to be more obedient to it than one who believes it to be entirely subjective, having its seat in human consciousness only. But whatever a person's opinion may be on this point of Ontology, the force he is really urged by is his own subjective feeling, and is exactly measured by its strength. No one's belief that duty is an objective reality is stronger than the belief that God is so; yet the belief in God, apart from the expectation of actual reward and punishment, only operates on conduct through, and in proportion to, the subjective religious feeling. The sanction, so far as it is disinterested, is always in the mind itself; and the notion therefore of the transcendental moralists must be, that this sanction will not exist in the mind unless it is believed to have its root out of the mind; and that if a person is able to say to himself, This which is restraining me, and which is called my conscience, is only a feeling in my own mind, he may possibly draw the conclusion that when the feeling ceases the obligation ceases, and that if he find the feeling inconvenient, he may disregard it, and endeavour to get rid of it. But is this danger confined to the utilitarian morality? Does the belief that moral obligation has its seat outside the mind make the feeling of it too strong to be got rid of? The fact is so far otherwise, that all moralists admit and lament the ease with which, in the generality of minds, conscience can be silenced or stifled. The question, Need I obey my conscience? is quite as often put to themselves by persons who never heard of the principle of utility, as by its adherents. Those whose conscientious feelings are so weak as to allow of their asking this question, if they answer it affirmatively, will not do so because they believe in the transcendental theory, but because of the external sanctions.

[7]   It is not necessary, for the present purpose, to decide whether the feeling of duty is innate or implanted. Assuming it to be innate, it is an open question to what objects it naturally attaches itself; for the philosophic supporters of that theory are now agreed that the intuitive perception is of principles of morality and not of the details. If there be anything innate in the matter, I see no reason why the feeling which is innate should not be that of regard to the pleasures and pains of others. If there is any principle of morals which is intuitively obligatory, I should say it must be that. If so, the intuitive ethics would coincide with the utilitarian, and there would be no further quarrel between them. Even as it is, the intuitive moralists, though they believe that there are other intuitive moral obligations, do already believe this to one; for they unanimously hold that a large *portion* of morality turns upon the consideration due to the interests of our fellow-creatures. Therefore, if the belief in the transcendental origin of moral obligation gives any additional efficacy to the internal sanction, it appears to me that the utilitarian principle has already the benefit of it.

[8]   On the other hand, if, as is my own belief, the moral feelings are not innate, but acquired, they are not for that reason the less natural. It is natural to man to speak, to reason, to build cities, to cultivate the ground, though these are acquired faculties. The moral feelings are not indeed a part of our nature, in the sense of being in any perceptible degree present in all of us; but this, unhappily, is a fact admitted by those who believe the most strenuously in their transcendental origin. Like the other acquired capacities above referred to, the moral faculty, if not a part of our nature, is a natural outgrowth from it; capable, like them, in a certain small degree, of springing up spontaneously; and susceptible of being brought by cultivation to a high degree of development. Unhappily it is also susceptible, by a sufficient use of the external sanctions and of the force of early impressions, of being cultivated in almost any direction: so that there is hardly anything so absurd or so mischievous that it may not, by means of these influences, be made to act on the human mind with all the authority of conscience. To doubt that the same potency might be given by the same means to the principle of utility, even if it had no foundation in human nature, would be flying in the face of all experience.

[9]   But moral associations which are wholly of artificial creation, when intellectual culture goes on, yield by degrees to the dissolving force of analysis: and if the feeling of duty, when associated with utility, would appear equally arbitrary; if there were no leading department of our nature, no powerful class of sentiments, with which that association would harmonise, which would make us feel it congenial, and incline us not only to foster it in others (for which we have abundant interested motives), but also to cherish it in ourselves; if there were not, in short, a natural basis of sentiment for utilitarian morality, it might well happen that this association also, even after it had been implanted by education, might be analysed away.

[10]   But there *is* this basis of powerful natural sentiment; and this it is which, when once the general happiness is recognised as the ethical standard, will con-

stitute the strength of the utilitarian morality. This firm foundation is that of the social feelings of mankind; the desire to be in unity with our fellow creatures, which is already a powerful principle in human nature, and happily one of those which tend to become stronger, even without express inculcation, from the influences of advancing civilisation. The social state is at once so natural, so necessary, and so habitual to man, that, except in some unusual circumstances or by an effort of voluntary abstraction, he never conceives himself otherwise than as a member of a body; and this association is riveted more and more, as mankind are further removed from the state of savage independence. Any condition, therefore, which is essential to a state of society, becomes more and more an inseparable part of every person's conception of the state of things which he is born into, and which is the destiny of a human being. Now, society between human beings, except in the relation of master and slave, is manifestly impossible on any other footing than that the interests of all are to be consulted. Society between equals can only exist on the understanding that the interests of all are to be regarded equally. And since in all states of civilisation, every person, except an absolute monarch, has equals, every one is obliged to live on these terms with somebody; and in every age some advance is made towards a state in which it will be impossible to live permanently on other terms with anybody. In this way people grow up unable to conceive as possible to them a state of total disregard of other people's interests. They are under a necessity of conceiving themselves as at least abstaining from all the grosser injuries, and (if only for their own protection) living in a state of constant protest against them. They are also familiar with the fact of co-operating with others and proposing to themselves a collective, not an individual interest as the aim (at least for the time being) of their actions. So long as they are co-operating, their ends are identified with those of others; there is at least a temporary feeling that the interests of others are their own interests. Not only does all strengthening of social ties, and all healthy growth of society, give to each individual a stronger personal interest in practically consulting the welfare of others; it also leads him to identify his *feelings* more and more with their good, or at least with an even greater degree of practical consideration for it. He comes, as though instinctively, to be conscious of himself as a being who *of course* pays regard to others. The good of others becomes to him a thing naturally and necessarily to be attended to, like any of the physical conditions of our existence. Now, whatever amount of this feeling a person has, he is urged by the strongest motives both of interest and of sympathy to demonstrate it, and to the utmost of his power encourage it in others; and even if he has none of it himself, he is as greatly interested as any one else that others should have it. Consequently the smallest germs of the feeling are laid hold of and nourished by the contagion of sympathy and the influences of education; and a complete web of corroborative association is woven round it, by the powerful agency of the external sanctions. This mode of conceiving ourselves and human life, as civilisation goes on, is felt to be more and more natural. Every step in political improvement renders it more so, by removing the sources of opposition of interest, and levelling those inequalities of legal privilege between individuals or classes, owing to which there are large portions of mankind whose happiness it is still practicable to disregard. In an improving state of the human mind, the influences are constantly on the increase, which tend to generate in each individual a feeling of unity with all the rest; which feeling, if perfect, would make him never think of, or desire, any beneficial condition for himself, in the benefits of which they are not included. If we now suppose this feeling of unity to be taught as a religion, and the whole force of education, of institutions, and of opinion, directed, as it once was in the case of religion, to make every person grow up from infancy surrounded on all sides both by the profession and by the practice of it, I think that no one, who can realise this conception, will feel any misgiving about the sufficiency of the ultimate sanction for the Happiness morality. To any ethical student who finds the realisation difficult, I recommend, as a means of facilitating it, the second of M. Comte's two principle works, the *Système de Politique Positive*. I entertain the strongest objections to the system of politics and morals set forth in that treatise; but I think it has superabundantly shown the possibility of giving to the service of humanity, even without the aid of belief in a Providence, both the psychical power and the social efficacy of a religion; making it take hold of human life, and colour all thought, feeling, and action, in a manner of which the greatest ascendancy ever exercised by any religion may be but a type and foretaste; and of which the danger is, not that it should be insufficient but that it should be so excessive as to interfere unduly with human freedom and individuality.

[11]   Neither is it necessary to the feeling which constitutes the binding force of the utilitarian morality on those who recognise it, to wait for those social influences which would make its obligation felt by mankind at large. In the comparatively early state of human advancement in which we now live, a person cannot indeed feel that entireness of sympathy with all others, which would make any real discordance in the general direction of their conduct in life impossible; but already a person in whom the social feeling is at all developed, cannot bring himself to think of the rest of his fellow creatures as struggling rivals with him for the means of happiness, whom he must desire to see defeated in their object in order that he may succeed in his. The deeply rooted conception which every individual even now has of himself as a social being, tends to make him feel it one of his natural wants that there should be harmony between his feelings and aims and those of his fellow creatures. If differences of opinion and of mental culture make it impossible for him to share many of their actual feelings – perhaps make him denounce and defy those feelings – he still needs to be conscious that his real aim and theirs do not conflict; that he is not opposing himself to what they really wish for, namely their own good, but is, on the contrary, promoting it. This feeling in most individuals is much inferior in strength to their selfish feelings, and is often wanting altogether. But to those who have it, it possesses all the characters of a natural feeling. It does not present itself to their minds as a superstition of education, or a law despotically imposed by the power of society, but as an attribute which it

would not be well for them to be without. This conviction is the ultimate sanction of the greatest happiness morality. This it is which makes any mind, of well-developed feelings, work with, and not against, the outward motives to care for others, afforded by what I have called the external sanctions; and when those sanctions are wanting, or act in an opposite direction, constitutes in itself a powerful internal binding force, in proportion to the sensitiveness and thoughtfulness of the character; since few but those whose mind is a moral blank, could bear to lay out their course of life on the plan of paying no regard to others except so far as their own private interest compels.

Chapter IV

Of What Sort of Proof the Principle of Utility is Susceptible

IT HAS already been remarked, that questions of ultimate ends do not admit of proof, in the ordinary acceptation of the term. To be incapable of proof by reasoning is common to all first principles; to the first premises of our knowledge, as well as to those of our conduct. But the former, being matters of fact, may be the subject of a direct appeal to the faculties which judge of fact – namely, our senses, and our internal consciousness. Can an appeal be made to the same faculties on questions of practical ends? Or by what other faculty is cognisance taken of them?

[2] Questions about ends are, in other words, questions what things are desirable. The utilitarian doctrine is, that happiness is desirable, and the only thing desirable, as an end; all other things being only desirable as means to that end. What ought to be required of this doctrine – what conditions is it requisite that the doctrine should fulfil – to make good its claim to be believed?

[3] The only proof capable of being given that an object is visible, is that people actually see it. The only proof that a sound is audible, is that people hear it: and so of the other sources of our experience. In like manner, I apprehend, the sole evidence it is possible to produce that anything is desirable, is that people do actually desire it. If the end which the utilitarian doctrine proposes to itself were not, in theory and in practice, acknowledged to be an end, nothing could ever convince any person that it was so. No reason can be given why the general happiness is desirable, except that each person, so far as he believes it to be attainable, desires his own happiness. This, however, being a fact, we have not only all the proof which the case admits of, but all which it is possible to require, that happiness is a good: that each person's happiness is a good to that person, and the general happiness, therefore, a good to the aggregate of all persons. Happiness has made out its title as one of the ends of conduct, and consequently one of the criteria of morality.

[4] But it has not, by this alone, proved itself to be the sole criterion. To do that, it would seem, by the same rule, necessary to show, not only that people

desire happiness, but that they never desire anything else. Now it is palpable that they do desire things which, in common language, are decidedly distinguished from happiness. They desire, for example, virtue, and the absence of vice, no less really than pleasure and the absence of pain. The desire of virtue is not as universal, but it is as authentic a fact, as the desire of happiness. And hence the opponents of the utilitarian standard deem that they have a right to infer that there are other ends of human action besides happiness, and that happiness is not the standard of approbation and disapprobation.

[5] But does the utilitarian doctrine deny that people desire virtue, or maintain that virtue is not a thing to be desired? The very reverse. It maintains not only that virtue is to be desired, but that it is to be desired disinterestedly, for itself. Whatever may be the opinion of utilitarian moralists as to the original conditions by which virtue is made virtue; however they may believe (as they do) that actions and dispositions are only virtuous because they promote another end than virtue; yet this being granted, and it having been decided, from considerations of this description, what *is* virtuous, they not only place virtue at the very head of the things which are good as means to the ultimate end, but they also recognise as a psychological fact the possibility of its being, to the individual, a good in itself, without looking to any end beyond it; and hold, that the mind is not in a right state, not in a state conformable to Utility, not in the state most conducive to the general happiness, unless it does love virtue in this manner – as a thing desirable in itself, even although, in the individual instance, it should not produce those other desirable consequences which it tends to produce, and on account of which it is held to be virtue. This opinion is not, in the smallest degree, a departure from the Happiness principle. The ingredients of happiness are very various, and each of them is desirable in itself, and not merely when considered as swelling an aggregate. The principle of utility does not mean that any given pleasure, as music, for instance, or any given exemption from pain, as for example health, is to be looked upon as means to a collective something termed happiness, and to be desired on that account. They are desired and desirable in and for themselves; besides being means, they are a part of the end. Virtue, according to the utilitarian doctrine, is not naturally and originally part of the end, but it is capable of becoming so; and in those who love it disinterestedly it has become so, and is desired and cherished, not as a means to happiness, but as a part of their happiness.

[6] To illustrate this farther, we may remember that virtue is not the only thing, originally a means, and which if it were not a means to anything else, would be and remain indifferent, but which by association with what it is a means to, comes to be desired for itself, and that too with the utmost intensity. What, for example, shall we say of the love of money? There is nothing originally more desirable about money than about any heap of glittering pebbles. Its worth is solely that of the things which it will buy; the desires for other things than itself, which it is a means of gratifying. Yet the love of money is not only one of the strongest moving forces of human life, but money is, in many cases, desired in and for itself;

the desire to possess it is often stronger than the desire to use it, and goes on increasing when all the desires which point to ends beyond it, to be compassed by it, are falling off. It may, then, be said truly, that money is desired not for the sake of an end, but as part of the end. From being a means to happiness, it has come to be itself a principal ingredient of the individual's conception of happiness. The same may be said of the majority of the great objects of human life – power, for example, or fame; except that to each of these there is a certain amount of immediate pleasure annexed, which has at least the semblance of being naturally inherent in them; a thing which cannot be said of money. Still, however, the strongest natural attraction, both of power and of fame, is the immense aid they give to the attainment of our other wishes; and it is the strong association thus generated between them and all our objects of desire, which gives to the direct desire of them the intensity it often assumes, so as in some characters to surpass in strength all other desires. In these cases the means have become a part of the end, and a more important part of it than any of the things which they are means to. What was once desired as an instrument for the attainment of happiness, has come to be desired for its own sake. In being desired for its own sake it is, however, desired as *part* of happiness. The person is made, or thinks he would be made, happy by its mere possession; and is made unhappy by failure to obtain it. The desire of it is not a different thing from the desire of happiness, any more than the love of music, or the desire of health. They are included in happiness. They are some of the elements of which the desire of happiness is made up. Happiness is not an abstract idea, but a concrete whole; and these are some of its parts. And the utilitarian standard sanctions and approves their being so. Life would be a poor thing, very ill provided with sources of happiness, if there were not this provision of nature, by which things originally indifferent, but conducive to, or otherwise associated with, the satisfaction of our primitive desires, become in themselves sources of pleasure more valuable than the primitive pleasures, both in permanency, in the space of human existence that they are capable of covering, and even in intensity.

[7]   Virtue, according to the utilitarian conception, is a good of this description. There was no original desire of it, or motive to it, save its conduciveness to pleasure, and especially to protection from pain. But through the association thus formed, it may be felt a good in itself, and desired as such with as great intensity as any other good; and with this difference between it and the love of money, of power, or of fame, that all of these may, and often do, render the individual noxious to the other members of the society to which he belongs, whereas there is nothing which makes him so much a blessing to them as the cultivation of the disinterested love of virtue. And consequently, the utilitarian standard, while it tolerates and approves those other acquired desires, up to the point beyond which they would be more injurious to the general happiness than promotive of it, enjoins and requires the cultivation of the love of virtue up to the greatest strength possible, as being above all things important to the general happiness.

[8]   It results from the preceding considerations, that there is in reality nothing desired except happiness. Whatever is desired otherwise than as a means to some end beyond itself, and ultimately to happiness, is desired as itself a part of happiness, and is not desired for itself until it has become so. Those who desire virtue for its own sake, desire it either because the consciousness of it is a pleasure, or because the consciousness of being without it is a pain, or for both reasons united; as in truth the pleasure and pain seldom exist separately, but almost always together, the same person feeling pleasure in the degree of virtue attained, and pain in not having attained more. If one of these gave him no pleasure, and the other no pain, he would not love or desire virtue, or would desire it only for the other benefits which it might produce to himself or to persons whom he cared for.

[9]   We have now, then, an answer to the question, of what sort of proof the principle of utility is susceptible. If the opinion which I have now stated is psychologically true – if human nature is so constituted as to desire nothing which is not either a part of happiness or a means of happiness, we can have no other proof, and we require no other, that these are the only things desirable. If so, happiness is the sole end of human action, and the promotion of it the test by which to judge of all human conduct; from whence it necessarily follows that it must be the criterion of morality, since a part is included in the whole.

[10]   And now to decide whether this is really so; whether mankind do desire nothing for itself but that which is a pleasure to them, or of which the absence is a pain; we have evidently arrived at a question of fact and experience, dependent, like all similar questions, upon evidence. It can only be determined by practised self-consciousness and self-observation, assisted by observation of others. I believe that these sources of evidence, impartially consulted, will declare that desiring a thing and finding it pleasant, aversion to it and thinking of it as painful, are phenomena entirely inseparable, or rather two parts of the same phenomenon; in strictness of language, two different modes of naming the same psychological fact: that to think of an object as desirable (unless for the sake of its consequences), and to think of it as pleasant, are one and the same thing; and that to desire anything, except in proportion as the idea of it is pleasant, is a physical and metaphysical impossibility.

[11]   So obvious does this appear to me, that I expect it will hardly be disputed: and the objection made will be, not that desire can possibly be directed to anything ultimately except pleasure and exemption from pain, but that the will is a different thing from desire; that a person of confirmed virtue, or any other person whose purposes are fixed, carries out his purposes without any thought of the pleasure he has in contemplating them, or expects to derive from their fulfilment; and persists in acting on them, even though these pleasures are much diminished, by changes in his character or decay of his passive sensibilities, or are outweighed by the pains which the pursuit of the purposes may bring upon him. All this I fully admit, and have stated it elsewhere, as positively and emphatically as any one. Will,

the active phenomenon, is a different thing from desire, the state of passive sensibility, and though originally an offshoot from it, may in time take root and detach itself from the parent stock; so much so, that in the case of an habitual purpose, instead of willing the thing because we desire it, we often desire it only because we will it. This, however, is but an instance of that familiar fact, the power of habit, and is nowise confined to the case of virtuous actions. Many indifferent things, which men originally did from a motive of some sort, they continue to do from habit. Sometimes this is done unconsciously, the consciousness coming only after the action: at other times with conscious volition, but volition which has become habitual, and is put into operation by the force of habit, in opposition perhaps to the deliberate preference, as often happens with those who have contracted habits of vicious or hurtful indulgence. Third and last comes the case in which the habitual act of will in the individual instance is not in contradiction to the general intention prevailing at other times, but in fulfilment of it; as in the case of the person of confirmed virtue, and of all who pursue deliberately and consistently any determinate end. The distinction between will and desire thus understood is an authentic and highly important psychological fact; but the fact consists solely in this – that will, like all other parts of our constitution, is amenable to habit, and that we may will from habit what we no longer desire for itself or desire only because we will it. It is not the less true that will, in the beginning, is entirely produced by desire; including in that term the repelling influence of pain as well as the attractive one of pleasure. Let us take into consideration, no longer the person who has a confirmed will to do right, but him in whom that virtuous will is still feeble, conquerable by temptation, and not to be fully relied on; by what means can it be strengthened? How can the will to be virtuous, where it does not exist in sufficient force, be implanted or awakened? Only by making the person *desire* virtue – by making him think of it in a pleasurable light, or of its absence in a painful one. It is by associating the doing right with pleasure, or the doing wrong with pain, or by eliciting and impressing and bringing home to the person's experience the pleasure naturally involved in the one or the pain in the other, that it is possible to call forth that will to be virtuous, which, when confirmed, acts without any thought of either pleasure or pain. Will is the child of desire, and passes out of the dominion of its parent only to come under that of habit. That which is the result of habit affords no presumption of being intrinsically good; and there would be no reason for wishing that the purpose of virtue should become independent of pleasure and pain, were it not that the influence of the pleasurable and painful associations which prompt to virtue is not sufficiently to be depended on for unerring constancy of action until it has acquired the support of habit. Both in feeling and in conduct, habit is the only thing which imparts certainty; and it is because of the importance to others of being able to rely absolutely on one's feelings and conduct, and to oneself of being able to rely on one's own, that the will to do right ought to be cultivated into this habitual independence. In other words, this state of the will is a means to good, not intrinsically a good; and does not contradict the doctrine that nothing is a good to human beings but in so far as it is either itself pleasurable, or a means of attaining pleasure or averting pain.

[12]   But if this doctrine be true, the principle of utility is proved. Whether it is so or not, must now be left to the consideration of the thoughtful reader.

Chapter V

On the Connection between Justice and Utility

I N ALL AGES of speculation, one of the strongest obstacles to the reception of the doctrine that Utility or Happiness is the criterion of right and wrong, has been drawn from the idea of justice. The powerful sentiment, and apparently clear perception, which that word recalls with a rapidity and certainty resembling an instinct, have seemed to the majority of thinkers to point to an inherent quality in things; to show that the just must have an existence in Nature as something absolute, generically distinct from every variety of the Expedient, and, in idea, opposed to it, though (as is commonly acknowledged) never, in the long run, disjoined from it in fact.

[2]   In the case of this, as of our other moral sentiments, there is no necessary connection between the question of its origin, and that of its binding force. That a feeling is bestowed on us by Nature, does not necessarily legitimate all its promptings. The feeling of justice might be a peculiar instinct, and might yet require, like our other instincts, to be controlled and enlightened by a higher reason. If we have intellectual instincts, leading us to judge in a particular way, as well as animal instincts that prompt us to act in a particular way, there is no necessity that the former should be more infallible in their sphere than the latter in theirs: it may as well happen that wrong judgments are occasionally suggested by those, as wrong actions by these. But though it is one thing to believe that we have natural feelings of justice, and another to acknowledge them as an ultimate criterion of conduct, these two opinions are very closely connected in point of fact. Mankind are always predisposed to believe that any subjective feeling, not otherwise accounted for, is a revelation of some objective reality. Our present object is to determine whether the reality, to which the feeling of justice corresponds, is one which needs any such special revelation; whether the justice or injustice of an action is a thing intrinsically peculiar, and distinct from all its other qualities, or only a combination of certain of those qualities, presented under a peculiar aspect. For the purpose of this inquiry it is practically important to consider whether the feeling itself, of justice and injustice, is *sui generis* like our

sensations of colour and taste, or a derivative feeling, formed by a combination of others. And this it is the more essential to examine, as people are in general willing enough to allow, that objectively the dictates of justice coincide with a part of the field of General Expediency; but inasmuch as the subjective mental feeling of justice is different from that which commonly attaches to simple expediency, and, except in extreme cases of the latter, is far more imperative in its demands, people find it difficult to see, in justice, only a particular kind or branch of general utility, and think that its superior binding force requires a totally different origin.

[3]   To throw light upon this question, it is necessary to attempt to ascertain what is the distinguishing character of justice, or of injustice: what is the quality, or whether there is any quality, attributed in common to all modes of conduct designated as unjust (for justice, like many other moral attributes, is best defined by its opposite), and distinguishing them from such modes of conduct as are disapproved, but without having that particular epithet of disapprobation applied to them. If in everything which men are accustomed to characterise as just or unjust, some one common attribute or collection of attributes is always present, we may judge whether this particular attribute or combination of attributes would be capable of gathering round it a sentiment of that peculiar character and intensity by virtue of the general laws of our emotional constitution, or whether the sentiment is inexplicable, and requires to be regarded as a special provision of Nature. If we find the former to be the case, we shall, in resolving this question, have resolved also the main problem: if the latter, we shall have to seek for some other mode of investigating it.

[4]   To find the common attributes of a variety of objects, it is necessary to begin by surveying the objects themselves in the concrete. Let us therefore advert successively to the various modes of action, and arrangements of human affairs, which are classed, by universal or widely spread opinion, as Just or as Unjust. The things well known to excite the sentiments associated with those names are of a very multifarious character. I shall pass them rapidly in review, without studying any particular arrangement.

[5]   In the first place, it is mostly considered unjust to deprive any one of his personal liberty, his property, or any other thing which belongs to him by law. Here, therefore, is one instance of the application of the terms just and unjust in a perfectly definite sense, namely, that it is just to respect, unjust to violate, the *legal rights* of any one. But this judgment admits of several exceptions, arising from the other forms in which the notions of justice and injustice present themselves. For example, the person who suffers the deprivation may (as the phrase is) have *forfeited* the rights which he is so deprived of: a case to which we shall return presently. But also,

[6]   Secondly, the legal rights of which he is deprived, may be rights which *ought* not to have belonged to him; in other words, the law which confers on him

these rights, may be a bad law. When it is so, or when (which is the same thing for our purpose) it is supposed to be so, opinions will differ as to the justice or injustice of infringing it. Some maintain that no law, however bad, ought to be disobeyed by an individual citizen; that his opposition to it, if shown at all, should only be shown in endeavouring to get it altered by competent authority. This opinion (which condemns many of the most illustrious benefactors of mankind, and would often protect pernicious institutions against the only weapons which, in the state of things existing at the time, have any chance of succeeding against them) is defended, by those who hold it, on grounds of expediency; principally on that of the importance, to the common interest of mankind, of maintaining inviolate the sentiment of submission to law. Other persons, again, hold the directly contrary opinion, that any law, judged to be bad, may blamelessly be disobeyed, even though it be not judged to be unjust, but only inexpedient; while others would confine the licence of disobedience to the case of unjust laws: but again, some say, that all laws which are inexpedient are unjust; since every law imposes some restriction on the natural liberty of mankind, which restriction is an injustice, unless legitimated by tending to their good. Among these diversities of opinion, it seems to be universally admitted that there may be unjust laws, and that law, consequently, is not the ultimate criterion of justice, but may give to one person a benefit, or impose on another an evil, which justice condemns. When, however, a law is thought to be unjust, it seems always to be regarded as being so in the same way in which a breach of law is unjust, namely, by infringing somebody's right; which, as it cannot in this case be a legal right, receives a different appellation, and is called a moral right. We may say, therefore, that a second case of injustice consists in taking or withholding from any person that to which he has a *moral right*.

[7]   Thirdly, it is universally considered just that each person should obtain that (whether good or evil) which he *deserves*; and unjust that he should obtain a good, or be made to undergo an evil, which he does not deserve. This is, perhaps, the clearest and most emphatic form in which the idea of justice is conceived by the general mind. As it involves the notion of desert, the question arises, what constitutes desert? Speaking in a general way, a person is understood to deserve good if he does right, evil if he does wrong; and in a more particular sense, to deserve good from those to whom he does or has done good, and evil from those to whom he does or has done evil. The precept of returning good for evil has never been regarded as a case of the fulfilment of justice, but as one in which the claims of justice are waived, in obedience to other considerations.

[8]   Fourthly, it is confessedly unjust to *break faith* with any one: to violate an engagement, either express or implied, or disappoint expectations raised by our conduct, at least if we have raised those expectations knowingly and voluntarily. Like the other obligations of justice already spoken of, this one is not regarded as absolute, but as capable of being overruled by a stronger obligation of justice on the other side; or by such conduct on the part of the person concerned as is

deemed to absolve us from our obligation to him, and to constitute a *forfeiture* of the benefit which he has been led to expect.

[9]   Fifthly, it is, by universal admission, inconsistent with justice to be *partial*; to show favour or preference to one person over another, in matters to which favour and preference do not properly apply. Impartiality, however, does not seem to be regarded as a duty in itself, but rather as instrumental to some other duty; for it is admitted that favour and preference are not always censurable, and indeed the cases in which they are condemned are rather the exception than the rule. A person would be more likely to be blamed than applauded for giving his family or friends no superiority in good offices over strangers, when he could do so without violating any other duty; and no one thinks it unjust to seek one person in preference to another as a friend, connection, or companion. Impartiality where rights are concerned is of course obligatory, but this is involved in the more general obligation of giving to every one his right. A tribunal, for example, must be impartial, because it is bound to award, without regard to any other consideration, a disputed object to the one of two parties who has the right to it. There are other cases in which impartiality means, being solely influenced by desert; as with those who, in the capacity of judges, preceptors, or parents, administer reward and punishment as such. There are cases, again, in which it means, being solely influenced by consideration for the public interest; as in making a selection among candidates for a government employment. Impartiality, in short, as an obligation of justice, may be said to mean, being exclusively influenced by the considerations which it is supposed ought to influence the particular case in hand; and resisting the solicitation of any motives which prompt to conduct different from what those considerations would dictate.

[10]   Nearly allied to the idea of impartiality is that of *equality*, which often enters as a component part both into the conception of justice and into the practice of it, and, in the eyes of many persons, constitutes its essence. But in this, still more than in any other case, the notion of justice varies in different persons, and always conforms in its variations to their notion of utility. Each person maintains that equality is the dictate of justice, except where he thinks that expediency requires inequality. The justice of giving equal protection to the rights of all, is maintained by those who support the most outrageous inequality in the rights themselves. Even in slave countries it is theoretically admitted that the rights of the slave, such as they are, ought to be as sacred as those of the master; and that a tribunal which fails to enforce them with equal strictness is wanting in justice; while, at the same time, institutions which leave to the slave scarcely any rights to enforce, are not deemed unjust, because they are not deemed inexpedient. Those who think that utility requires distinctions of rank, do not consider it unjust that riches and social privileges should be unequally dispensed; but those who think this inequality inexpedient, think it unjust also. Whoever thinks that government is necessary, sees no injustice in as much inequality as is constituted by giving to the magistrate powers not granted to other people. Even among those who hold

levelling doctrines, there are as many questions of justice as there are differences of opinion about expediency. Some Communists consider it unjust that the produce of the labour of the community should be shared on any other principle than that of exact equality; others think it just that those should receive most whose needs are greatest; while others hold that those who work harder, or who produce more, or whose services are more valuable to the community, may justly claim a larger quota in the division of the produce. And the sense of natural justice may be plausibly appealed to in behalf of every one of these opinions.

[11]   Among so many diverse applications of the term justice, which yet is not regarded as ambiguous, it is a matter of some difficulty to seize the mental link which holds them together, and on which the moral sentiment adhering to the term essentially depends. Perhaps, in this embarrassment, some help may be derived from the history of the word, as indicated by its etymology.

[12]   In most, if not in all, languages, the etymology of the word which corresponds to Just, points to an origin connected either with positive law, or with that which was in most cases the primitive form of law – authoritative custom. *Justum* is a form of *jussum*, that which has been ordered. *Jus* is of the same origin. *Dikaion* comes from *dike*, of which the principle meaning, at least in the historical ages of Greece, was a suit at law. Originally, indeed, it meant only the mode or *manner* of doing things, but it early came to mean the *prescribed* manner; that which the recognized authorities, patriarchal, judicial, or political, would enforce. *Recht*, from which came *right* and *righteous*, is synonymous with law. The original meaning indeed of *recht* did not point to law, but to physical straightness; as *wrong* and its Latin equivalents meant twisted or *tortuous*, and from this it is argued that right did not originally mean law, but on the contrary law meant right. But however this may be, that fact that *recht* and *droit* because restricted in their meaning to positive law, although much which is not required by law is equally necessary to moral straightness or rectitude, is as significant of the original character of moral ideas as if the derivation had been the reverse way. The courts of justice, the administration of justice, are the courts and the administration of law. *La justice*, in French, is the established term for judicature. There can, I think, be no doubt that the *idée mère*, the primitive element, in the formation of the notion of justice, was conformity to law. It constituted the entire idea among the Hebrews, up to the birth of Christianity; as might be expected in the case of a people whose laws attempted to embrace all subjects on which precepts were required, and who believed those laws to be a direct emanation from the Supreme Being. But other nations, and in particular the Greeks and Romans, who knew that their laws had been made originally, and still continued to be made, by men, were not afraid to admit that those men might make bad laws; might do, by law, the same things, and from the same motives, which if done by individuals without the sanction of law, would be called unjust. And hence the sentiment of injustice came to be attached, not to all violations of law, but only to violations of such laws as *ought* to exist, including such as ought to exist, but do not; and to laws

themselves, if supposed to be contrary to what ought to be law. In this manner the idea of law and of its injunctions was still predominant in the notion of justice, even when the laws actually in force ceased to be accepted as the standard of it.

[13]   It is true that mankind consider the idea of justice and its obligations as applicable to many things which neither are, nor is it desired that they should be, regulated by law. Nobody desires that laws should interfere with the whole detail of private life; yet every one allows that in all daily conduct a person may and does show himself to be either just or unjust. But even here, the idea of the breach of what ought to be law, still lingers in a modified shape. It would always give us pleasure, and chime in with our feelings of fitness, that acts which we deem unjust should be punished, though we do not always think it expedient that this should be done by the tribunals. We forego that gratification on account of incidental inconveniences. We should be glad to see just conduct enforced and injustice repressed, even in the minutest details, if we were not, with reason, afraid of trusting the magistrate with so unlimited an amount of power over individuals. When we think that a person is bound in justice to do a thing, it is an ordinary form of language to say, that he ought to be compelled to do it. We should be gratified to see the obligation enforced by anybody who had the power. If we see that its enforcement by law would be inexpedient, we lament the impossibility, we consider the impunity given to injustice as an evil, and strive to make amends for it by bringing a strong expression of our own and the public disapprobation to bear upon the offender. Thus the idea of legal constraint is still the generating idea of the notion of justice, though undergoing several transformations before that notion, as it exists in an advanced state of society, becomes complete.

[14]   The above is, I think, a true account, as far as it goes, of the origin and progressive growth of the idea of justice. But we must observe, that it contains, as yet, nothing to distinguish that obligation from moral obligation in general. For the truth is, that the idea of penal sanction, which is the essence of law, enters not only into the conception of injustice, but into that of any kind of wrong. We do not call anything wrong, unless we mean to imply that a person ought to be punished in some way or other for doing it; if not by law, by the opinion of his fellow-creatures; if not by opinion, by the reproaches of his own conscience. This seems the real turning point of the distinction between morality and simple expediency. It is a part of the notion of Duty in every one of its forms, that a person may rightfully be compelled to fulfil it. Duty is a thing which may be *exacted* from a person, as one exacts a debt. Unless we think that it might be exacted from him, we do not call it his duty. Reasons of prudence, or the interest of other people, may militate against actually exacting it; but the person himself, it is clearly understood, would not be entitled to complain. There are other things, on the contrary, which we wish that people should do, which we like or admire them for doing, perhaps dislike or despise them for not doing, but yet admit that they are not bound to do; it is not a case of moral obligation; we do not blame them, that is, we do not think that they are proper objects of punishment. How we come by

these ideas of deserving and not deserving punishment, will appear, perhaps, in the sequel; but I think there is no doubt that this distinction lies at the bottom of the notions of right and wrong; that we call any conduct wrong, or employ, instead, some other term of dislike or disparagement, according as we think that the person ought, or ought not, to be punished for it; and we say that it would be right to do so and so, or merely that it would be desirable or laudable, according as we would wish to see the person whom it concerns, compelled, or only persuaded and exhorted, to act in that manner.*

[15]   This, therefore, being the characteristic difference which marks off, not justice, but morality in general, from the remaining provinces of Expediency and Worthiness; the character is still to be sought which distinguishes justice from other branches of morality. Now it is known that ethical writers divide moral duties into two classes, denoted by the ill-chosen expressions, duties of perfect and of imperfect obligation; the latter being those in which, though the act is obligatory, the particular occasions of performing it are left to our choice, as in the case of charity or beneficence, which we are indeed bound to practise, but not towards any definite person, nor at any prescribed time. In the more precise language of philosophic jurists, duties of perfect obligation are those duties in virtue of which a correlative *right* resides in some person or persons; duties of imperfect obligation are those moral obligations which do not give birth to any right. I think it will be found that this distinction exactly coincides with that which exists between justice and the other obligations of morality. In our survey of the various popular acceptations of justice, the term appeared generally to involve the idea of a personal right – a claim on the part of one or more individuals, like that which the law gives when it confers a proprietary or other legal right. Whether the injustice consists in depriving a person of a possession, or in breaking faith with him, or in treating him worse than he deserves, or worse than other people who have no greater claims, in each case the supposition implies two things – a wrong done, and some assignable person who is wronged. Injustice may also be done by treating a person better than others; but the wrong in this case is to his competitors, who are also assignable persons. It seems to me that this feature in the case – a right in some person, correlative to the moral obligation – constitutes the specific difference between justice, and generosity or beneficence. Justice implies something which it is not only right to do, and wrong not to do, but which some individual person can claim from us as his moral right. No one has a moral right to our generosity or beneficence, because we are not morally bound to practise those virtues towards any given individual. And it will be found with respect to this, as with respect to every correct definition, that the instances which seem to conflict with it are those which most confirm it. For if a moralist attempts, as some have

* See this point enforced and illustrated by Professor Bain, in an admirable chapter (entitled "The Ethical Emotions, or the Moral Sense"), of the second of the two treatises composing his elaborate and profound work on the Mind.

done, to make out that mankind generally, though not any given individual, have a right to all the good we can do them, he at once, by that thesis, includes generosity and beneficence within the category of justice. He is obliged to say, that our utmost exertions are *due* to our fellow creatures, thus assimilating them to a debt; or that nothing less can be a sufficient *return* for what society does for us, thus classing the case as one of gratitude; both of which are acknowledged cases of justice. Wherever there is right, the case is one of justice, and not of the virtue of beneficence: and whoever does not place the distinction between justice and morality in general, where we have now placed it, will be found to make no distinction between them at all, but to merge all morality in justice.

[16]   Having thus endeavoured to determine the distinctive elements which enter into the composition of the idea of justice, we are ready to enter on the inquiry, whether the feeling, which accompanies the idea, is attached to it by a special dispensation of nature, or whether it could have grown up, by any known laws, out of the idea itself; and in particular, whether it can have originated in considerations of general expediency.

[17]   I conceive that the sentiment itself does not arise from anything which would commonly, or correctly, be termed an idea of expediency; but that though the sentiment does not, whatever is moral in it does.

[18]   We have seen that the two essential ingredients in the sentiment of justice are, the desire to punish a person who has done harm, and the knowledge or belief that there is some definite individual or individuals to whom harm has been done.

[19]   Now it appears to me, that the desire to punish a person who has done harm to some individual is a spontaneous outgrowth from two sentiments, both in the highest degree natural, and which either are or resemble instincts; the impulse of self-defence, and the feeling of sympathy.

[20]   It is natural to resent, and to repel or retaliate, any harm done or attempted against ourselves, or against those with whom we sympathise. The origin of this sentiment it is not necessary here to discuss. Whether it be an instinct or a result of intelligence, it is, we know, common to all animal nature; for every animal tries to hurt those who have hurt, or who it thinks are about to hurt, itself or its young. Human beings, on this point, only differ from other animals in two particulars. First, in being capable of sympathising, not solely with their offspring, or, like some of the more noble animals, with some superior animal who is kind to them, but with all human, and even with all sentient, beings. Secondly, in having a more developed intelligence, which gives a wider range to the whole of their sentiments, whether self-regarding or sympathetic. By virtue of his superior intelligence, even apart from his superior range of sympathy, a human being is capable of apprehending a community of interest between himself and the human society of which he forms a part, such that any conduct which threatens the security of the society generally, is threatening to his own, and calls forth his instinct (if instinct it be) of self-defence. The same superiority of intelligence joined to the

power of sympathising with human beings generally, enables him to attach himself to the collective idea of his tribe, his country, or mankind, in such a manner that any act hurtful to them, rouses his instinct of sympathy, and urges him to resistance.

[21]   The sentiment of justice, in that one of its elements which consists of the desire to punish, is thus, I conceive, the natural feeling of retaliation or vengeance, rendered by intellect and sympathy applicable to those injuries, that is, to those hurts, which wound us through, or in common with, society at large. This sentiment, in itself, has nothing moral in it; what is moral is, the exclusive subordination of it to the social sympathies, so as to wait on and obey their call. For the natural feeling tends to make us resent indiscriminately whatever any one does that is disagreeable to us; but when moralised by the social feeling, it only acts in the directions conformable to the general good: just persons resenting a hurt to society, though not otherwise a hurt to themselves, and not resenting a hurt to themselves, however painful, unless it be of the kind which society has a common interest with them in the repression of.

[22]   It is no objection against this doctrine to say, that when we feel our sentiment of justice outraged, we are not thinking of society at large, or of any collective interest, but only of the individual case. It is common enough certainly, though the reverse of commendable, to feel resentment merely because we have suffered pain; but a person whose resentment is really a moral feeling, that is, who considers whether an act is blamable before he allows himself to resent it – such a person, though he may not say expressly to himself that he is standing up for the interest of society, certainly does feel that he is asserting a rule which is for the benefit of others as well as for his own. If he is not feeling this – if he is regarding the act solely as it affects him individually – he is not consciously just; he is not concerning himself about the justice of his actions. This is admitted even by anti-utilitarian moralists. When Kant (as before remarked) propounds as the fundamental principle of morals, "So act, that thy rule of conduct might be adopted as a law by all rational beings," he virtually acknowledges that the interest of mankind collectively, or at least of mankind indiscriminately, must be in the mind of the agent when conscientiously deciding on the morality of the act. Otherwise he uses words without a meaning: for, that a rule even of utter selfishness could not *possibly* be adopted by all rational beings – that there is any insuperable obstacle in the nature of things to its adoption – cannot be even plausibly maintained. To give any meaning to Kant's principle, the sense put upon it must be, that we ought to shape our conduct by a rule which all rational beings might adopt *with benefit to their collective interest.*

[23]   To recapitulate: the idea of justice supposes two things; a rule of conduct, and a sentiment which sanctions the rule. The first must be supposed common to all mankind, and intended for their good. The other (the sentiment) is a desire that punishment may be suffered by those who infringe the rule. There is involved, in addition, the conception of some definite person who suffers by the

infringement; whose rights (to use the expression appropriated to the case) are violated by it. And the sentiment of justice appears to me to be, the animal desire to repel or retaliate a hurt or damage to oneself, or to those with whom one sympathises, widened so as to include all persons, by the human capacity of enlarged sympathy, and the human conception of intelligent self-interest. From the latter elements, the feeling derives its morality; from the former, its peculiar impressiveness, and energy of self-assertion.

[24]   I have, throughout, treated the idea of a *right* residing in the injured person, and violated by the injury, not as a separate element in the composition of the idea and sentiment, but as one of the forms in which the other two elements clothe themselves. These elements are, a hurt to some assignable person or persons on the one hand, and a demand for punishment on the other. An examination of our own minds, I think, will show, that these two things include all that we mean when we speak of violation of a right. When we call anything a person's right, we mean that he has a valid claim on society to protect him in the possession of it, either by the force of law, or by that of education and opinion. If he has what we consider a sufficient claim, on whatever account, to have something guaranteed to him by society, we say that he has a right to it. If we desire to prove that anything does not belong to him by right, we think this done as soon as it is admitted that society ought not to take measures for securing it to him, but should leave it to chance, or to his own exertions. Thus, a person is said to have a right to what he can earn in fair professional competition; because society ought not to allow any other person to hinder him from endeavouring to earn in that manner as much as he can. But he has not a right to three hundred a-year, though he may happen to be earning it; because society is not called on to provide that he shall earn that sum. On the contrary, if he owns ten thousand pounds three per cent stock, he *has* a right to three hundred a-year; because society has come under an obligation to provide him with an income of that amount.

[25]   To have a right, then, is, I conceive, to have something which society ought to defend me in the possession of. If the objector goes on to ask, why it ought, I can give him no other reason than general utility. If that expression does not seem to convey a sufficient feeling of the strength of the obligation, nor to account for the peculiar energy of the feeling, it is because there goes to the composition of the sentiment, not a rational only, but also an animal element, the thirst for retaliation; and this thirst derives its intensity, as well as its moral justification, from the extraordinarily important and impressive kind of utility which is concerned. The interest involved is that of security, to every one's feelings the most vital of all interests. Nearly all other earthly benefits are needed by one person, not needed by another; and many of them can, if necessary, be cheerfully foregone, or replaced by something else; but security no human being can possibly do without; on it we depend for all our immunity from evil, and for the whole value of all and every good, beyond the passing moment; since nothing but the gratification of the instant could be of any worth to us, if we could be deprived

of anything the next instant by whoever was momentarily stronger than ourselves. Now this most indispensable of all necessaries, after physical nutriment, cannot be had, unless the machinery for providing it is kept unintermittedly in active play. Our notion, therefore, of the claim we have on our fellow-creatures to join in making safe for us the very groundwork of our existence, gathers feelings around it so much more intense than those concerned in any of the more common cases of utility, that the difference in degree (as is often the case in psychology) becomes a real difference in kind. The claim assumes that character of absoluteness, that apparent infinity, and incommensurability with all other considerations, which constitute the distinction between the feeling of right and wrong and that of ordinary expediency and inexpediency. The feelings concerned are so powerful, and we count so positively on finding a responsive feeling in others (all being alike interested), that *ought* and *should* grow into *must*, and recognised indispensability becomes a moral necessity, analogous to physical, and often not inferior to it in binding force exhorted.

[26]   If the preceding analysis, or something resembling it, be not the correct account of the notion of justice; if justice be totally independent of utility, and be a standard *per se*, which the mind can recognise by simple introspection of itself; it is hard to understand why that internal oracle is so ambiguous, and why so many things appear either just or unjust, according to the light in which they are regarded.

[27]   We are continually informed that Utility is an uncertain standard, which every different person interprets differently, and that there is no safety but in the immutable, ineffaceable, and unmistakable dictates of justice, which carry their evidence in themselves, and are independent of the fluctuations of opinion. One would suppose from this that on questions of justice there could be no controversy; that if we take that for our rule, its application to any given case could leave us in as little doubt as a mathematical demonstration. So far is this from being the fact, that there is as much difference of opinion, and as fierce discussion, about what is just, as about what is useful to society. Not only have different nations and individuals different notions of justice, but in the mind of one and the same individual, justice is not some one rule, principle, or maxim, but many, which do not always coincide in their dictates, and in choosing between which, he is guided either by some extraneous standard, or by his own personal predilections.

[28]   For instance, there are some who say, that it is unjust to punish any one for the sake of example to others; that punishment is just, only when intended for the good of the sufferer himself. Others maintain the extreme reverse, contending that to punish persons who have attained years of discretion, for their own benefit, is despotism and injustice, since if the matter at issue is solely their own good, no one has a right to control their own judgment of it; but that they may justly be punished to prevent evil to others, this being an exercise of the legitimate right of self-defence. Mr. Owen, again, affirms that it is unjust to punish at

all; for the criminal did not make his own character; his education, and the circumstances which surround him, have made him a criminal, and for these he is not responsible. All these opinions are extremely plausible; and so long as the question is argued as one of justice simply, without going down to the principles which lie under justice and are the source of its authority, I am unable to see how any of these reasoners can be refuted. For in truth every one of the three builds upon rules of justice confessedly true. The first appeals to the acknowledged injustice of singling out an individual, and making a sacrifice, without his consent, for other people's benefit. The second relies on the acknowledged justice of self-defence, and the admitted injustice of forcing one person to conform to another's notions of what constitutes his good. The Owenite invokes the admitted principle, that it is unjust to punish any one for what he cannot help. Each is triumphant so long as he is not compelled to take into consideration any other maxims of justice than the one he has selected; but as soon as their several maxims are brought face to face, each disputant seems to have exactly as much to say for himself as the others. No one of them can carry out his own notion of justice without trampling upon another equally binding. These are difficulties; they have always been felt to be such; and many devices have been invented to turn rather than to overcome them. As a refuge from the last of the three, men imagined what they called the freedom of the will; fancying that they could not justify punishing a man whose will is in a thoroughly hateful state, unless it be supposed to have come into that state through no influence of anterior circumstances. To escape from the other difficulties, a favourite contrivance has been the fiction of a contract, whereby at some unknown period all the members of society engaged to obey the laws, and consented to be punished for any disobedience to them, thereby giving to their legislators the right, which it is assumed they would not otherwise have had, of punishing them, either for their own good or for that of society. This happy thought was considered to get rid of the whole difficulty, and to legitimate the infliction of punishment, in virtue of another received maxim of justice, *volenti non fit injuri*; that is not unjust which is done with the consent of the person who is supposed to be hurt by it. I need hardly remark, that even if the consent were not a mere fiction, this maxim is not superior in authority to the others which it is brought in to supersede. It is, on the contrary, an instructive specimen of the loose and irregular manner in which supposed principles of justice grow up. This particular one evidently came into use as a help to the coarse exigencies of courts of law, which are sometimes obliged to be content with very uncertain presumptions, on account of the greater evils which would often arise from any attempt on their part to cut finer. But even courts of law are not able to adhere consistently to the maxim, for they allow voluntary engagements to be set aside on the ground of fraud, and sometimes on that of mere mistake or misinformation.

[29]   Again, when the legitimacy of inflicting punishment is admitted, how many conflicting conceptions of justice come to light in discussing the proper apportionment of punishment to offences. No rule on this subject recommends

itself so strongly to the primitive and spontaneous sentiment of justice, as the *lex talionis,* an eye for an eye and a tooth for a tooth. Though this principle of the Jewish and of the Mahometan law has been generally abandoned in Europe as a practical maxim, there is, I suspect, in most minds, a secret hankering after it; and when retribution accidentally falls on an offender in that precise shape, the general feeling of satisfaction evinced bears witness how natural is the sentiment to which this repayment in kind is acceptable. With many, the test of justice in penal infliction is that the punishment should be proportioned to the offence; meaning that it should be exactly measured by the moral guilt of the culprit (whatever be their standard for measuring moral guilt): the consideration, what amount of punishment is necessary to deter from the offence, having nothing to do with the question of justice, in their estimation: while there are others to whom that consideration is all in all; who maintain that it is not just, at least for man, to inflict on a fellow creature, whatever may be his offences, any amount of suffering beyond the least that will suffice to prevent him from repeating, and others from imitating, his misconduct.

[30]   To take another example from a subject already once referred to. In a co-operative industrial association, is it just or not that talent or skill should give a title to superior remuneration? On the negative side of the question it is argued, that whoever does the best he can, deserves equally well, and ought not in justice to be put in a position of inferiority for no fault of his own; that superior abilities have already advantages more than enough, in the admiration they excite, the personal influence they command, and the internal sources of satisfaction attending them, without adding to these a superior share of the world's goods; and that society is bound in justice rather to make compensation to the less favoured, for this unmerited inequality of advantages, than to aggravate it. On the contrary side it is contended, that society receives more from the more efficient labourer; that his services being more useful, society owes him a larger return for them; that a greater share of the joint result is actually his work, and not to allow his claim to it is a kind of robbery; that if he is only to receive as much as others, he can only be justly required to produce as much, and to give a smaller amount of time and exertion, proportioned to his superior efficiency. Who shall decide between these appeals to conflicting principles of justice? Justice has in this case two sides to it, which it is impossible to bring into harmony, and the two disputants have chosen opposite sides; the one looks to what it is just that the individual should receive, the other to what it is just that the community should give. Each, from his own point of view, is unanswerable; and any choice between them, on grounds of justice, must be perfectly arbitrary. Social utility alone can decide the preference.

[31]   How many, again, and how irreconcilable, are the standards of justice to which reference is made in discussing the repartition of taxation. One opinion is, that payment to the State should be in numerical proportion to pecuniary means. Others think that justice dictates what they term graduated taxation; taking a higher percentage from those who have more to spare. In point of natural justice

a strong case might be made for disregarding means altogether, and taking the same absolute sum (whenever it could be got) from every one: as the subscribers to a mess, or to a club, all pay the same sum for the same privileges, whether they can all equally afford it or not. Since the protection (it might be said) of law and government is afforded to, and is equally required by all, there is no injustice in making all buy it at the same price. It is reckoned justice, not injustice, that a dealer should charge to all customers the same price for the same article, not a price varying according to their means of payment. This doctrine, as applied to taxation, finds no advocates, because it conflicts strongly with men's feelings of humanity and perceptions of social expediency; but the principle of justice which it invokes is as true and as binding as those which can be appealed to against it. Accordingly it exerts a tacit influence on the line of defence employed for other modes of assessing taxation. People feel obliged to argue that the State does more for the rich than for the poor, as a justification for its taking more from them: though this is in reality not true, for the rich would be far better able to protect themselves, in the absence of law or government, than the poor, and indeed would probably be successful in converting the poor into their slaves. Others, again, so far defer to the same conception of justice, as to maintain that all should pay an equal capitation tax for the protection of their persons (these being of equal value to all), and an unequal tax for the protection of their property, which is unequal. To this others reply, that the all of one man is as valuable to him as the all of another. From these confusions there is no other mode of extrication than the utilitarian.

[32]   Is, then the difference between the just and the Expedient a merely imaginary distinction? Have mankind been under a delusion in thinking that justice is a more sacred thing than policy, and that the latter ought only to be listened to after the former has been satisfied? By no means. The exposition we have given of the nature and origin of the sentiment, recognises a real distinction; and no one of those who profess the most sublime contempt for the consequences of actions as an element in their morality, attaches more importance to the distinction than I do. While I dispute the pretensions of any theory which sets up an imaginary standard of justice not grounded on utility, I account the justice which is grounded on utility to be the chief part, and incomparably the most sacred and binding part, of all morality. Justice is a name for certain classes of moral rules, which concern the essentials of human well-being more nearly, and are therefore of more absolute obligation, than any other rules for the guidance of life; and the notion which we have found to be of the essence of the idea of justice, that of a right residing in an individual implies and testifies to this more binding obligation.

[33]   The moral rules which forbid mankind to hurt one another (in which we must never forget to include wrongful interference with each other's freedom) are more vital to human well-being than any maxims, however important, which

only point out the best mode of managing some department of human affairs. They have also the peculiarity, that they are the main element in determining the whole of the social feelings of mankind. It is their observance which alone preserves peace among human beings: if obedience to them were not the rule, and disobedience the exception, every one would see in every one else a probable enemy, against whom he must be perpetually guarding himself. What is hardly less important, these are the precepts which mankind have the strongest and the most direct inducements for impressing upon one another. By merely giving to each other prudential instruction or exhortation, they may gain, or think they gain, nothing: in inculcating on each other the duty of positive beneficence they have an unmistakable interest, but far less in degree: a person may possibly not need the benefits of others; but he always needs that they should not do him hurt. Thus the moralities which protect every individual from being harmed by others, either directly or by being hindered in his freedom of pursuing his own good, are at once those which he himself has most at heart, and those which he has the strongest interest in publishing and enforcing by word and deed. It is by a person's observance of these that his fitness to exist as one of the fellowship of human beings is tested and decided; for on that depends his being a nuisance or not to those with whom he is in contact. Now it is these moralities primarily which compose the obligations of justice. The most marked cases of injustice, and those which give the tone to the feeling of repugnance which characterises the sentiment, are acts of wrongful aggression, or wrongful exercise of power over some one; the next are those which consist in wrongfully withholding from him something which is his due; in both cases, inflicting on him a positive hurt, either in the form of direct suffering, or of the privation of some good which he had reasonable ground, either of a physical or of a social kind, for counting upon.

[34]   The same powerful motives which command the observance of these primary moralities, enjoin the punishment of those who violate them; and as the impulses of self-defence, of defence of others, and of vengeance, are all called forth against such persons, retribution, or evil for evil, becomes closely connected with the sentiment of justice, and is universally included in the idea. Good for good is also one of the dictates of justice; and this, though its social utility is evident, and though it carries with it a natural human feeling, has not at first sight that obvious connection with hurt or injury, which, existing in the most elementary cases of just and unjust, is the source of the characteristic intensity of the sentiment. But the connection, though less obvious, is not less real. He who accepts benefits, and denies a return of them when needed, inflicts a real hurt, by disappointing one of the most natural and reasonable of expectations, and one which he must at least tacitly have encouraged, otherwise the benefits would seldom have been conferred. The important rank, among human evils and wrongs, of the disappointment of expectation, is shown in the fact that it constitutes the principal criminality of two such highly immoral acts as a breach of friendship and a breach of promise. Few

hurts which human beings can sustain are greater, and none wound more, than when that on which they habitually and with full assurance relied, fails them in the hour of need; and few wrongs are greater than this mere withholding of good; none excite more resentment, either in the person suffering, or in a sympathising spectator. The principle, therefore, of giving to each what they deserve, that is, good for good as well as evil for evil, is not only included within the idea of justice as we have defined it, but is a proper object of that intensity of sentiment, which places the just, in human estimation, above the simply Expedient.

[35]   Most of the maxims of justice current in the world, and commonly appealed to in its transactions, are simply instrumental to carrying into effect the principles of justice which we have now spoken of. That a person is only responsible for what he has done voluntarily, or could voluntarily have avoided; that it is unjust to condemn any person unheard; that the punishment ought to be proportioned to the offence, and the like, are maxims intended to prevent the just principle of evil for evil from being perverted to the infliction of evil without that justification. The greater part of these common maxims have come into use from the practice of courts of justice, which have been naturally led to a more complete recognition and elaboration than was likely to suggest itself to others, of the rules necessary to enable them to fulfil their double function, of inflicting punishment when due, and of awarding to each person his right.

[36]   That first of judicial virtues, impartiality, is an obligation of justice, partly for the reason last mentioned; as being a necessary condition of the fulfilment of the other obligations of justice. But this is not the only source of the exalted rank, among human obligations, of those maxims of equality and impartiality, which, both in popular estimation and in that of the most enlightened, are included among the precepts of justice. In one point of view, they may be considered as corollaries from the principles already laid down. If it is a duty to do to each according to his deserts, returning good for good as well as repressing evil by evil, it necessarily follows that we should treat all equally well (when no higher duty forbids) who have deserved equally well of us, and that society should treat all equally well who have deserved equally well of it, that is, who have deserved equally well absolutely. This is the highest abstract standard of social and distributive justice; towards which all institutions, and the efforts of all virtuous citizens, should be made in the utmost possible degree to converge. But this great moral duty rests upon a still deeper foundation, being a direct emanation from the first principle of morals, and not a mere logical corollary from secondary or derivative doctrines. It is involved in the very meaning of Utility, or the Greatest Happiness Principle. That principle is a mere form of words without rational signification, unless one person's happiness, supposed equal in degree (with the proper allowance made for kind), is counted for exactly as much as another's. Those conditions being supplied, Bentham's dictum, "everybody to count for one, nobody for more than one," might be written under the principle of utility as an

explanatory commentary.* The equal claim of everybody to happiness in the estimation of the moralist and the legislator, involves an equal claim to all the means of happiness, except in so far as the inevitable conditions of human life, and the general interest, in which that of every individual is included, set limits to the maxim; and those limits ought to be strictly construed. As every other maxim of justice, so this is by no means applied or held applicable universally; on the contrary, as I have already remarked, it bends to every person's ideas of social expediency. But in whatever case it is deemed applicable at all, it is held to be the dictate of justice. All persons are deemed to have a *right* to equality of treatment, except when some recognised social expediency requires the reverse. And hence all social inequalities which have ceased to be considered expedient, assume the character not of simple inexpediency, but of injustice, and appear so tyrannical, that people are apt to wonder how they ever could have been tolerated; forgetful that they themselves perhaps tolerate other inequalities under an equally mistaken

* This implication, in the first principle of the utilitarian scheme, of perfect impartiality between persons, is regarded by Mr. Herbert Spencer (in his *Social Statics*) as a disproof of the pretensions of utility to be a sufficient guide to right; since (he says) the principle of utility presupposes the anterior principle, that everybody has an equal right to happiness. It may be more correctly described as supposing that equal amounts of happiness are equally desirable, whether felt by the same or by different persons. This, however, is not a presupposition; not a premise needful to support the principle of utility, but the very principle itself; for what is the principle of utility, if it be not that "happiness" and "desirable" are synonymous terms? If there is any anterior principle implied, it can be no other than this, that the truths of arithmetic are applicable to the valuation of happiness, as of all other measurable quantities.

(Mr. Herbert Spencer, in a private communication on the subject of the preceding Note, objects to being considered an opponent of utilitarianism, and states that he regards happiness as the ultimate end of morality; but deems that end only partially attainable by empirical generalisations from the observed results of conduct, and completely attainable only by deducing, from the laws of life and the conditions of existence, what kinds of action necessarily tend to produce happiness, and what kinds to produce unhappiness. What the exception of the word "necessarily," I have no dissent to express from this doctrine; and (omitting that word) I am not aware that any modern advocate of utilitarianism is of a different opinion. Bentham, certainly, to whom in the *Social Statics* Mr. Spencer particularly referred, is, least of all writers, chargeable with unwillingness to deduce the effect of actions on happiness from the laws of human nature and the universal conditions of human life. The common charge against him is of relying too exclusively upon such deductions, and declining altogether to be bound by the generalisations from specific experience which Mr. Spencer thinks that utilitarians generally confine themselves to. My own opinion (and, as I collect, Mr. Spencer's) is, that in ethics, as in all other branches of scientific study, the consilience of the results of both these processes, each corroborating and verifying the other, is requisite to give to any general proposition the kind degree of evidence which constitutes scientific proof.).

notion of expediency, the correction of which would make that which they approve seem quite as monstrous as what they have at last learnt to condemn. The entire history of social improvement has been a series of transitions, by which one custom or institution after another, from being a supposed primary necessity of social existence, has passed into the rank of a universally stigmatised injustice and tyranny. So it has been with the distinctions of slaves and freemen, nobles and serfs, patricians and plebeians; and so it will be, and in part already is, with the aristocracies of colour, race, and sex.

[37]　It appears from what has been said, that justice is a name for certain moral requirements, which, regarded collectively, stand higher in the scale of social utility, and are therefore of more paramount obligation, than any others; though particular cases may occur in which some other social duty is so important, as to overrule any one of the general maxims of justice. Thus, to save a life, it may not only be allowable, but a duty, to steal, or take by force, the necessary food or medicine, or to kidnap, and compel to officiate, the only qualified medical practitioner. In such cases, as we do not call anything justice which is not a virtue, we usually say, not that justice must give way to some other moral principle, but that what is just in ordinary cases is, by reason of that other principle, not just in the particular case. By this useful accommodation of language, the character of indefeasibility attributed to justice is kept up, and we are saved from the necessity of maintaining that there can be laudable injustice.

[38]　The considerations which have now been adduced resolve, I conceive, the only real difficulty in the utilitarian theory of morals. It has always been evident that all cases of justice are also cases of expediency: the difference is in the peculiar sentiment which attaches to the former, as contradistinguished from the latter. If this characteristic sentiment has been sufficiently accounted for; if there is no necessity to assume for it any peculiarity of origin; if it is simply the natural feeling of resentment, moralised by being made coextensive with the demands of social good; and if this feeling not only does but ought to exist in all the classes of cases to which the idea of justice corresponds; that idea no longer presents itself as a stumbling-block to the utilitarian ethics. Justice remains the appropriate name for certain social utilities which are vastly more important, and therefore more absolute and imperative, than any others are as a class (though not more so than others may be in particular cases); and which, therefore, ought to be, as well as naturally are, guarded by a sentiment not only different in degree, but also in kind; distinguished from the milder feeling which attaches to the mere idea of promoting human pleasure or convenience, at once by the more definite nature of its commands, and by the sterner character of its sanctions.

Part III

Essays on the Text

Chapter 4

Mill's Theory of Value

Wendy Donner

Introduction

Utilitarianism is an intriguingly intricate moral philosophy with many facets, and it is open to a plurality of readings and interpretations. In this multifarious landscape, John Stuart Mill's version of utilitarianism still stands out as one of the more complex varieties. It is an exemplar of intricacy and its complex structure invites reflection and dialogue on an assortment of theoretical puzzles and questions about its plausibility and most accurate interpretation. Mill's theory is rich and substantial. It is constructed for the purpose, if not the mission, of ready application to a wide range of social and political questions. It is undoubtedly an activist and reformist theory, well suited to Mill's own lifelong commitments to social and political campaigns and issues of his day.

Despite its intricacy, which does perplex and challenge, its core is pristinely simple and strikingly compelling. The starting point and the anchor are the reality of suffering in the world and the awareness this brings for the ethical life. The foundational claim is that the starting point of ethics is this suffering and the aspirations and obligations to alleviate suffering and promote happiness that flow from this in ethical life. Mill's statement of the foundational principle of utilitarianism as a moral theory states this unequivocally.

> The creed which accepts as the foundation of morals, Utility, or the Greatest Happiness Principle, holds that actions are right in proportion as they tend to promote happiness, wrong as they tend to promote the reverse of happiness. (Mill 1861, reprinted as Part II of this volume, Ch. II, para. 2. Citations to this work will simply be by roman numeral for chapter and arabic numeral for paragraph.)

Mill's classic utilitarian theory thus contends that actions are judged to be right or wrong according to their consequences. Utilitarianism is a form of consequentialism, because it is by referring to the consequences of actions that we morally assess them. In a consequentialist moral theory, actions are right if they produce good consequences and they are wrong if they result in bad consequences. Mill analyses and unpacks good or value as happiness, and bad as unhappiness or suffering.

The principle of utility functions as the ultimate standard and foundational principle of morality. However, in Mill's utilitarianism, the principle of utility serves a much broader purpose than that of simply grounding morality. It is a general principle of the good, and does full duty as the ultimate standard for all practical reasoning, for all of the "practice of life" (Mill 1843: 951). This generality of function has significant implications, which are sometimes overlooked, for the rest of Mill's utilitarianism. Here is Mill's statement of the principle clarifying its status as a principle of good. "The utilitarian doctrine is, that happiness is desirable, and the only thing desirable, as an end; all other things being only desirable as means to that end" (IV, 2). He adds that "by happiness is intended pleasure, and the absence of pain; by unhappiness, pain, and the privation of pleasure" (II, 2). He expands this meaning in claiming that

> pleasure, and freedom from pain, are the only things desirable as ends; and . . . all desirable things (which are as numerous in the utilitarian scheme as in any other scheme) are desirable either for the pleasure inherent in themselves, or as means to the promotion of pleasure and the prevention of pain. (II, 2)

The full distinctiveness of Mill's theory emerges in the examination of the details of the nature of good. The wide reach of this principle of good in a utilitarian consequentialist theory is unsurprising. Much depends upon the conception of this good, and I now turn to an investigation of the nature of good.

Qualitative Hedonism

Jeremy Bentham, James Mill, and John Stuart Mill are all classical utilitarian philosophers, sharing core concepts, frameworks, and principles. While the singularity of Mill's theory of value is indisputable, in acknowledging this distinctiveness it is crucial not to overlook this core common ground. Mill adhered to the basic principles that Bentham advocated and thought that Bentham was right about the essentials. The shared core is that the good for human beings consists in experiences or states of consciousness of pleasure or happiness. Hedonism maintains that the only things that are intrinsically good are pleasurable or happy states of experience. This statement of the basic claim of hedonism leaves open further questions that need exploring.

The differences appear in the detailed analysis of the nature of states of pleasure or happiness. All these philosophers hold to "mental-state" accounts of utility, locating value in states of mind and experiences such as pleasure, happiness, satisfaction, enjoyment, or well-being. It is convenient in some respects to label Mill's value theory as qualitative hedonism, in part to allow a ready comparison with Bentham's avowedly quantitative hedonism. But as the use of this label can be misleading, it is important that I signal early and clearly that what counts for the philosophical discussion depends upon an accurate understanding of the substance of his views, and not the label we apply to those views. It is also important, in explicating and exploring Mill's views in *Utilitarianism,* that I make full and free use of his voluminous body of work on this subject in other writings for filling in the background and context and for completeness of understanding.

Mill was the designated heir of the Benthamite utilitarian philosophical family lineage. His father James Mill designed his childhood education to train him for this responsibility. Yet Mill's own philosophical theory of value is singular in large measure because of Mill's own acute awareness of the limitations and weaknesses of his philosophical forebear's formulation of utilitarianism, and of the effects of the limitations on his own education and development (Mill 1873: 137–92). Many of those weaknesses Mill located in Bentham's theory of value and especially in his conception of the good. Since in this philosophical tradition the concepts of human nature and of character are intimately linked and connected to the concept of good for agents with this nature, the younger Mill traced the flaws in the view of intrinsic value back to flaws in the Benthamite depiction of character and human nature. (See Mill 1833: 5–18, 1838: 94–100.) These two are interwoven and cannot be disentangled. He also departed from Bentham's method of measuring utility, the notorious felicific calculus, which he regarded as being too crude a measurement instrument.

One promising point of embarkation, for a consideration of Mill's differences with Bentham, is Mill's comment in *Utilitarianism* that critics of hedonism dislike hedonism and characterize it as "a doctrine worthy only of swine" (II, 3). He answers:

> The accusation supposes human beings to be capable of no pleasures except those of which swine are capable . . . a beast's pleasures do not satisfy a human being's conceptions of happiness. Human beings have faculties more elevated than the animal appetites, and when once made conscious of them, do not regard anything as happiness which does not include their gratification. (II, 4)

In unraveling the meaning of this we come to the heart of his disputes with his mentor. For he was affected by this objection, and sensitive that it might apply to Bentham's theory of value. In distancing himself, he broke new ground in his presentation of the good for humans. Bentham's brand of hedonism is vulnerable, Mill feared, because Bentham's hedonism explicitly allows only one sort of good-making characteristic or feature – namely quantity – to be taken into account in assessing how much value a particular state of mind is judged to have. In focusing only on quantity, Bentham's theory also tends to focus on the simple pleasurable sensations and components of experience. Mill distances himself from Bentham's quantitative theory in several pivotal respects.

In the first place, although the things that are valuable are satisfying or pleasurable states of experience or consciousness, Mill's expansive conception of good, reconstructed to overcome Benthamite limitations, differs from Bentham in a pivotal way. While Bentham contends that simple sensations of pleasure are the paradigm mental states that are valuable, Mill demurs. Mill proposes that value is contained in complex, heterogeneous states of consciousness which are the products of the workings of psychological laws of association on these simple mental states. Sensations and ideas are linked through association and in the process of psychological development these originally simple mental states evolve into more complex states of experience. Mill thinks that association often operates as a quasi-chemical process to create chemical unions of elements in which the original parts or elements merge into a new and complex whole. He says:

> When many impressions or ideas are operating in the mind together, there sometimes takes place a process of a similar kind to chemical combination. When impressions have been so often experienced in conjunction, that each of them calls up readily and instantaneously the ideas of the whole group, those ideas sometimes melt and coalesce into one another, and appear not several ideas, but one. (Mill 1843: 853)

The complexes that result occupy an important place in Mill's moral psychology and his value theory. They are the paradigm bearers of value, rather than the simple ideas that generate them.

Secondly, Mill contends that limiting the good-making characteristics of valuable states of consciousness to their quantity is misguided. Mill argues that the quality (or kind) as well as the quantity are both correctly seen as the good-making properties which determine the value of these satisfying states of consciousness.

Thirdly, the measurement of utility is of central concern for utilitarianism. The procedures for measuring the value of the states of consciousness that are under consideration widen the distance between Bentham and Mill. Mill's method for measuring value relies upon the judgments of "competent agents." One key question is thus the exploration of what Mill means by a competent agent. I argue that Mill's notion of a competent agent is an agent who has undergone an education best understood as a process of development and self-development. This conception of a competent agent is at the very core of Mill's ethical theory. While an extensive examination of Mill's philosophy of education is beyond the scope of this essay, I take up this question below in the section on education. I have explored Mill's views on the education of competent agents more thoroughly elsewhere. (See Donner 1991, 1998; Donner and Fumerton 2000.)

To facilitate understanding, it is helpful to keep in mind that, although the bearers of value are pleasurable mental states, what we are seeking to promote and measure is utility or value. In Mill's system, complex mental states are the paradigm entities that are valuable. As these are complex, they have a multitude of features that can be observed through mindful introspection. People can be trained and educated to become adept and skillful at noting their various properties and components. In this introspective scrutiny, many of the properties that come to attention have nothing to do with the value of the experience. And others do come to attention as those that are good-making and contribute to the value of the experience. Bentham maintains that only the quantity (primarily intensity and duration) count in the reckoning of value or satisfying experiences. Mill contends that, in addition to quantity, the quality or kind of the experience also counts in this reckoning. Their shared common ground is that they both contend that these named features have a dual nature and function. They are both empirical features, that is, features of the consciousness that can be empirically and phenomenally picked out by a discerning, trained awareness. But at the same time, they are also normative, or good-making, or productive of value. This discernment can be done better or worse, well or badly, depending upon the cultivation and education in this ability. This training to discern and appreciate certain properties of experience is one of the basic building blocks of the education and training of competent agents in Mill's system. This means that they are appropriately or correctly picked out or discerned by a trained introspective mind as the basis of value. While value is grounded in these empirical and phenomenal features, and these provide an empirical base for value, the features are not identical with value and they do not constitute value.

Because few would dispute that in many typical cases a greater quantity of happiness or satisfaction is better than a lesser, the trained, discriminative judgments involved in coming to an assessment about what the quantity "amounts to" in Bentham's system may seem too obvious to merit dwelling upon. But pausing here is helpful in understanding what Mill is proposing. When we explore further Bentham's good-making and empirical feature of quantity, we find that there is no simple characteristic of quantity. Instead, Bentham's felicific calculus, his method of measuring value, breaks down quantity into several components. Although he names seven "circumstances to be taken into the account in estimating the value of a pleasure or pain" (Bentham in Troyer 2003: 19) most commentators collapse these and focus on the first two, namely, the intensity and the duration. Here I pass over many of the problems with measurement long associated with the felicific calculus. I zero in on the point that trained discrimination is called on and necessary even to judge in a rough and ready manner the amount of, at least, the intensity. But even supposing that adequate judgments of intensity with the definite units required by Bentham's system are available, a further explicitly normative judgment is required in order to arrive at the overall value of the pleasure.

This is because there is no quantity *simpliciter*; ineluctably, there are only properties such as intensity and duration. There is no simple empirical or phenomenal property of quantity, composed of one element that can be measured. Quantity is unavoidably a compound feature of experience, comprised of at least the features of intensity and duration. Bentham assumes too readily that these two features of intensity and duration should be given equal weight. What hides in the background, but must be brought to the foreground for analysis and made conspicuous, is Bentham's assumed normative judgment that the intensity and the duration of a pleasure count equally in estimating and calculating its value. But this cannot simply be assumed, as it is a disputable claim. We may well ask why intensity and duration should count equally. It is possible and indeed plausible to construct scenarios in which a few brief periods of extraordinary happiness or ecstatic bliss are taken to be the central defining moments of a life. In such scenarios some people would be willing to make enormous sacrifices of other periods of happiness in order to attain and achieve these brief moments of intense satisfaction. Lives of adventurers are plausibly interpreted in this light. It is also possible and plausible to construct scenarios in which the feature of duration is given overriding weight. In such scenarios the agents choose to eschew or abstain from intense pleasures in order to pursue and protect the peaceful and calm enjoyments that are constant and enduring. It is not required that such cases be typical or common in order to make the point that Bentham's measurement procedure is not merely one of straightforward calculation. From these scenarios we can draw out the point that different agents, similarly trained and educated, can be expected to differ in their judgments, assessments, and weightings of intensity and duration. What I claim must be noted is that a normative judgment about how to weigh these two separate components of quantity (for there is no simple property quantity) is unavoidable. No straightforward empirical calculation of quantity without this normative weighting judgment can be obtained. Moreover, agents of different character and outlook will inevitably differ about the best way to weigh these features, according to whether they are bold and exuberant thrill-seekers, to take one extreme, or peaceful contemplatives, to take the other. Pluralism and diversity of judgment are unavoidable.

This clarification of the requirements of Bentham's calculus is helpful in approaching Mill's proposals. Mill claims that quality, as well as quantity, is a good-making feature of pleasurable experience. He says that by quality of experience he means kind. In *Utilitarianism* he says:

> It is quite compatible with the principle of utility to recognize the fact, that some *kinds* of pleasure are more desirable and more valuable than others. It would be absurd that while, in estimating all other things, quality is considered as well as quantity, the estimation of pleasures should be supposed to depend on quantity alone. (II, 4)

> What is there to decide whether a particular pleasure is worth purchasing at the cost of a particular pain, except the feelings and judgment of the experienced? When, therefore, those feelings and judgment declare the pleasures derived from the higher faculties to be preferable *in kind*, apart from the question of intensity, to those of which the animal nature, disjoined from the higher faculties, is susceptible, they are entitled on this subject to the same regard. (II, 8)

According to the Greatest Happiness Principle . . . the ultimate end . . . is an existence exempt as far as possible from pain, and as rich as possible in enjoyments, both in point of quantity and quality. (II, 10)

Mill mirrors Bentham in maintaining that the relevant properties of experiences are both empirical and normative. Much confusion about Mill's meaning has its source in a failure of critics and commentators to note that in Mill's philosophy quality and value are not synonymous. Value, Mill holds, is what we are trying to promote or produce and what we measure when we follow the principle of utility. The quality of pleasurable experience is best understood as its kind, and indeed Mill says, as explicitly as possible, that by quality he means kind of pleasure: "it is quite compatible with the principle of utility to recognize the fact, that some *kinds* of pleasure are . . . more valuable than others" (II, 4). In Mill's system, value or good is produced by the two basic good-making properties, quantity (intensity and duration) and quality (kind). Experiences are ranked on the scale of value; in other words what is being measured is the value of experiences. The scales are not cardinal, as in Bentham's system, for Mill maintains that these sorts of value judgment do not lend themselves to cardinal measurement. Mill allows for different categories of kind to be brought into the measurement procedure. In his most basic statements of the theory, the qualities or kinds of happiness that are the most valuable are those that develop and exercise the higher human capacities and faculties. (See Donner 1991; Brink 1992; Crisp 1997.) Put alternatively, the exercise of the intellectual and moral virtues or excellences exemplify the most valuable kinds of happiness. This claim explicitly ties Mill's theory in with the lineage of virtue ethics, which makes the exercise of the human excellences or virtues a focal point of ethics and politics. (See Semmel 1984; Berkowitz 1999.) Mill's standard example is that "the pleasures derived from the higher faculties [are] preferable *in kind*" (II, 8). Thus kinds can be classified as those resulting from the exercise of the lower to the exercise of the higher human faculties. But kinds of pleasure are also classified by cause or source and by phenomenal differences in the experience. Causal and intentional properties form their own categories of kinds. Mill's theory is characterized by its flexibility in part because he identifies quality and kind, and yet also has a pliant view of the categories of kinds.

Bentham's measurement procedure combines empirical, factual judgments and discriminations about the amount of intensity and duration with incontrovertible normative judgments about how they are to be weighted and then integrated onto the primary scale of value, which is what we are measuring. Mill's measurement procedure follows Bentham to an extent and then takes a radically new direction. Mill's procedure must deal with combining the dimensions of intensity and duration, but his procedure must also have a process for integrating judgments of quality (kind) onto the primary scale of value. Agents must make normative judgments, not just about how to weigh intensity and duration, but also about how to weigh quality against quantity in combining them on the primary scale. There is a more extensive normative component in Mill's measurement procedure. The further normative judgment that Mill's procedure calls for is that some kinds (qualities) of satisfactions are more valuable, and thus should be ranked more highly on the central scale of value. Mill's frequent references to "higher" pleasures are thus best understood as meaning pleasures of a kind (quality) that is more valuable. The measurement procedure leads Mill in the new direction of eliciting the judgments of competent agents to resolve, determine, and arrive at overall judgments of the value of pleasurable experiences. These judgments are best understood as being evidential, and thus they may be mistaken; indeed, Mill's expectation of progress over time has built into it the expectation that judgments are regularly discovered to be mistaken. The method allows for a vote among judges in cases of disagreement, in the public realm. As the diversity and pluralism of contemporary societies increase, a philosophy that explicitly allows for and expects diversity among educated and trained agents is plausible and helpful; one that expects conformity is not. Roger Crisp says:

> Because the views of the judges are only evidential, it is of course conceivable that they may be mistaken, and Mill implicitly accepts this in allowing for disagreement among them . . . Mill is claiming not that the majority *must* be right, but that it is only reasonable to respect the decision of the majority. (1997: 37)

The caveat to this claim is, of course, that in the area of life defended in *On Liberty*, where our actions do not affect the vital interests or rights of others, our own judgment in the end is respected.

All of these roads lead to the central role of a philosophy of education, to explain the proper education of developed and self-developed agents. It also leads to deep links with virtue ethics. And this distinctive and new direction of the theory leads directly to some persistent objections to Mill's qualitative hedonism.

Objections to Mill's Qualitative Hedonism: Internal Inconsistency and Value Pluralism

Mill's revision of Bentham's hedonism and his attempts to distance himself from the problems he perceived in the Benthamite theory of value have not always been well received in the discussions of his theory. Indeed, his bold revisionism and his inclusion of quality as a good-making property have become the subject of an extensive literature, much of it highly critical. Mill's shift away from quantitative hedonism produces a theory notable or notorious for its complexity and its openness to a variety of readings and interpretations. Mill's procedure for measuring value is similarly intricate and complex, and open to a range of interpretations and attendant objections. However, I contend that many of the most persistent and often repeated criticisms of Mill are misguided and based upon confusion. One result of this focus upon confused objections, I contend, has been to misdirect attention away from the objections to Mill's value theory which are more intractable and more deeply challenging and puzzling. These more substantial objections are put by value pluralists, who argue that things other than happiness are valuable in themselves.

One of the most persistent objections is that Mill's qualitative hedonism is internally inconsistent or alternatively that Mill's theory abandons hedonism by including quality in the measurement of the value of pleasurable experience. According to this perspective, if you are a hedonist, then the only property that can count in measuring the value is quantity, or how much of the pleasurable experience there is. This objection is bluntly stated by F. H. Bradley:

> If you are to prefer a higher pleasure to a lower without reference to quantity – then there is an end altogether of the principle which puts the measure in the surplus of pleasure to the whole sentient creation. (1962: 119)

Although this objection put by Bradley is persistently raised, its persistence does not reflect its strength. It is based upon a misinterpretation of the basic claim of hedonism, which is that pleasurable experience is the only thing that is good in itself. I argue that it is a separate question what dimensions of properties of these experiences produce their value and should be taken into account in the measurement of their value. This objection to Mill's value theory falls prey to the error of conflating two separate questions: (1) What things are intrinsically valuable? (pleasurable mental states) and (2) What properties of these mental states are productive of their value? A position on the first question leaves undetermined an answer to the second.

In assuming the very claim that needs to be argued, namely, that only quantity matters in assessing the overall value of pleasure, Bradley simply begs the question against Mill. Mill has a classic response in anticipation of this objection that has occupied such a prominent place in the literature. Mill says:

> It would be absurd that while, in estimating all other things, quality is considered as well as quantity, the estimation of pleasures should be supposed to depend on quantity alone. (II, 4)

It is indeed absurd to assume as the baseline position that if you value satisfying experiences, then the only thing about them that matters is how much or what quantity you have. Few, if any, actual rational moral agents care only about the amount of happiness they have. Mill's theory of value is constructed as a guide for actual agents in living worthwhile lives. He apprehends clearly that quantity does not capture the whole picture, and he constructs an account that more accurately reflects and guides judgments of practical wisdom. Roger Crisp sees the similarities of Mill's perspective and Aristotelian virtue accounts:

> Those who can judge the value of experiences correctly are those who are not only
> sensitive to the salient features of those experiences, particularly their intensity
> and nature, but able to attach to those features the evaluative weight they deserve.
> (1997: 39)

It simply does not follow from the basic claim of hedonism, namely, that the only
intrinsically valuable things are experiences of happiness, that we are committed
to the further claim that only the amount of happiness matters. This is clearly mistaken. Moreover, it is deeply at odds with how reflective people make comparative choices about good things, beautiful things, noble things, and other similar
value choices. In such choices, the kind as well as the amount is standardly taken
into account in making value judgments. The anomalous perspective in these
practical and rational judgments in daily life is the approach that only quantity
matters. (For other noteworthy discussions of these questions, see Berger 1984;
Riley 1988; Skorupski 1989; Brink 1992; Long 1992; Crisp 1997; Scarre 1997;
West 2004.)

There are substantive and persistent challenges and objections to Mill's value
theory which are not as easily laid to rest. Thoughtful readers will find themselves
puzzling over these. Value pluralism presents one such challenge to all forms of
hedonism. Value pluralism maintains that all forms of hedonism are too limited in
the list of things allowed onto the list of intrinsically valuable things. Surely, the
value pluralist contends, other things like virtue, knowledge or wisdom, and
enlightenment are, at least on some occasions, valuable in themselves, apart from
any connection to or presence of pleasure or satisfaction.

Mill's reply draws upon his psychological theory of associationism. He uses
virtue as an example.

> To illustrate this further, we may remember that virtue is not the only thing, origi-
> nally a means, and which if it were not a means to anything else, would be and remain
> indifferent, but which by association with what it is a means to, comes to be desired
> for itself. (IV, 6)

Mill's point is that through psychological association virtue becomes part of
our happiness. Originally we desire virtue as a means to happiness, but through
psychological association virtue becomes pleasurable and so a component of happiness. Virtue is pleasurable especially when a person has developed and exercises
the moral and intellectual capacities. I claim that the development and exercise of
the virtues is so interwoven with happiness in Mill's system that this response is
plausible.

A bigger test to his system is the example of knowledge. Although the development and exercise of the intellectual virtues is also interwoven with happiness,
yet we can construct examples of human knowledge that seem to lack this connection to human well-being, and that even seem strongly connected with deep

and massive harm and suffering. One immediate example is the knowledge that led to the construction of the atomic bomb. The horror inflicted upon Hiroshima seems to be a clear example of knowledge separated and severed from human well-being. The proliferation of nuclear weapons and other horrifying weapons of mass destruction are further examples. We can add in knowledge severed from well-being with examples like that expertise that destroys the natural environment. Viewed in this light, examples of knowledge severed from well-being and satisfaction are plentiful. But is this what value pluralists intend to propound? This is not the sort of counterexample to hedonism to which they appeal. The objection from pluralists is, rather, looking for knowledge that is valuable in itself, and knowledge leading to mass destruction does not seem to fit the bill. At this point the question arises as to where the burden of proof lies, as well as the question what impact these examples should have. The opponents of hedonism reply that the sorts of examples they have in mind are decidedly not those that cause deep suffering (which also have a connection to well-being, albeit a negative one). The sorts of examples rather are those valuable in themselves, apart from happiness, and not as a means to something further, as would be the case in knowledge as instrumentally, rather than intrinsically, valuable.

Is Mill correct in asserting this essential link to the happiness experienced from these other purported good things? In his favor, a very strong case can be made that in cases of other good things, if a link to happiness is not present we are inclined to question the intrinsic nature of the value. Whether this applies to all such proposed examples is a good question to ponder. This is the sort of question to which a definitive answer seems elusive, for both supporters and opponents of qualitative hedonism.

But, while counterexamples to Mill's theory can be constructed in which the link to happiness may seem neutral, are we not entitled to more from the value pluralist? Do examples in the absence of a more complete alternative theory constitute a compelling objection to Mill? For the claims of value pluralism to be convincing, we need the apparatus of a theory, not simply examples in isolation from a theoretical structure. A contrary case needs also to be constructed showing how virtue and knowledge are valuable apart from this connection to happiness. Generally what occurs in these discussions is that value pluralists point to proposed examples without making the extensive positive case for the claim that they are good in themselves. This would need to include an analysis of how knowledge can be good in itself in cases in which massive suffering results. For if knowledge is indeed valuable in itself, then must it not be valuable even in the cases in which it has no link to happiness, as well as in cases in which it results in great suffering? Perhaps this is too stringent a requirement. But, at minimum, there must be an analysis similar to that proffered by Mill, setting out the good-making features of knowledge, or an alternative apparatus. So Mill's argument that there must be connections to happiness in order to claim that knowledge is valuable is bolstered by some counterexamples to value pluralism.

Perhaps the value pluralist will respond that we don't know what good conse-quences this knowledge will provide in the future. But this line of reply supports hedonism, since it appeals in the end to enhancement of human happiness and undercuts the objection. Does value pluralism claim that knowledge is a good even if it leads to horrific suffering? Or merely that there are some examples of knowl-edge that are neutral with regard to well-being, yet good nonetheless? We may be led to the conclusion that Mill's case is far stronger than that of the opponents.

A thorough understanding of Mill's value theory needs an examination, not just of his views on the nature of value, but also of his approach to measuring the value at the heart of his system. His liberal philosophy of education explains the process of developing competent agents.

Development and Self-Development: Liberal Democratic Education

Mill sets out an expansive conception of good and he develops a method for mea-suring the value of satisfying experiences that is consonant with this enlarged view. Mill's method for measuring good relies on the judgments of competent agents who have undergone an education best understood as a process of development and self-development.

Mill signals his method of value measurement in *Utilitarianism*. He says:

> If I am asked, what I mean by difference in quality of pleasures, or what makes one pleasure more valuable than another, merely as a pleasure, except its being greater in amount, there is but one possible answer. Of two pleasures, if there be one to which all or almost all who have experience of both give a decided preference, irrespective of any feeling of moral obligation to prefer it, that is the more desirable pleasure. If one of the two is, by those who are competently acquainted with both, placed so far above the other that they prefer it, even though knowing it to be attended with a greater amount of discontent, and would not resign it for any quantity of the other pleasure which their nature is capable of, we are justified in ascribing to the preferred enjoyment a superiority in quality, so far outweighing quantity as to render it, in comparison, of small account. (II, 5)

> From this verdict of the only competent judges, I apprehend there can be no appeal. On a question which is the best worth having of two pleasures, or which of two modes of existence is the most grateful to the feelings, apart from its moral attrib-utes and from its consequences, the judgment of those who are qualified by knowl-edge of both, or, if they differ, that of the majority among them, must be admitted as final. (II, 8)

Mill is not primarily concerned with judgments about particular pleasures and satisfactions. The primary focus of his theory is as much about good character and good lives as it is about particular satisfactions. Because of the broad scope of concern, and the education needed to be a competent agent, Mill focused much of his attention in his writings on his philosophy of education. Here I can only sketch the broad outlines of his approach, which I have elaborated elsewhere. (See Donner 1991, 1998; Donner and Fumerton 2000.)

He believes that agents who have been properly socialized and educated are better equipped and more likely to lead satisfying and worthwhile lives in the private sphere, as well as to engage as responsible and active citizens in the public domain. We are entitled to the social resources and the access to cooperative and collective endeavors to allow us to lead lives of self-development as adults. To be self-developed is both an essential element of, and an essential precondition for, appreciating the most valuable kinds of happiness. Members of society who have been denied the basic education needed to become self-developed agents, or competent agents with the training and ability to make astute judgments of value, are wronged by their society. Although this topic is beyond the scope of this essay, I contend that the form of political liberalism consonant with Mill's value theory is a radically egalitarian one (Donner 1991: 160–87). People have a right to liberty of self-development and are wronged and harmed if they are shut out from an appropriate education.

Thus a lot of theoretical weight is put on the philosophy of education in Mill's theory. The process of development in childhood is the first stage of the education and socialization of competent agents. In this part of the process, the generic human intellectual, affective, and moral capacities are nurtured. These generic capacities are tendencies and potentials that can be stifled and blocked or they can be nurtured and encouraged. Mill sees the development of human emotional capacities as the foundation for all forms of development. He traces his own well-known "mental crisis," a serious bout of depression in his early adult years, to the lack of nurturing of feeling in his own education. He took corrective action to restore balance in his own philosophy of education and protect a proper place for "internal culture" of feeling (Mill 1873: 147). This recognition of the need for emotional development does not lead Mill to ignore intellectual culture, and he is well-known for his emphasis on the value of intellectual enjoyments and mental development. The process of moral development educates children to connect sympathetically to others and to enjoy their happiness. The capacity for compassion is the result. He claims that this feeling of sympathy and connection is firmly rooted in human nature. He says:

> This firm foundation is that of the social feelings of mankind; the desire to be in unity with our fellow creatures, which is already a powerful principle in human nature, and happily one of those which tend to become stronger, even without express inculcation, from the influences of advancing civilization. The social state is at once so natural, so necessary, and so habitual to man, that, except in some unusual circumstances or by an effort of voluntary abstraction, he never conceives himself than as a member of a body. (IV, 10)

He rejects the view of moral agents as primarily rationally self-interested. He is always careful to balance the intellectual and individualist side with the moral and social side and to deplore the creation of a hierarchy among them. Mill claims that moral development must always accompany mental development, and this has important implications for his conception of self-development as well as for his liberal political philosophy.

When children reach adulthood the process of development evolves into, and continues as, self-development. In self-development, the higher-order capacities of individuality, autonomy, sociality, and cooperativeness are built up on the groundwork of the generic human capacities. The higher-order capacities must also be balanced. The essential liberal capacity of autonomy is the ability to reflect on, choose, endorse, and revise the character, relationships, projects, and life plans most reflective of individual character. Individuality is the capacity to discover and explore the range of individual abilities and talents. While Mill does not believe that individuals have fixed essences, there is a range of potential characters and plans of life most in harmony with individual characters. (See Ten 1980: 68—85; Gray 1983: 70–89; Berger 1984: 226–78; Crisp 1997: 195–200.)

Mill is well known for his defence of individuality and freedom in *On Liberty* (1859). However, Millian individuals are not atomistic but are rooted in their communities. According to Mill, value is located in each individual member of a community and the value of a community is constructed from the value of individual community members. Millian autonomous individuals are self-determining, creating and controlling the contours of their lives, and their choices and commitments reflect their particularity. Careful and intricate balance of the individual and the social carries through into the realm of higher-order capacities.

This model of self-development has powerful implications for Mill's form of liberalism, for since a certain threshold level of self-development is needed in order to lead a good life, to deny some people the opportunity of self-development is to violate some of their most vital interests – and thus their basic rights. Since almost all members of society have the potential to attain the status of self-development, the social context and institutions have a large influence in determining whether these potentials develop. According to Mill's moral and political philosophy, people have the right to liberty of self-development, and their rights are violated if their society actively bars them or does not take action to provide the means to develop and exercise their human capacities.

Judgments of value based upon these procedures have some measure of legitimacy or authority. But the authority of the judgments is not, in the long term, final or definitive, as these judgments can be mistaken and overturned by later evaluations. The judgments can be challenged and they are progressive; there is the expectation of change, improvement, and progress over time. There is also the expectation of disagreement, dispute, dissent, plurality and diversity of views and judgments. This process, and the agents and their judgments, even highly educated ones, are all fallible, as the argument of *On Liberty* takes great pains to establish. However, educated agents are the best situated and have the greatest chance to make correct discriminations and judgments.

I interpret Mill's method of assessing the value of satisfactions as laying out a comprehensive approach that allows in principle for the inclusion and comparability of the full range of the good-making features of enjoyments. This full range includes all of the areas of daily life that fall under what Mill calls the Art of Life: morality, prudence, and nobility, or "the Right, the Expedient, and the Beautiful or Noble, in human conduct and works" (Mill 1843: 949). It also includes a vast array of what Mill calls the moral arts: the practical arts of daily living. My interpretation is consistent with Mill's own understanding of the broad reach of the principle of utility as the general principle of the good that guides and justifies all practical judgments about the ends of life. In Book VI of the *Logic*, in the section "Teleology, or the Doctrine of Ends," he says:

> there must be some standard by which to determine the goodness or badness, absolute and comparative, of ends, or objects of desire. And whatever that standard is, there can be but one. (1843: 951)

He explains that a foundation for the moral part of the Art of Life, if found,

> would provide only for that portion of the field of conduct which is properly called moral. For the remainder of the practice of life some general principle, or standard, must still be sought; and if that principle be rightly chosen, it will be found, I apprehend, to serve quite as well for the ultimate principle of Morality, as for that of Prudence, Policy, or Taste. (1843: 951)

This remark is made at the end of the *Logic*, a work that is not as widely read as many of Mill's writings. It explains the comment in *Utilitarianism* that he is concerned with "the theory of life on which this theory of morality is grounded – namely, that pleasure, and freedom from pain, are the only things desirable as ends" (II, 2).

The principle of utility is a general principle of the good with a wide jurisdiction over all of the areas of private and public life and all of the arts of life. The implications of this are far-reaching, for if the principle is to fulfill its function, the conceptions of the good at its basis must be general enough to carry into all of these areas of public and private life. The evaluative judgments and assessments of satisfactions and pursuits must be appropriate for all these different areas of life, and judgments of value must be sensitively attuned to the different contexts under perusal. The education required to make such judgments of the good becomes of central importance as a fulcrum of the theory.

This approach could not then, without missing the spirit of the principle of utility and the range of areas under its jurisdiction, restrict the domain of the kinds of satisfactions that can be scrutinized and compared for value or disvalue. Mill undoubtedly himself regards the enjoyments of intellectual activity and pursuit of justice as primary examples of the highly valuable pleasures that develop and exercise the higher human capacities. However, it is important, I contend, to interpret his comments on the high value of these enjoyments as simply providing enduring examples of the application of the principles of his theory. Since his value theory is a general one, it is a mistake to restrict or to try to determine in advance the good-making properties that are to be assessed and compared.

Jonathan Riley's reading of Mill on the values of different kinds of enjoyments is an example of an interpretation that is prone to be too restrictive. Riley's reading permits only four kinds of enjoyments: "'utilities of justice' . . . 'private utilities' (including 'aesthetic utilities') . . . 'utilities of charity,' and . . . 'merely expedient utilities'" (1988: 87). These fixed categories of kind are too rigid to convey accurately the complexity of Mill's actual position on the myriad kinds of satisfactions which may be enjoyed and evaluated. Riley's interpretation is also restrictive in arguing for the lexical dominance of some kinds of utilities or enjoyments, and is especially problematic in its claim that different kinds of utilities cannot be compared. Riley contends that "each kind of utility is non-comparable with other kinds in terms of quantity or intensity" (1988: 166). However, this is difficult to uphold as a general approach to value measurement and lacks plausibility. In the course of daily life agents are constantly called upon to make such comparisons, and they do so successfully, albeit in a rough and ready way. Mill's intention is to argue for a general and comprehensive method that can be used to construct actual agents' plans of life and to guide actual value assessments.

Self-Development and Virtue Ethics

Mill's commitments to a progressive conception of human nature and to a concept of the good for humans that is fundamentally oriented to self-development connect his theory to the tradition of virtue ethics. The focus on the developments and exercise of the human excellences as an ongoing lifelong pursuit is reminiscent of the priorities of ethics of virtue. This is not surprising considered in the light of the priority given in Mill's own childhood education to exposure to classical Greek philosophy. The spirit of Aristotelian virtue ethics pervades and permeates Mill's ethics, and Mill emphasizes its powerful influence on his outlook in the *Autobiography* (1873). Mill's extensive and elaborate explanation of the educational processes of development and self-development can be read as setting out a program for the cultivation, inculcation, and development of essential mental and moral virtues. Although Mill gives these Aristotelian ideas a liberal egalitarian face, he follows Aristotle in propounding the claims that a good human life must be one that allows for the development and exercise of the human mental and moral excellences. (See Crisp and Slote 1997; Berkowitz 1999; Urbinati 2002.) He writes extensively about activities developing these traits in both public and private realms. The emphasis upon the political virtues in Mill's theory is striking, and his commitment to active participatory democracy is another example of pursuing avenues for the practice of the virtues in the public domain that is redolent of virtue theories. *On Liberty* and *Consideration on Representative Government* (1861a: 371–577) are perhaps the two best-known writings of this type, but there are many other writings in which Mill sets out these arguments. Mill sees active participation in the political and social life of the community as one of the main arenas for the exercise of these excellences. Particularly in his later writings on economics, Mill argues for participatory and democratic workplace partnerships and associations, and hopes that this would bring about "the conversion of each human being's daily occupation into a school of the social sympathies and the practical intelligence" (1848: 792). These are training grounds for developing traits and habits of cooperation and compassion.

In Mill's theory the foundations remain utilitarian, for the exercise of the virtues provides the best chance of promoting happiness for all. But the characterization of human happiness is essentially interwoven with virtue. Roger Crisp and Michael Slote note that virtue ethics puts the focus on agents and their lives and character. They ask, "is it possible for utilitarians . . . to enlarge the focus of their own theories to incorporate agents' lives as a whole, their characters as well as . . . their actions?" (1997: 3). In the case of Mill's utilitarianism, the answer is clearly in the affirmative. It would be incomprehensible to Mill to reach for understanding the good for humans without according a prime place to virtuous character traits and capacities. Virtues are admirable character traits that are generally productive of good and that have become habitual, through association with pleasure (Berger 1984: 99–100). The development of admirable character traits that become habitual through practice and participation is one key mark of an ethics of virtue.

A second mark of virtue ethics is the employment of exemplars or models for students to emulate in these practices. These models embody and teach ideals that others use as examples to follow. Mill himself gives many examples to illustrate his intentions regarding appropriate models or exemplars of the intellectual and moral virtues. In the essay "Theism," Mill proposes Christ as an ideal of virtue for others to emulate. He draws attention to those who have used Christ "as the ideal representative and guide of humanity." He adds:

> nor, even now, would it be easy, even for an unbeliever, to find a better translation of the rule of virtue from the abstract into the concrete, than to endeavour so to live that Christ would approve our life. (1874: 488)

Such models and examples can be more personal, as Mill demonstrates in his dedication to, and depiction of, his wife Harriet Taylor Mill as his inspiration. She is "the friend and wife whose exalted sense of truth and right was my strongest incitement" (1859: 216). *On Liberty* uses a range of examples of this sort, including both specific examples like Christ and Socrates and general examples of persons with highly developed individuality as models. Such persons "set an example" of "more enlightened conduct" (p. 267). He explains that:

> Many have let themselves be guided . . . by the counsels and influence of a more highly gifted and instructed One or Few. The initiation of all wise or noble things, comes and must come from individuals . . . The honour and glory of the average man is that he is capable of following that initiative; that he can respond internally to wise and noble things, and be led to them with his eyes open. (1859: 269)

Mill is quick to add that he is advocating emulation of models, and he is not proposing "hero-worship" or forceful imposition of values.

> All he can claim is, freedom to point out the way. The power of compelling others into it, is not only inconsistent with the freedom and development of all the rest, but corrupting to the strong man himself. (1859: 269)

The richness of Mill's approach to education understood as development and self-development explains why he had confidence in the measurement procedure he proposed in his theory and in the judgments of competent agents to evaluate and measure value. His liberal philosophy of education is substantial. But doubts remain. Mill's method of assessing value, and the philosophy of education it mandates, raise a slew of questions to ponder and objections to consider. In the brief space of this essay, I can but indicate these further questions briefly.

One significant challenge is the objection that Mill's system is elitist. If the development and exercise of the higher human capacities and the education that is needed are prerequisites for appreciating the most valuable satisfactions, then the elitist argument could be that those who have had this education are better able to judge and appreciate value, and even to impose their judgments on others. But the response to this comes from Mill's deepest commitments and the fundamental egalitarianism of his theory. It follows from the basic tenets of his theory that people are wronged if they are denied this education, and doubly wronged, then, if their self-development is further impaired by having the judgment of others imposed, rather than simply offered as a model. The argument of *On Liberty* adds power to the reply to the elitist, for the benefits of individuality and autonomy cannot be obtained on the elitist model.

Another substantial objection is that, although the education process is designed to produce autonomous and reliable judges of value, yet the very process of education will have favored certain sorts of enjoyments (most notably the intellectual ones) and thus there will be a built-in bias or predetermination for self-developed agents to favor some enjoyments over others. This brings us face to face with the bedrock question of how to educate citizens to lead autonomous lives. It is a problem faced by all liberal democracies, and the only answer and counter is to encourage the sort of education for freedom that Mill proposes, and back up the commitment with effective development of autonomy. (See Baum 2000.) Mill's theory cannot escape this common puzzle faced by all democratic educational philosophies, and yet his bottom-line commitment to educate all citizens for freedom provides the most promising avenues to meet these challenges.

Mill's value theory continues to challenge and intrigue contemporary students of moral and political philosophy. His theory defies attempts at easy categorization, and its intricacy is designed to provide a framework for practical wisdom and for living well. It is an activist theory, constructed to be used and tested in the light of its application to daily life. If ethical life is as complex as it seems to be in contemporary pluralistic and diverse communities, then we need a theory as sophisticated as Mill's to guide our reflections and judgments.

References

Baum, Bruce (2000) *Rereading Power and Freedom in J. S. Mill*. Toronto: University of Toronto Press.

Berger, Fred (1984) *Happiness, Justice, and Freedom: The Moral and Political Philosophy of John Stuart Mill*. Berkeley: University of California Press.

Berkowitz, Peter (1999) *Virtue and the Making of Modern Liberalism*. Princeton: Princeton University Press.

Bradley, F. H. (1962) *Ethical Studies*, 2nd edn. London: Oxford University Press.

Brink, David O. (1992) "Mill's deliberative utilitarianism," *Philosophy and Public Affairs* 21, pp. 67–103.

Crisp, Roger (1997) *Mill on Utilitarianism*. London: Routledge.

Crisp, Roger, and Michael Slote (1997) *Virtue Ethics*. Oxford: Oxford University Press.

Donner, Wendy (1991) *The Liberal Self: John Stuart Mill's Moral and Political Philosophy*. Ithaca: Cornell University Press.

——(1998) "Mill's utilitarianism," in John Skorupski (ed.) *The Cambridge Companion to Mill* (pp. 255–92). Cambridge: Cambridge University Press.

Donner, Wendy, and Richard Fumerton (2000) "John Stuart Mill," in Steven M. Emmanuel (ed.) *The Blackwell Guide to the Modern Philosophers* (pp. 343–69). Oxford: Blackwell.

Gray, John (1983) *Mill on Liberty: a Defence*, London: Routledge.

Long, Roderick T. (1992) "Mill's higher pleasures and the choice of character," *Utilitas* 4, pp. 279–97.

Mill, John Stuart (1833) "Remarks on Bentham's philosophy," in J. M. Robson (ed.) *Collected Works of John Stuart Mill*, Vol. X: *Essays on Ethics, Religion, and Society* (pp. 3–18). Toronto: University of Toronto Press, 1969.

——(1838) "Bentham," in J. M. Robson (ed.) *Collected Works of John Stuart Mill*, Vol. X: *Essays on Ethics, Religion, and Society* (pp. 75–115). Toronto: University of Toronto Press, 1969.

——(1843) *A System of Logic Ratiocinative and Inductive*, in J. M. Robson (ed.) *Collected Works of John Stuart Mill*, Vols. VII–VIII. Toronto: University of Toronto Press, 1973.

——(1848) *Principles of Political Economy*, in J. M. Robson (ed.) *Collected Works of John Stuart Mill*, Vols. II–III. Toronto: University of Toronto Press, 1965.

——(1859) *On Liberty*, in J. M. Robson (ed.) *Collected Works of John Stuart Mill*, Vols. XVIII–XIX: *Essays on Politics and Society* (pp. 213–310). Toronto: University of Toronto Press, 1977.

——(1861a) *Considerations on Representative Government*, in J. M. Robson (ed.) *Collected Works of John Stuart Mill*, Vols. XVIII–XIX: *Essays on Politics and Society* (pp. 371–577). Toronto: University of Toronto Press, 1977.

——(1861b) *Utilitarianism*, in J. M. Robson (ed.) *Collected Works of John Stuart Mill*, Vol. X: *Essays on Ethics, Religion, and Society* (pp. 203–59). Toronto: University of Toronto Press, 1969. (Reprinted as Part II of this volume; citations are to chapter in roman numerals and to paragraph in arabic numerals.)

——(1873) *Autobiography*, in J. M. Robson and Jack Stillinger (eds.) *Collected Works of John Stuart Mill*, Vol. I: *Autobiography and Literary Essays* (pp. 1–290). Toronto: University of Toronto Press, 1981.

——(1874) "Theism," in J. M. Robson (ed.) *Collected Works of John Stuart Mill*, Vol. X: *Essays on Ethics, Religion, and Society* (pp. 429–89). Toronto: University of Toronto Press, 1969.

——(1963–91) *Collected Works of John Stuart Mill*, 33 vols., ed. J. M. Robson. Toronto: University of Toronto Press.

Riley, Jonathan (1988) *Liberal Utilitarianism: Social Choice Theory and J. S. Mill's Philosophy*. Cambridge: Cambridge University Press.

Scarre, Geoffrey (1997) "Donner and Riley on qualitative hedonism," *Utilitas* 9, pp. 351–60.

Semmel, Bernard (1984) *John Stuart Mill and the Pursuit of Virtue*. New Haven: Yale University Press.

Skorupski, John (1989) *John Stuart Mill*. London: Routledge.

Ten, C. L. (1980) *Mill on Liberty*. Oxford: Oxford University Press.

Troyer, John (ed.) (2003) *The Classical Utilitarians: Bentham and Mill*. Indianapolis: Hackett.

Urbinati, Nadia (2002) *Mill on Democracy: From the Athenian Polis to Representative Government*. Chicago: University of Chicago Press.

West, Henry (2004) *An Introduction to Mill's Utilitarian Ethics*. Cambridge: Cambridge University Press.

Further reading

Anderson, Elizabeth (1991) "John Stuart Mill and experiments in living," *Ethics* 102, pp. 4–26.

Bentham, Jeremy (1962) *The Works of Jeremy Bentham*, 10 vols., ed. John Bowring. New York: Russell & Russell.

——(1970) *The Collected Works of Jeremy Bentham*, ed. J. H. Burns and H. L. A. Hart, Vol. 1: *An Introduction to the Principles of Morals and Legislation*. London: Athlone Press.

Bronaugh, Richard (1974) "The utility of quality: an understanding of Mill," *Canadian Journal of Philosophy* 4, pp. 317–25.

Cooper, Wesley E., Kai Nielsen, and Steven C. Patten (eds.) (1979) *New Essays on John Stuart Mill and Utilitarianism, Canadian Journal of Philosophy*, suppl. vol. 5, pp. 1–19.

Donner, Wendy (1993) "John Stuart Mill's liberal feminism," *Philosophical Studies* 69, pp. 155–66.

Donner, Wendy, Amy Schmitter, and Nathan Tarcov (2003) "Enlightenment liberalism," in Randall Curran (ed.) *The Blackwell Companion to the Philosophy of Education* (pp. 73–93). Oxford: Blackwell.

Edwards, Rem (1979) *Pleasures and Pains: A Theory of Qualitative Hedonism*. Ithaca: Cornell University Press.

Eisenach, Eldon J. (1998) *Mill and the Moral Character of Liberalism*. University Park, PA: Pennsylvania State University Press.

Griffin, James (1986) *Well-being: its Meaning, Measurement and Moral Importance*. Oxford: Clarendon Press.

Gutmann, Amy (1987) *Democratic Education*. Princeton: Princeton University Press.

Hoag, Robert W. (1986) "Happiness and freedom: recent work on John Stuart Mill," *Philosophy and Public Affairs* 15, pp. 188–99.

——(1992) "J. S. Mill's language of pleasures," *Utilitas* 4, pp. 247–78.

Lyons, David (1994) *Rights, Welfare, and Mill's Moral Theory*. Oxford: Clarendon Press.

——(ed.) (1997) *Mill's* Utilitarianism: *Critical Essays*. Lanham, MD: Rowman & Littlefield.

Macpherson, C. B. (1977) *The Life and Times of Liberal Democracy*. Oxford: Oxford University Press.

Mill, James (1869) [1829] *An Analysis of the Phenomena of the Human Mind*, 2nd edn., 2 vols., ed. John Stuart Mill. London: Longmans, Green & Dyer. (Reprinted New York: Augustus M. Kelly, 1967.)

Mill, John Stuart, Harriet Taylor Mill, and Helen Taylor (1994) *Sexual Equality*, ed. Ann P. Robson and John M. Robson. Toronto: University of Toronto Press.

Pateman, Carole (1970) *Participation and Democratic Theory*. Cambridge: Cambridge University Press.

Riley, Jonathan (1993) "On quantities and qualities of pleasure," *Utilitas* 5, pp. 291–300.

——(1998) *Mill on Liberty*. London: Routledge.

Robson, John M. (1968) *The Improvement of Mankind*. Toronto: University of Toronto Press.

Ryan, Alan (1988) *The Philosophy of John Stuart Mill*, 2nd edn. New York: Macmillan.

Skorupski, John (ed.) (1998) *The Cambridge Companion to Mill*. Cambridge: Cambridge University Press.

Sosa, Ernest (1969) "Mill's *Utilitarianism*," in James M. Smith and Ernest Sosa (eds.) *Mill's* Utilitarianism (pp. 154–72). Belmont, CA: Wadsworth.

Stafford, William (1998) *John Stuart Mill*. New York: St Martin's Press.

Sumner, L. W. (1979) "The good and the right," in Wesley E. Cooper, Kai Nielsen, and Steven C. Patten (eds.) *New Essays on John Stuart Mill and Utilitarianism, Canadian Journal of Philosophy*, suppl. vol. 5, pp. 99–114.

——(1992) "Welfare, happiness, and pleasure," *Utilitas* 4, pp. 199–206.

Weinstock, Daniel (1996) "Making sense of Mill," *Dialogue* 35, pp. 791–804.

West, Henry R. (1972) "Reconstructing Mill's "proof" of the principle of utility," *Mind* 81, pp. 256–7.

——(1976) "Mill's qualitative hedonism," *Philosophy* 51, pp. 101–5.
——(1982) "Mill's 'proof' of the principle of utility," in Harlan B. Miller and William H. Williams (eds.) *The Limits of Utilitarianism.* Minneapolis: University of Minnesota Press.
Wilson, Fred (1990) *Psychological Analysis and the Philosophy of John Stuart Mill.* Toronto: University of Toronto Press.

Chapter 5

Mill's Theory of Morally Correct Action

Alan E. Fuchs

Introduction

John Stuart Mill's essay *Utilitarianism* has been and will probably continue to be one the most widely read treatises in moral philosophy. Rare is the college course in ethics that does not study at least parts of this deceptively short and seemingly straightforward defense of the utilitarian moral theory. It is therefore remarkable that even after over a century and a half of such meticulous scrutiny and after the publication of hundreds of scholarly articles analyzing almost every line of its text, vigorous controversies still rage concerning the proper interpretation of some of its most basic arguments and claims. In this chapter, I will examine briefly the major disputes concerning Mill's theory of morally correct action, that is, his "criterion" or "test" of what is morally "right and wrong" (Mill 1861, Ch. I, paras. 1–2. References to this work, found in Part II of this volume, will simply be by roman numeral referring to chapter, and arabic numeral referring to paragraph within that chapter.). My primary goal will be to evaluate the major interpretations of Mill's thinking, leaving it to other authors in this volume to assess the plausibility and viability of Mill's theory as a sound moral theory.

There is no dispute that Mill was a *consequentialist*. To understand what that claim means, we first have to distinguish two different kinds of normative or evaluative questions. The first group asks what kinds of things or states-of-affairs are intrinsically worthwhile or valuable, or what is desirable in and for itself and not merely as a means to some other valued or desirable state. Contemporary philosophers label any systematic specification of what is valuable in this sense, a theory of the *good*. An historically important example of such a theory of the good is hedonism, the view that pleasure (and the absence of pain) is the highest good. The second set of evaluative questions is concerned with how everyone should and should not act. What is it that we always ought or ought not to do? Are there any general kinds of activities that we have a duty or obligation to perform? These are the questions concerning morally correct activity, and a systematic account of all such conduct constitutes a theory of the *right*.

It is clear from the above that a theory of the right might be formulated without any essential references to a theory of the good. One could, for example, hold that it was always morally right to obey the will of God, while leaving open the question as to which things were intrinsically good. But John Stuart Mill, along with many other theorists, thought it obvious that the "right" should be defined in terms of the "good." According to such a *consequentialist* (or "teleological") view, the morally right action is the one that directly or indirectly brings about the best consequences, the most good. A complete consequentialist moral theory, such as Mill's utilitarianism, will therefore have two components, a theory of the good, which specifies the good or the end to be sought, and a theory of the right, which dictates how we should act in order to maximize that good. In this chapter I will focus exclusively on Mill's theory of the right, assuming that something close to Wendy Donner's account of his notion of the good ("utility" or "happiness") is correct. (See 4: MILL'S THEORY OF VALUE, and Donner 1991.)

But exactly how does Mill relate the right to the good? Here is where controversies and questions arise. One set of critics reaffirms the traditional interpretation that Mill held a direct consequentialist view. According to this so-called *act-consequentialism*, the morally right action is that particular act which, among the alternatives open to the agent, is most likely to bring about the greatest possible good. Moreover, since utilitarianism holds that happiness (or "utility") is the greatest good, the morally obligatory action becomes that act which would most likely produce the greatest possible amount of happiness or utility. This version of act-consequentialism is dubbed *act-utilitarianism*. Moral rules, if they are used at all in this theory, serve merely as "rules of thumb," that is, as guidelines that help the act-utilitarian agent to determine quickly and accurately which actions are, as a matter of fact, most likely to produce the most utility on each occasion. Therefore, such rules could (and indeed should) be violated if and when we are sure that doing so in a particular case would directly bring about the greatest good. (See, for example, Berger 1984: ch. 3.)

Other commentators argue that moral rules play a much more fundamental role in Mill's theory of the right. According to the *rule-consequentialist* interpretation of his theory, individual actions are morally right (or wrong) if and only if they were required (or prohibited) by a valid moral rule. The valid moral rules are, in turn, those precepts the recognition of which would produce the greatest good. Rule-consequentialism with a hedonistic theory of the good, as in Mill, is called *rule-utilitarianism*. There are numerous differences among the suggested rule-utilitarian accounts of the right, but in all versions of rule-utilitarianism a justified moral rule cannot be violated on a particular occasion merely because one is reasonably certain that a marginal increase in overall utility would result from doing so. (See, for example, Urmson 1953.)

More recently, some scholars have suggested that Mill's theory of the morally right is more complex than either act- or rule-utilitarianism. They point out that Mill's "Principle of Utility" is best understood not as theory of the right, but as a theory of the good. As such it merely affirms that the greatest happiness is the sole intrinsic good. Mill's theory of the right is therefore free to endorse several practices and modes of evaluation as practical means to realizing that end. Henry West, for example, finds both act- and rule-utilitarian elements in Mill's theory of morally correct activity (West 2004: 77).

Mill as an Act-Utilitarian

Let us now examine each of these interpretations, focusing briefly on their respective treatment of moral rules. *Act-utilitarianism* does seem to reflect the criterion of morally correct action that Mill presents early in the second chapter of *Utilitarianism*, where he declares that "the creed which accepts as the foundation of morals 'utility' or the 'greatest happiness principle' holds that actions are right in proportion as they tend to promote happiness; wrong as the tend to produce the reverse of happiness" (II, 2). It would appear that Mill directs us here to evaluate every possible action in terms of *its* predictable consequences and then to perform that action which our calculations have shown will most likely lead to the greatest possible good.

This act-utilitarian account formulates a theoretical criterion or standard for morally right action. It does not, however, necessarily establish the practical precepts or guidelines that an act-utilitarian agent might want to or might need to follow in order to actually determine the utility-maximizing or "optimific" act. Indeed, most act-utilitarians concede that for several reasons a policy of adhering to certain "rules of thumb" (which will resemble ordinary moral rules such as "don't lie" and "keep your promises") would probably yield greater happiness than following a policy or strategy of always trying to maximize the good directly. Mill, for example, quotes a criticism of utilitarianism according to which "there is not enough time, previous to action, for calculating and weighing the effects of any line of conduct on the general happiness" (II, 24). This critique also suggests that utilitarian agents, having to spend so much of their lives calculating the likely consequences of every possible action, would seemingly have little or no time left for the actual engagement in any of their more desirable pursuits. Others have argued that because some of the effects of individual actions are often far-reaching and may include subtle ramifications that go far beyond the direct results of the acts itself, predicting the true consequences of each choice would surely exceed the intellectual and scientific resources available to the typical agent. Another alleged problem is that individuals, given the task of estimating the effects of contemplated particular acts both to themselves and to others, are likely to show bias, exaggerating the beneficial consequences to themselves and discounting the deleterious effects on others, once again assuring that their choices will not actually maximize the aggregate good (II, 25).

Mill's apparent response to these and other related critiques is to endorse the use of rules or secondary principles as simplified guides to calculation. Mill seems to argue that secondary principles, based on the observed tendencies of similar actions in the past, will provide present agents with more reliable predictions of the actual beneficial and deleterious results of their contemplated actions than would reliance on any of their own estimates. Thus he remarks, in response to the first criticism,

> that there *has* been ample time, namely, the whole past duration of the human species. During all that time mankind have been learning by experience the tendencies of actions; on which experience all the prudence as well as all the morality of life are dependent. (II, 24, emphasis added)

Similarly, the rule "Don't lie" is based on the observation that "honesty is the best policy," in that telling the truth has invariably had better effects than lying and is likely to continue to do so. Consequently, telling the truth in any particular case will probably produce the best consequences, even if it now looks as if a greater good would result from violating the rule on the present occasion. Therefore, in recognition of these considerations, the careful act-utilitarian will resort to a policy that forbids breaking any of these rules of thumb merely to provide a marginal increase in utility. Indeed, adherents of this practical strategy, convinced of the much greater reliability of the rules' predictions over their own, will, in practice, reject almost any temptation to disobey the rule in the name of maximizing utility directly. Consequently, the behavior of such an agent might be practically indistinguishable from that of a true rule-utilitarian. (See Berger 1984: 67.) In theory, however, the act-utilitarian is always open to the argument that since one's moral obligation is always to do that which really is most likely to maximize the good, one should always be open to a convincing argument that by violating a moral rule one can, in a particular instance, maximize utility; and, in such a case, one should do so.

Advocates of an act-utilitarian reading of Mill's theory of the right point to a couple of significant passages in support of their interpretation. The most important text is of course the statement of the utilitarian "creed" quoted above. It surely seems to articulate a clear utilitarian test to be applied to each individual action. Defenders of the act-utilitarian interpretation, however, acknowledge that in that same second chapter of *Utilitarianism*, Mill also identifies morally correct action with the observance of utility based moral *rules*, as when he defines the "standard of morality" as "the rules and precepts for human conduct by the observance of which [a good life] . . . might be, to the greatest extent possible, secured to all mankind" (II, 10), or when he insists that "there is no case of moral obligation in which some secondary principle is not involved" (II, 25). They contend, however, that all such references by Mill to the use of moral rules are to be understood as invoking rules of thumb as part of a practical policy and not as essential components of a theory of what makes right actions right. They point out, for example, that Mill likens the use of moral rules to the mariner's use of the Nautical Almanac. Although it would be theoretically possible for sailors to calculate for themselves all of the astronomical data necessary to navigate successfully, it is surely sound policy for them to use the results of others' calculations to help them reach their destinations (II, 24). Moreover, these interpreters note that Mill recognized exceptions to all moral rules (presumably in those cases where following the rule would give rise to grave consequences), which is what one would expect were one treating moral rules as mere rules of thumb.

> It is not the fault of any creed, but of the complicated nature of human affairs, that rules of conduct cannot be so framed as to require no exception, and that hardly any kind of action can safely be laid down as either always obligatory or always condemnable. There is no ethical creed which does not temper the rigidity of its laws by giving a certain latitude, under the moral responsibility of the agent, for accommodation to peculiarities of circumstances. (II, 25)

Furthermore, on those occasions when moral rules come into conflict with each other, Mill apparently endorses a direct act-consequentialist appeal to utility in order to determine which of the conflicting rules should determine what should in that instance be done. Again, this is the result we would expect were moral rules serving merely as strategic rules of thumb in an act-utilitarian theory (II, 25).

Additional support for the act-utilitarian interpretation of practical precepts comes from several of Mill's writings in which he reflects upon the need for flexibility in using any general rule that is based on the social sciences. In his *A System of Logic*, for example, Mill seemingly offers a textbook account of rules functioning as rules of thumb.

> By a wise practitioner, therefore, rules of conduct will only be considered as provisional. Being made for the most numerous cases, or for those of most ordinary occurrence, they point out the manner in which it will be least perilous to act, where time or means do not exist for analysing the actual circumstances of the case, or where we cannot trust our judgement in estimating them. But they do not at all supersede the propriety of going through (when circumstances permit) the scientific process requisite for framing a rule from the data of the particular case before us. (Mill 1843: 946. See also Mill 1837: 161.)

Finally, scholars of Mill's writings often turn to his letters to help interpret his views, since Mill was an active correspondent who frequently responded to philosophical questions and critiques raised by his friends and critics. For example, both D.G. Brown (1974: 68) and Roger Crisp (1998: 17–18) think that the following remarks, which Mill wrote in a letter to John Venn in 1872, clearly demonstrate Mill's commitment to act-utilitarianism:

I agree with you that the right way of testing actions by their consequences, is to test them by the natural consequences of the particular actions, and not by those which would follow if every one did the same. But, for the most part, consideration of what would happen if everyone did the same, is the only means we have of discovering the tendency of the act in the particular case. (Mill 1972: 1881)

Mill as a Rule-Utilitarian

As noted above, rule-utilitarianism is a consequentialist theory. It does not, however, evaluate particular actions in terms of their direct promotion of the good, but rather by the requirements, permissions, and prohibitions of valid moral rules. Utility is therefore promoted indirectly, for the valid moral rules are those the recognition and adoption of which will bring about the greatest good. There have been numerous alternative formulations of this basic idea, but since Mill did not distinguish clearly among them and since our focus is on the interpretation of Mill rather than on the best formulation of utilitarianism as a viable contemporary moral theory, I will highlight only two. (But see 11: RIGHT, WRONG, AND RULE-CONSEQUENTIALISM, and Lyons 1965.) The first, called *utilitarian generalization*, is exemplified in an important passage in *Utilitarianism*. There, Mill asserts that the morality of at least some kinds of actions is determined *not* by the consequences of the single performance of a particular action, but rather by the utility of the universal or general performance of acts of that type. Mill notes that

> in the case of . . . things which people forbear to do from moral considerations, *though the consequence in the particular case might be beneficial* – it would be unworthy of an intelligent agent not to be consciously aware that the action is of a class which, if practiced generally, would be generally injurious, and that this is the ground of the obligation to abstain from it. (II, 19, emphasis added)

Thus, for example, though it might maximize total utility for a single individual not to pay her taxes – she would avoid a significant loss of well-being without causing any measurable drop in public services either to herself or to the rest of her community – we morally condemn her "free-loading" because of the disastrous consequences that would befall a society in which all citizens failed to pay their taxes. The idea that we should consider "what would happen if everyone did the same?" is surely not a new one. Mill even thinks that it is the operant idea behind Kant's famous categorical imperative (I, 4).

It should be noted in passing that the passage from *Utilitarianism* quoted in the previous paragraph gives an explicit and unequivocal rejection of act-utilitarianism as the correct formulation of Mill's theory. For Mill says there that an individual action may maximize utility but still be morally wrong if it is proscribed by a valid moral rule. He is similarly explicit in his rejection of act-utilitarianism at the end of his *A System of Logic,* where he argues that an action can be morally right even if it produces more harm than good:

> There are many virtuous actions, and even virtuous modes of action . . . by which happiness in the particular instance is sacrificed, more pain being produced than pleasure. But conduct of which this can be truly asserted, admits of justification only because it can be shown that on the whole more happiness will exist in the world if feelings are cultivated which will make people, in certain cases, regardless of happiness. (1843: 952)

Moreover, in a letter to Henry Brandreth, Mill clearly endorses rule- rather than act-utilitarian justifications of moral obligations:

> The duty of truth as a positive duty is also to be considered on the ground of whether more good or harm would follow to mankind in general if it were generally disregarded and *not merely whether good or harm would follow in a particular case.* (Mill 1972: 1234, emphasis added)

While Mill often employs utilitarian generalization arguments, he sometimes complains that they give an incomplete account of all of the relevant considerations that must be assessed in determining our moral duty. For example, he finds "great fault" with Bentham for confounding the "principle of utility with the principle of specific consequences" and for basing his estimation

> of the approbation or blame due to a particular kind of action from a calculation solely of the consequences to which that very action, if practiced generally, would itself lead. (Mill 1833: 7–8)

Mill does not deny that consideration of such generalized consequences is relevant to the moral evaluation of acts of that type, but he insists that other factors, such as the general influence of such actions on the character of the agents performing them, and the utility of having social rules praising or blaming conduct of that sort, must also be factored into the assessment. Mill therefore seems to appeal to a second type of rule-utilitarian theory, one that does not evaluate moral rules in comparative isolation, as in utilitarian generalization, but rather considers them as component parts of a more complex *ideal moral code*, a set of rules that together *would* maximize utility if it was adopted and followed by the overwhelming majority of the members of a society. Morally correct actions, in this view, are those required by the rules of such a code, while wrong or permissible actions would similarly be defined in terms of its rules. Such an ideal moral code would allow rules with different levels of urgency as well as precepts of more or less limited scope. The code might also contain general procedures for the resolution of conflicts among its rules, and, perhaps, certain rules that relied upon essential conceptual relationships with each other by, for example, defining legal or moral rights in terms of rules regulating certain forms of permissible social coercion. And since this code would have to be widely disseminated, understood, and internalized by most of the citizens of an actual society, there would be limits on the complexity and number of its rules. I agree with Richard Brandt, one of the leading proponents of this type of theory, that Mill held such an ideal moral code form of rule-utilitarianism as his theory of morally correct actions or duties (Brandt 1967: 57–8).

Mill gives several reasons why the rules of morality should be "taken seriously," that is, why they should be upheld even on those occasions when it would definitely produce a marginal increase in utility to break them. The foremost argument which he offers is based on everyone's need for guaranteed expectations of security. The moral rules that insure everyone's freedom from bodily harm are literally essential for those individuals' well-being. Rules ensuring such security must therefore be understood, internalized, and enforced as unconditional rights, not subject to the possibility of case-by-case exceptions based on ad hoc calculations.

> Security, no human being can possibly do without; on it we depend for all our immunity from evil and for the whole value of all and every good, beyond the passing moment.

This security, he argues, is the "groundwork of our existence," and therefore the rules protecting it must have a "character of absoluteness" and an apparent "incommensurability with all other considerations" (V, 25). Such rules cannot be mere rules of thumb. Mill makes that clear when he discusses the proposed murder of an individual so odious that "were such a man to be assassinated, the balance of traceable consequences would be greatly in favour of the act." Nonetheless, Mill insists, we may not kill such a man, because the consequences to any society whose moral code would permit such case-by-case exemptions from the moral rules prohibiting murder would be disastrous. If people were not punished for killing and taught not to kill, and if it

> were thought allowable for any one to put to death at pleasure any human being whom he believes that the world would be well rid of, nobody's life would be safe. (Mill 1852: 181–2)

Mill uses other arguments that rely on the value of having easily understood, widely internalized, and strictly enforced rules that enable individuals to form expectations of how others can be counted on to behave toward each other.

> Such, for example, is the rule of veracity; [or] that of not infringing the legal rights of others; and so forth; concerning which it is obvious that although many cases exist in which a deviation from the rule would in the particular case produce more good than evil, it is necessary for general security . . . that the rules should be inflexibly observed. (1843:1154–5)

Similarly, he apparently recognizes that many mutually advantageous cooperative endeavors would be unstable without coercive moral rules, because it might not otherwise be in the interest of each of the participating parties to contribute his or her fair share of the required burdens. More generally, he recognizes the need for supporting the expectations that individuals create by expressly or tacitly promising to return a good for a good that one has received (V, 34).

Mill further argues for a rule- rather than act-utilitarian conception of moral duties because of the enormous importance that he gives to individual liberty. The argument here is complex and will be discussed by others in this volume. Very briefly, Mill contends that only by adherence to strict rules guaranteeing individual liberty can we bring about the conditions under which individuals capable of achieving his rich notion of happiness will develop and flourish. (See 4: MILL'S THEORY OF VALUE, and Mill 1859: ch. III.)

Moral Rules, Justice, and Supererogation

Perhaps the most decisive argument for interpreting Mill as a strict rule-utilitarian is contained in his account of justice in Chapter V of *Utilitarianism*. There, Mill observes that justice is conceptually tied to the idea of punishment: "The idea of legal constraint is . . . the generating idea of the notion of justice" (V, 13). He immediately notes, however, that such an account fails to explain the unique quality of justice as opposed to the broader category of moral obligations in general, because, he contends, *all* moral wrongs are conceptually tied to the idea of punishment.

> We do not call anything wrong unless we mean to imply that a person ought to be punished in some way or other for doing it – if not by law, by the opinion of his fellow creatures; if not by opinion by the reproaches of his own conscience. (V, 14)

This entails that anyone who commits a moral wrong is a fit subject for the coercive force of either the external or internal sanctions that Mill discussed in Chapter III of *Utilitarianism*. The identification of moral obligations with a liability to punishment, he remarks, "seems to be the real turning point of the distinction between morality and simple expediency" (V, 14). It is important to emphasize that once again Mill fully recognizes, here, a class of actions that are expedient (or conducive to the good), but nonetheless *not* morally obligatory. There may be things, he says, which we wish that people should do, which we like or admire them for doing, perhaps dislike or despise them for not doing, but yet admit that they are not bound to do; it is not a case of moral obligation; we do not blame them, that is, we do not think that they are proper objects of punishment (V, 14).

Mill is clearly referring here to so-called *supererogatory* acts, actions that go "beyond the call of duty," such as heroic acts of bravery (as when one risks one's own life in order to save the lives of others) or of saint-like altruism (as when a person sacrifices almost all of his or her wealth in order to relieve starvation in underdeveloped countries). Elsewhere, Mill argues similarly that

> it is not good that persons should be bound, by other people's opinion, to do every-thing that they would deserve praise for doing. There is a standard of altruism to which all should be required to come up, and a degree beyond it which is not oblig-atory, but meritorious. (1865: 337)

Sanctions, such as the inculcated pangs of conscience, should be invoked only for the former (1865: 338–9).

Since liability to punishment is for Mill the distinguishing feature that separates moral obligations in general from actions that are the merely expedient, what then is the distinctive feature of those moral obligations that are matters of *justice*? Mill's account invokes the Kantian distinction between perfect duties, which are owed to assignable individuals (who therefore have correlative rights to the performance of those duties), and "imperfect" duties which are not associated with anyone's assignable rights and which therefore give everyone considerable discretion as to when and how to meet their obligations. Mill identifies the realm of the perfect duties with that of the precepts of justice, and he links the domain of the imper-fect duties with the remaining (non-justice) realm of moral obligations, such as the less stringent requirements of ordinary, non-heroic charity or beneficence. (See the figure "The Art of Life.") Since Mill further analyzes the notion of a "right" as any valid claim which the right-holder has on society to have something guaranteed to him or her by means of social or external forms of coercion, the duties of justice will necessarily be associated with a liability to socially organized "external" forms of punishment, while the merely moral imperfect obligations

The Art of Life

Greatest Good = Happiness			
Moral obligations Liability to punishment		**Simple expediency** No liability to punishment	**Aesthetics** No liability to punishment
Justice Perfect duties, Correlative rights, External and internal coercion e.g. security and liberty	**Other moral duties** Imperfect duties, No correlative rights, Internal coercion only e.g. ordinary beneficence	e.g. supererogatory acts, certain policy matters	e.g. nobility of character, matters of taste

will be subjected only to internal forms of compulsion such as feelings of guilt or shame

David Lyons has pointed out that Mill's division of the moral landscape into (at least) the separate realms of justice, moral obligations, and acts of "simple expediency," logically requires the recognition and strict enforcement of social rules. Lyons shows that for Mill,

> to call an act wrong is to imply that guilt feelings, and perhaps other sanctions, would be warranted against it. But sanctions assume coercive rules. To show an act wrong, therefore, is to show that a coercive rule against it would be justified. The justification of a coercive social rule establishes a moral obligation, breach of which is wrong. (Lyons 1976: 105, 109)

This is perhaps obvious in the realm of the perfect duties of justice, where the notion of coercing actions not yet performed clearly presupposes a socially promulgated and widely internalized set of rules linking unjust acts with corresponding sanctions. But Lyons argues that even in the realm of the informal rules constituting the non-justice realm of morality, the idea of being morally wrong entails the operation of coercive rules:

> For there to be informal social rules, the corresponding value must be internalized widely with the group. Thus, the judgment that a certain set of informal rules would be justified implies approval of the same values being generally internalized. (1976: 108)

The foregoing analysis relates several moral concepts to each other. As such, it makes no essential reference to utility or to any other substantive moral principle. Utility is invoked only when Mill comes to specify which kinds of actions fall into each evaluative category. For example, is a certain level of aid to others to be regarded as a requirement of justice, an imperfect moral duty, or a not-required, but very commendable act of supererogation? These classifications would begin with the recognition that making an interest into a moral right is a costly endeavor. It authorizes sanctions that will be burdensome to enforce and which may involve the limitation of individual liberties, both quite disutilitarian results. Consequently, only the most vital human interests (which Mill identifies here as our need for security and liberty) will be so essential to the general welfare that the benefit of protecting them as rights outweighs the costs of so treating them. Therefore, only these limited interests are recognized as rights in a utility-maximizing moral code. The benefits that could have been derived from the protection of less vital interests, such as those promoted by the imperfect duties of moderate beneficence, however, would not justify the costs of using external, organized, social coercion in their support, and they consequently would *not* be treated as rights. Nonetheless, since there is some significant social value to be gained by requiring such actions, it would be useful on balance for society to promulgate informal moral precepts that would be internalized by individuals and which would thereby "punish" transgressions of these moral rules with internal sanctions such as feelings of shame and guilt. (See Mill 1972: 649.)

Finally, although there would be some value gained by requiring everyone always to perform the most expedient action open to them, enforcement of such a proposed duty (by external or internal sanctions) would entail enormous costs that would far exceed any benefits to be gained. Therefore, a utility maximizing code would not regard supererogatory acts as moral duties at all, nor would it more generally require individuals on each occasion to perform the most expedient action. Using this kind of rule-consequentialist, cost–benefit reasoning, Mill further specifies the limited content of the realm of the perfect duties of justice. In *On Liberty*, Mill tries to show that utility would be maximized if we restrict the grounds for permissible "external" social coercion (and therefore the extent of our moral obligations of justice) to the prevention of harm to others. His notion of harm, however, has to be understood as a *wrongful* harm, that is, as a setback to "certain interests which, either by express legal provision or by tacit understanding ought to be considered as *rights*" (1859: 276, emphasis added). (On the notion of a wrongful harm, see Feinberg 1984: 34–6.) Most duties of justice will therefore be negative, enjoining us in various ways from interfering with other individuals' pursuit of their own good. But Mill did maintain that under certain circumstances people have rights to some kinds of positive aid, so that they too would be wrongfully harmed by failure to be aided in that manner. (See 8: MILL'S THEORY OF RIGHTS.)

Mill's Theory of the Right and "The Art of Life"

The distinction noted above between moral obligation and supererogation demonstrates conclusively that Mill does not regard the maximization of utility on each occasion as his criterion of morally correct action, that is, as his theory of the right. Rather, the "greatest happiness" principle constitutes his theory of the good, his specification of the ultimately desirable state of affairs. As such, he is committed to evaluating all practical endeavors and policies in terms of their efficacy in bringing about the greatest good. As we have just seen, Mill thinks that at least for a limited range of particularly important interests, strict adherence to the rules constitutive of morality will bring about the greatest good. But Mill also recognizes other important aspects of our practical lives, such as the cultivation of personal character traits and the implementation of public policies, that, while not strictly matters of moral obligation, would nonetheless play vital roles in any comprehensive attempt to realize the greatest good. Indeed, Mill sketches such a wide-ranging, hierarchically arranged set of practices in *A System of Logic*. Morality, he notes there, is but one of several practical "arts," each of which uses the results of scientific observations to formulate practical rules as means of ultimately realizing the desired end of happiness. There is, he says,

> [a] body of doctrine, which is properly the Art of Life in its three departments, Morality, Prudence or Policy, and Aesthetics; the Right, The Expedient, and the Beautiful or Noble, in human conduct and works. (1843: 949)

In the longer of his two essays on Bentham, Mill makes a similar, but not identical, distinction among three ways to evaluate human activity, "its moral aspect, or that of its right and wrong; its aesthetic aspect, or that of its beauty; [and] its sympathetic aspect, or that of its lovableness" (1838: 112–13). Although these different dimensions of assessment often cohere (say in a person with an admirable character who regularly performs morally right actions), they need not (as when an evil person may happen to do the morally correct thing). If, as we have just seen, Mill recognized several perspectives from which we should evaluate people and their conduct in addition to the practice of morality narrowly conceived, what are we to do when the precepts of morality come into conflict with those of another "art"? For example, what are we to do if an expedient public policy decision conflicts with a requirement of justice? Lyons once asserted that we are left with a perplexing conflict, since Mill's Principle of Utility would have us do the expedient act, while his theory of morality says that we must follow *its* decrees (Lyons 1976: 119). Later he argued that since utility is the *summum bonum*, considerations of expediency would have to have priority over moral duties and rights (Lyons 1982). Sumner similarly foresees conflicts between the right and the good, although he thinks that such conflicts would be confined to rare situations in which following a moral rule would lead to disastrous results. In such cases, Sumner also thinks Mill would have us choose the best over the right, and we should therefore (reluctantly) do the morally wrong thing! (Sumner 1979: 112–14). West's subtle interpretation is similar, in that he too stresses the diversity of evaluative perspectives in Mill's total normative system. He goes further, however, arguing that not only are act-utilitarian calculations necessary to adjudicate conflicts between the requirements of morality and those of the other practices in the art of life, but that such direct appeals to utility actually play an important role in determining the morally right action itself. So while he fully recognizes that Mill's theory of moral duty predominantly relies upon strict rule-utilitarian arguments, West also claims that there are at least three kinds of cases in which the morally right action is determined by act-utilitarian deliberation. The three cases are (1) where we need to resolve conflicts between two or more valid moral rules, (2) where simple exceptions to a given rule are required by considerations of expediency, and (3) where we are faced with a totally new situation for which there are no applicable moral rules (West 2004: 87).

Let us examine these three cases in turn. As we noted above, Mill clearly recognized exceptions to all moral rules, typically treating these exceptions as the results of conflicts between two or more conflicting duties. "There exists no moral system under which there do not arise unequivocal cases of conflicting obligation" (II, 25). Moreover, Mill apparently suggests that the resolution of these conflicts, that is, the determination of one's overall duty in such cases, is to be determined in each instance by a direct appeal to utility: "If utility is the ultimate source of moral obligations, utility may be invoked to decide between them when their demands are incompatible" (II, 25). I do not believe, however, that Mill would have us resort to act-utilitarian reasoning when resolving conflicts between two (or more) valid moral rules. I understand him, rather, as treating such potential conflicts as requiring limitations on the scope or range of applicability of each of the abutting rules, so that there really is no ultimate conflict between them. For example, Mill considers the apparent conflict between our rule against lying and our duty to protect innocent lives (by, for example, keeping bad news from a dangerously ill person) (II, 23). But Mill does not say that we should simply weigh the consequences of each possible alternative in each such instance and then perform the individually most expedient alternative. Rather, he contends, the ideal rule prohibiting lying does not apply to cases in which an innocent person's life is at stake. Recognition of the great utility accruing from enforcement of the duty to save innocent life leads the ideal moral code to endorse the general rule "Don't lie, except to save innocent lives" rather than the unencumbered rule "Don't lie," since there is greater utility in adopting the former rather than the latter as the appropriate rule for *all* such cases. However, in order to retain most of the great social benefit we derive from the rule prohibiting prevarication, any such rule-defined general exceptions to the rule must be carefully limited:

> But in order that the exception may not extend itself beyond the need, and may have the least possible effect in weakening reliance on veracity, it ought to be recognized and, if possible its *limits defined*; and if the principle of utility is good for anything, it must be good for weighing these conflicting utilities against one another and *marking out the region* within which one or the other preponderates. (II, 23, emphasis added)

Similarly, in "Whewell on moral philosophy," Mill grants that all rules, including those against homicide, have exceptions. But, as in *Utilitarianism*, he states that such exceptions are not to be decided on a case-by-case act-utilitarian basis, but rather on a rule-utilitarian determination of the proper scope and defined limits of the rules in question:

> The essential is, that the exception should be itself a general rule; so that, being of definite extent, and not leaving the expediencies to the partial judgement of the agent in the individual case, it may not shake the stability of the wider rule in the cases to which the reason of the exception does not extend. (1852: 183. See also Mill 1843: 1155.)

In the penultimate paragraph of *Utilitarianism*, Mill applies a similar analysis to the apparent conflicts that arise even between the usually paramount requirements of justice and the obligation to save innocent lives.

> To save a life, it may not only be allowable, but a duty to steal or take by force the necessary food or medicine, or to kidnap and compel to officiate the only qualified medical practitioner. (V, 37)

Mill's analysis of these examples appears to proffer only a linguistic recommendation, suggesting how to describe needed exceptions to otherwise absolutely binding rules of justice.

> In such cases . . . we usually say, not that justice must give way to some other moral principle, but that what is just in ordinary cases is, by reason of that other principle, not just in the particular case. By this useful accommodation of language, the character of indefeasibility attributed to justice is kept up, and we are saved from the necessity of maintaining that there can be laudable injustice. (V, 37)

I would suggest, however, that this passage further illustrates the results of using rule-utilitarian considerations to delineate limits to the range of applicability of potentially conflicting moral rules. In this case, the justified extent of the right of private property is limited somewhat by the utility of curtailing that right with a built-in general exception for all situations in which innocent life is at stake. Such an amended rule would have greater utility than the more simplistic principle establishing and enforcing an absolute exception-less right to one's property, and the former is therefore, on rule-utilitarian grounds, the morally correct specification of the rule.

West's second class of cases envisions the need to violate a valid secondary principle or rule, not because it comes into conflict any other valid rule, but simply because violating it would, in a particular instance, maximize utility. Mill himself does not consider any such case, arguing that exceptions to moral rules are only necessitated by conflicts with other moral rules. However, West claims that Mill would have (or should have?) acknowledged exceptions based on simple expediency. For example, West argues that an individual would be morally culpable if, in discharging his obligation to be charitable, he donated funds to minimally needy members of his own community, neglecting the greater needs of the starving poor in foreign lands (2004: 88). But, while *we* might agree with West's moral assessment of this example, Mill, I believe, would not have. For him, as we have seen, ordinary acts of beneficence are "imperfect" duties. Therefore, as long as donors make reasonably generous charitable contributions, they have considerable discretion in selecting the beneficiaries of their gifts. Morally requiring maximally beneficial charitable contributions from them would obliterate the distinction between morally obligatory conduct and the supererogatory. Similarly, *we* might agree with West, in another example that he offers, that a person should not selfishly or frivolously choose his or her occupation. But the author of *On Liberty* would insist that individuals should be free from any form of societal punishment when autonomously choosing their own "modes of existence," and therefore, assuming that they do not violate any other person's rights, they should be under no moral obligation to choose the most socially beneficial profession.

In arguing that Mill does not allow exceptions to individual moral rules in order to maximize utility on particular occasions, I do not deny that he would allow exceptions if following a rule would lead to a disaster or catastrophe (Sumner 1979: 113–14). What is less clear is whether Mill would treat such cases as particular act-utilitarian justified exceptions to an otherwise applicable moral rule, or rather as conflicts between two competing rules. Most "disastrous" consequences that might result from following a moral rule (such as death to an innocent person or loss of liberty to an entire democratic nation) would likely violate some precepts of justice, since they would constitute wrongful harms from which their victims would have rights to be free. If that were indeed the case, then this second class of alleged exceptions to rules would collapse back into the first class discussed above, and we could similarly conclude that Mill's treatment of them was basically rule- rather than act-utilitarian. But even if one insisted that there were cases in which breaking a rule was necessary to avert a catastrophe and that there were no other relevant moral rules present, one still could argue that Mill need not revert to act-utilitarian grounds for making the exception. The question a Millian rule-utilitarian would ask is: Would the rule with a general built-in exception for averting disaster bring about greater utility than that same rule without such an exception? If so, then that exception becomes a part of the correct moral precept, and therefore invoking it would not really constitute a violation of the optimific, revised rule at all.

West's third class of cases suggests that in order to determine the morally correct thing to do when there are no applicable "prescribed" rules we must calculate the consequences of each possible individual action as required in act-utilitarianism. This raises a significant issue, for under any realistic set of actual moral rules, many situations are likely to arise in which no extant rule speaks to the situation at hand. Mill does seem to support the use of ad hoc, case-by-case calculations in situations of this kind, arguing that we cannot act like judges whose function is to apply the given law rigidly to the particular case. Rather, he likens our role in such cases to that of the legislator or administrator whose judgment should "be formed on the merits of the particular case," an apparent appeal to act-utilitarian deliberation. However, legislators and administrators usually do not make rulings limited to individual isolated cases; they more typically enact general laws, rules, and regulations governing broad classes of activity. Indeed, Mill's elaboration of the process to be followed in the cases under consideration explicitly results in the promulgation of general precepts, and it seems to lay down a rule-utilitarian procedure for determining those rules. Mill first directs us to focus on the end of maximizing happiness, but then, he says, we are to use science to inquire what are the *kinds* of actions by which this end . . . is capable of being realized. When Science has framed propositions, which are the completed expression of the whole of the conditions necessary to the desired end, these are handed over to Art, which has nothing further to do but to transform them into corresponding *rules of conduct*. (1843: 1155, emphasis added)

Therefore, as moral "legislators," writing, as it were, a part of the ideal moral code, we would consider the expected consequences of the general performance of the kind of action proposed, as in utilitarian generalization. But that would not exhaust our analysis. We must also determine if the contemplated action is of a kind that would justify making it into a coercive law, and if so, what kind of sanctions would be most expedient to impose for acts of its kind. We would also have to take into account possible indirect consequences of making such a rule, such as the influence it might have on the character of individuals affected by it, and we would have to predict the ease or difficulty of obtaining wide social acceptance for the proposed rules. But all of these considerations involve rule- rather than act-utilitarian deliberations.

We have stressed throughout this chapter that Mill's delimitation of the realm of "moral" evaluation is significantly narrower than our ordinary one. *We* naturally assess virtuous or less than virtuous character traits in moral terms, and we regard matters of sexual and other aspects of personal conduct as reflecting "moral values." Most of us would find it almost odd to follow Mill's analysis and regard the noble and admirable deeds of saints and heroes as outside of the sphere of moral evaluation. I leave it to others to determine whether Mill's sharp focus on his limited notion of morality improves or detracts from his entire utilitarian theory. Mill himself, I believe, felt some tension between his carefully circumscribed notion and the more common, broader denotation of the term "moral," and he himself sometimes lapses into that broader usage. Indeed, Mill sometimes uses "moral" even more broadly than we ordinarily would, identifying it with almost every kind of practical activity. Thus, throughout Book VI of *A System of Logic*, Mill refers to all of the social sciences (including economics, history, psychology, and political science) as "moral sciences." Were Mill consistently to embrace this extremely wide concept of "morality" (that is, to identify morality with all of practical reason), West would surely be correct in concluding that Mill's theory of moral activity contained elements of both act- and rule-utilitarianism (along with aspects of virtue ethics and other norms as well). But I hope to have shown that there is a preponderance of grounds for concluding that Mill offered his account of "the field of conduct that is *properly called moral*" as referring to but a part, albeit the most important part, of his utility-maximizing, all-encompassing "art of life" (Mill 1843: 951, emphasis added).

In conclusion, let us return to the question of what we should do if the dictates of morality come into conflict with any of the other utility maximizing practices in Mill's Art of Life, such as those of "expediency" or "policy." Since we have seen that he generally regards morally right actions as those specified by the rules of a rule-utilitarian ideal moral code, it follows that the precepts of moral duty must be upheld against all attempts to justify violation of those rules merely in the name of simple expediency. Mill strongly suggests, moreover, that when conduct falls under the rules of moral obligation, particularly that part of morality that comprises the perfect duties of justice, the rules are to be followed, even if that action conflicts with any of the other dimensions of practical reason. Toward the end of *Utilitarianism*, for example, Mill argues that "justice is a *more sacred thing than policy*, and . . . the latter ought only to be listened to after the former has been satisfied." Somewhat further on he affirms that "justice is a name for a certain classes of moral rules . . . [that are] *of more absolute obligation, than any other rules for the guidance of life*." And that is because

> the *moral rules* which forbid mankind to hurt one another (in which we must never forget to include wrongful interference with each other's freedom) *are more vital to human well-being than any maxims, however important, which only point out the best mode of managing some department of human affairs*. (V, 33, emphasis added. See also V, 25.)

Moreover, in the later essay on Bentham, immediately after noting the three main aspects in terms of which we can appraise actions, Mill clearly asserts that "the moral view" is "unquestionably the first and most important mode of looking at them," and that the "moral standard ought . . . to be paramount" (1838: 112–13).

Mill seems to have fully anticipated the possibly tragic strains that may confront a person when the various elements of the art of life pull in opposing directions, as when the obligation to tell the truth in a court of law may conflict with the virtue of being loyal to a friend on trial, or when the duty to fight in a clearly just war may force one to destroy cultural treasures of great beauty. But Mill concludes, I believe, that if an action is definitely one's moral duty (after all morally extenuating circumstances have been duly considered), it must be done. The apparent severity of this conclusion is softened somewhat, however, by recalling that for Mill the extent of our moral duties is comparatively narrow, and that when our moral obligations are satisfied, or when (as will usually be the case) they do not even apply to the question in hand, the other practices of the art of life such as The Expedient and the Noble may hold sway and directly lead us to the *summum bonum* of the greatest happiness.

References

Berger, Fred R. (1984) *Happiness, Justice, and Freedom: The Moral and Political Philosophy of John Stuart Mill*. Berkeley: University of California Press.

Brandt, Richard B. (1967) "Some merits of one form of rule-utilitarianism," *University of Colorado Studies* 3, pp. 39–65.

Brown, D. G. (1974) "Mill's act-utilitarianism," *Philosophical Quarterly* 24, pp. 67–8.

Crisp, Roger (ed.) (1998) *J. S. Mill's* Utilitarianism. Oxford: Oxford University Press.

Donner, Wendy (1991) *The Liberal Self: John Stuart Mill's Moral and Political Philosophy*. Ithaca: Cornell University Press.

Feinberg, Joel (1984) *Harm to Others*. Oxford: Oxford University Press.

Lyons, David (1965) *Forms and Limits of Utilitarianism*. Oxford: Oxford University Press.

——(1976) "Mill's theory of morality," *Nous* 10, pp. 101–20.

——(1982) "Utility and rights," in J. R. Pennock and J. W. Chapman (eds.) *Ethics, Economics, and the Law* (pp. 107–38). New York: New York University Press.

Mill, John Stuart (1833) "Remarks on Bentham's philosophy," in J. M. Robson (ed.) *Collected Works of John Stuart Mill*, Vol. X: *Essays on Ethics, Religion, and Society* (pp. 3–18). Toronto: University of Toronto Press, 1969.

——(1837) "Carlyle's French revolution," in J. M. Robson (ed.) *Collected Works of John Stuart Mill*, Vol. XX: *Essays on French History and Historians* (pp. 131–66). Toronto: University of Toronto Press, 1985.

——(1838) "Bentham," in J. M. Robson (ed.) *Collected Works of John Stuart Mill*, Vol. X: *Essays on Ethics, Religion, and Society* (pp. 75–115). Toronto: University of Toronto Press, 1969.

——(1843) *A System of Logic Ratiocinative and Inductive*, in J. M. Robson (ed.) *Collected Works of John Stuart Mill*, Vols. VII–VIII. Toronto: University of Toronto Press, 1973.

——(1852) "Whewell on moral philosophy," in J. M. Robson (ed.) *Collected Works of John Stuart Mill*, Vol. X: *Essays on Ethics, Religion, and Society* (pp. 165–201). Toronto: University of Toronto Press, 1969.

——(1859) *On Liberty*, in J. M. Robson (ed.) *Collected Works of John Stuart Mill*, Vols. XVIII–XIX: *Essays on Politics and Society* (pp. 213–310). Toronto: University of Toronto Press, 1977.

——(1861) *Utilitarianism*, in J. M. Robson (ed.) *Collected Works of John Stuart Mill*, Vol. X: *Essays on Ethics, Religion, and Society* (pp. 203–59). Toronto: University of Toronto Press, 1969. (Reprinted as Part II of this volume; citations are to chapter by roman numeral and to paragraph by arabic numeral.)

——(1865) *August Comte and Positivism*, in J. M. Robson (ed.) *Collected Works of John Stuart Mill*, Vol. X: *Essays on Ethics, Religion, and Society* (pp. 261–368). Toronto: University of Toronto Press, 1969.

——(1972) *Later Letters of John Stuart Mill 1849–1873*, ed. Francis Mineka and Dwight N. Lindley, in J. M. Robson (ed.) *Collected Works of John Stuart Mill*, Vols. XIV–XVII. Toronto: University of Toronto Press.

Sumner, L. W. (1979) "The good and the right," in Wesley Cooper, Kai Nielsen, and Steven Patten (eds.) *New Essays on John Stuart Mill and Utilitarianism, Canadian Journal of Philosophy*, suppl. vol. V, pp. 99–114.

Urmson, J. O. (1953) "The interpretation of the philosophy of J. S. Mill," *Philosophical Quarterly* 3, pp. 33–40.

West, Henry R. (2004) *An Introduction to Mill's Utilitarian Ethics*. Cambridge: Cambridge University Press.

Further reading

Brown, D. G. (1973) "What is Mill's principle of utility?," *Canadian Journal of Philosophy* 3, pp. 1–12.

Cupples, Brian (1972) "A defense of the received interpretation of J. S. Mill," *Australasian Journal of Philosophy* 50, pp. 131–7.

Dryer, D. P. (1969) "Mill's utilitarianism," in J. M. Robson (ed.) *Collected Works of John Stuart Mill*, Vol. X (pp. lxiii–cxiii). Toronto: University of Toronto Press.

Gaus, Gerald (1980) "Mill's theory of moral rules," *Australasian Journal of Philosophy* 58, pp. 265–79.

Rawls, John (1955) "Two concepts of rules," *Philosophical Review* 64, pp. 3–32.

Ryan, Alan (1988) *The Philosophy of John Stuart Mill*, 2nd edn. New York: Macmillan.

Smart, J. J. C. (1973) "An outline of a system of utilitarian ethics," in J. J. C. Smart and Bernard Williams, *Utilitarianism: For and Against*. Cambridge: Cambridge University Press.

Sosa, Ernest (1969) "Mill's *Utilitarianism*," in James Smith and Ernest Sosa (eds.) *Mill's Utilitarianism: Text and Criticism* (pp. 154–72). Belmont, CA: Wadsworth.

Chapter 6

Mill's Theory of Sanctions

Dale E. Miller

Definitions

In Chapter III of *Utilitarianism* Mill turns to the subject of motivational psychology. His goal in this chapter is to show that no special problems would be involved in getting people to obey utilitarianism, for they would have the same sorts of motives to do so as to obey conventional or "traditional" morality. Mill opens the chapter by writing:

> The question is often asked, and properly so, in regard to any supposed moral standard – What is its sanction? what are the motives to obey it? or more specifically, what is the source of its obligation? whence does it derive its binding force? (Mill 1861, reprinted as Part II of this volume, Ch. III, para. 1. Future citations to this work will simply indicate chapter by roman numeral, paragraph by arabic numeral.)

He aims to answer this question with respect to utilitarianism. Some of his ways of wording it may be puzzling, however. What does he mean by the "sanction" of a moral theory? And why is a theory's "source of . . . obligation" a matter of people's motives to obey it? Is not the source of this obligation just the fact that the theory is better than any others? And does not Mill attempt to show, in Chapter IV, that this is true of utilitarianism?

In order to understand Mill's language here, one must know a little about both his understanding of motivational psychology and the work of some earlier writers in the utilitarian tradition. Like the other classical British empiricists, Mill subscribes to a general psychological theory called "associationism." Associationism holds that when we experience any state of consciousness it is because that state is associated in our mind with one that preceded it; the first state summoned up the latter one, so to speak. (The only exceptions are sensations, which are produced by states of our bodies in accordance with physiological laws.) Mental states can be associated through their similarity or through our having frequently experienced them together. To take some simple examples: seeing a dog may make you think about a dog of the same breed that you saw earlier or seeing your own dog may make you think of the toy that you have often seen it carrying. In each of these examples, a sensation is summoning up a thought or idea, but desires, emotions, feelings of pleasure and pain, and even volitions (choices about what to do) can also summon up and be summoned up by other mental states with which they are associated (Mill 1843: 856).

Mill's view of motivational psychology is generally similar to that of the eighteenth-century philosopher David Hume. When we deliberate about how to act, Mill thinks, this choice will be determined by our desires (and aversions – an aversion to something is essentially just a desire to avoid it). Of the different possible actions that we consider, we will choose the one that seems to us at the time to be the best way of satisfying our desires overall. Obviously this will depend on what desires we have and their relative strengths; it will also depend on our beliefs about what would result from our various possible actions. Not all of our actions are preceded by deliberation, however. Mill observes that if we have chosen to act a certain way often enough then we may continue to act the same way out of habit, even if the desires that originally moved us to act should fade (IV, 11).

The notions of pleasure and pain have an even more fundamental place in Mill's theory of motivational psychology than those of desire and habit. Jeremy Bentham began his *Introduction to the Principles of Morals and Legislation* by writing that:

> Nature has placed mankind under the government of two sovereign masters, pain and pleasure. It is for them alone to point out what we ought to do, as well as to determine what we shall do. (1948: 1)

Bentham believed that all that we desire for its own sake is pleasure and freedom from pain, and that whenever we choose some action it is because we expect that the choice will result in our enjoying some future pleasure or avoiding some future pain. Mill agrees with Bentham that pleasure and pain ultimately determine how we act, although when we come to the "internal sanction" we will see that he dissents from some aspects of Bentham's account of exactly how they do so. Mill may not share Bentham's view that we desire nothing but pleasure and the absence of pain for its own sake, although we will not be able to explore this important and interesting question at any length here. Yet even if Mill *does* believe that we can desire other things for their own sakes, he would still maintain that pleasure and pain are ultimately responsible for the formation of these desires. To put it briefly, in Chapter IV of *Utilitarianism*, Mill says that through the association of ideas we can come to desire for their own sakes things that were at first desired only as means to pleasure and freedom from pain; virtue and money are examples of things that he believes some people come to desire for their own sakes. His account of this phenomenon is ambiguous, however. When he says that a person can come to desire money, for its own sake, for example, it is not entirely clear whether he means that the person may begin to desire money itself, as opposed to any pleasure, or that the person may begin to take pleasure in the mere consciousness of possessing money (and of course, to desire this new pleasure). On one reading Mill thinks that we desire something other than pleasure and on the other reading he does not. Whichever reading one favors, however, it is still true that the new desire comes into being only because the idea of money has been associated with feelings of pleasure. Fred Berger takes Mill to believe that occurrent pleasures and pains are capable of causing desires and aversions that have objects other than pleasures and pains, but not all of the passages that Berger adduces in favor of this interpretation lend it genuine support, for several of them can more easily be read in other ways. (See Berger 1978, and 1984: 12–16.)

Now we can return to Mill's terminology. His choice of words at the beginning of Chapter III reflects the influence of Bentham as well as that of another earlier utilitarian, the legal theorist John Austin. Bentham defined sanctions simply as "sources of pain and pleasure" (1948: 24–5). Precise classifications were an obsession with Bentham, and he distinguished between four different sanctions: the physical, the political, the moral, and the religious. In other words, Bentham was saying that all of our pleasures and pains come from four general sources: nature, the government, other individuals, and God. Austin's definition of "sanction" was somewhat narrower. In his seminal book *The Province of Jurisprudence Determined*, which collects a series of lectures that J. S. Mill attended, he said that sanctions should be understood strictly as punishments or other sources of pain that are directed against a person for failing to do what he or she has been told to do. Austin then connected the notion of sanctions with that of obligation by saying that all it means for a person to be under an obligation to do something is that sanctions will be imposed on him or her for failing to do it (Austin 2000: 14–18).

Like Bentham, Mill uses "sanction" to refer to sources of both pleasure and pain. Because he believes that "pain is a stronger thing than pleasure, and punishment vastly more efficacious than reward," however, he is primarily interested, in Chapter III, in ways that people who act contrarily to the utilitarian theory of morality could be made to suffer for it (1865: 459). Given this, perhaps it is no surprise that he uses "obligation"' in the Austinian sense in this chapter. In this sense, it is the fact that people can be made to suffer pain as a consequence of failing to obey utilitarianism's dictates that is the "source of its obligation."

Yet while Austin's definition of "obligation" may have its uses, on a moment's reflection it should be clear that it differs from our ordinary way of using the word. H. L. A. Hart, a sympathetic critic of Austin, notes that Austin's definition entails that we are obligated to turn our money over to a robber who threatens us with a weapon. This does not fit the way we actually speak; we might say that we were "obliged" to give our money to a mugger, but not that we were obligated to do so (Hart 1994: 82–5). Perhaps our ordinary notion of obligation involves the idea that a person who fails to do something that he or she is obligated to do *should* suffer in some way for it, but for this it is neither necessary nor sufficient that he or she actually will. (In fact, in the course of examining the internal sanction we will see that Mill says something like this himself.) It is elsewhere in the essay, especially in Chapter IV, where Mill makes the case for our having an obligation to obey utilitarianism in the usual sense of "obligation."

The External Sanctions

Mill recognizes a wider variety of sanctions than Bentham, and although he is less concerned with categorizing them he does divide them into two classes, the external and the internal. The external sanctions are sources of pain or pleasure in whose operation others are directly involved:

> They are, the hope of favour and the fear of displeasure, from our fellow creatures or from the Ruler of the Universe, along with whatever we may have of sympathy or affection for them, or of love and awe of Him, inclining us to do his will independently of selfish consequences. (III, 3)

From this we can see that the external sanctions can be further divided into two groups. Some derive from the ability of others to harm us when they do not approve of our behavior or to reward us if they do. The rest involve a sympathetic fellow feeling, or indeed "co-feeling," that we sometimes have with other people. Since people will tend to reward us for promoting their happiness and to punish us for causing them pain, and since it pleases us to please those with whom we sympathize, it is clear how these external sanctions could be a source of motives to promote others' happiness. In addition to that, if we assume, as Mill suggests that we should, "that God desires, above all things, the happiness of his creatures, and that this was his purpose in their creation" (II, 22), we see how those who believe in a supreme being would be motivated. Of course, if there are people with whom one does not sympathize or from whom one need not fear retaliation, or if one does not believe in a supreme being (as Mill probably did not), then the external sanctions may give one little or no reason to care about their happiness. Mill's acute awareness of this point explains a great deal about his ethical, social, and political philosophy. One of his primary concerns in his practical philosophy is that of how to ensure that each person has a due regard for the happiness of everyone whom his or her actions might affect. In particular, he thinks that moral progress depends on encouraging individuals to sympathize with wider circles of people.

Mill's understanding of sympathy is much like that of Hume, who thinks of it as "a disposition we have to feel what others are feeling" (Stroud 1977: 197). In a review of a book by his friend Alexander Bain, Mill describes it a little more broadly as the disposition or capacity "of taking on the emotions, or mental states generally, of others" (1859a: 362). Mill is actually presenting Bain's conception of sympathy, but it is clear in context that Mill agrees. Today we might use "empathy" instead of "sympathy" to describe this capacity for sharing others' thoughts and feelings, although there does not seem to be any consensus among contemporary psychologists about how empathy and sympathy are to be distinguished (Omdahl 1995: 15). Because we have the capacity for sympathy, Mill writes, "The idea of the pain of another is naturally painful; the idea of the pleasure of another is naturally pleasurable" (1835: 60). Insofar as we sympathize with someone else, therefore, the thought of their happiness is a source of happiness to us and the thought of their unhappiness makes us unhappy.

As the final quotation in the preceding paragraph indicates, Mill thinks that we are sympathetic by nature. When we direct our attention to what another person is feeling, we have a natural tendency to feel the same (although we may not always do so, for the tendency may be counteracted). That is not to say, though, that we are naturally inclined to pay attention to what others feel. Mill's father James wrote, with John Stuart's agreement:

> It is well known that the pains of and pleasures of another person affect us; that is, associate with themselves the ideas of our own pains and pleasures, with more or less intensity, *according to the attention which we bestow upon his pains or pleasures*. (James Mill 1878: 219, emphasis added)

Sometimes a person will display feelings in a way that arrests our attention, but otherwise we must learn to pay attention; "the good of others becomes our pleasure because we have learnt to find pleasure in it" (Mill 1852: 184). Mill explains:

> There is no selfishness equal to that of children, as everyone who is acquainted with children well knows . . . The pains of others, though naturally painful to us, are not so until we have realised them by an act of imagination, implying voluntary attention; and that no young child ever pays, while under the impulse of a present desire. (1835: 60–1)

Nearly everyone develops the habit of paying some regard to the feelings of at least a few people who are close to them, such as family members, but many have little sympathy for anyone outside of this narrow circle of intimates:

> [S]ympathetic characters, left uncultivated, and given up to their sympathetic instincts, are as selfish as others. The difference is in the *kind* of selfishness: theirs is not solitary but sympathetic selfishness; *l'egoïsme à deux, à trois*, or *à quatre*; and they may be very amiable and delightful to those with whom they sympathize, and grossly unjust and unfeeling to the rest of the world. (1874a: 394)

Mill finds this kind of "sympathetic selfishness" to be very common among his male contemporaries:

> One of the commonest types of character among us is that of a man whose ambition is self-regarding; who has no higher purpose in life than to enrich or raise in the world himself or his family; who never dreams of making the good of his fellow creatures or his country a habitual object . . . (1867: 253)

He actually believes, however, that women are even more prone to be in this condition than men, not because of any "natural" difference between the sexes, but because women are seldom placed in positions in which they are forced to pay attention to the feelings of anyone outside of their families. This teaches them that "the individuals connected with them are . . . the only ones whose interest they are called upon to care for" (1869: 321, 329).

Mill believes that the moral improvement of mankind depends on encouraging individuals to form the habit of paying attention to, and hence sympathizing with, the feelings of broader groups of people. If the lower classes have no political or economic power then their feelings can be safely ignored; so the fact that his society is moving in the direction of greater social and political equality represents progress in this regard:

> Not only does all strengthening of social ties, and all healthy growth of society, give to each individual a stronger personal interest in practically consulting the welfare of others; it also leads him to identify his feelings more and more with their good, or at least with an even greater degree of practical consideration for it . . . This mode of conceiving ourselves and human life, as civilisation goes on, is felt to be more and more natural. Every step in political improvement renders it more so, by removing the sources of opposition of interest, and levelling those inequalities of legal privilege between individuals or classes, owing to which there are large portions of mankind whose happiness it is still practicable to disregard. (III, 10)

Mill advocates a variety of measures that he thinks will encourage each individual to form the habit of paying attention to the feelings of others. The classroom portion of this program of education consists mainly of the study of poetry, and of the other arts insofar as they share with poetry its essential feature of the "delineation of states of feeling" (Mill 1833b: 347). Learning to appreciate art requires learning to concentrate one's attention on the feelings of someone else. (See Paul 1998: 104.) More important, though, is what happens outside the classroom. One consideration Mill offers in support of many of the reform measures he advocates is the fact that they would put people in situations where they would be forced to attend to the feelings of people outside their immediate circle or even their economic class. Examples include the enfranchisement of women, mandatory public service for citizens, and the removal of barriers to worker ownership of firms. (See Miller 2000 and 2003b.) It seems that from a utilitarian standpoint what would be most desirable is for each individual to sympathize to some degree with the entirety of humanity, and Mill believes that it may eventually be possible to bring even this about:

Let it be remembered that if individual life is short, the life of the human species is not short – its indefinite duration is practically equivalent to endlessness; and being combined with indefinite capability of improvement, it offers to the imagination and sympathies a large enough object to satisfy any reasonable demand for grandeur of aspiration . . . Nor let it be thought that only the more eminent of our species, in mind and heart, are capable of identifying their feelings with the entire life of the human race. This noble capability implies indeed a certain cultivation, but not superior to that which might be, and certainly will be if human improvement continues, the lot of all. (1874b: 420)

(The section just concluded is a reworked version of a discussion that originally appeared in Miller 2003c. There I go on to consider how a person's sympathy with the feelings of others might impede his or her exercise of the individuality that Mill celebrates in *On Liberty*.)

The Internal Sanction

Mill discusses just one internal sanction in Chapter III of *Utilitarianism*. It is the source of the painful "feeling of duty," which is

a mass of feeling which must be broken through in order to do what violates our standard of right, and which, if we do nevertheless violate that standard, will probably have to be encountered afterwards in the form of remorse. (III, 4. See Miller 1998 for a discussion of Mill's account of other "internal" sources of pleasure and pain – those responsible for feelings such as pride and shame – as well as the internal sanction of duty.)

This sanction is an internal enforcer of moral rules or principles; a person can be said to have internalized whatever rules or principles his or her conscience enforces. The internal sanction is "the essence of Conscience," Mill writes, despite the fact that "in that complex phenomenon as it actually exists, the simple fact is in general all encrusted over with collateral associations" (III, 4); the terms "conscience" and "internal sanction" will be used interchangeably below. The conscience is the "ultimate sanction of the principle of utility" to which Mill refers in the title of the chapter, despite the fact that he takes this "spring of action" to be missing from Bentham's understanding of our motivational psychology altogether.

Accounting for conscience's power to affect our behavior within the framework of the Humean theory of motivation is more difficult than it might at first appear. The motivational force of after-the-fact guilt or remorse is straightforward; since we have a desire not to experience such painful feelings, we have a motive to avoid acts that we expect will give rise to them. (Of course, we may have other desires that are, at least momentarily, stronger, which is why we do not always listen to our consciences.) More difficult for a Humean to explain, though, is the ability of pain experienced when a person is merely contemplating some action to deter him or her from choosing it. Mill's solution to this puzzle can be found in the critical essay "Remarks on Bentham's philosophy," where he writes that, in addition to the possibility of a person being motivated to refrain from an immoral act by his aversion to remorse, it is just as possible:

> that he recoils from the very thought of committing the act; the idea of placing himself in such a situation is so painful, that he cannot dwell upon it long enough to have even the physical power of perpetrating the crime. His conduct is determined by pain; but by a pain which precedes the act, not by one which is expected to follow it. Not only *may* this be so, but unless it be so, the man is not truly virtuous. (1833a: 12)

So simply contemplating an act can be so painful that the agent cannot even bear to weigh the motives he does have. The pain can cause him to stop deliberating before he can settle on the act. (See also Miller 1998.)

Mill distinguishes between two schools of thought concerning the origin of the internal sanction. One is a view known as "moral intuitionism." This view can take different forms, but generally speaking the intuitionists to whom Mill is responding believe that the conscience is "innate" – that we are born with it, so to speak. They hold that there are particular moral rules or principles that the conscience is inherently disposed to enforce, so that it is natural for everyone to feel discomfort at the thought of violating them, discomfort that takes the form of guilt when it is experienced after the fact. Unsurprisingly, the rules or principles that intuitionists take to have this connection with the feeling of duty tend to be ones that are widely accepted within their own society; in the case of the intuitionists who are Mill's primary targets, they are the rules or principles that constitute Victorian conventional morality. These intuitionists commonly reason that if our consciences are innate then they must have been given to us by God, and this leads them to regard the feeling of duty as an infallible source of moral knowledge: by noticing when our conscience makes us feel uneasy, we can know what things are in fact wrong. The other view, which is Mill's, is that the conscience is acquired; it is a product of experience. He describes the conscience as being "implanted," but his choice of word is unfortunate. The intuitionist can also say that the conscience is implanted – by God.

In Chapter III, Mill is willing to grant the intuitionists, for the sake of argument, that the conscience is innate. He maintains that, if this is the case, at least as good of a case can be made for utilitarianism's being "intuitively obligatory" as for the same's being true of any other view of morality. Mill's efforts to show that the conscience might be innately "programmed" to prod us to obey utilitarianism is unpersuasive, however, because it is too difficult to reconcile Mill's view that the vast majority of people need to revise their views about morality in significant ways with the intuitionist view that our consciences are infallible moral guides. Intuitionism characteristically upholds received ideas about morality, as has already been noted. If each person's conscience urges him or her to cleave to a particular morality, it is hard to see how any rival moral view could ever become widely accepted. In contrast, Mill's utilitarianism clearly is a revisionist moral theory, one that is somewhat at odds with widely accepted views about morality. In Chapter II of *Utilitarianism* it emerges that Mill takes utilitarianism to have a two-level structure, with the abstract principle that happiness should be maximized occupying the higher level and providing the justification for more concrete lower-level rules or principles. Exactly what relation we take Mill to posit between these levels depends on whether we read him as an act- or a rule-utilitarian, which is a question broached elsewhere in this volume, but he does tell us explicitly that while happiness-maximization is "the fundamental principle of morality, we require subordinate principles to apply it by" (III, 24). He allows that conventional morality may serve as a first approximation of the lower-level rules or principles that utilitarianism would endorse, because beliefs about the effects of different types of behavior on human happiness always influence the evolution of conventional morality (I, 4). Yet it is most definitely not Mill's view that utilitarianism endorses Victorian conventional morality as it stands (nor, surely, would he think that it endorses the conventional moralities of any twenty-first-century societies). As he also says in Chapter II,

> [T]hat the received code of ethics is by no means of divine right; and that mankind have still much to learn as to the effects of actions on the general happiness, I admit, or rather, earnestly maintain. The corollaries from the principle of utility, like the precepts of every practical art, admit of indefinite improvement, and, in a progressive state of the human mind, their improvement is perpetually going on. (II, 24)

Hence for Mill's purposes the question of where the conscience comes from is a more important one than he admits. It is only by showing that the conscience is acquired by experience, and hence can be "cultivated" in different directions, that he can explain how the feeling of duty can be used to enforce somewhat different moral rules than those to which it already commonly attaches. Mill makes a variety of criticisms of the sort of intuitionism that regards the feeling of duty as an innate and reliable moral guide. It impedes moral progress, he says, because it teaches people that there is no need to question whatever moral views they happen to hold already. (See, for example, Mill 1859b: 220, 284.) He asserts that it is indeterminate, furthermore, because the intuitionists with whom he is familiar teach that there are multiple moral rules or principles that we are obligated to obey, but have nothing to say about what to do when these rules conflict (as they often do) (I, 3). In addition, he insists that intuitionism by itself has no power to explain what distinguishes right actions from wrong ones, and that on those occasions when intuitionists have tried to explain this they inevitably fell back on utilitarian reasoning (I, 4). Mill's chief objection to intuitionism, however, is simply that associationism can explain how common experiences that nearly everyone shares would give rise to the conscience. Mill holds that we should not regard any faculty as an infallible source of intuitive knowledge if it is possible to give a scientific account of that faculty's origin (which is not to say that we can so treat it if no such account can be given) (Skorupski 1989: 21–30). Since this is possible in the case of the conscience, Mill reasons, we should not regard the conscience as a font of intuitive knowledge of right and wrong.

Mill believes that we initially acquire the internal sanction as a result of being punished after breaking rules that we have been told to obey. We come to associate the violation of certain rules of conduct with painful punishment, and eventually we internalize the activity of punishment. This may be the complete explanation of how the conscience is implanted in some people. As Mill puts it in an 1859 letter, "innumerable associations of pain with doing wrong . . . may produce a general & intense feeling of recoil from wrongdoing," and this is "a sufficient account" of the basis of the sanction "as it exists in many minds." However, this is not "the normal form of moral feeling." There is usually more to the story than this, a second source of associations between wrongdoing and punishment that is a "natural outgrowth of the social nature of man." When we know that people with whom we sympathize would want to see us punished if we were to violate certain rules of conduct, then we may sympathize with their desire for our punishment:

> I feel conscious that if I violate certain laws, other people must necessarily or naturally desire that I sh^d be punished for the violation. I also feel that I sh^d desire them to be punished if they violated the same laws toward me. From these feelings & from the sociality of my nature I place myself in their situation, & sympathize in their desire that I sh^d be punished; & (even apart from benevolence) the painfulness of not being in union with them makes me shrink from pursuing a line of conduct which would make my ends, wishes, and purposes habitually conflict with theirs. (1972: 650)

The passage continues:

> To this fellow feeling with man may of course be added (if I may so express myself) fellow feeling with God, & recoil from the idea of not being in union with Him. May I add, that even to an unbeliever there may be a feeling similar in nature towards an *ideal* God? As there may be towards an ideally perfect man, or towards our friends who are no more, even if we do not feel assured of their immortality. All these feelings are immensely increased in strength by reflected influence from other persons who feel the same.

Mill takes this second source of associations between punishment and wrongdoing to have a very particular significance. During a period of depression that he suffered around the time that he turned 20, Mill was struck by the fact that the habit of analytical thinking that had been instilled in him by James Mill had the power to dissolve mental associations, when it became apparent that they resulted merely from the deliberate efforts of others:

> [M]y teachers had occupied themselves but superficially with the means of forming and keeping up these salutary associations. They seemed to have trusted altogether to the old familiar instruments, praise and blame, reward and punishment. Now I did not doubt that by these means, begun early and applied unremittingly, intense associations of pain and pleasure, especially of pain, might be created, and might produce desires and aversions capable of lasting undiminished to the end of life. But there must always be something artificial and casual in associations thus produced ... [T]he very excellence of analysis ... is that ... it enables us mentally to separate ideas which have only casually clung together ... Analytic habits may thus even strengthen the associations between causes and effects, means and ends, but tend altogether to weaken those which are, to speak familiarly, a *mere* matter of feeling. (1873: 141, 143)

For people who associate wrongdoing with punishment only because of the actual punishments that they have undergone, the internal sanction is highly vulnerable to this sort of dissolution, for "moral associations which are wholly of artificial creation, when intellectual culture goes on, yield by degrees to the dissolving force of analysis" (III, 9; see also Mill 1873: 141ff.).

The recognition that analytical thinking has this kind of corrosive power does not turn Mill against it. The question is simply how to cope with its sometimes undesirable side effect. Mill's general answer involves the early cultivation of the feelings, which was missing from his own upbringing. In describing how his early "mental crisis" (his phrase) affected his philosophical views, Mill writes:

> I never turned recreant to intellectual culture, or ceased to consider the power and practice of analysis as an essential condition both of individual and of social improvement. But I thought that it had consequences which required to be corrected, by joining other kinds of cultivation with it. The maintenance of a due balance among the faculties, now seemed to me of primary importance. The cultivation of the feelings became one of the cardinal points in my ethical and philosophical creed. (1873: 145)

With respect to the specific mental association that constitutes the internal sanction of duty, Mill believes that our sympathy with the desire of others to punish us when we transgress against them will serve to protect it against dissolution by analytical thinking. We recognize that this desire on their part is entirely natural – at one point Mill calls it the "normal action of their natural sentiments" – and for this reason we recognize that the association between wrongdoing and pain is far from being "artificial and casual" (1865: 455). Mill also discusses this desire in Chapter V of *Utilitarianism*; it is the basis of what he there calls the "sentiment of justice." This is the point of the somewhat obscure passage in *Utilitarianism* in which he writes that:

> if the feeling of duty, when associated with utility, would appear equally arbitrary; if there were no leading department of our nature, no powerful class of sentiments, with which that association would harmonise, which would make us feel it congenial, and incline us not only to foster it in others (for which we have abundant interested motives), but also to cherish it in ourselves; if there were not, in short, a natural basis of sentiment for utilitarian morality, it might well happen that this association also, even after it had been implanted by education, might be analysed away.

> But there *is* this basis of powerful natural sentiment; and this it is which, when once the general happiness is recognised as the ethical standard, will constitute the strength of the utilitarian morality. This firm foundation is that of the social feelings of mankind; the desire to be in unity with our fellow creatures, which is already a powerful principle in human nature, and happily one of those which tend to become stronger, even without express inculcation, from the influences of advancing civilisation. (III, 9, 10)

Mill thinks sympathy will function to prevent the conscience from being analyzed away only to the extent that the rules or principles it enforces approximate the utilitarian theory of morality. Only when a morality serves to promote the happiness of others will their desire for us to be punished when we disobey it seem natural. So Mill's claim is not merely that the internal sanction can direct people to obey utilitarianism as well as it can any competing moral view; it is that the conscience of someone who has internalized the utilitarian morality would be especially resistant to the corrosive influence of analytical thinking. However, if there are groups of people with whom we lack sympathy, then rules or principles that would prevent us from damaging their interests will receive no support from this quarter. So here is an additional reason for Mill to think that moral progress depends upon the broadening of sympathy.

One final point about the internal sanction: In Chapter V of *Utilitarianism*, Mill says something very interesting about the conceptual relation between the feeling of duty and morally wrong action:

> We do not call anything wrong, unless we mean to imply that a person ought to be punished in some way or other for doing it; if not by law, by the opinion of his fellow-creatures; if not by opinion, by the reproaches of his own conscience. (V, 14)

This apparently entails that a person's conscience ought to act up if and only if he or she has done, or is thinking about doing, something wrong. This may sound like a truism, but given that Mill is a utilitarian it has some interesting implications. First, as is obvious, it seems to mean that whether Mill is an act- or a rule-utilitarian makes a real difference to what sorts of things he thinks our consciences ought to "punish" us for having done. If he believes that every action that fails to maximize happiness is wrong, for example, then he appears to be committed to saying that every such action ought to be followed by guilt. (See Miller 2003a, where I use this argument against one form of act-utilitarianism.) Matters grow even more interesting if we assume that Mill holds the usual utilitarian view about punishment, which is that it should be administered only when this is itself happiness-maximizing, and that he applies this to the conscience as well. On the basis of this assumption, some interpreters have attributed a view to Mill that reverses the normal order of explanation between immorality and the feeling of duty. These commentators take him to hold that whether an action is wrong depends on whether it would be happiness-maximizing for a person's conscience to enforce a rule or principle that proscribes it. (See, for example, Lyons 1976: 101–20, and Gray 1996.)

Conclusion

Mill's theory of sanctions, and his understanding of the psychology of human action more generally, are among the least-discussed elements of his utilitarianism. They are, however, more complex, sophisticated, and interesting than many philosophers realize, especially when one also takes into account the way in which Mill's views were further developed by his friend and follower Alexander Bain. (See Bain 1977.) Some aspects of Mill's work in psychology may be a little dated now; for example, contemporary theorists are likely to think that he overstates how much the association of ideas can explain. With theories as with buildings, however, the fact that the foundation needs some work does not necessarily mean that the superstructure is unsound. We can still learn something from Mill about the psychology of moral motivation.

References

Austin, John (2000) *The Province of Jurisprudence Determined*. New York: Prometheus.

Bain, Alexander (1977) *The Emotions and the Will*. Washington: University Publication of America.

Bentham, Jeremy (1948) *An Introduction to the Principles of Morals and Legislation*. New York: Hafner.

Berger, Fred R. (1978) "Mill's concept of happiness," *Interpretation* 7, pp. 95–117.

——(1984) *Happiness, Justice and Freedom: the Moral and Political Philosophy of John Stuart Mill*. Berkeley: University of California Press.

Gray, John (1996) *Mill on Liberty: a Defence*, 2nd edn. London: Routledge.

Hart, H. L. A. (1994) *The Concept of Law*, 2nd edn. Oxford: Clarendon Press.

Lyons, David (1976) "Mill's theory of morality," *Nous* 10, pp. 101–20.

Mill, James (1878) *Analysis of the Phenomena of the Human Mind*, 2nd edn. London: Longmans, Green, Reader, & Dyer.

Mill, John Stuart (1833a) "Remarks on Bentham's philosophy," in J. M. Robson (ed.) *Collected Works of John Stuart Mill*, Vol. X: *Essays on Ethics, Religion, and Society* (pp. 3–18). Toronto: University of Toronto Press, 1969.

——(1833b) "Thoughts on poetry and its varieties," in J. M. Robson and Jack Stillinger (eds.) *Collected Works of John Stuart Mill*, Vol. I: *Autobiography and Literary Essays* (pp. 341–65). Toronto: University of Toronto Press, 1981.

——(1835) "Sedgwick's discourse," in J. M. Robson (ed.) *Collected Works of John Stuart Mill*, Vol. X: *Essays on Ethics, Religion, and Society* (pp. 31–74). Toronto: University of Toronto Press, 1969.

——(1843) *A System of Logic Ratiocinative and Inductive*, in J. M. Robson (ed.) *Collected Works of John Stuart Mill*, Vols. VII–VIII. Toronto: University Of Toronto Press, 1973.

——(1852) "Whewell on moral philosophy," in J. M. Robson (ed.) *Collected Works of John Stuart Mill*, Vol. X: *Essays on Ethics, Religion, and Society* (pp. 165–201). Toronto: University of Toronto Press, 1969.

——(1859a) "Bain's psychology," in J. M. Robson (ed.) *Collected Works of John Stuart Mill*, Vol. XI: *Essays on Philosophy and the Classics* (pp. 339–73). Toronto: University of Toronto Press, 1978.

——(1859b) *On Liberty*, in J. M. Robson (ed.) *Collected Works of John Stuart Mill*, Vols. XVIII–XIX: *Essays on Politics and Society* (pp. 213–310). Toronto: University of Toronto Press, 1977.

——(1861) *Utilitarianism*, in J. M. Robson (ed.) *Collected Works of John Stuart Mill*, Vol. X: *Essays on Ethics, Religion, and Society* (pp. 203–59). Toronto: University of Toronto Press, 1969. (Reprinted as Part II of this volume; citations are by roman numeral for chapter and arabic numeral for paragraph within the chapter.)

——(1865) *An Examination of Sir William Hamilton's Philosophy and of the Principal Philosophical Questions Discussed in his Writings*, in J. M. Robson (ed.) *Collected Works of John Stuart Mill*, Vol. IX. Toronto: University of Toronto Press, 1979.

——(1867) "Inaugural address delivered to the university of St Andrews," in J. M. Robson (ed.) *Collected Works of John Stuart Mill*, Vol. XXI: *Essays on Equality, Law, and Education* (pp. 215–57). Toronto: University of Toronto Press, 1984.

——(1869) *The Subjection of Women*, in J. M. Robson (ed.) *Collected Works of John Stuart Mill*, Vol. XXI: *Essays on Equality, Law, and Education* (pp. 259–340). Toronto: University of Toronto Press, 1984.

——(1873) *Autobiography*, in J. M. Robson and Jack Stillinger (eds.) *Collected Works of John Stuart Mill*, Vol. I: *Autobiography and Literary Essays* (pp. 1–290). Toronto: University of Toronto Press, 1981.

——(1874a) "Nature," in *Three Essays on Religion*, in J. M. Robson (ed.) *Collected Works of John Stuart Mill*, Vol. X: *Essays on Ethics, Religion, and Society* (pp. 373–402). Toronto: University of Toronto Press, 1969.

——(1874b) "Utility of religion," in *Three Essays on Religion*, in J. M. Robson (ed.) *Collected Works of John Stuart Mill*, Vol. X: *Essays on Ethics, Religion, and Society* (pp. 403–28). Toronto: University of Toronto Press, 1969.

——(1972) Letter to William George Ward, 28 November 1859, in Francis E. Mineka and Dwight N. Lindley (eds.) *Collected Works of John Stuart Mill*, Vols. XIV–XVII: *The Later Letters of John Stuart Mill 1849–1873* (pp. 646–50). Toronto: University of Toronto Press.

Miller, Dale E. (1998) "Internal sanctions in Mill's psychology," *Utilitas* 10, pp. 68–81.

——(2000) "John Stuart Mill's civic liberalism," *History of Political Thought* 21, pp. 88–113.

——(2003a) "Actual-consequence act utilitarianism and the best possible persons," *Ratio* 16, pp. 49–62.

——(2003b) "Mill's "socialism," *Politics, Philosophy and Economics* 2, pp. 213–38.

——(2003c) "Sympathy versus spontaneity: a tension in Mill's conception of human perfection," *International Journal of Politics and Ethics* 3, pp. 173–88.

Omdahl, Becky Lynn (1995) *Cognitive Appraisal, Emotion, and Empathy.* Mahwah, NJ: Lawrence Erlbaum.

Paul, L. A. (1998) "The worm at the root of the passions: poetry and sympathy in Mill's utilitarianism," *Utilitas* 10, pp. 83–104.

Skorupski, John (1989) *John Stuart Mill.* New York: Routledge.

Stroud, Barry (1977) *Hume.* London: Routledge & Kegan Paul.

Chapter 7

Mill's "Proof" of the Principle of Utility

Henry R. West

Utilitarianism is a "consequentialist" doctrine: that actions are right or wrong in proportion as they produce good or bad consequences. Mill's version is also a "hedonistic" doctrine. Consequences are good insofar as they have more happiness or less unhappiness; bad, as they have more unhappiness or less happiness; and by happiness and unhappiness, Mill means pleasure and pain. In English, the words "happiness" and "unhappiness" do not have the same connotations as "pleasure" and "pain." "Happiness" implies feeling good about one's life as well as feeling good. "Happiness" is found in relationships with friends and loved ones and in a sense of accomplishment. "Pleasure" seems to be something that is momentary and more sensational. But according to Mill's psychology, a happy life consists in many pleasures and few pains. The happiness of relationships with friends and loved ones is reducible to the joys and satisfactions in the moments of one's life that arise from these relationships. The happiness of a sense of accomplishment consists of the pleasurable states of consciousness that arise from a sense of accomplishment. The happiness of self-respect and the unhappiness of self-disrespect consist of the pleasurable and painful states of consciousness that these involve. This reduction of happiness and unhappiness to pleasures and pains is a controversial element in Mill's philosophy. I leave it to the reader to think about that reduction. In what follows, it will be assumed.

In Chapter IV of *Utilitarianism*, Mill addresses himself to the question "Of what sort of proof the principle of utility is susceptible." The "principle of utility" is that happiness is desirable, and the only thing desirable, as an end, all other things being desirable only as means to that end. In other words, Mill is discussing the proof for his hedonistic theory of intrinsic value, of what is good and bad in itself, all other values being derived from the intrinsic value and disvalue of pleasure and pain. (There has been controversy about what to count as Mill's "principle." Brown (1973) is persuasive.)

In Chapter I, Mill had explained that:

this cannot be proof in the ordinary and popular meaning of the term. Questions of ultimate ends are not amenable to direct proof. Whatever can be proved to be good, must be so by being shown to be a means to something admitted to be good without proof. (Mill 1861: Ch. I, para. 5. Citations to this work, reprinted as Part II of this volume, will be simply by roman numeral for chapter, arabic numeral for paragraph.)

But he then goes on to say:

We are not, however, to infer that its acceptance or rejection must depend on blind impulse or arbitrary choice . . . The subject is within the cognizance of the rational faculty; and neither does that faculty deal with it solely in the way of intuition. Considerations may be capable of determining the intellect either to give or withhold its assent to the doctrine, and this is equivalent to proof. (I, 5)

The argument in the twelve paragraphs of Chapter IV, if successful, is one of the most important arguments in all of moral philosophy, for it would establish hedonism, in the broad meaning that Mill attaches to pleasure, as the value foundation for all of life and for morality as a part of that. In this "proof" Mill appeals to introspective psychology. He does not claim that it is a proof in the sense of a logical deduction. It is merely claimed that the only evidence available to judge what is intrinsically good, when properly analyzed, supports the utilitarian theory of value. At the end of this chapter, some attention will be given to alternatives to this psychological approach. First, we need to analyze Mill's argument.

To be incapable of proof by reasoning, Mill says, is common to all first principles, those of knowledge as well as those of conduct. But the former, being matters of fact, may be subject to a direct appeal to the faculties that judge of fact: namely, our senses and our internal consciousness. For questions of practical ends, appeal must be made to the faculty of desire:

The only proof capable of being given that an object is visible is that people actually see it. The only proof that a sound is audible, is that people hear it: and so of the other sources of our experience. In like manner, I apprehend, the sole evidence it is possible to produce that anything is desirable, is that people do actually desire it. (IV, 3)

Here Mill has been accused of the "fallacy of equivocation," confusing "desirable" meaning "capable of being desired" with "desirable" meaning "worthy of being desired" (McCloskey 1971: 62). Mill was the author of a logic textbook, the most prominent one written in the nineteenth century. Isn't it more likely that he is being misinterpreted, rather than that he made an obvious logical blunder? Mill is clearly making a distinction between matters of fact (knowledge) and matters of conduct (practical ends). His claim is that the evidence for either must be something in human experience. In the one case it is sensory information. In the other case it is appetitive information: what people desire.

Appealing to this evidence, Mill thinks that it is obvious that happiness is at least one thing that is desirable:

> No reason can be given why the general happiness is desirable, except that each person, so far as he [or she] believes it to be attainable, desires his [or her] own happiness. This, however, being a fact, we have not only all the proof which the case admits of, but all which it is possible to require, that happiness is a good: that each person's happiness is a good to that person, and the general happiness, therefore, a good to the aggregate of all persons. Happiness has made out its title as *one* of the ends of conduct, and consequently one of the criteria of morality. (IV, 3)

In this passage, Mill has been accused by critics of the "fallacy of composition": of over-generalizing from what is true of one member of a collective to all members of the collective. It is claimed that Mill argues that since each desires his own happiness, we all desire the happiness of all (McCloskey 1971: 62). But that is not Mill's argument. He does not say that all persons desire the happiness of all. He is claiming that on the basis of each person desiring his or her own happiness, we can conclude that the happiness of each of those persons is a good for each of those persons individually, and, therefore, if one is seeking to identify what is good for an aggregate of individuals, their happiness will be one ingredient. He is claiming that just as the happiness of an individual is at least one element in the welfare of that individual, so the happiness of an aggregate of individuals would be at least one element in the welfare of the aggregate of those individuals. Mill makes this explicit in a letter concerning this passage:

> when I said that the general happiness is a good to the aggregate of all persons I did not mean that every human being's happiness is a good to every other human being though I think that in a good state of society and education it would be so. I merely meant in this particular sentence to argue that since A's happiness is a good, B's a good, C's a good, etc., the sum of all these goods must be a good. (1972: 1414)

Mill is thus saying that if happiness is desirable for one individual, on the basis of the evidence of that individual's desire, then it is desirable for each individual based on the desire of each individual. There is no fallacy here.

Isn't Mill correct so far? All people want to be happy as an end in itself, whatever else they may want; so happiness is one kind of thing that is good as an end in itself.

The more difficult part of Mill's "proof" is to argue that happiness is the only kind of thing that is good in itself. People seem to desire other things, such as wealth, fame, friendship, and self-respect, not merely as means to happiness but as ends. Mill's task is to argue that these are desired as "parts" of happiness, or that they are sought as a matter of habit without there being any longer genuine desire for them. Mill holds a variation of what is called "psychological hedonism": that all motivation is due to pleasure or pain, either concurrent, in prospect, or in the past. His is not the simple version of psychological hedonism that all motivation is attraction to future pleasure or aversion to future pain. He says that pleasure (or pain) is not always the conscious object of desires and not all motives are anticipation of pleasure or of pain:

> [A] motive does not mean always, or solely, the anticipation of a pleasure or of a pain . . . As we proceed in the formation of habits, and become accustomed to will a particular act or a particular course of conduct because it is pleasurable, we at last continue to will it without any reference to its being pleasurable. (1843: 842)

This can still be called "psychological hedonism," I think, because Mill believes that all habits are derived from desires, and desires for and aversions from objects other than pleasure and pain are ultimately based on conditioning or "association" with pleasure and pain.

Mill can thus argue that objects that are not currently sought either as means of happiness or as a part of happiness have become ends of conduct derivatively:

> Will is the child of desire, and passes out of the dominion of its parent only to come under that of habit. That which is the result of habit affords no presumption of being intrinsically good. (IV, 11)

An example of this habit formation would be obsessive or addictive behavior that is even contrary to conscious desire, or any pattern of behavior that has become habitual and is done without thought or deliberation. Mill's claim, then, leaves him with everything that affords any presumption of being intrinsically good as being also an object of conscious desire.

Mill may here underplay the role of genetics in human behavior. There may be much human motivation that is the product of natural selection, having survival value or having once had survival value and now producing behavior without ever going through the process of being an object of conscious desire. Some emotional reactions to situations may be genetically based. In fact Mill believes that sympathy is genetic. We naturally feel pleasure when we are aware that others feel pleasure and we naturally feel pain when we are aware that others are in pain. We can develop these natural reactions or we can suppress them, but they are among our natural endowments. But Mill would say that we must critically evaluate such reactions before they provide any presumption of being evidence of what is intrinsically good. In Chapter V, he says that there is a natural feeling of retaliation or vengeance, but he says that this sentiment, in itself, has nothing moral in it (V, 31). So, just as he claims that what is the result of habit provides no presumption of being intrinsically good, he might claim that what is the result of instinct has no presumption of being intrinsically good.

If this were Mill's reply, wouldn't the same criticism be made of his appeal to pleasure and pain as the original sources of our desires? The answer, I believe, is that Mill is not claiming that pleasure and pain are intrinsically desirable and undesirable because they are the *original* sources of our motivation. I think that he is claiming that they are intrinsically good and bad because when we attend to the objects of our conscious desires, they are the common denominator.

In paragraphs 4–10 of Chapter IV, Mill asserts that every object of conscious desire is associated with pleasure or the absence of pain, either as a means or an end. Many desires are acquired, such as the desire for virtue or the possession of money, and have come to be desired through the mechanism of their association with pleasure or the absence of pain. But whether acquired or not, the ends of the desires can be regarded as experiences or states of affairs with a pleasure component. They are pleasures or "parts of happiness" (IV, 6). Although they may fall under various other descriptions, it is the fact that they are ingredients of happiness that provides a unified account of desire.

It is tempting to read into Mill the claim that it is the agreeable quality of the state of consciousness desired that is the real object of desire, although it is palpable that people "do desire things, which in common language, are decidedly distinguished from happiness" (IV, 4). But in his examples, the desire for music, health, etc., Mill regards music, etc., not just pleasure, as an object of desire, although at the same time there may be desire for the pleasure of music, or there may be pleasure at the anticipation of music, or pleasure in anticipation of the pleasure of music. Mill does not need to make the strong, and implausible, claim that desire is only for the pleasure of music and not also for music. He only needs to claim that, as a psychological fact, music, health, etc., would not be desired, as an end, if no pleasure or freedom from pain or past association with pleasure or freedom from pain were connected with them.

Desire is evidence of desirability, but it does not confer desirability. This is obvious in the case of things desired as means. On reflection, it is also obvious in the case of things desired as ends. The possession of money is desired as an end by the miser. This desire does not make the possession of money as an end a rational desire. The evidence of desire must be analyzed. Some desires are destructive. But if analysis of the miser's desire for possession of money is that the miser desires it as part of his [or her] happiness – that he [or she] would be made happy by its possession or unhappy by its loss – we have evidence that pleasure and pain provide a comprehensive theory that identifies the pleasure or pain inherent in desired things as what makes them desirable or undesirable. The pleasures and pains inherent in them do not themselves have to be discriminated as the sole *objects* of desires and aversions. We can then criticize the miser's way of life to assert that the miser would be happier, and therefore have a more desirable life, if the he or she valued other things as ends. (See 4: MILL'S THEORY OF VALUE.)

Some commentators have thought that Mill reduces the relation between desire and pleasure to a trivial one in the passage where he says

desiring a thing and finding it pleasant, aversion to it and thinking of it as painful, are phenomena entirely inseparable, or rather two parts of the same phenomenon –

in strictness of language, two different modes of naming the same psychological fact; that to think of an object as desirable (unless for the sake of its consequences), and to think of it as pleasant, are one and the same thing; and that to desire anything, except in proportion as the idea of it is pleasant, is a physical and metaphysical impossibility. (IV, 10)

This statement is certainly puzzling to the twenty-first-century reader, but in context Mill is asking the reader to engage in "practiced self-consciousness and self-observation" (IV, 10). He is asserting an empirical generalization, to be confirmed by introspective analysis, not a statement based on identity of meaning of the terms. Supporting this is that for Mill the term "metaphysical" is a term for "psychological" (Mandelbaum 1968: 39). The term "metaphysical" has changed its meaning from the way that it was used by Mill. The question of whether desire (for something as an end) is inseparable from pleasure is a psychological, not a linguistic issue. Mill is asserting that there is a complex state of consciousness when one desires an object as an end. One element is the desire for it. Another element is to think of it as pleasant. The state of consciousness is one complex thing, and the desire aspect and the idea of it as pleasant are two aspects of it. There is one complex psychological fact with two "parts." That these two parts occur together, are "inseparable," is to be found by introspective analysis, not by the meaning of the descriptions.

Mill claims that the objects of desire, described as music, health, virtue, etc., are desired as "parts" of happiness. What does that mean? Mill says, "The ingredients of happiness are very various, and each of them is desirable in itself, and not merely when considered as swelling an aggregate" (IV, 5). He continues:

They are some of the elements of which the desire of happiness is made up. Happiness is not an abstract idea, but a concrete whole; and these are some of its parts. (IV, 6)

Mill seems to be saying that the happiness of our lives is made up of many various pleasures, with different sources. He says that life would be a poor thing, very ill provided with sources of happiness, if there were no difference between the sources. Through association with our primitive desires, things which were originally indifferent have become sources of pleasure more valuable than the primitive pleasures. Remember that Mill thinks that there are higher and lower pleasures, and many of these sources based on conditioning are sources of higher pleasures.

There are really two parts to Mill's theory of how desires are connected with pleasures. One is the "associationist" psychological theory, according to which ideas and activities that are originally indifferent – neither pleasurable nor painful – come to be pleasurable or painful. For example, the desire for power in an adult is due to the experience of the feeling of power being conjoined with pleasure, and powerlessness conjoined with pain. After frequent associations, power comes to be sought for its own sake, and means are chosen to its attainment without paying attention to the pleasure associated with it or the pain associated with its absence. If pleasure and pain are the *causes* of one's coming to desire power or fame as ends, then they are necessary conditions for such desires. It is therefore psychologically impossible to desire something as an end unless it has first been associated with pleasure or avoidance of pain. This theory was probably persuasive to Mill. But it is not the only argument, nor the most important, for establishing Mill's conclusion.

The second part of Mill's argument is to engage in "practiced self-consciousness and self-observation, assisted by observation of others" (IV, 10). On self-observation, it will be found that many of the things that we desire, we desire not as ends but as means. Some others are parts of very complex desires, such as the desire for self-respect, and we would not desire them unless they contributed to the object of that desire, not as means but as "parts" of it. To test Mill's claim, we need to take some end that is believed to be desired as an end independent of pleasure and pain. Aristotle claimed that we would desire seeing, remembering, knowing, and possessing the virtues even if they brought no pleasure. Would we? The self-examination required is difficult, because theses things *do* bring pleasure or avoidance of pain. It is extremely difficult to be sure that we desire them independently. Seeing, for example, is a source of the pleasure of seeing beautiful objects, recognizing the faces of our friends and family, and its absence would make us more dependent upon others for physical guidance to avoid painful injuries. So suppose that seeing was painful. Would we still want to see as an end, or only for its instrumental utility? Perhaps we would, because it is a part of consciousness, and consciousness is our life. But it may be that life itself is pleasurable, and if it weren't, we would want an end to it. James Griffin gives the example of Sigmund Freud refusing to take pain-killing drugs in order to think clearly at the very end of his life: "I prefer," Freud said, "to think in torment than not to be able to think clearly" (Griffin 1986: 8). This would seem to be an example refuting hedonism based on the evidence of desire. How might Mill answer it?

There are at least three answers that Mill might give. First, he might say that Freud really is getting, or thinks that he is getting, more pleasure from thinking clearly and the self-respect that accompanies it than he is suffering pain. Thus the pain is outweighed by pleasure. Mill's theory of higher pleasures would support this answer. The pleasures Freud is getting from thinking clearly and from self-respect are higher pleasures and can outweigh a greater quantity of pain. Second, he might say that although under sedation he would not feel pain of being reduced to a subhuman non-rational state, his pain on *anticipation* of being in such a state prevents him from choosing it. Third, Mill might say that Freud is a victim of habit. He has consistently found his happiness in his intellectual life, and without realizing it, he is acting on the basis of that habit, rationalizing it by claiming that he prefers it. Each of these answers is a psychological explanation. A committed hedonist might give a different answer. A committed hedonist might say that Freud simply has mistaken values. He prefers to endure the torment because he thinks that life's value is in thinking clearly. But it isn't. Its value is in having more pleasure and less pain; so if the torment outweighs the pleasure of thinking clearly, then Freud is simply making a mistake. I leave it to the reader to see if any of these answers is satisfactory.

Alternatives to Mill's Methodology

Mill's "proof" depends upon the evidence of desire. Is there any alternative approach to the question of intrinsic value? In some of Mill's other writings, he considers three other foundations for ethics: Nature, the Will of God, and Intuition.

Mill's argument against Nature can be easily summarized. "Nature" has two meanings: it either means everything that occurs, and therefore it gives no guidance for human conduct, or it means what occurs apart from human intervention. Mill thinks that in the latter sense, to follow Nature is irrational and immoral. It is irrational because all human action consists in altering, and all useful action in improving, the spontaneous course of Nature. It is immoral because the course of Nature, judged by human standards, is atrocious. For example, killing, "the most criminal act recognized by human laws, Nature does once to every being that lives; and in a large proportion of cases, after protracted tortures" (1874: 385). Focusing on a human activity, Mill was an advocate for artificial means of contraception for birth control. He believed that the high birth-rate of the working-classes was a source of great misery. Many parents could not support their large families, and the sheer growth in the working class population kept down wages. To think that sex without artificial means of contraceptive is intrinsically good because it is natural is to Mill a mistake, leading to poverty and unnecessary suffering. Masters of slaves have always claimed that their authority was natural, and men have claimed that the subjection of women to them is natural. Whatever is customary has seemed natural, but customs should be subjected to critical analysis.

A second candidate for intrinsic value, the Will of God, requires, in the first place, belief that there is a higher power with a Will, and, in the second, the belief that one can know what that Will is. Different religions have different conceptions of God and disagreements about God's Will. Mill asks why one should obey one's Maker. Is it because God is righteous and merciful? If so, then these are values independent of God's Will. If anyone believes that God wills evil, then more respect is due that person if he or she acts otherwise. If God's Will is supposed to define what is righteous, then to say that God is righteous is a truism, simply saying that God wills what God wills.

A third candidate is Intuitionism, the claim that we can simply know, immediately, what is intrinsically good. Mill's arguments are primarily directed against the "moral sense" philosophers, who believed that we can know intuitively that certain kinds of actions are right and certain kinds are wrong, independent of their consequences. Mill claimed that they generally take the received rules of morality as a priori true, and he thought that this was an obstacle to a progressive morality. He believed that the subjection of women, cruelty to animals, the class system with its aristocratic privileges, on the one hand, and poverty and disenfranchisement, on the other, needed to be changed. The claim that one could intuit that those of the male gender or those of noble birth should have special powers and privileges is a hindrance to moral improvement.

Other philosophers, such as G. E. Moore, have claimed that one intuits what is intrinsically good. Moore's intuitions led him to claim that things such as knowledge and beauty are intrinsically good, independent of pleasure and pain, and, in the case of beauty, even independent of human experience. His argument for this is: if one imagines a world, unknown by a sentient being, which is beautiful, and another which is ugly, one would judge that the universe is better if the beautiful one exists and the ugly one does not. The problem with this thought-experiment is that one feels pleasure at the thought of the beautiful world and pain at the thought of the ugly one. So one's judgment is not independent of pleasure and pain. Mill could reply to this the way that he replied to the moral sense theorists. According to Mill, appeal to desire as the basis for judgments of intrinsic value makes the issue one of psychological analysis. According to the intuitionists, one either agrees with their intuitions or disagrees. There seems no basis for empirical evidence or rational debate.

Conclusion

In this chapter, I have attempted to describe the project of Mill's "proof," and to assert that it does not contain gross logical fallacies. His appeal is to experience, known by introspective analysis of one's desires. His claim is that by careful analysis and the observations of others, one finds that all things that are desired are desired as means to, or as "parts" of, happiness, and things to which one is averse are aversions to sources of pain, either as causes of pain or, one might say, "parts" of unhappiness. When this project is carried out, happiness and unhappiness seem to be the common denominators of our desires and aversions for things in themselves. Pleasure is the kind of thing that is desired, and pain is the kind of thing to which one is averse, although these are found in diverse kinds of experience. To the extent, then, that one seeks to achieve the welfare of oneself or of others, promoting happiness and reducing unhappiness are the ends to be sought. This is not a logical proof in the sense that its negation involves a contradiction. But it is an argument from experience which Mill claims is adequate to convince the intellect.

References and further reading

Brown, D. G. (1973) "What is Mill's principle of utility?," *Canadian Journal of Philosophy* 3, pp. 1–12. Reprinted in David Lyons (ed.) *Mill's* Utilitarianism: *Critical Essays* (pp. 9–24). Lanham, MD: Rowman & Littlefield.

Griffin, James (1986) *Well-being.* Oxford: Oxford University Press.

Mandelbaum, M. (1968) "On interpreting Mill's *Utilitarianism,*" *Journal of the History of Philosophy* 8, pp. 35–46.

McCloskey, H. J. (1971) *John Stuart Mill: a Critical Study.* London and Basingstoke: Macmillan.

Mill, John Stuart (1843) *A System of Logic Ratiocinative and Inductive,* in J. M. Robson (ed.) *Collected Works of John Stuart Mill,* Vols. VII–VIII. Toronto: Toronto University Press, 1973.

——(1861) *Utilitarianism,* in J. M. Robson (ed.) *Collected Works of John Stuart Mill,* Vol. X: *Essays on Ethics, Religion, and Society* (pp. 203–59). Toronto: University of Toronto Press, 1969. (Reprinted as Part II of this volume; citations are by roman numeral for chapter, arabic for paragraph within the chapter.)

——(1874) "Nature," in J. M. Robson (ed.) *Collected Works of John Stuart Mill,* Vol. X: *Essays on Ethics, Religion, and Society* (pp. 373–402). Toronto: University of Toronto Press, 1969.

——(1972) Letters, in Francis E. Mineka and Dwight N. Lindley (eds.) *Collected Works of John Stuart Mill,* Vols. XIV–XVII: *The Later Letters of John Stuart Mill 1849–1873.* Toronto: University of Toronto Press.

West, Henry R. (2004) *An Introduction to Mill's Utilitarian Ethics.* Cambridge: Cambridge University Press.

Chapter 8

Mill's Theory of Rights

L. W. Sumner

Those who have not read to the end of *Utilitarianism* may be surprised to learn that John Stuart Mill has a theory of rights. After all, the claim that people have rights which must be respected is usually associated with a deontological moral framework, not with the utilitarianism which it was Mill's business to articulate and defend. Furthermore, it is widely known that Jeremy Bentham, Mill's utilitarian predecessor, heaped scorn on the very idea of a moral right. And yet there it is, midway through the final chapter of *Utilitarianism*, the one devoted to the topic of justice, an extended treatment of moral duties and moral rights. These are far from being the best-known passages in the work – that honor must belong to the distinction between higher and lower pleasures or the "proof" of the principle of utility – but for understanding the shape of Mill's moral theory, and its application to concrete moral/political issues, they may be the most important.

The main purpose of this chapter is to outline Mill's views about rights and to show how they are connected to his utilitarianism. But it will be helpful to begin by exploring more carefully why the very idea of a utilitarian theory of rights seems odd. Readers are right to suspect that there is something about utilitarianism as a moral theory and rights as a moral concept which make for an unlikely fit. If this is so, then one question we will need to answer is how Mill thought they could ever be combined.

Rights and Goals

One important part of our moral thinking has to do with the promotion of states of affairs which we deem to be worthwhile or valuable for their own sake: well-being, or autonomy, or virtue, or equality, or whatever. It is this part of our thinking which is well captured by the broad family of consequentialist ethical theories. Basically, our reasoning here takes a cost–benefit form: it counts in favor of a course of action, or a social policy, that it will bring about an intrinsically good state of affairs (a benefit) and counts against it that it will produce an intrinsically bad one (a cost). It is most natural here to think of rankings of options in terms of better and worse, measured by whatever values are taken to be in play. The best – the maximizing – option is then the one which will return the best overall balance of benefits over costs.

On the other hand, we also tend to think that some means that might be used to achieve valuable goals are unjustifiable because they exploit or victimize particular individuals or groups. The natural way of expressing this thought is to say that these parties have rights which constrain or limit the pursuit of social goals, rights which must (at least sometimes) be respected even though a valuable goal would be better promoted by ignoring or infringing them. Rights then function morally as safeguards for the security or integrity of individuals or groups in the face of collective endeavors. It is this part of our moral thinking which is well captured by deontological theories, and rights therefore seem most at home in such theories.

The idea that rights impose constraints on the pursuit of collective goals serves to identify in a preliminary way their moral/political function, and also begins to explain their perennial appeal. But it is not yet sufficient to show how rights are distinctive or unique. Duties and obligations impose similar constraints: if I have an obligation to pay my income tax then that is what I must do even though more good might result from my donating the money to Doctors Without Borders. So what is the particular way in which rights limit our promotion of valuable states of affairs? And what exactly is the relationship between rights and duties? We need to look more closely at the anatomy of rights.

A simple example will serve to get us started. Suppose that you have borrowed my copy of Mill's *Utilitarianism* with the promise to return it by Saturday, and Saturday has arrived. I now have a claim, held against you, that you give me back the book, and you have a duty, owed to me, to do so. My claim (against you) and your duty (to me) are identical: they are the same normative relationship between us, viewed (as it were) from opposite ends. In that relationship I am the subject of the right (the right-holder), you are its object (the duty-bearer), and your returning the book is the content of the right (what I have a claim to have done; what you have a duty to do). In general, A's claim against B that B do X is logically equivalent to B's duty toward A to do X: claims and duties are in this way correlative. Claims are always of the form that something be done: the actions which make up their content must be those of another, never those of the right-holder herself. Since my right against you has the form of a claim, we may call it a *claim-right*. Claim-rights constitute one important class of rights, exemplified primarily by contractual rights (held against assignable parties) and by rights to security of the person (held against everyone in general).

However, not all rights are claim-rights. Another example will make this clear. I own my copy of *Utilitarianism*, which implies (among other things) that I have the right to read it when I want to. This right has the same subject (me) as my claim-right, but a different content and a different object. Its content is once again an action, but this time an action on my part rather than yours (or someone else's): it is a right *to do* rather than a right *to have done*. For this reason my right involves, not a claim (against someone else) but what it is common instead to refer to as a liberty. To say that I have the liberty to read my copy of *Utilitarianism* is to say that I am under no obligation not to read it, or that my reading it is permissible. Actually, it is implicitly to say more than this, since my right to read the book (when I want to) is usually accompanied by my right not to read it (when I don't want to). I therefore have two distinct liberties: to read the book and not to read it. We normally treat these as the two sides of one (complex) liberty: to read it or not, as I choose. In general, A's liberty to do X (or not) is logically equivalent to the absence both of A's duty to do X and A's duty not to do X. Since my right to read my copy of *Utilitarianism* (or not) has the form of a liberty, we may call it a *liberty-right*. Liberty-rights constitute another important class of rights, exemplified primarily by property rights and by rights to various freedoms (of thought, belief, conscience, expression, etc.).

So far we have located a subject and a content for my liberty-right, but not an object. Against whom is this right held? In the case of claim-rights the answer to this question is straightforward: whoever bears the duty which is equivalent to the claim. Because claim-rights specify duties, and because these duties are assigned to particular parties (or to everyone in general), claim-rights enable us easily to locate their objects. But my liberty-right to read my book involves on the face of it no claim (or duty); the liberty in question just consists in the absence of duties on my part. It is therefore not so obviously held *against* anyone. And indeed if we restrict ourselves just to its stipulated content, that is true: it is a right which imposes no duties. However, we know that property rights are typically protected by duties imposed on others: for instance, duties not to interfere with the use or enjoyment of the property in question. By virtue of my property right I have more than just the bare unprotected liberty to read (or not read) my book as I please; this liberty is safeguarded by what H. L. A. Hart has usefully called a "protective perimeter" of duties imposed on others (Hart 1982: 171–3). You therefore (along with everyone else) have the duty not to interfere with my peaceful reading of my book (by stealing it, defacing it, blindfolding me, etc.). We learn therefore the lesson that liberty-rights are not as simple as they seem: they involve a complex bundle of liberties (held by the subject) and duties (imposed on others). The others who bear these duties are the (implicit) objects of the right.

We now have the conceptual resources on hand to see exactly how rights can limit the pursuit of valuable goals. The complex structure of rights reveals two distinct ways in which this can happen. First, by imposing duties on their objects, claim-rights limit the freedom of others to choose the best, or maximizing, option; they must (at least sometimes) do what the claim-right requires even when they would promote the goal better by not doing so. Second, by conferring liberties on their subjects, liberty-rights secure the freedom of right-holders not to choose the best, or maximizing, option; they may (at least sometimes) choose to do what the liberty-right permits even when they would promote the goal better by not doing so. Rights therefore impose constraints on others (who must not promote the best outcome) and allow options to their holders (who need not do so). By these means rights define protected spaces in which individuals are able to pursue their own personal projects or have their personal interests safeguarded, free from the demands of larger collective enterprises. Rights are obstacles put in the way of cost–benefit maximizing.

The qualifiers "at least sometimes" in the preceding paragraph deserve some brief attention. They signal that neither the duties which claim-rights impose on others nor the liberties which liberty-rights confer on their holders need be absolute. And this brings us to a fourth dimension of a right (besides its subject, object, and content), namely its strength. The strength of a right is its level of resistance to rival normative considerations, such as the promotion of worthwhile goals. A right will insulate its holder to some extent against the necessity of taking these considerations into account, but it will also typically have a threshold above which they dominate or override the right. Should it turn out, for instance, that you need my copy of *Utilitarianism* in order to check a citation, without which your dissertation may fail and your career may be ruined, then your duty to return it on time (and my claim that it be returned) may be overridden, even if I want the book back. Likewise, the same degree of urgency may override my liberty-right to use the book when I please. Rights raise thresholds against the pursuit of valuable goals but these thresholds are seldom insurmountable. Some particularly important rights (against torture, perhaps, or slavery, or genocide) may be absolute, but most are not.

With all this in hand, let us return to Mill. It is clear from the earlier chapters of *Utilitarianism* that Mill believed that one particular state of affairs is intrinsically valuable: "The utilitarian doctrine is, that happiness is desirable, and the only thing desirable, as an end; all other things being only desirable as means to that end" (Mill 1861, reprinted as Part II of this volume, Ch. IV, para. 2. Citations will be simply to chapter by roman numeral and paragraph by arabic numeral.). Furthermore, he linked the moral quality of actions to the promotion of this end:

> The creed which accepts as the foundation of morals, Utility, or the Greatest Happiness Principle, holds that actions are right in proportion as they tend to promote happiness, wrong as they tend to promote the reverse of happiness. (II, 2)

Mill therefore seems to treat maximizing the balance of happiness over unhappiness (or, since he was a hedonist about happiness, pleasure over pain) as the justifying goal of action. The right thing to do is always whatever will best promote that goal.

However, it is equally clear from Chapter V of *Utilitarianism* that Mill had in mind something like the conception of rights which was sketched above. In the course of his analysis of the concept of justice, Mill first links it with the notion of duty or obligation, understood in the following way:

> It is part of the notion of Duty in every one of its forms, that a person may right-fully be compelled to fulfil it. Duty is a thing which may be *exacted* from a person, as one exacts a debt. (V, 14)

Mill therefore clearly had the concept of duty as a normative (legal or moral) requirement. However, he thought that this concept was too general in its appli-cation to pick out the particular class of duties of justice. For this purpose we need to focus on "those duties in virtue of which a correlative *right* resides in some person or persons." Mill then uses this concept of a right to complete his analy-sis of justice:

> It seems to me that this feature in the case – a right in some person, correlative to the moral obligation – constitutes the specific difference between justice, and gen-erosity or beneficence. Justice implies something which it is not only right to do, and wrong not to do, but which some individual person can claim from us as his moral right. (V, 15)

(The notion of a right which Mill is working with here is what we earlier identi-fied as a claim-right, but it will be obvious later that he also had the notion of a liberty-right.)

Having the concept of a right is one thing; taking rights seriously within the framework of one's moral theory another. However, it is clear that Mill also passes this test. Later in Chapter V Mill defends the importance of justice, and therefore of the rights which constitute it:

> justice is a name for certain moral requirements, which regarded collectively, stand higher in the scale of social utility, and are therefore of more paramount obligation, than any others. (V, 37)

Mill therefore seems to endorse both strands of our moral thinking: both the pro-motion of a valuable social goal (the greatest happiness) and respect for rights. From the former perspective he seems committed to saying that an action is right just in case it is optimal. From the latter perspective he seems committed to saying that we have duties (of justice) to respect rights, even on occasions when doing so will not be optimal. Since this appears to be a contradiction, we must ask how Mill can reconcile these two commitments. How can a utilitarian have a theory of rights?

Rules, Rights, and Utility

In answering this question it is important to distinguish two distinct stages in Mill's theory of rights: his analysis of the concept of a moral right and his account of how such rights are to be justified. As we shall see, his utilitarianism comes into play at the second stage but not at the first. The concept of a moral right which Mill articulates is entirely neutral as far as a substantive ethical theory is concerned; it can as easily be accepted by a deontologist as a utilitarian. We therefore begin with it.

Because Mill's project in *Utilitarianism* is to construct and defend an ethical framework, he needs to make sense of the idea, not just of a right in general, but of a *moral* right in particular. Bentham's objections were specifically to this idea; he had no difficulty with the notion of a legal right, which could be grounded in a system of positive law, but he thought that moral rights were suspect precisely because they lacked this grounding. So one thing Mill is trying to explain in Chapter V is how rights could be moral – how there could be such things as moral rights. As noted above, he comes to the concept of a right via two other concepts: those of duty and justice. Mill thought that the concept of duty could serve to demarcate the distinctive realm of morality (the right), as opposed to that of expediency (the good or admirable), because of its analytic connection with the idea of a sanction. "For the truth is," Mill tells us,

> that the idea of penal sanction, which is the essence of law, enters not only into the conception of injustice, but into that of any kind of wrong. We do not call anything wrong, unless we mean to imply that a person ought to be punished in some way or other for doing it; if not by law, by the opinion of his fellow creatures; if not by opinion, by the reproaches of his own conscience. (V, 14)

A wrong, for Mill, is a violation of a duty or obligation. It is therefore the connection between wrongs and sanctions that leads Mill to say, as noted above, that "It is a part of the notion of duty in every one of its forms, that a person may rightfully be compelled to fulfil it" (V, 14). The compulsion takes the form of the application, or threat, of a sanction.

The model which Mill clearly has in mind here is that of a legal duty. Paradigmatic legal duties are those imposed by a system of laws backed by the threat of punishment. However, the range of sanctions which Mill recognized included not only formal legal penalties but also such informal reactions as negative public opinion. He therefore had the idea of duties imposed by rules other than legal ones, such as the rules of a social morality whose "enforcement" might take the form of disapproval, blame, or ostracism. Let us call any rule system in force within a given social group *conventional*; a legal system is then but one particular form of conventional rule system, distinguished by such features as compulsory jurisdiction and a range of particularly severe penalties for infractions. It is this broader concept of a conventional duty – a duty imposed by a conventional rule system – which Mill links to that of a sanction (whether formal or informal).

Thus far Mill has identified the concept of a duty, but not a moral duty. It is obvious that moral duties are not a particular species of conventional duties: it is no contradiction to say that we have a moral duty to do something though, as it happens, no conventional rule system, including the conventional morality currently in place, imposes it on us. It is precisely this independence of the idea of a moral duty from actually existing rule systems that allows us to use it to critique such systems. So a further step is needed in order to get Mill to the concept of a moral duty. It is this step which Mill takes when he says that

> we do not call anything wrong [that is, a violation of duty], unless we mean to imply that a person *ought* to be punished in some way or other for doing it. (V, 14; emphasis added)

So in addition to the notion of a sanction being applied following the breach of a conventional duty we now have the further idea that this ought to happen, i.e., that the application would be *justified*. Since Mill is seeking the concept of a moral right, it is natural to think that the justification in question must be a moral one. Putting all the pieces together, we get something like the following picture. The existence of a conventional duty depends on the existence of the conventional rules (and sanctions) which impose the duty. By contrast, the existence of a moral duty depends on there being a moral justification for the existence of such rules (and sanctions). Moral duties are not identical to conventional duties, but they are identical to those conventional duties whose existence is morally justified.

Mill's account thus seems able to explain what makes a duty a moral duty. The next step is to extend it to the case of moral rights. Recall that Mill's concern, in Chapter V of *Utilitarianism*, is not with the entire domain of morality (which he regarded as demarcated by the concept of a moral duty) but with the particular sub-domain of justice. Mill locates this sub-domain by first partitioning duties into two sets:

> duties of perfect obligation are those duties in virtue of which a correlative *right* resides in some person or persons; duties of imperfect obligation are those moral obligations which do not give birth to any right. (V, 15)

He then identifies the realm of justice with the realm of perfect obligations, and thus rights:

> It seems to me that this feature in the case – a right in some person, correlative to the moral obligation – constitutes the specific difference between justice, and generosity or beneficence. Justice implies something which it is not only right to do, and wrong not to do, but which some individual person can claim from us as his moral right. (V, 15)

Mill's analysis has therefore led him from the concept of a moral duty through the concept of justice to that of a moral right. His resultant account of this last concept takes the following form:

> When we call anything a person's right, we mean that he has a valid claim on society to protect him in the possession of it, either by the force of law, or by that of education and opinion. (V, 24)

There are in this account three distinct elements: (1) a conventional right, (2) some form of sanction which protects the right, and (3) having a valid claim to this protection. The third element adds the by now familiar requirement that the possession of the conventional right be morally justified. If we pull all the pieces together the result is a concept of a moral right which mirrors Mill's concept of a moral duty: I have a moral right just in case my possession of the corresponding conventional right is, or would be, morally justified.

It is worth emphasizing again at this point that Mill's account of the nature of moral rights is a piece of conceptual analysis and is therefore entirely independent of his substantive ethical theory. Mill himself clearly distinguished between his conceptual and substantive commitments:

> To have a right, then, is, I conceive, to have something which society ought to defend me in the possession of. If the objector goes on to ask why it ought, I can give him no other reason than general utility. (V, 25)

Unsurprisingly, then, the justification for rights which Mill himself favors is utilitarian. More precisely, he favors a utilitarian justification for the social policy of establishing and enforcing some set of conventional rights. Establishing the rights will involve incorporating them into a conventional rule system, whether this be a legal system or a system of conventional morality. Enforcing them will require backing the rules with sanctions, whether formal (legal penalties) or informal (social disapproval). Besides these external sanctions, Mill also recognizes the role of the internal sanctions of conscience, operating through such mechanisms as shame and guilt. A justification of rights is therefore a justification of an entire social system that acknowledges and protects those rights. For Mill, what appeal could there be in order to justify such a system other than to utility?

Mill's primary aim in the final chapter of *Utilitarianism* is to make sense of the idea of justice, and of rights, within the framework of his utilitarianism. As such, he does not provide an extensive account in this setting of the kinds of rights which he regards as justifiable on grounds of utility. However, he does close the chapter with a sketch of what he has in mind. "Justice," he tells us,

> is a name for certain classes of moral rules, which concern the essentials of human well-being more nearly, and are therefore of more absolute obligation, than any other

rules for the guidance of life; and the notion which we have found to be of the essence
of the idea of justice, that of a right residing in an individual, implies and testifies to
this more binding obligation. (V, 32)

What this suggests, then, is that a justifiable system of rights would protect "the
essentials of human well-being." But what are these essentials? What Mill has
chiefly in mind are rights against being harmed by others, where he interprets
harm to include not just the infliction of physical injury but also interference with
personal freedom and disappointment of legitimate expectations. We should therefore expect Mill's roster of moral rights to include most of the standard items in
rights manifestos, especially rights to life, liberty, and security of the person, as
well as contractual and property rights.

Mill's claim, therefore, is that a society will do a better job of protecting the
well-being of its citizens – a better job of maximizing general happiness – if it puts
in place a system of conventional rights, including legal rights, which are backed
by sanctions. This account provides part of the answer to the question how a utilitarian can also take rights seriously. But it is only part of the answer, since it operates entirely on the societal level. If Mill's claim is correct (and it is surely plausible)
then it explains why a society dedicated to promoting general utility should take
rights seriously by embedding them in such instruments as private, public, and
constitutional law. It also explains why respect for rights should be part of that
society's conventional morality, thus why a system of moral education should
include internalizing rules which forbid violating the rights of others. But it does
not explain why individuals should follow those rules, and respect those rights,
when doing so will produce less utility than breaking the rules and violating the
rights. We must remind ourselves here of the tension, indeed apparent contradiction, between commitment to a utilitarian goal and respect for rights. Mill, we are
supposing, thinks that the best – indeed the right – thing to do is whatever will
maximize happiness. Rights, however, are obstacles to maximizing happiness, since
they either require or permit us to act in non-maximizing ways. So the remaining
question for Mill is: why should individuals committed to the utilitarian goal
respect the rights of others when doing so will disserve that very goal?

Answering this question will take us, at least briefly, beyond the confines of
Mill's theory of rights into his general theory of the right. So far I have been
assuming that this theory is act-utilitarian in structure: that is, whether an action
is right or wrong depends solely on its consequences, and specifically on its utility.
It is this act-utilitarian theory of the right which appears to be inconsistent with
a theory of rights, since it appears to require individuals to choose the best (maximizing) course of action even if that involves violating rights. One way out of this
dilemma, of course, would be to reject the act-utilitarian interpretation of Mill's
theory of the right. Perhaps, for instance, Mill is some kind of rule-utilitarian, in
which case whether an action is right or wrong would depend not on its utility
but on the utility of the rule which requires it. If, as we are supposing, rules which

protect rights have great utility, this would provide a way of rescuing Mill's consistency, since actions in conformity with those rules would be right even if they
were not themselves maximizing. Some commentators have indeed suggested that
Mill is better read as a rule- than an act-utilitarian. (See, for instance, Urmson
1953.) But I believe that this interpretation is mistaken, and in any case there are
well-known objections to most of the familiar forms of rule-utilitarianism. There
must be a better way than this of reconciling Mill's utilitarianism with his commitment to rights.

The rule-utilitarian reading of Mill is based primarily on some things that he
says, in Chapter II of *Utilitarianism*, about the role of "secondary principles" in
our moral thinking. Mill is there responding to a practical objection to his theory
of the right: "that there is not time, previous to action, for calculating and weighing the effects of any line of conduct on the general happiness" (II, 24). To this
objection Mill scornfully replies that "there has been ample time, namely the whole
past duration of the human species" to learn by experience "the tendencies of
actions; on which experience all the prudence, as well as all the morality of life, is
dependent." These "tendencies" are codified in moral rules which are "taught to
the young, and enforced by law and opinion." Mill then continues:

> The corollaries from the principle of utility, like the precepts of every practical art,
> admit of indefinite improvement, and, in a progressive state of the human mind, their
> improvement is perpetually going on. But to consider the rules of morality as improv-
> able, is one thing; to pass over the intermediate generalizations entirely, and endeav-
> our to test each individual action directly by the first principle, is another. It is a
> strange notion that the acknowledgement of a first principle is inconsistent with the
> admission of secondary ones . . . The proposition that happiness is the end and aim
> of morality, does not mean that no road ought to be laid down to that goal, or that
> persons going thither should not be advised to take one direction rather than another
> . . . Whatever we adopt as the fundamental principle of morality, we require sub-
> ordinate principles to apply it by . . . (II, 24)

Mill therefore seems to think that ordinarily in our moral deliberations about
what to do we should be guided by the appropriate rule or "secondary principle"
– the one conformity to which experience has shown to be utility-maximizing –
rather than by a case-by-case calculation of utilities. However, he does acknowledge two circumstances in which reference back to the "first principle" is called
for: (1) when we appear to be confronted with an exception to the rule and (2)
when two or more rules conflict. It is in these cases – but only in these – that we
must decide what to do on the basis of a comparison of the utilities of the options
available to us. Now it is easy to see why these passages have led some to suppose
that Mill is a rule-, rather than an act-, utilitarian; after all, he does suggest that
in our moral decision-making we should largely rely on the utility of rules rather
than that of particular actions. However, the rule-utilitarian reading makes little
sense of the cases in which Mill endorses just such a reference to the utilities of

actions. For this reason (among others) I think that Mill had some other role for rules in mind.

To get at this role we need to make a distinction between two functions which a moral principle, or a moral theory, might have. On the one hand, it might state a *criterion* of the right: a set of necessary and sufficient conditions for an action (or a policy, or whatever) to be right. The principle of utility can be construed in this way, i.e., as stipulating that an action is right just in case it will maximize utility. Call this an *objective* principle (or theory) of the right. On the other hand, a principle might provide a *decision procedure* to be used in our moral deliberation: a standard or guideline adherence to which will lead us to do what is right. The principle of utility can also be construed in this way, i.e., as suggesting that on particular occasions of moral choice agents should compare the utilities of the actions available to them and choose the best (maximizing) alternative. Call this a *subjective* principle (or theory) of the right. The force of this distinction is that an objective criterion may or may not support the use of that very same principle as a subjective decision procedure. If our objective principle is act-utilitarian then it will require us to adopt whatever decision procedure will lead us most reliably to satisfy that principle. That decision procedure might just tell agents to apply the objective criterion on every occasion, i.e., always to decide on the basis of a calculation of utilities. But it also might not: agents might do better, in terms of the objective criterion, to adopt some other decision procedure, for instance, one that incorporates some degree of adherence to moral rules. We may call a theory which employs the same principle both as criterion and as decision procedure a *direct* theory (since it tells agents just to apply the criterion directly in each particular case). Conversely, a theory which recommends some other decision procedure as a means of satisfying the criterion is an *indirect* theory (since it tells agents to satisfy the criterion by not directly applying it).

I have suggested above that Mill's objective theory of the right is act-utilitarian, rather than rule-utilitarian, in character. However, Mill's comments on the role of "secondary principles" strongly suggest that he rejected the idea that, at least on most occasions, agents should simply apply the act-utilitarian criterion directly. His reasons for rejecting this option appeal to the costliness of the direct procedure (in terms of time expenditure), the fallibility of moral agents, and their tendency toward self-preference. Instead, he seems to support an indirect strategy for utility maximization which requires adherence to (utility-maximizing) rules except in those cases where they either conflict or admit of exceptions. This complex strategy thus consists of a set of moral rules with thresholds above which direct appeal to utility is called for. The justification for this indirect decision procedure is itself utilitarian: in the long run its adoption will have better consequences than would a direct procedure. However, there is no guarantee that it will lead agents to do the best – i.e., the right – thing on every occasion. On the contrary, it will sometimes require agents to conform to a rule even when defection would be utility-maximizing. And it will do this because, in the long run, less utility will be produced by deciding on every occasion whether to conform to the rule or defect.

If this picture of Mill's thought is correct, as I think it is, then we have the resources to explain how he can simultaneously endorse an act utilitarian theory of the right and commitment to a strong set of moral rights. His act-utilitarianism is objective, but not subjective. The decision procedure he favors, as a means of satisfying his own act utilitarian goal, requires commitment to a set of internalized moral rules which will be adhered to in all non-exceptional circumstances. Among these rules we should expect pride of place to be given to those "which concern the essentials of human well-being more nearly, and are therefore of more absolute obligation, than any other rules for the guidance of life." But these are precisely the rules of justice which require respect for rights. Mill therefore expects us to cultivate dispositions which will lead us to respect rights even when doing so will lead to utility losses on particular occasions, because of the utility gains which such dispositions will yield over the long run.

Rights and Liberty

The foregoing lays out in a very general and abstract way a solution to the seeming incompatibility of Mill's act-utilitarianism and his endorsement of moral rights. However, it might be useful at this point to see how all of this might play out in a more concrete way. Although Mill sets out his general theory of rights and their justification in the final chapter of *Utilitarianism*, his most sustained defence of a particular set of rights takes place in a different, and equally famous, work: the essay *On Liberty*. The aim of that essay is to find a general principle which will define the limits of social interference with the activities of individuals or, what comes to the same thing, the limits of individual liberty of action. The kinds of social interference Mill has in mind include not only the formal mechanisms available to the state through its legal system, but also the more informal ways in which dissident minorities can be oppressed or silenced by dominant social groups – what Mill calls "the tyranny of the majority." The principle of liberty which he defends is well known:

> the only purpose for which power can be rightfully exercised over any member of a civilized community, against his will, is to prevent harm to others. His own good, either physical or moral, is not a sufficient warrant. (1859: 223)

Because this principle defines the limits of individual liberty in terms of harm to others, it has come to be known as the *harm principle*. The harm principle states that where harm to others is involved, individuals may rightfully be subject to coercion or control, while in their purely personal conduct, where no such harm is involved, their liberty must be protected.

It should be clear that the function of the harm principle is to confer on individuals a very extensive liberty-right: basically, the right to do anything they please as long as their conduct will not cause harm to others. As such, it imposes on others (including the state) the duty not to interfere coercively in an agent's purely self-regarding conduct. The sphere of liberty protected by the principle includes two classes of actions: those which cause harm, but only to the agent herself, and those which cause no harm to anyone. The duty of non-interference which it imposes therefore precludes two justifications for limiting individual liberty: paternalism (restraints on actions harmful only to self) and moralism (restraints on harmless actions on the ground that they are immoral).

One striking feature of Mill's harm principle, and of the liberty-right which it confers, is its absolutism. At the beginning of the paragraph in *On Liberty* where he introduces the principle, Mill says that it is to "govern absolutely the dealings of society with the individual in the way of compulsion and control." Then, toward the end of the same paragraph, Mill reasserts its stringency: "in the part [of his conduct] which merely concerns himself, [the individual's] independence is, of right, absolute." Mill clearly intends the limits the principle sets to social interference to trump all competing arguments in favor of such interference. Once it has been determined, therefore, that someone's conduct belongs to the personal part of her life, then there can be no further question as to whether she should be at liberty to engage in it. In particular, whether she has a right to such liberty is not to be decided by any calculation of the costs and benefits of social interference in that particular instance. The harm principle states that if the conduct is personal then it is protected from interference – period.

In a perfectly ordinary sense, then, Mill offers individuals a principled defence of liberty in their personal lives, one which excludes case-by-case utilitarian calculation. At the same time, however, the justification Mill offers for the harm principle itself is utilitarian:

> It is proper to state that I forego any advantage which could be derived to my argument from the idea of abstract right, as a thing independent of utility. I regard utility as the ultimate appeal on all ethical questions; but it must be utility in the largest sense, grounded on the permanent interests of man as a progressive being. (1859: 224)

The argument *to* the harm principle (from Mill's general ethical theory) is therefore utilitarian, while arguments *from* that principle (to particular cases) are deontological. Mill defends a policy of respecting an absolute right to liberty in the personal sphere of life on the basis of a cost–benefit calculation: such a policy will have better consequences than any alternative, including the alternative of determining, by means of a cost–benefit calculation, whether to respect individual liberty on each particular occasion. He therefore offers a utilitarian argument for excluding further utilitarian arguments about whether to interfere in people's per-

sonal lives. An absolute right to liberty – one which trumps social utility – is justified on the ground of social utility. As far as I am aware, Mill never claimed that
violation of such a right would be misguided or counterproductive in every
instance. Such a claim would in any case be very implausible. It is not implausible (though it may be false) that the best policy is to act as though such a violation is always wrong, on the ground that things will turn out for the best that way
in the long run. One of the implications of defending such a policy is that it will
sometimes lead to mistakes: it will prohibit interference in some cases in which it
would have been the optimal course of action. But Mill's argument must be that
the alternative policy of deciding whether to interfere on the basis of a case-by-
case calculation of consequences will in the long run have worse consequences.

Mill's defence of his principle of liberty therefore nicely exemplifies the structure of an indirect utilitarian justification of rights. Connecting the argument of
On Liberty in this way to the general theory of rights articulated in *Utilitarianism* has the added benefit of laying to rest doubts which many of Mill's commentators have expressed about the consistency of the two works. (See, for
instance, Ten 1980.) Mill was a great moral and political philosopher and, where
one is available, we should always prefer an interpretation of his thought which
shows that it is free of contradictions.

See also 5: MILL'S THEORY OF MORALLY CORRECT ACTION; 6: MILL'S THEORY
OF SANCTIONS.

References

Hart, H. L. A. (1982) *Essays on Bentham: Studies in Jurisprudence and Political Theory*.
  Oxford: Clarendon Press.
Mill, John Stuart (1861) *Utilitarianism*, in J. M. Robson (ed.) *Collected Works of John
  Stuart Mill*, Vol. X: *Essays on Ethics, Religion, and Society* (pp. 203–59). Toronto:
  University of Toronto Press, 1969. (Reprinted as Part II of this volume; citations
  are to chapter by roman numeral and to paragraph by arabic numeral.)
——(1859) *On Liberty*, in J. M. Robson (ed.) *Collected Works of John Stuart Mill*, Vol.
  XVIII: *Essays on Politics and Society* (pp. 213–310). Toronto: University of Toronto Press,
  1977.
Ten, C. L. (1980) *Mill on Liberty*. Oxford: Clarendon Press.
Urmson, J. O. (1953) "The interpretation of the moral philosophy of J. S. Mill,"
  Philosophical Quarterly 3, pp. 33–9.

Further reading

Berger, F. R. (1979) "John Stuart Mill on justice and fairness," in W. E. Cooper, K. Nielsen,
  and S. C. Patten (eds.) *New Essays on John Stuart Mill and Utilitarianism* (pp. 115–36).
  Guelph: Canadian Association for Publishing in Philosophy.

Dryer, D. P. (1979) "Justice, liberty, and the principle of utility in Mill," in W. E. Cooper, K. Nielsen, and S. C. Patten (eds.) *New Essays on John Stuart Mill and Utilitarianism* (pp. 63–73). Guelph: Canadian Association for Publishing in Philosophy.

Dworkin, R. (1977) *Taking Rights Seriously*. Cambridge, MA: Harvard University Press.

Lyons, D. (1977) "Human rights and the general welfare," *Philosophy and Public Affairs* 6, pp. 113–29.

Railton, P. (1984) "Alienation, consequentialism, and the demands of morality," *Philosophy and Public Affairs* 13, pp. 134–71.

Sumner, L. W. (1979) "The good and the right," in W. E. Cooper, K. Nielsen, and S. C. Patten (eds.) *New Essays on John Stuart Mill and Utilitarianism* (pp. 99–114). Guelph: Canadian Association for Publishing in Philosophy.

——(1987) *The Moral Foundation of Rights*. Oxford: Clarendon Press.

——(2004) *The Hateful and the Obscene: Studies in the Limits of Free Expression*. Toronto: University of Toronto Press.

Wellman, C. (1985) *A Theory of Rights: Persons under Laws, Institutions, and Morals*. Totowa, NJ: Rowman & Allanheld.

Part IV

Influence and Contemporary Issues

Chapter 9

Contemporary Criticisms of Utilitarianism: a Response

William H. Shaw

Introduction

Utilitarianism represents an old and distinguished tradition in moral philosophy, the influence of which extends to law, economics, public policy, and other realms, and is evident in much of our everyday moral thinking. Beginning with Bentham and continuing down to the present day, many able philosophers have expounded, defended, and enriched the utilitarian theory – Mill, of course, being perhaps the most famous of these. Today the utilitarian tradition is as alive as ever, and the theory is at the center of a number of contemporary debates in ethics, with critical discussions of it continuing to fill the leading professional journals.

In my judgment, utilitarianism offers the most promising approach to normative ethics, one that is coherent, fruitful, and more appealing morally and philosophically than any rival theory. But ethics is a rich and contested field, and no moral theory can claim to have offered considerations compelling enough to have won a consensus in its favor among philosophers. Indeed, serious objections have been lodged against all normative theories. This is particularly true of utilitarianism, which because of its historical importance and present influence has attracted more than its share of critical attention. Indeed, many contemporary philosophers believe that utilitarianism offers a profoundly flawed view of right and wrong. If utilitarianism is to stand as a credible theory, let alone prove itself to be more satisfactory than alterative ethical approaches, then it must rebut these objections and overcome the reservations of its critics.

In this essay, I endeavor to defend utilitarianism against the most significant and frequently voiced objections to it. To deal with all possible opposition to the theory, indeed, even to disarm completely the main criticisms is too large a task for a single essay. Still, I aim to show that the most common and influential objections are far from fatal and, indeed, often seriously misguided. In doing so, I hope also to display the rich and frequently subtle normative resources that utilitarianism has at its command, thereby enhancing one's appreciation of its practical, moral, and theoretical viability. But what I have to say falls short of a complete brief for utilitarianism because I do not elaborate the positive case for it or critique rival ethical theories. And I focus most of my attention on defending utilitarianism's consequentialist orientation to ethics as opposed to its welfarist theory of value (these terms are explained in the next section).

Understanding Utilitarianism

As contemporary moral theorists interpret it, utilitarianism has two distinct philosophical components. The first of these is *welfarism*. This is the value thesis that individual welfare or well-being is all that ultimately matters; it is the sole good, the only thing that is intrinsically valuable or valuable for its own sake. Anything else that we think of as good for people – friendship, say, or individual freedom – is good only because, and to the extent that, it contributes to their well-being. (Like other early utilitarians, Bentham and Mill equated happiness with pleasure and unhappiness with pain, and they were concerned with happiness only because they identified it with well-being or what is good for people. Today utilitarians agree that happiness is not the only, and perhaps not the best, way to understand well-being. For convenience, however, I shall go on using "happiness," "well-being," and "welfare" interchangeably, but what really matters for utilitarianism is well-being whether or not one understands it in terms of happiness.)

Utilitarianism holds that a state of affairs is good or bad to some degree (and better or worse than some other state of affairs) only in virtue of the well-being of the lives of particular individuals, and it goes on to affirm that each person's well-being is equally valuable, that his happiness or unhappiness, her pleasure or pain, carries the same weight as that of any other person. Thus, total net happiness is simply the sum of everyone's happiness or unhappiness, with more happiness here counterbalancing less happiness there. Underlying this, of course, is the assumption that in principle we can compare people's different levels of well-being. But one shouldn't interpret this assumption too rigorously. Utilitarians have always granted that interpersonal comparisons of welfare are difficult, and they can even concede that some issues of comparison and addition may be irresolvable in principle. Utilitarians need believe only that we can rank many states of affairs as better or worse.

The second philosophical component of utilitarianism is its consequentialist or teleological (goal-oriented) approach to right and wrong. *Consequentialism* is the thesis that the rightness or wrongness of actions is a function of their consequences or, more precisely, that our actions are right or wrong because, and only because, of the goodness or badness of their consequences. For utilitarians and other consequentialists it is not an action's intrinsic nature or whether it is an instance of a certain permitted or forbidden type of act (for example, the keeping of a promise or the telling of a lie) that determines its rightness or wrongness, but rather its specific consequences in a particular situation. Utilitarianism, however, is not only a consequentialist theory. It is also a maximizing doctrine because it requires us always to act so as to bring about as much well-being as possible.

Taken together, then, utilitarianism's consequentialism and its welfarist value theory lead it to affirm the following basic moral principle:

> An action is right if and only if it brings about at least as much net happiness as any other action the agent could have performed; otherwise it is wrong.

The Most Common Criticism of Utilitarianism

We can never know for certain all the consequences of the things we do, still less the future results of every possible action that we might have performed at any given time. The fact that the causal ramifications of actions extend indefinitely into the future compounds this problem, seeming to thwart any claim to know what course of conduct is best. Talking in terms of probabilities does not eliminate this problem because we can rarely do more than guess at comparative likelihoods, and in any case we are always liable to overlook some possible outcomes and fail to consider some alternative courses of action. Furthermore, as previously noted, comparing people's levels of well-being is tricky and imprecise at best, and when many people are involved, the matter may seem hopelessly complex. Finally, even if we had all the relevant information and could perform the necessary calculations, there would rarely be time to do so before we had to act. Critics of utilitarianism frequently seize on these facts to argue that utilitarianism is unusable as a guide to action. This is the most common criticism of utilitarianism.

Utilitarians have several pertinent responses. First, they can concede the above points and yet argue that they do not impugn the utilitarian goal of maximizing well-being. The correctness of that goal is not undermined by shortfalls in our knowledge of how best to attain it. Well-being is still what we should aim at, however difficult it may be to see the best way to bring it about.

Second, utilitarians can point out that human beings are already well acquainted with the nature and typical causes of happiness and unhappiness. On the basis of thousands of years of collective experience, we understand many of the sources of suffering and satisfaction, and we know various things that conduce to people's lives going well and various things that thwart their flourishing. In line with this point, Mill's *Utilitarianism* ridicules people who

> talk . . . as if, at the moment when some man feels tempted to meddle with the property or life of another, he had to begin considering for the first time whether murder and theft are injurious to human happiness . . . It is truly a whimsical supposition that,

> if mankind were agreed in considering utility to be the test of morality, they would remain without any agreement as to what *is* useful . . . There is no difficulty in proving any ethical standard whatever to work ill if we suppose universal idiocy to be conjoined with it. (Mill 1861, reprinted as Part II of this volume, Ch. II, para. 24. Subsequent citations are simply by roman numeral for chapter and arabic numeral for paragraph.)

Our knowledge of the future is far from certain, and we can, it seems, measure and compare people's happiness only coarsely. However, we are not altogether in the dark about which kinds of action tend to promote human well-being and which kinds do not, and that knowledge will frequently suffice to justify our acting one way rather than another.

Mill's point also answers the complaint that "there is not time, previous to action, for calculating and weighing the effects of any line of conduct on the general happiness" (II, 24). In ordinary circumstances we can and should follow certain well-established rules or guidelines that can generally be relied upon to produce the best results. We can, for example, make it a practice to tell the truth and keep our promises, rather than try to calculate possible pleasures and pains in every routine case, because we know that in general telling the truth and keeping promises result in more happiness than lying and breaking promises. In this vein, Mill emphasized the necessity of "intermediate generalizations" or "corollaries from the principle of utility":

> To inform a traveler respecting the place of his ultimate destination is not to forbid the use of landmarks and direction-posts on the way. The proposition that happiness is the end and aim of morality does not mean that no road ought to be laid down to that goal . . . Whatever we adopt as the fundamental principle of morality, we require subordinate principles to apply it by. (II, 24)

Besides answering the no-time-to-calculate criticism, relying on "subordinate principles" alleviates another problem. Conscientious agents can make mistakes in their calculations, and bias can infect the reasoning of even a sincere utilitarian, especially when his or her own interests are at stake. In normal circumstances, however, one is less likely to err and more likely to promote happiness by sticking to certain settled guidelines than by trying to calculate from scratch the consequences of various courses of action.

A Deeper Objection: Utilitarianism Requires Immoral Conduct

Even if utilitarianism surmounts these practical objections, its critics identify a deeper and more profound reason for rejecting the theory: namely, that it sometimes requires us to do immoral things.

According to the utilitarian principle, rightness and wrongness turn on the specific, comparative consequences of the various courses of action available to the agent. Without knowing something about the particular situation in which the agent must act, we cannot judge ahead of time whether acting a certain way will be right or wrong. We cannot say absolutely or on the basis of some sort of a priori reasoning that actions of a certain type are always right or always wrong. Utilitarians see this flexibility as a strong point of their normative standard, but their critics view it as a fatal flaw: the utilitarian goal of maximizing well-being, they argue, can sometimes necessitate the agent's acting immorally. The critics concede that it generally conduces to total well-being for people to tell the truth, keep their promises, and refrain from killing or injuring other people, from damaging their property, or from violating their rights. But there can be exceptions, and in unusual circumstances, promoting overall welfare might call for the agent to do something we normally consider quite wrong.

For this reason, the critics believe that we must repudiate utilitarianism. To make their case, they often elaborate various imaginary scenarios or "counterexamples" in which circumstances conspire to require a welfare-maximizing agent to behave in some appalling way – for example, by killing an innocent person, torturing a young child, framing a suspect for a crime he did not commit, or supporting slavery or some other system of extreme social and economic inequalities. Thus the critics might ask us to imagine an old and miserably depressed tramp, whose future will be one of continued unhappiness, and who has no family or friends. If it can be done painlessly and without anyone noticing, and assuming that the killer would enjoy doing it or that he or others would benefit from the tramp's death in some way, then murdering the tramp would appear to be justified on utilitarian grounds. Yet surely, the critics argue, killing him would be foul and wicked, and because utilitarianism would condone it, one must reject the theory.

The Utilitarian Response

Utilitarians begin their reply to this sort of attack by arguing that their theory does not mandate the conduct the critic says it does. They challenge the facts imagined in these cases, arguing that it is preposterous to suppose that killing or torturing an innocent person, for example, could possibly be the single most effective thing one could do to promote long-term social well-being. Is there really absolutely nothing else the agent could do that would have better results? The more dreadful the action or policy the critic envisions, the less believable it becomes that carrying it out would bring about more good than anything else one could do. Consider the allegation that a slave system might somehow maximize collective welfare and that therefore utilitarians would be obliged, wrongly, to support it. Given all that we know about human history, psychology, and social dynamics, how could it possibly promote "utility in the largest sense, grounded in the permanent interests of man as a progressive being" (Mill 1978: 10) for society to adopt slavery? Slaves inevitably suffer from their lot and chafe against their chains, and they can be terrorized by the threat of future punishment in a way that no animal can. Moreover, even otherwise decent people tend to exploit those over whom they have absolute power. If we keep in mind real people and the ways in which the world really works, it becomes utterly fantastic to suppose that slavery might promote the long-term collective well-being of humanity better than any alternative way of organizing society.

Assume, however, that the critic refuses to allow the utilitarian to challenge the hypothesized facts of the example. He or she simply insists that the facts are as stipulated and that somehow or other conduct or policies we normally consider morally repugnant really would maximize total welfare. In response, of course, utilitarians must acknowledge that their principle entails that it is right to perform that action, whatever it is, that produces the most good overall. But they deny that the imagined conflict with ordinary morality provides a compelling reason for rejecting utilitarianism.

Suppose, first, that in order to offer a plausible scenario, the critic asks us to imagine that it would maximize welfare to perform an action that, although normally considered wrongful, is not absolutely horrific: lying to an acquaintance, perhaps, or breaking a casual promise, or hurting a small child. In these cases, the utilitarian will point out that, assuming the stakes are high enough – perhaps twisting the arm of a hysterical young girl is really the only way to make her quickly tell us where a terrorist, whom she has mistakenly befriended, is hiding – then it's doubtful that ordinary, commonsense morality would condemn the action. Everyday morality is not absolutist; it recognizes that unusual circumstances can sometimes justify breaking the ordinary moral rules, that in rare cases it really can be right, all things considered, to tell a lie, break a promise, or cause an innocent person pain.

To this, however, the critic is likely to respond that although commonsense morality permits us to override its rules when the benefits of doing so are great, it does not license us merely to obtain only a small increase in overall welfare – 1001 units of benefit from breaking a promise, say, as opposed to 1000 units from keeping it. (Ross 1930: 35; Hooker 2000: 145–6). It's doubtful, of course, that one can give meaningful content to the hypothesis that breaking a promise produces one-tenth of a percent more good than keeping it, and even if the goodness of states of affairs could be ranked as exactly as this, no one could claim to know these rankings with the imagined degree of precision. Nevertheless, suppose that in the long run and all things considered (including the effect on one's reputation, the willingness of others to trust one, and potential damage to the general practice of promising) slightly more good would come from breaking a promise than from keeping it and that the agent knows this for a fact. The critics believe that this conflicts with our ordinary moral ideas, but when one colors in some realistic details – skipping my promised lunch with Gretchen when my day is extremely busy and I have arranged for her best friend Alice to show up at the restaurant in my stead – then it is far from clear that breaking the promise would be so patently immoral that any moral theory that permits or requires it must forfeit one's allegiance. Moreover, utilitarians will argue that there is nothing sacrosanct about ordinary morality. If its rules sometimes conflict with utilitarianism, then we should adjust our ordinary moral thinking or at least have a greater appreciation of the limits of its applicability.

To be sure, if the imagined welfare-maximizing action is truly horrific or unconscionable (torturing an innocent person, for example), then it becomes harder to dismiss our ordinary moral instincts, which rebel against such conduct. Where the stakes are high, however, ordinary morality itself may be stumped. Is it right or wrong to torture to death an innocent person if doing so will somehow stop a war in which tens of thousands will otherwise die? Questions like this are not ones that the rules of everyday morality were designed to answer. But if the welfare benefit of the awful conduct is only marginal – killing a healthy hospital patient in order to use her organs to save the lives of three others – then doing so would undoubtedly contradict everyday moral thinking.

Here, though, utilitarianism can endorse our ordinary moral sentiments without abandoning its own standard of right. In other words, utilitarians can maintain that it's a good thing that doctors refuse to even entertain the idea of killing healthy patients, that Michael opposes slavery categorically and across the board, and that Rebecca would never, ever, conspire to frame someone for a crime he didn't commit, no matter how much benefit was alleged to flow from doing so. The reason is simple. Although it is possible that performing some ghastly deed might be the best course of conduct in a far-fetched set of circumstances imagined by the critic of utilitarianism, these are not circumstances real people will ever encounter. In the world as it actually is, we do much better if people are dead set against doing atrocious things, if they instinctively reject the possibility that supporting slavery, framing an innocent person, killing a healthy patient for his organs, torturing a child, and so on, might be the right course of action. People who feel and act this way will, of course, do the non-utilitarian thing in the fanciful circumstances imagined by the critic of utilitarianism. But they will act the right way in the world they actually live in, a world in which such dreadful actions diminish net happiness. Indeed, the more strongly and categorically people oppose such conduct, the more likely they are to behave, in the real world, in happiness-promoting ways.

An example: the wrongfulness of killing

From a utilitarian perspective, the negative consequences of intentional homicide are obvious. In addition to whatever pain the victim suffers, killing the person deprives him of future well-being, and it typically brings sorrow and grief to family and friends. Moreover, fear of being murdered can quickly and easily spread worry and insecurity throughout society. All societies firmly prohibit killing other people, at least under ordinary circumstances, and there is a fully compelling utilitarian case for their doing so. Without such a prohibition, social existence would barely be possible.

Now consider again the case of the old tramp, whose murder would, according to the critic of utilitarianism, optimally promote net well-being. Even if the supposed facts are exactly as the critic imagines – and that's a very big *if* – one is unlikely to know, or have compelling grounds for believing, that this is so, all things considered and in the long run. Furthermore, teaching people that it is permissible to kill others whenever they are firmly convinced that doing so is for the best would have disastrous social consequences. "If it were thought allowable for any one to put to death at pleasure any human being whom he believes that the world would be well rid of," Mill writes, then "nobody's life would be safe" (1852: 182). Moreover, a readiness to kill other people, even in the cause of promoting the good of all, represents a disposition that utilitarians would strive hard to discourage in favor of attitudes and sentiments (like a respect for life) that tend to promote welfare. Real utilitarians cannot love and assist others as they should and yet be as ready to kill people as the unhappy tramp case imagines.

Utilitarianism in Practice

Utilitarianism's basic criterion of rightness is straightforward: an action is right if and only if nothing the agent could have done instead would have brought about more well-being. However, as we are beginning to see, the theory's practical implications can be surprisingly subtle.

Praise and blame

For utilitarians, whether an agent acted wrongly is distinct from the question whether he or she should be blamed or criticized for so acting (and, if so, how severely). Utilitarians apply their normative standard to questions of blame or praise just as they do to questions of rightness or wrongness. In particular, they will ask whether it will best promote happiness to criticize someone for failing to maximize happiness. Blame, criticism, and rebuke, although hurtful, can have good results by encouraging both the agent and others to do better in the future, whereas neglecting to reproach misconduct increases the likelihood that the agent (or others) will act in the same unsatisfactory way in the future. However, in some circumstances to blame or criticize someone for acting wrongly would be pointless or even counterproductive, for example, if the person acted wrongly accidentally, was innocently misinformed, or was suffering from emotional distress. In such circumstances, chastising the person for not living up to the utilitarian standard might do more harm than good.

Suppose that a well-intentioned agent acted in a welfare-promoting way, but that she could have produced even more good had she acted in some other way. Should utilitarians criticize her? Depending on the circumstances, the answer may well be "no." Imagine that she acted in a way that was unselfish, showed regard for others, and accomplished much good, or suppose that she could have produced more happiness only by violating a generally accepted rule, the following of which usually produces good results. Or imagine that pursuing the second course of conduct would have required a disregard for self-interest or for the interests of those who are near and dear to her that is more than we can normally or reasonably expect from human beings. In these cases, blame would seem to have little or no point. Indeed, we may even want to encourage others to follow her example (that is, to adhere to the same rule or act from the same motive) when they encounter similar situations. Praising an agent for an action that fails to live up to the utilitarian standard can sometimes be right. This is because utilitarians applaud instances of act-types they want to encourage, and they commend those motivations, dispositions, and character traits they want to reinforce.

Motives, dispositions, and character traits

Utilitarians take an instrumental approach to motives. Good motives are those that tend to produce right conduct whereas bad motives are those that tend to produce wrongful conduct. And they assess habits, dispositions, attitudes, behavioral patterns, and character traits in the same instrumental way: they determine which ones are good, and how good they are, by looking at the actions they lead to. It doesn't follow from this, however, that utilitarians believe that a moral agent's only motivation or sole concern ought to be the impartial maximization of happiness. As Mill writes,

> It is the business of ethics to tell us what are our duties, or by what test we may know them; but no system of ethics requires that the sole motive of all we do shall be a feeling of duty. (II, 19)

Indeed, he and other utilitarian writers have long urged that more good may come from people acting from other, more particular motivations, commitments, and dispositions than from their acting only and always on a desire to promote the general good.

As we have seen, a utilitarian should not try to compute the probabilities of all possible outcomes before each and every action. Even if this were humanly possible, it would be absurd and counterproductive. Stopping and calculating generally lead to poor results. One usually does better by acting from good habits or doing what has proved right in similar situations or what seems intuitively to be the best course of conduct. Thus, utilitarianism implies that one should not always reason as a utilitarian or, at least, that one should not always reason in a fully and directly utilitarian way. Better results may come from our acting from principles, procedures, or motives other than the basic utilitarian one. This last statement may sound paradoxical, but the utilitarian standard itself determines in what circumstances we should employ that standard as our direct guide to acting. The proper criterion for assessing actions is one matter; in what ways we should deliberate, reason, or otherwise decide what to do (so as to meet that criterion as best we can) is another issue altogether.

Utilitarians will naturally want to guide their lives, make decisions, and base their actions on those principles, motives, and habits that produce the best results over the long run. Which principles, motives, and habits these are is a contingent matter, but utilitarians believe that one often does best to focus on the welfare of that limited number of human beings to whom one is closely connected. One reason is that one is rarely in a position to promote happiness on a wider scale. As Mill explains:

> The great majority of good actions are intended not for the benefit of the world, but for that of individuals, of which the good of the world is made up; and the thoughts of the most virtuous man need not on these occasions travel beyond the particular persons concerned . . . the occasions on which any person (except one in a thousand) has it in his power to [promote happiness] on an extended scale, in other words, to be a public benefactor, are but exceptional; and on these occasions alone is he called on to consider public utility; in every other case, private utility, the interest or happiness of some few persons is all he has to attend to. (II, 19)

In other words, people generally produce more happiness when they are motivated by and focus on the welfare of those relatively few people with whom their lives are intertwined and whose good they can directly affect, rather than on happiness in general. Nor should we forget that the agent's own happiness is also part of the general good; indeed, it will usually be the part that he or she has the greatest power to affect, one way or another. To quote Mill again, "the good of all can only be pursued with any success by each person's taking as his particular department the good of the only individual whose requirements he can thoroughly know," namely himself (1972: 762).

Following moral rules

Although utilitarianism bases morality on one fundamental principle, it also stresses the importance of following rules, guidelines, or "subordinate principles" that can generally be relied upon to produce good results. We should, for instance, make it an instinctive practice to tell the truth and keep our promises because doing so produces better results than does case-by-case calculation. Relying on such secondary rules counteracts the fact that we can easily err in estimating the value and likelihood of particular results. In general and over the long haul, we are less likely to go wrong and more likely to promote good by cleaving to well-established welfare-promoting rules than by trying to maximize happiness in each and every action we perform. Moreover, when secondary rules are well known and generally followed, people know what others are going to do in certain routine and easily recognizable situations, and they can rely on this knowledge when acting. This improves social coordination and makes society more stable and secure.

An analogy with traffic laws and regulations illuminates these points. Society's goal, let us assume, is that the overall flow of automotive traffic maximize benefit by getting everyone to his or her destination as safely and promptly as possible. Now imagine a traffic system with just one law or rule: Drive your vehicle so as to maximize welfare. It's easy to see that such a one-rule traffic system would be far from ideal and that we would do much better with a variety of more specific traffic regulations. Without secondary rules telling them, for example, to drive on the right side of the road and obey traffic signals, drivers would be left to do whatever they thought best at any given moment, depending on their interpretation of the traffic situation and their calculation of the probable results of alternative actions. Some philosophers seem to think that if people were clever enough and well informed enough, and if time and effort were no consideration, secondary rules would be unnecessary. But this is a mistake because the optimal course of action for me depends on what I expect others to do, and vice versa, and expectations can only be coordinated by a system of rules to which people routinely adhere without regard to consequences. Furthermore, contemporary utilitarians generally agree that the full benefit of secondary rules can be reaped only when they are treated as moral rules and not merely as rules of thumb or practical aids to decision-making. Having people strongly inclined to act in certain rule-designated ways, to feel guilty about failing to do so, and to invoke those rules to assess the conduct of others can have enormous utility. This is because it produces good results to have people strongly disposed to act in certain predictable ways, ways that generally (but perhaps not always) maximize expected benefit. "Any other plan," writes Mill,

> would not only leave everybody uncertain what to expect, but would involve perpetual quarrelling: and hence general rules must be laid down for people's conduct to one another, or in other words, rights and obligations must ... be recognised. (1972: 762)

Moreover, utilitarians will not readily license people to override these basic moral rules. The reason is obvious, as Mill explains:

> If one person may break through the rule on his own judgment, the same liberty cannot be refused to others; and since no one could rely on the rule's being observed, the rule would cease to exist. (1852: 182)

Agents who genuinely embrace a rule as part of their personal moral code will not break it whenever they believe that doing so will marginally increase overall happiness; indeed, in normal circumstances they will not even entertain the idea of doing so. For their part, utilitarians will be more concerned to instill in people a firm disposition to follow certain basic rules (the general utility of which has been established), than they will be desirous of harvesting the extra welfare that might hypothetically come from people shrewdly deviating from those rules. Utilitarians will not criticize or blame a person for adhering to a moral rule endorsed by their theory in the rare case in which diverging from it would have had better results and the person was in a position to know this. Criticizing someone for misapplying a rule or disregarding a generally recognized exception to it makes sense. But it's counterproductive to fault people for following, in the appropriate circumstances, the very moral rules to which one wishes them to have a staunch, internalized commitment.

Living life as a utilitarian

As they go through life, thoughtful people inevitably survey their own characters, assess their traits and dispositions, and reflect on the kind of person they want to be and on the kind of people they wish others to be. They will ponder how best to raise and educate their children, and they will sometimes takes steps to modify and improve their own habits, traits, and dispositions. Utilitarians approach these issues with a desire to identify the attitudes, motivations, and patterns of behavior that conduce to the well-being of both the agent and others, and they want to understand the costs and psychological feasibility of trying to cultivate those dispositions.

Some critics of utilitarianism seem to believe that the theory requires people to shed their personal interests and normal human attachments in order to devote themselves entirely to maximizing general well-being. With so much good waiting to be done, they argue, utilitarians should be working around the clock, and not wasting time dallying with friends, going to the movies, or reading Plato. But an impossible personality type cannot be the utilitarian ideal for the simple reason that it is impossible. Perhaps, though, utilitarians should strive to come as close to this ideal as they can, even if no human being can fully achieve it. But this conclusion is wrong for two reasons.

The first is pragmatic. Such an effort, so against the grain of human nature, is bound to collapse. With great exertion, perhaps, one might sustain the sort of utilitarian fanaticism envisioned by the critics for a year or two, but a collapse of these efforts seems inevitable, most likely followed by a repudiation of the whole endeavor.

The second reason is deeper. The ideal that the critics attribute to utilitarianism overlooks the fact that people's personal attachments and relationships, and their particular commitments, projects, and interests, are cardinal components of their well-being. To strip oneself of these things, even if it were possible, would be not only to denude oneself of the very things that give meaning, zest, and interest to life, but also to undermine the sources of one's identity and self-understanding. "Free development of individuality is one of the leading essentials of well-being," Mill correctly observes, and the liberty to live life as one sees fit is "quite the chief ingredient of individual and social progress" (1978: 54). Accordingly, utilitarianism favors people's developing close relationships and acting directly on the basis of their concerns for friends and loved ones, and it seeks to protect individual choice and autonomy and to give people reasonably wide scope to live as they wish, free from criticism or punishment as long as they adhere to the basic moral rules and refrain from harming others. As Mill writes:

> Mankind . . . obtain a greater sum of happiness when each pursues his own, under the rules and conditions required by the good of the rest, than when each makes the good of the rest his only object, and allows himself no personal pleasures not indispensable to the preservation of his faculties. (1865: 337)

Some Final Criticisms of Utilitarianism

Utilitarians approach issues of character and conduct from several distinct angles. First, about any action they can ask whether it was right in the sense of maximizing well-being. Second, they can ask whether it was an action the agent should have performed, knowing what she knew (or should have known) and feeling the obligation she should have felt to adhere to the rules that utilitarians would want people to stick to in her society. Third, utilitarians can ask whether the agent's motivations are ones that should be reinforced and strengthened, or weakened and discouraged, and they can ask this same question about the broader character traits of which these motivations are an aspect. Finally, if the action fell short in any of these respects, utilitarians can ask whether the agent should be criticized and, if so, how much. This will involve taking into account, among other things, how badly the agent acted, whether there were extenuating factors, what the alternatives were, and what could reasonably have been expected from someone in the agent's shoes, and, most important, the likely effects of criticizing the agent (and others like her) for the conduct in question. Looking at the matter from these various angles produces a nuanced, multidimensional moral assessment.

Given a fuller understanding of how utilitarianism works, many standard objections lose traction. Still, even an indirect and sophisticated utilitarianism of the sort I have outlined has its detractors. I conclude by briefly reviewing and responding to some of their criticisms.

The first is that utilitarianism, as presented, is ambiguous. It delivers no unqualified answers, no simple and definitive instructions to the moral agent. A given course of conduct, for instance, may fail the stringent utilitarian standard of rightness, but yet accord with rules, and flow from character traits, that utilitarians approve and seek to reinforce. But, the critic charges, this leaves the practical implications of utilitarianism far too open-ended. I think, to the contrary, that the multifaceted and wide-ranging character of utilitarian normative appraisal is a strong point of the theory, one that makes it faithful to the complicated reality of our moral lives. And although in theory discrepancies can emerge between assessments given from different utilitarian vantage points, in practice this poses little problem.

Some critics doubt this, however. They find this complex utilitarian approach with its multiple levels of assessment unsatisfactory on the grounds that it is philosophically unstable and psychologically unsustainable. They argue that one cannot coherently shift back and forth between a focus on rules, motives, and character traits, on the one hand, and an act-oriented perspective, on the other. One cannot be genuinely committed to the rules and principles to which utilitarians would want one to adhere when one knows that they are grounded only in the imperative to promote well-being. Likewise, you cannot be deeply and sincerely devoted to your friends and loved ones or properly attached to your own projects and life-goals if you believe that the value of these things ultimately lies only in the contribution they make to human flourishing. You are bound to end up looking at them, the critics contend, in an alienated and instrumental way.

I think, to the contrary, that one can be firmly committed to one's principles, properly involved with one's own projects, and warmly attached to the good of one's friends and loved ones, and use these commitments and attachments as direct reasons for acting one way or another, while at the same time knowing that these undertakings are ultimately justified solely on grounds of utility. Indeed, far from being a psychologically or philosophically unsustainable stance, the ideal of the examined life, upheld by philosophers since Socrates, seems to require that one be able, at least sometimes, to step back and examine the reasons for, and justification of, the principles and commitments one has embraced (perhaps modifying them in the process). Nor is there reason for thinking that such critical reflection, when undertaken from a utilitarian perspective, undercuts in a self-defeating way the commitments it endorses. One's across-the-board opposition to torture or slavery will not be weakened by understanding that it rests on an appreciation of the suffering and loss of human well-being that these practices have always brought with them. Indeed, such knowledge can only strengthen that opposition, and the fuller and more detailed that knowledge, the better.

Yet other critics take a different tack. They contend that, despite the apparently rich and multilevel character of utilitarian assessment, at the end of the day an individual utilitarian is still obliged to act in whatever way would directly and immediately maximize well-being, regardless of the rules that utilitarians would want people to follow or the dispositions, habits, and character traits they would wish to strengthen in them. But this criticism simply ignores everything that was said in the previous section. Sophisticated utilitarians know that the motivations and dispositions they have and the rules they follow are for the best; they know that the most sensible way for them (and others) to live precludes their trying to maximize utility with each and every action they perform. These utilitarians will not feel guilty about, nor criticize other people for, sticking to rules or acting from motives and dispositions that their theory approves of. Indeed, if their moral instincts are as well formed as they should be, these utilitarians will simply not be the kind of people who could bring themselves, say, to torture a small child, even if you could somehow convince them intellectually that this would be for the best.

Some opponents of utilitarianism charge, however, that even if in practice the theory has no untoward consequences – that is, even if it never in fact requires agents to do morally dreadful things – nevertheless its basic standard is wrong in principle. The critic contends, in other words, that it is still possible in theory, even if not in the real world, that an action or policy that is profoundly immoral could promote total happiness better than any alternative action or policy and thus be approved by the basic utilitarian standard. But, the critic concludes, this is unacceptable. If utilitarianism or any other theory entails that conduct we know to be wrong could ever, under any imaginable circumstances, turn out to be permissible, then we must reject the theory. In response, utilitarians will point out that the critic's own hypothesis entails that utilitarianism would permit slavery, for instance, only in a world in which human nature is quite different from what we know it to be, and they will argue that a theory's implications for conduct in such a world is an irrelevant basis of critique. By analogy, from a utilitarian perspective it's wrong to go around sticking pins in people, but things would be different if human beings had skins as thick as an elephant's hide and consequently didn't mind being stuck. Not only would this be an absurd basis for rejecting utilitarianism, but also it ignores the power of the theory to explain quite specifically why it is wrong, in the world as it actually is, to stick pins in people: namely, because it startles, hurts, and distresses them.

The critic, however, may persist by arguing that utilitarianism is giving us the right answer, but for the wrong reason. When it condemns an action as wrongful, utilitarianism does so because the action thwarts or tends to thwart human well-being, and not because it is inherently evil, unjust, or wrong, treats people merely as means or violates their rights, affronts human dignity, contradicts the categorical imperative, or tramples on moral principles everyone knows to be true. For utilitarians, of course, these familiar normative constructs are not theoretically basic. Whatever validity they have depends ultimately on their being translated into a utilitarian framework. The critic is free to object to this, but the objection depends on the critic's elaborating and defending an alternative normative perspective, one that proves more plausible than utilitarianism. Perhaps this can be done, and nothing in this essay shows that it can't be. But utilitarianism is not refuted by the mere existence of alternative theories that regard, as basic, concepts that utilitarianism takes as secondary to the principle of utility.

References

Hooker, Brad (2000) *Ideal Code, Real World*. Oxford: Oxford University Press.

Mill, John Stuart (1852) "Whewell on moral philosophy," in J. M. Robson (ed.) *Collected Works of John Stuart Mill*, Vol. X: *Essays on Ethics, Religion, and Society* (pp. 165–201). Toronto: University of Toronto Press, 1969.

—— (1861) *Utilitarianism*, in J. M. Robson (ed.) *Collected Works of John Stuart Mill*, Vol. X: *Essays on Ethics, Religion, and Society* (pp. 203–59). Toronto: University of Toronto Press, 1969. (Reprinted in Part II of this volume; citations are by roman numeral for chapter, arabic numeral for paragraph.)

—— (1865) *August Comte and Positivism*, in J. M. Robson (ed.) *Collected Works of John Stuart Mill*, Vol. X: *Essays on Ethics, Religion, and Society* (pp. 261–368). Toronto: University of Toronto Press, 1969.

—— (1972) Letters, in F. E. Mineka and D. N. Lindley (eds.) *Collected Works of John Stuart Mill*, Vols. XIV–XVII: *The Later Letters of John Stuart Mill, 1849–1873*. Toronto: University of Toronto Press.

—— (1978) [1859] *On Liberty*. Indianapolis: Hackett.

Ross, W. D. (1930) *The Right and the Good*. Oxford: Oxford University Press.

Chapter 10

The Scalar Approach to Utilitarianism

Alastair Norcross

Introduction

Consequentialist theories such as utilitarianism have traditionally been viewed as theories of right action. Consequentialists have employed theories of value, theories that tell us what things are good and bad, in functions that tell us what actions are right and wrong. The dominant consequentialist function from the good to the right, at least since Sidgwick, has been maximization: an act is right if and only if it produces at least as much good as any alternative available to the agent, otherwise it is wrong. According to this maximizing function, rightness and wrongness are not matters of degree. Consequentialists are not alone on this score. Deontologists concur that rightness and wrongness are not matters of degree. There is an important difference, though. In typical deontological theories, properties that make an action right and wrong – e.g., being a keeping of a binding promise, a killing of an innocent person, or a telling of a lie – are *not* naturally thought of as matters of degree. So one wouldn't expect the rightness or wrongness of an act to be a matter of degree for deontology. But this is not the case with consequentialism. Goodness and badness, especially in the utilitarian value theory, are clearly matters of degree. So the property of an act that makes it right or wrong – how much good it produces relative to available alternatives – *is* naturally thought of as a matter of degree. Why, then, is rightness and wrongness not a matter of degree?

I will argue that, from the point of view of a consequentialist, actions should be evaluated purely in terms that admit of degrees. My argument is directed towards those who are already attracted to consequentialism. I am not undertaking to argue for consequentialism against any rival moral theory. Perhaps, though, some who have rejected consequentialism because of its views on rightness and wrongness may be more attracted to a theory constructed along the lines that I suggest.

I shall conduct my discussion in terms of utilitarianism, since this is the most popular form of consequentialism, and the one to which I adhere. However, since none of my points rely on a specifically utilitarian value theory, my argument applies quite generally to consequentialist theories.

The Demandingness Objection

Since, according to maximizing utilitarianism, any act that fails to maximize is wrong, there appears to be no place for actions that are morally admirable but not required, and agents will often be required to perform acts of great self-sacrifice. This gives rise to the common charge that maximizing utilitarianism is too demanding. But how, exactly, are we to take this criticism? Utilitarianism is too demanding *for what*? If I take up a hobby, say mountain climbing, I may well decide that it is too demanding *for me*. By that, I mean that I am simply not willing to accept the demands of this hobby. I may, therefore, decide to adopt the less demanding hobby of reading about mountain climbing instead. However, unless we adopt a radically subjectivist view of the nature of morality, according to which I am free simply to pick whichever moral theory pleases me, this approach will not work for the claim that utilitarianism is too demanding. When critics object to what they see as utilitarianism's demands, they are not simply declaring themselves unwilling to accept these demands, but are claiming that morality doesn't, in fact, make such demands. We are not, they claim, actually required to sacrifice our own interests for the good of others, at least not as much as utilitarianism tells us. Furthermore, there really are times when we can go above and beyond the call of duty. Since utilitarianism seems to deny these claims, it must be rejected.

How should a utilitarian respond to this line of criticism? One perfectly respectable response is simply to deny the claims at the heart of it. We might insist that morality really is very demanding, in precisely the way utilitarianism says it is. But doesn't this fly in the face of common sense? Well, perhaps it does, but so what? Until relatively recently, moral "common sense" viewed women as having an inferior moral status to men, and some races as having an inferior status to others. These judgments were not restricted to the philosophically unsophisticated. Such illustrious philosophers as Aristotle and Hume accepted positions of this nature. Many utilitarians (myself included) believe that the interests of sentient non-human animals should be given equal consideration in moral decisions with the interests of humans. This claim certainly conflicts with the "common sense" of many (probably most) humans, and many (perhaps most) philosophers. It should not, on that account alone, be rejected. Indeed, very few philosophers base their rejection of a principle of equal consideration for non-human animals merely on its conflict with "common sense." Furthermore, it is worth noting that one of the main contemporary alternatives to a (roughly) consequentialist approach to morality is often referred to as "common-sense morality." Those who employ this phrase do not intend the label itself to constitute an argument against consequentialism.

As I said, a perfectly respectable utilitarian response to the criticism that utilitarianism is too demanding is simply to insist that morality really is very demanding. However, there are powerful reasons to take a different approach altogether. Instead of either maintaining the demands of maximizing utilitarianism, or altering the theory to modify its demands, we should reject the notion that morality issues demands at all. In order to see why this might be an attractive option, I will briefly examine the alleged category of supererogatory actions, and an attempted modification of utilitarianism to accommodate it.

Maximizing utilitarianism, since it classifies as wrong all acts that fail to maximize, leaves no room for supererogation. A supererogatory act is generally characterized as an act which is not required, but which is in some way better than the alternatives. For example, a doctor, who hears of an epidemic in a remote village may choose to go to the assistance of the people who are suffering there, although in doing so he will be putting himself at great risk (Feinberg 1961: 276–88). Such an action does not seem to be morally required of the doctor, but it produces more utility than the morally permissible alternative of remaining in his home town. The category of the supererogatory embodies two connected intuitions that are at odds with maximizing utilitarianism. First, it seems that people sometimes go beyond the call of duty. Maximizing utilitarianism would not allow that. To do your duty is to do the best thing you can possibly do. And second, people who fail to make certain extreme sacrifices for the greater good are usually not wrong. It seems harsh to demand or expect that the doctor sacrifice his life for the villagers.

The utilitarian can avoid these consequences by retreating to a form of satisficing utilitarianism (Slote 1985: ch. 3). For example, one can allow that the boundary between right and wrong can in some cases be located on the scale at some point short of the best. This would allow that an agent can do her duty without performing the best action available to her, and it would make it possible for her to go beyond the call of duty. The position of the boundary between right and wrong may be affected by such factors as how much self-sacrifice is required of the agent by the various options, and how much utility or disutility they will produce. For example, it may be perfectly permissible for the doctor to stay at home, even though the best option would have been to go and help with the epidemic. On the other hand, if all the doctor could do and needed to do to save the villagers were to send a box of tablets or a textbook on diseases, then he would be required to do all he could to save them. Satisficing versions of utilitarianism, no less than the traditional ones, assume that the rightness of an action is an all-or-nothing property. If an action does not produce at least the required amount of good, then it is wrong; otherwise it is right. On a maximizing theory the required amount is the most good available. On a non-maximizing theory what is required may be less than the best. Both forms of utilitarianism share the view that a moral miss is as good as a mile. If you don't produce as much good as is required, then you do something wrong, and that's all there is to it, at least as far as right and wrong are concerned.

Scalar Utilitarianism

Here's an argument for the view that rightness and wrongness isn't an all-or-nothing affair. Let us call this, following Slote (1985: ch. 5) "scalar morality." Suppose that we have some obligations of beneficence, e.g. the wealthy are required to give up a minimal proportion of their incomes for the support of the poor and hungry. (Most people, including deontologists such as Kant and Ross, would accept this.) Suppose Jones is obligated to give 10 percent of his income to charity. The difference between giving 8 percent and 9 percent is approximately the same, in some obvious physical sense, as the difference between giving 9 percent and 10 percent, or between giving 11 percent and 12 percent. Such similarities should be reflected in moral similarities. A moral theory which says that there is a *really significant* moral difference between giving 9 percent and 10 percent, but *not* between giving 11 percent and 12 percent, looks misguided. At least, no utilitarian should accept this. She will be equally concerned about the difference between giving 11 percent and 12 percent as the difference between giving 9 percent and 10 percent. To see this, suppose that Jones were torn between giving 11 percent and 12 percent and that Smith were torn between giving 9 percent and 10 percent. The utilitarian will tell you to spend the same amount of time persuading each to give the larger sum, assuming that other things are equal. This is because she is concerned with certain sorts of consequences, in this case, with getting money to people who need it. An extra $5,000 from Jones (who has already given 11 percent) would satisfy this goal as well as an extra $5,000 from Smith (who has given 9 percent). It does not matter whether the $5,000 comes from one who has already given 11 percent or from one who has given a mere 9 percent.

An all-or-nothing theory of right and wrong would have to say that there was a *threshold*, e.g., at 10 percent, such that if one chose to give 9 percent one would be wrong, whereas if one chose to give 10 percent one would be right. If this distinction is to be interesting, it must say that there is a *big* difference between right and wrong, between giving 9 percent and giving 10 percent, and a small(er) difference between similarly spaced pairs of right actions, or pairs of wrong actions. The difference between giving 9 percent and 8 percent is just the difference between a wrong action and a slightly worse one; and the difference between giving 11 percent and 12 percent is just the difference between one supererogatory act and a slightly better one. In fact, if the difference between right and wrong is at all significant, it must be possible for it to offset at least some differences in goodness. For example, if the threshold for rightness in a case of charitable giving were \$10,000 for both Smith and Jones, the difference between Smith giving \$10,000 and giving \$9,000 must be more significant than the difference between Jones giving \$9,000 and giving somewhat less than \$8,000. But suppose that Smith is wavering between giving \$10,000 and giving \$9,000, and that Jones is wavering between giving \$9,000 and giving \$7,999. No utilitarian would consider it more important to persuade Smith to give the higher amount than to persuade Jones to give the higher amount. This doesn't just apply to actions. No utilitarian would consider it better that (or would hope more fervently that, etc.) Smith opts for the higher amount than that Jones opts for the higher amount.

A related reason to reject an all-or-nothing line between right and wrong is that the choice of any point on the scale of possible options as a threshold for rightness will be *arbitrary*. Even maximization is subject to this criticism. One might think that the difference between the best and the next best option constitutes a really significant moral difference, quite apart from the difference in goodness between the options. We do, after all, attach great significance to the difference between winning a race and coming second, even if the two runners are separated by only a fraction of a second. We certainly don't attach anything like the same significance to the difference between finishing, say, seventh and eighth, even when a much larger interval separates the runners. True enough, but I don't think that it shows that there really is a greater significance in the difference between first and second than in any other difference. We do, after all, also attach great significance to finishing in the top three. We give medals to the top three and to no others. We could just as easily honor the top three equally and not distinguish between them. When we draw these lines – between the first and the rest, or between the top three and the rest, or between the final four and the others – we seem be laying down arbitrary conventions. And saying that giving 10 percent is right and giving only 9 percent is wrong seems analogously conventional and arbitrary.

By contrast, good and bad are scalar concepts, but as with many other scalar concepts, such as rich and tall, we speak of a state of affairs as good or bad (*simpliciter*). This distinction is not arbitrary or conventional. The utilitarian can give a fairly natural account of the distinction between good and bad states of affairs. For example: consider each morally significant being included in the state of affairs. Determine whether her conscious experience is better or worse than no experience. Assign it a positive number if it is better, and a negative one if it is worse. Then add together the numbers of all morally significant beings in the state of affairs. If the sum if positive, the state of affairs is good. If it is negative, the state of affairs is bad.

Note that although this gives an account of a real distinction between good and bad, it doesn't give us reason to attach much significance to the distinction. It doesn't make the difference between a minimally good state of affairs and a minimally bad state of affairs more significant than the difference between pairs of good states of affairs or between bad states of affairs. To see this, imagine that you are consulted by two highly powerful amoral gods, Bart and Lisa. Bart is trying to decide whether to create a world that is ever so slightly good overall (+1) or one that is ever so slightly bad overall (−1). Lisa is trying to decide whether to create a world that is clearly, but not spectacularly, good (+1), or one that is clearly *spectacularly* good (+1 *billion*). They each intend to flip a coin, unless you convince them one way or the other in the next five minutes. You can only talk to one of them. Isn't it clearly more important to convince Lisa to opt for the better of her two choices than to convince Bart to opt for the better of his two choices?

However, if utilitarianism only gives an account of goodness, how do we go about determining our moral obligations and duties? It's all very well to know how good my different options are, but this doesn't tell me what morality requires of me. Traditional maximizing versions of utilitarianism, though harsh, are perfectly clear on the question of moral obligation. My obligation is to do the best I can. Even a satisficing version can be clear about how much good it is my duty to produce. How could a utilitarian, or other consequentialist, theory count as a moral theory, if it didn't give an account of duty and obligation? After all, isn't the central task of a moral theory to give an account of moral duty and obligation?

Utilitarians, and consequentialists in general, at least in the twentieth century onwards, seem to have agreed with deontologists that their central task was to give an account of moral obligation. They have disagreed, of course, sometimes vehemently, over what actually is morally required. Armed with an account of the good, utilitarians have proceeded to give an account of the right by means of a simple algorithm from the good to the right. In addition to telling us what is good and bad, they have told us that morality requires us to produce a certain amount of good, usually as much as possible, that we have a moral obligation to produce a certain amount of good, that any act that produces that much good is right, and any act that produces less good is wrong. And in doing so they have played into the hands of their deontological opponents.

A deontologist, as I said earlier, is typically concerned with such properties of an action as whether it is a killing of an innocent person, or a telling of a lie, or a keeping of a promise. Such properties do not usually come in degrees. (A notable exception is raised by the so-called duty of beneficence.) It is hard, therefore, to construct an argument against particular deontological duties along the lines of my argument against particular utility thresholds. If a utilitarian claims that one has an obligation to produce x amount of utility, it is hard to see how there can be a significant utilitarian distinction between an act that produces x utility and one that produces slightly less. If a deontologist claims that one has an obligation to keep one's promises, a similar problem does not arise. Between an act of promise-keeping and an alternative act that does not involve promise-keeping, there is clearly a significant deontological distinction, no matter how similar in other respects the latter act may be to the former. A utilitarian may, of course, claim that he is concerned not simply with utility, but with maximal utility.

Whether an act produces at least as much utility as any alternative is not a matter of degree. But why should a utilitarian be concerned with maximal utility, or any other specific amount?

To be sure, a utilitarian cannot produce an account of duty and obligation to rival the deontologist's, unless he claims that there are morally significant utility thresholds. But why does he want to give a rival account of duty and obligation at all? Why not instead regard utilitarianism as a far more radical alternative to deontology, and simply reject the claim that duties or obligations constitute any part of fundamental morality, let alone the central part? My suggestion is that utilitarianism should be treated simply as a theory of the goodness of states of affairs and of the comparative value of actions, which rates alternative possible actions in comparison with each other. This system of evaluation yields information about which alternatives are better than which and by how much. In the example of the doctor, this account will say that the best thing to do is to go and help with the epidemic, but it will say neither that he is required to do so, nor that he is completely unstained morally if he fails to do so.

If a utilitarian has an account of goodness and badness, according to which they are scalar phenomena, why not say something similar about right and wrong: that they are scalar phenomena but that there is a point (perhaps a fuzzy point) at which wrong shades into right? Well, what would that point be? I said earlier that differences in goodness should be reflected by differences in rightness. Perhaps the dividing line between right and wrong is just the dividing line between good and bad. In fact, Mill's statement of the principle of utility might seem to suggest such an approach:

> The creed which accepts as the foundation of morals, Utility, or the Greatest Happiness Principle, holds that actions are right in proportion as they tend to promote happiness, wrong as they tend to produce the reverse of happiness. (Mill 1861, reprinted as Part II of this volume, Ch. II, para. 2; citations are simply by roman numeral for chapter and arabic numeral for paragraph)

There are, of course, notorious difficulties with interpreting Mill's statement. Talk of tendencies of actions to promote happiness, for example, could lead to a form of rule-utilitarianism. However, since my concern in this paper is not to offer an interpretation of Mill, I will set aside issues of scholarship, and focus instead on the suggestion that an action is right just in case it is good, and wrong just in case it is bad. There are two reasons to reject this suggestion. The first is that it seems to collapse the concepts of right and wrong into those of good and bad respectively, and hence, to make the former pair redundant. The second is that, on the account of good and bad states of affairs I offered the utilitarian, it is not clear that there is any satisfactory account of the difference between good and bad actions with which to equate the difference between right and wrong actions. (See Norcross 1997.)

Wrongness as Blameworthiness

We tend to blame and punish agents for their wrong actions and not for actions that are not wrong. And we tend to consider it wrong to blame or punish someone for an action that was not wrong. Perhaps, then, a utilitarian (or other theorist) can analyze wrongness in terms of blameworthiness. Consider this well-known passage from Mill:

> We do not call anything wrong, unless we mean to imply that a person ought to be punished in some way or other for doing it; if not by law, by the opinion of his fellow-creatures; if not by opinion, by the reproaches of his own conscience. (V, 14)

Although, as I said earlier, my main concern is not Mill scholarship, it is worth noting that a close reading of the paragraphs immediately preceding this passage suggests that Mill is not here proposing an *analysis* of wrongness that fits with utilitarianism. He is, rather, pointing out some features of the ordinary usage of the term "wrong." Nonetheless, an analysis of wrongness in terms of punishment is worth considering. This suggests the possibility of a scalar conception of wrongness. Since censure (and other forms of punishment) comes in degrees, then perhaps wrongness might also come in degrees.

Consider the following definition of wrong action:

WA: An action is wrong if and only if it is appropriate to impose various sanctions on the agent.

What does it mean to say that it is "appropriate" to sanction? Since appropriateness is a normative notion, the most natural understanding is to think of it as meaning "obligatory." (Alternatively, we could understand it as meaning "permissible." I shall focus on the obligatory reading here, since it is the most popular. The chief objection to the obligatory reading also applies to the permissibility reading.) In that case, WA would be:

WA1: An action is wrong if and only if we ought to impose various sanctions on the agent.

But if WA is to be understood as WA1, it leads to a definitional circle or regress. It tells us to understand what is wrong in terms of what it is wrong not to do. (I take it that "wrong" and "ought not to be done" are interchangeable.) But we don't have a better grasp on the notion of "ought to sanction" than we have on the notions of "ought to keep promises" or "ought to feed the hungry." Trying to understand the wrongness of one action in terms of the wrongness of other actions is unenlightening.

There is an alternative account of appropriateness according to which it is still normative. That account says that an action is appropriate if and only if it is optimific. WA would then amount to:

WA2: An action is wrong if and only if it is optimific to punish the agent.

This suggestion avoids the uninformative circularity of WA1. Let us suppose that WA2 expresses the sort of connection between wrongness and censure that people have in mind. Can it provide the utilitarian with a distinction between badness and wrongness?

I believe that WA2 is not available to the utilitarian as a way of distinguishing wrong actions from bad actions. For he cannot identify wrong actions with actions which it is optimific to sanction. To see this consider what Sidgwick says about praise.

> From a Utilitarian point of view, as has been before said, we must mean by calling a quality, "deserving of praise," that it is expedient to praise it, with a view to its future production: accordingly, in distributing our praise of human qualities, on utilitarian principles, we have to consider primarily not the usefulness of the quality, but the usefulness of the praise. (Sidgwick 1962: 428)

The utilitarian will, of course, say the same about censure as Sidgwick says about praise: we should assess whether it is good to punish or blame someone by assessing the utility of doing so. Punishing and blaming are actions just like promise-keeping and killing and, like those actions, their value is determined by their consequences, their power to produce utility.

If there is a conceptual connection of the sort asserted by WA2 between an action's being wrong and its being appropriate to punish the agent, and if Sidgwick's account of when it is appropriate to punish is correct, then we should be able to determine whether an act is wrong by determining whether punishing the agent of that act will produce more utility than not. On the other hand, if there is good reason to reject this method of deciding whether someone has done wrong, then there is reason to reject WA2.

I submit that there is reason to reject the claim that the *wrongness* of an action is determined by whether punishing the agent would produce more utility than not. This is because our concept of wrongness is constrained by one or both of the following principles which conflict with WA2:

1: If action *x* is wrong, then an action *y* done by someone in exactly similar circumstances, with the same intention and the same consequences, is also wrong.

We might call this the principle of universalizability. It might, however, be optimific to punish the agent of *x* but not the agent of *y*. Hence, according to WA2, *x* would be wrong, but *y* would not.

2: If someone does the best she can, and does very well indeed, then she has done nothing wrong.

But it can sometimes be optimific to punish a utility-maximizer. For example, imagine that Agnes has always produced as much utility as it was possible for her to produce. Moreover, none of her actions has led to any unfortunate consequences, such as someone's untimely death or suffering. Punishing her as a scapegoat might nevertheless produce more utility than not doing so. It is absurd to say that she has done something wrong just in virtue of the fact that it is appropriate or optimific to punish her.

Given any one of these constraints on any recognizable understanding of wrongness, the utilitarian cannot say that whether an action is wrong is determined by whether it is optimific to punish the agent for doing it. (The principles I have expressed here would produce conflicts with a satisficing version of WA2 as well.)

It might be objected that the conflict between principles (1) and (2) and WA2 can be explained away if we see the relationship between the concepts of wrongness and censure as less simple than the one we have suggested. Instead of saying that wrongness is a necessary and sufficient condition for the appropriateness of censure, it might be urged, we need a connection that allows for exceptions. Why not say that wrongness makes it prima facie appropriate to censure the agent? This prima facie appropriateness can be outweighed by such factors as the agent's motivational state or very extreme consequences of, say, not punishing an innocent person. We recognize intuitively that the appropriateness of punishing or blaming someone for doing wrong is occasionally outweighed by other considerations, e.g., if the agent has suffered a great deal as a result of his action. So the suggestion is:

WA3:   An action is wrong if and only if it is prima facie appropriate to blame its agent.

Presumably also, the fact that an agent has done no wrong is a prima facie reason not to punish the agent. Both kinds of reasons can be overridden, particularly in the sorts of bizarre cases that philosophers come up with. This would account for our disinclination to say that Agnes did something wrong, even if we grant that it was appropriate to punish her.

This suggestion will not work, however. The utilitarian does not think it is prima facie appropriate to blame the agent of every wrong action, or prima facie appropriate not to blame someone who has done no wrong. This is because the *sole* determinant of the appropriateness of blame or punishment is how much utility will be produced by doing so. Imagine someone (say, Agnes) who has done no wrong. Suppose that punishing her will produce very slightly more utility than not doing so. The utilitarian will judge that punishing her is better than not. If her innocence did create a presumption against punishing her, then that presumption should be enough to outweigh the very slight gain in utility. But this is not how the utilitarian sees things.

I submit that there can be no conceptual connection, for the utilitarian, between wrongness and punishability or blameworthiness.

Even if we reject a conceptual connection between wrongness and punishment, isn't there a simple conceptual analysis of *rightness* in terms of reasons? If a utilitarian accepts that one possible action is better than another just in case it has better consequences, must she not also accept that there is more (moral) reason to perform the better action? Furthermore, must she not accept that there is the most (moral) reason to perform the *best* action available to the agent? But doesn't "(morally) right" simply mean "supported by the strongest (moral) reasons" or "what we have most (moral) reason to do"? In which case, we seem to have arrived back at the maximizing conception of rightness.

The problem with this suggestion is that it is highly implausible that there is such a simple conceptual connection between rightness and maximal reason. Consider the example of supererogation discussed above. Supererogatory acts are supposed to be morally superior to their merely permissible alternatives. There will be more (moral) reason to perform putative supererogatory acts than to perform their morally inferior alternatives. But if "right" simply means "supported by the strongest reasons," supererogatory acts will be right (unless there are even better alternatives) and the morally inferior, but supposedly acceptable, alternative acts will be wrong. But if "right" and "duty" are equated, then, by definition, there can be no acts that go "above and beyond" duty, in the sense of being better than duty. So it would seem that those who argue for the category of supererogatory actions are simply confused about the meanings of words. But this is highly implausible. Likewise, those who criticize utilitarianism's maximizing account of rightness as being too demanding are surely not simply mistaken as to the meaning of the word "right."

Rightness and Goodness as Guides to Action

If utilitarianism is interpreted as a scalar theory, which doesn't issue any demands at all, it clearly can't be criticized for being too demanding. Does this mean that the scalar utilitarian must agree with the critic who claims (1) we are not frequently required to sacrifice our own interests for the good of others; and (2) there really are times when we can go above and beyond the call of duty? Strictly speaking, the answers are "yes" to (1), and "no" to (2). (1) It may frequently be *better* to sacrifice our interests for the good of others than to perform any action that preserves our interests. Sometimes it may be *much* better to do so. However, these facts don't entail any further facts to the effect that we are *required* to do so. (2) As for supererogation, the scalar utilitarian will deny the existence of duty as a fundamental moral category, and so will deny the possibility of actions that go "beyond" our duty, in the sense of being better than whatever duty demands. The intuition that drives the belief in supererogation can, however, be explained in terms of actions that are considerably better than what would be expected of a reasonably decent person in the circumstances.

At this point, someone might object that I have thrown out the baby with the bathwater. To be sure, scalar utilitarianism isn't too demanding; it's not nearly demanding enough! How can a theory that makes no demands fulfill the central function of morality, which is to guide our actions?

Utilitarianism should not be seen as giving an account of right action, in the sense of an action *demanded* by morality, but only as giving an account of what states of affairs are good and which actions are better than which other possible alternatives and by how much. The fundamental moral fact about an action is how good it is relative to other available alternatives. Once a range of options has been evaluated in terms of goodness, all the morally relevant facts about those options have been discovered. There is no further fact of the form "*x* is right," "*x* is to-be-done," or "*x* is demanded by morality."

This is not to say that it is a bad thing for people to use the phrases such as "right," "wrong," "ought to be done," or "demanded by morality," in their moral decision-making, and even to set up systems of punishment and blame which assume that there is a clear and significant line between right and wrong. It may well be that societies that believe in such a line are happier than societies that don't. It might still be useful to employ the notions of rightness and wrongness for the purposes of everyday decision-making. If it is practically desirable that people should think that rightness is an all-or-nothing property, my proposed treatment of utilitarianism suggests an approach to the question of what function to employ to move from the good to the right. In different societies the results of employing different functions may well be different. These different results will themselves be comparable in terms of goodness. And so different functions can be assessed as better or worse depending on the results of employing them.

It is clear that the notions of right and wrong play a central role in the moral thinking of many. It will be instructive to see why this so. There are two main reasons for the concentration on rightness as an all-or-nothing property of actions: (1) a long list of examples which present a choice between options which differ greatly in goodness; (2) the imperatival model of morality. Let's consider (1). When faced with a choice between helping a little old lady across the road, and mugging her, it is usually much better to help her across the road. If these are the only two options presented, it is easy to classify helping the old lady as the "right" thing to do, and mugging her as "wrong." Even when there are other bad options, such as kidnapping her or killing and eating her, the gap between the best of these and helping her across the road is so great that there is no question as to what to do. When we move from considering choices such as these to considering choices between options which are much closer in value, such as helping the old lady or giving blood, it is easy to assume that one choice *must* be wrong and the other right.

Let us move now to (2). Morality is commonly thought of as some sort of guide to life. People look to morality to tell them what to do in various circumstances, and so they see it as issuing commands. When they obey these, they do the right thing, and when they disobey, they do a wrong thing. This is the form of some simple versions of divine command ethics and some other forms of deontology. Part of the motivation for accepting such a theory is that it seems to give one a simple, easily applicable practical guide. Problems arise, of course, when someone finds herself in a situation in which she is subject to two different commands, either of which can be obeyed, but not both. In these cases we could say that there is a higher-order command for one rather than the other to be done, or that the agent cannot help doing wrong. The effect of allowing higher-order commands is to complicate the basic commands; so "do not kill" becomes "do not kill, unless . . .". The effect of allowing that there could be situations in which an agent cannot help doing wrong is to admit that morality may not always help us to make difficult choices. In either case, one of the motivations for accepting an imperatival model of morality – simplicity, and thus ease of application – is undermined.

Unless one does espouse a simple form of divine command theory, according to which the deity's commands should be obeyed just because they are the deity's commands, it seems that the main justification for the imperatival model of morality is pragmatic. After all, if we don't have the justification that the commands issue from a deity, it is always legitimate to ask what grounds them. That certain states of affairs are good or bad, and therefore should or should not be brought about, seems like a far more plausible candidate to be a fundamental moral fact than that someone should act in a certain way. However, it is generally easier to make choices if one sees oneself as following instructions. It may well be, then, that the imperatival model of morality, with the attendant prominence of the notions of right and wrong, has a part to play at the level of application. It may in fact be highly desirable that most people's moral thinking is conducted in terms of right and wrong. On the other hand, it may be desirable that everyone abandon the notions of right and wrong. I do not wish to argue for either option here, since the issue could probably only be settled by extensive empirical research.

The approach of the last few paragraphs might seem merely to relocate a problem to a different level. I have been claiming that, although morality doesn't actually tell us what we ought to do, there may be pragmatic benefits in adopting moral practices that include demands. Societies that adopt such practices may be better (happier, more flourishing, etc.) than those that don't. But surely this doesn't solve anything. We want to know whether we *ought* to adopt such practices. Scalar utilitarianism seems to be silent on that question. Since scalar utilitarianism doesn't tell us what we ought to do, it can't guide our actions (including our choices of what moral practices to adopt or encourage in society). But any adequate moral theory must guide our actions. Therefore the theory should be rejected. This argument has three premises:

1   If a theory doesn't guide our action, it is no good.
2   If a theory doesn't tell us what we ought to do, it doesn't guide our action.
3   Utilitarianism, as I have described it, does not tell us what we ought to do.

To assess this argument we need to disambiguate its first premise. The expression "guide our action" can mean several things. If it means "tell us what we ought to do" then premise (1) is question-begging. I shall construe it to mean something more like, "provide us with reasons for acting." On that reading, I shall concede (1), and shall argue that (2) is false. Here is Sidgwick in defense of something like (2):

> Further, when I speak of the cognition or judgment that "X ought to be done" – in the stricter ethical sense of the term ought – as a "dictate" or "precept" of reason to the persons to whom it relates, I imply that in rational beings as such this cognition gives an impulse or motive to action: though in human beings, of course, this is only one motive among others which are liable to conflict with it, and is not always – perhaps not usually – a predominant motive. (1962: 34)

As Sidgwick acknowledges, this reason can be overridden by other reasons, but when it is, it still exerts its pull in the form of guilt or uneasiness.

Sidgwick's point rests on internalism, the view that moral beliefs are essentially motivating. Internalism is controversial. Instead of coming down on one side or the other of this controversy, I shall argue that, whether one accepts internalism or externalism, the fact that a state of affairs is bad gives reason to avoid producing it as much as would the fact that producing it is wrong.

Suppose internalism is correct. In that case the belief that an act is wrong gives one a reason not to do it. Furthermore, such a reason is necessarily a motivating reason. It seems that the utilitarian internalist should take the position that the belief that a state of affairs is *bad* is also a motivating reason to avoid producing it, and the belief that one state of affairs is *better than the other* may well give the believer a stronger reason to produce the first than the second. If the fact that an act is wrong gives us reason to avoid it, then the fact that it involves the production of a bad state of affairs, by itself, gives us reason to avoid it.

Now let's suppose externalism is true. In that case the fact that an act is wrong gives one a motivating reason to avoid doing it *if one cares about avoiding wrongdoing*. If this is what wrongness amounts to, then it seems no defect in a theory that it lacks a concept of wrongness. For it may be true that one cannot consistently want to avoid doing wrong, believe that an act is wrong, and do the act without feeling guilt. But this doesn't provide a distinctive account of wrongness, because we can replace each occurrence of the word "wrong" and its cognates in the above sentence with other moral terms such as "an action which produces less than the best possible consequences" or "much worse than readily available alternatives" and the principle remains true. If the agent cares about doing the best he can, then he will be motivated to do so, feel guilt if he doesn't, and so on. It is true that few of us care about doing the best we can. But then, many of us do not care about doing what we ought either.

Whether internalism is correct or not, it looks as if premise (2) in the above argument is false. Abolishing the notion of "ought" will not seriously undermine the action-guiding nature of morality. The fact that one action is better than another gives us a moral reason to prefer the first to the second. Morality thus guides action in a scalar fashion. This should come as no surprise. Other action-guiding reasons also come in degrees. Prudential reasons certainly seem to function in this way. My judgment that cauliflower is better for me than pizza will guide my action differently depending on how much better I judge cauliflower to be than pizza. Whether moral facts are reasons for all who recognize them (the debate over internalism) is an issue beyond the scope of this paper, but whether they are or not, the significance each of us gives to such moral reasons relative to other reasons, such as prudential and aesthetic reasons, is not something which can be settled by a moral theory.

There are two other reasons I have encountered for requiring utilitarianism to provide an account of the right. The first might be expressed like this:

If utilitarianism is not a theory of the right, it must only be a theory of the good. Different consequentialist theories will be different theories of the good. But then how do we explain the difference between consequentialist and non-consequentialist theories in general?

I can still claim this distinctive feature for consequentialism: it includes the view that the relative value of an action depends entirely on the goodness of its consequences. Of the acts available to the agent, the best action will be the one that produces the best consequences, the next best will be the one that produces the next best consequences, and so on. I can also claim that the better the action, the stronger the moral reason to perform it. This distinguishes consequentialism from deontology, which allows that one may have a stronger moral reason to perform an action which produces worse consequences. For example, if faced with a choice between killing one and letting five die, the deontologist may acknowledge that five deaths are worse than one, but insist that the better behavior is to allow the five to die. According to that view, morality provides stronger reasons for allowing five deaths than for killing one. One advantage of the suggestion I offer here over, say, the view that it is of the essence of consequentialism to insist that the agent ought always to do whatever will produce the best consequences, is that it allows satisficing consequentialists and scalar consequentialists to count as consequentialists.

I have also encountered the following reason for requiring utilitarianism to provide an account of the right as well as the good: the utilitarian will have to provide a function from the good to the right in order to compare her theory with various deontological alternatives. Our chief method for comparing moral theories, according to this suggestion, consists in comparing their judgments about which acts are right or wrong. It is true that contemporary discussions of the relative merits of utilitarianism and deontology have often focused on particular examples, asking of the different theories what options are right or wrong. However, to assume that a moral theory must provide an account of the right in order to be subjected to critical scrutiny begs the question against my proposed treatment of utilitarianism. That utilitarians have felt the need to provide accounts of rightness is testimony to the pervasion of deontological approaches to ethics. Part of what makes utilitarianism such a radical alternative to deontology, in my view, is its claim that right and wrong are not fundamental ethical concepts.

References and further reading

Bennett, Jonathan (1993) "Negation and abstention: two theories of allowing," *Ethics* 104, pp. 75–96.

Feinberg, Joel (1961) "Supererogation and rules," *Ethics* 71, pp. 276–88.

Mill, John Stuart (1861) *Utilitarianism*. Reprinted as Part II of this volume.

Norcross, Alastair (1997) "Good and bad actions," *Philosophical Review* 106, pp. 1–34.

Sidgwick, Henry (1962) *The Methods of Ethics*, 7th edn. Chicago: University of Chicago Press.

Slote, Michael (1985) *Common-sense Morality and Consequentialism*. Boston: Routledge & Kegan Paul.

Chapter 11

Right, Wrong, and Rule-Consequentialism

Brad Hooker

Introduction

In 1712, George Berkeley wrote, "In framing the general laws of nature, it is granted we must be entirely guided by the public good of mankind, but not in the ordinary moral actions of our lives . . . The rule is framed with respect to the good of mankind; but our practice must be always shaped immediately by the rule" (Berkeley 1972: 217–27). There we find an early espousal of rule-utilitarianism. Rules are to be selected on the basis of their aggregate net benefits; actions are to be evaluated by the rules thus selected.

Rule-utilitarianism has been the most prominent kind of rule-consequentialism. Rule-utilitarians judge rules by only one kind of consequence: utility, impartially considered. To consider utility impartially is to give the same weight to a benefit or harm to any individual as is given to the same size benefit or harm to anyone else.

I know of no rule-consequentialists who think utility unimportant. The live question between various kinds of rule-consequentialists is whether utility is the only factor by which to judge rules. Rule-utilitarians say that it is. Other kinds of rule-consequentialists say that it is not.

By far the most common kind of not purely utilitarian rule-consequentialism is one that assesses rules not only by how much utility results but also by how equally that utility is distributed. Some philosophers interpret the classic utilitarians' slogan "the greatest good for the greatest number" as vaguely suggesting this "utility-plus-equality" test. Whether or not that is what the classic utilitarians at least sometimes had in mind, later I will explain why rule-consequentialists might want, or might not want, to consider not only how much utility results from a set of rules but also how that utility is distributed.

In the next two sections of this essay, I discuss two different ways to argue for rule-consequentialism. I will then show how rule-consequentialism is superior to scalar consequentialism. In four subsequent sections, I explain how rule-consequentialism is best formulated. In the last of these four sections, I take up the questions from the previous paragraph about distribution. I then turn to objections to rule-consequentialism. In the essay's penultimate section, I discuss objections that have been especially influential but have now been successfully answered. In the final section, I list some objections that move to the fore once the older objections fall.

The Consequentialist Argument for Rule-Consequentialism

Suppose we start with the general idea that the central or overriding goal of morality is to produce good consequences impartially considered. From that general idea, we might infer that the best moral theory for people to accept is whatever one will result in the best consequences.

That inference needs explanation. If the goal of morality is to produce good consequences impartially considered, then presumably the point of people's having moral commitments is to produce good consequences. Having moral commitments is partly a matter of having dispositions to act and react in certain ways, and partly a matter of having moral beliefs connected with those dispositions. Now consider a set of moral beliefs that form a system and that indicate what counts morally for or against actions in any situation. Such a set of moral beliefs constitutes a moral theory. So the thought that the central or overriding goal of morality is to produce good consequences might lead to the thought that the best moral theory for people to accept is whatever one will result in the best consequences.

Which moral theory is the one that, if people accept it, the best consequences will result? An initial thought might be that the theory whose acceptance would produce the best consequences is a version of maximizing act-consequentialism, i.e., the theory that an act is morally right if and only if it results in the best consequences. Wouldn't a theory that requires each individual always to produce the best consequences be the theory that, if accepted, would produce the best consequences?

Well, in part the answer depends on whether accepting a moral theory involves trying consciously to use it. It might seem natural to suppose that, if one accepts act-consequentialism as the criterion of right and wrong, then one will try to make moral decisions by first calculating the expected value of the different consequences of various alternatives and then choosing the available act favored by this calculation. That is, the simplest and most obvious version of act-consequentialism puts forward an act-consequentialist criterion of right and wrong and an act-consequentialist procedure for everyday moral decision-making.

However, in fact, very few act-consequentialists recommend the procedure of always calculating the expected value of alternative possible actions so to choose what to do on the basis of that calculation. Such a decision procedure is unwise for a number of different reasons. Below, in barest outline, are some of the main ones.

Very often agents lack information about the probable effects of particular alternatives they are choosing among. For example, I might not have any idea whether my starting to wear my cowboy boots to class will impress (or even be noticed by) the students.

Furthermore, even if agents do know the probabilities of the possible consequences, they may not have a good grasp of the respective values of those consequences. Jack and Jill might reasonably predict that going on vacation together will cause them to fall in love, and then coming home will cause them to fall out of love. But they might not be able to make confident judgments about whether such adventures would have more value than disvalue, or vice versa.

Obviously, there is the related problem that agents very often lack time or energy to collect information about the probabilities and values of all possible consequences of the alternatives. And even where agents could spare the time and energy to collect information, there is the risk of missing opportunities while collecting the information. There is also the sheer cost in time and attention of calculating the expected values of the consequences.

There is also the risk of mistakes in calculations. Human limitations and biases might well make us unreliable calculators of the expected overall consequences of our alternatives. A striking fact is that most people believe that the political party that would benefit them most would also benefit the country as a whole. This is strong evidence that people's attempts at impartial calculation regularly go awry. So if people regularly try to choose acts that they have calculated will produce the best consequences impartially considered, in fact very often what they will be doing is "rationalizing" the choice of acts that benefit themselves.

For that reason, perhaps there would not be enough mutual trust in a society of people trying to make decisions on the basis of act-consequentialism. We need firm assurances that others won't physically attack us, steal from us, or break promises to us. We need firmer assurances than we would get from knowing that everyone would be attempting to make every decision in act-consequentialist fashion. Indeed, it has often been argued that we need firmer such assurances than we would have in a society of even the most rigorous and conscientious of act-consequentialists. (See Hodgson 1967 and Warnock 1971.)

Let me make one more point about getting everyone to be willing to make every decision in as impartial a way as the act-consequentialist procedure would require. There would be enormous costs associated with getting everyone to be so impartial. The "raw material" for moral education is of course very young children. They are motivated mainly by immediate self-gratification and by the desire to identify with authority figures such as parents. Moral education is largely a matter of transforming children from that state to one where they are willing to forgo benefits for themselves for the sake of others. But if they were to become as impartial as the act-consequentialist decision procedure would require, then they would have to be willing to give up any benefit for themselves when doing so would benefit someone else more, even if only a little more. Imagine the costs in terms of time and energy and attention that would be involved in getting humans beings to have internalized that degree of altruism.

Many people do become very altruistic, at least to the extent of caring deeply about family and friends. If everyone is to become impartial, one way of doing this is to increase their concern for strangers up to the level of their concern for their family, friends, and even themselves. But given the limits of human nature, it might be impossible to increase people's concern for strangers up to the level of their concern for their family, their friends, and themselves. So the only way to get people to become completely impartial might instead be to suppress their concern for their family, friends, and themselves down to the level of their concern for strangers. But if that were done, then the world would be populated by people with fairly weak concerns about everything. It is hard to believe this would be a very happy world. So, if the realistic choice is between a world where everyone cares strongly about some others but only weakly about the rest, or a world where everyone cares equally but weakly about everyone, the better world might be the first of these.

We have seen a number of reasons that act-consequentialists might oppose a moral decision procedure of always calculating the expected value of alternative possible actions and choosing what to do on the basis of that calculation. Operating such a decision procedure would take more information, time, energy, powers of reasoning, and impartiality than people have, or could cost-effectively be brought to have.

So what kind of moral thinking would in fact maximize the good? One standard answer is that, at least normally, agents should decide how to act by referring to tried and true rules such as "Don't harm others," "Don't steal," "Keep your promises," "Tell the truth," etc. And what moral theory should people hold? Well, some have argued that in fact rule-consequentialism is the ideal theory to support such rules.

Let us then review this argument for rule-consequentialism. The argument begins with the idea that the goal of morality is to produce the best consequences. It moves on to the suggestion that the moral theory whose acceptance would produce the best consequences is rule-consequentialism. Call this the consequentialist argument for rule-consequentialism.

The consequentialist argument for rule-consequentialism has three weaknesses. The first is that the consequentialist argument for rule-consequentialism may be wrong to claim that the moral theory whose acceptance would produce the best consequences is rule-consequentialism. Actually, I think a very good case can be made that here the consequentialist argument for rule-consequentialism is not wrong. But I admit that the issue is hardly settled.

The second weakness in the consequentialist argument for rule-consequentialism is that the argument starts with a consequentialist premise, namely that the goal of morality is to produce the best consequences. This consequentialist premise is questioned by many. It needs defense. The consequentialist argument for rule-consequentialism cannot provide that defense. In a way, the consequentialist argument for rule-consequentialism starts further downsteam than it should.

The third weakness in the consequentialist argument for rule-consequentialism is that it conflates practical questions with epistemic ones. The question of which moral theory is the one whose acceptance would produce the best consequences is largely a question about the practical consequences of people's having this or that set of beliefs. The question of which moral theory is correct seems to be a different question. Because the questions are different, they might get different answers. For example, theory A might be the moral theory whose acceptance would produce the best consequences. The correct moral theory might instead be theory B. In short, this section's argument for rule-consequentialism unjustifiably supposes that the moral theory whose acceptance would produce the best consequences is also the correct moral theory.

The Reflective Equilibrium Argument for Rule-Consequentialism

The other argument for rule-consequentialism does not start from a consequentialist premise. It starts instead from the idea that, other things being at least roughly equal, a moral theory is justified to us if it identifies a fundamental moral principle that both explains why our more specific considered moral convictions are correct and provides some impartial justification for those convictions. To use the term that John Rawls made famous, we seek "reflective equilibrium" between abstract moral theory and more specific moral convictions. (See Rawls 1951, 1971, 1975.) Rule-consequentialism puts itself forward as a theory that can explain why our more specific considered moral convictions are correct and that can provide some impartial justification for them.

The idea that we should test proposed moral theories against our convictions strikes many as preposterous. Why not assume all our moral convictions are incorrect, or at least reserve judgment on them? Looking back at history, we see that many people's convictions were wrongheaded. We ourselves might be similarly mistaken. Surely there is some more reliable fulcrum in moral thinking than contemporary prejudice.

On the other hand, some moral judgments seem virtually impossible to deny. One is that torturing people for fun is wrong. Another is that the fact that an act would make an innocent person suffer counts morally against it, that is, counts towards the act's being morally wrong. These and other convictions of about the same level of specificity seem so secure that any moral theory had better agree with them. No moral theory seizes our confidence to the extent that we would be willing to take that theory's side in a fight against such convictions.

So, how well do rule-consequentialism's implications match our convictions? We have convictions that there are negative moral duties not to physically harm others, not to steal, not to break promises, positive moral duties to aid family and friends with one's own resources, and weaker positive duties to help strangers, including those who will never be in a position to reciprocate. Let us crudely divide these into two groups: prohibitions on action, and duties to aid.

Rule-consequentialism claims that individual acts of murder, torture, promise-breaking, and so on can be wrong even when they result in somewhat more good than not doing them would. The rule-consequentialist reason for this is that the general internalization of a code prohibiting murder, torture, promise-breaking, and so on would clearly result in more good than general internalization of a code with no prohibitions on such acts.

Rule-consequentialism also holds that, over time, agents should help those in greater need, especially the worst off, even if the personal sacrifices involved in helping them add up to a significant sacrifice for the agents. The sacrifice to the agents is to be assessed aggregately (that is, by how much sacrifice is required over a span of one's life), not iteratively (that is, by how much sacrifice is required for each individual action in a series of actions). (For the iterative/aggregative distinction, see Cullity 1995 and Scanlon 1998.) This general rule would apply in all sorts of cases. It isn't about merely what the rich should do. So, although it would apply when a rich person can help a poor one, it would also apply when a poor person can help another poor one, and even when a poor person can help a rich one. The reason this rule does not become excessively demanding is that sacrifice is to be assessed aggregatively, not iteratively. Agents would of course *be allowed* to make sacrifices beyond the "significant aggregative personal cost" threshold, but would not be *required* to go beyond this threshold, even to save lives, except where sacrifice of the agent's life is necessary to save the world, or even just some significant proportion of humanity.

Rule-consequentialists contend that their theory does a better job of cohering with these convictions and providing some impartial justification for them than its rival theories do. Let me illustrate by considering three of rule-consequentialism's consequentialist rivals – maximizing-act-consequentialism, satisficing-act-consequentialism (Slote 1984, 1985, 1989, 1992), and scalar consequentialism. (See 10: THE SCALAR APPROACH TO UTILITARIANISM.)

Maximizing-act-consequentialism insists that the only acts that are morally required – or permissible – are ones that bring about the best consequences. This is a claim that satisficing-act-consequentialism rejects on the grounds that it is too restrictive about which acts are morally permissible. Satisficing-act-consequentialism maintains that an act is morally permissible if and only if that act's (expected) results are good enough. As long as its threshold for good enough consequences is set a fair distance from the best consequences, satisficing-act-consequentialism will hold that many more acts are morally permissible than just the ones with the best consequences. Satisficing-act-consequentialism seems correct that maximizing-act-consequentialism is too restrictive.

Furthermore, maximizing-act-consequentialism very often demands more self-sacrifice for the sake of others than seems reasonable to demand. Making extreme sacrifices for others is highly admirable, but often beyond what true duty requires. So an attraction of satisficing-act-consequentialism is that the theory is less demanding than maximizing-act-consequentialism.

However, satisficing-act-consequentialism is open to devastating counterexamples – that is, examples where our considered moral convictions go strongly against the theory. Here is an example I have borrowed (and slightly altered) from Tim Mulgan (Mulgan 2001: 129–42). Suppose I can push one button that would save fifty people from terrible pain, or I can push another button that would save forty-nine from terrible pain, or I can do nothing, which would save none of them from any pain. Maximizing-act-consequentialism tells me to push the button that will save all fifty from terrible pain. Satisficing-act-consequentialism presumably tells me that saving fifty would be good but saving forty-nine would also be permissible.

Satisficing-act-consequentialism's claim about that case seems plausible if there is a significant enough cost to me in saving the extra person from the terrible pain. But let us build into the example that there is no cost to me whatever I choose in this situation. Thus, in this case, maximizing-act-consequentialism is not at all demanding. Still, satisficing-act-consequentialism says that doing less than the best is morally permissible even in this case. That conclusion conflicts sharply with the confident conviction most of us have that, at least in such cost-free situations, failing to help people is morally wrong. So satisficing-act-consequentialism does not sit in reflective equilibrium with our confident moral convictions.

Scalar consequentialism is much more radical than satisficing-act-consequentialism. As Norcross says a number of times, the scalar approach claims that duty, obligation, right and wrong are not fundamental moral categories. Scalar consequentialism offers to make do with just the concepts morally better and morally worse. In effect, it rejects the concepts morally required, morally permissible, and morally wrong.

Of course there is difficulty about which acts are permissible and which ones are not. Rejecting the very distinction between permissible and wrong, however, creates enormously greater difficulties. First of all, we have very confident convictions that certain acts are morally wrong, for example torturing people for fun. Second, we have very confident convictions that certain properties of acts count towards the act's being morally wrong. The example mentioned above is that an act that would make an innocent person suffer counts towards the act's being morally wrong. Scalar consequentialism seems ill equipped to agree with such convictions, since scalar consequentialism abandons the very idea of wrongness.

Furthermore, as Mill suggested, the distinction between permissible and wrong action is closely connected with the imposition of sanctions. Guilt, blame, and social exclusion, and sometimes other forms of punishment are appropriately attached to impermissible (that is, wrong) action, and not appropriately attached to permissible action. So if the very distinction between permissible and wrong action disappears, then with it go the practices of imposing guilt, blame, and other sanctions. Scalar consequentialism thus seems to call for a radical transformation of our moral conceptual scheme.

Let me drive home this point by stressing just how counterintuitive the act-utilitarian and scalar utilitarian views of blame are. As Norcross rightly indicates, Sidgwick saw that the strictly act-utilitarian approach to blame is that an agent is not to be blamed just because he or she fails to maximize utility; rather, the agent is to be blamed just if blaming that agent will maximize utility. Well, true, blame and other forms of punishment really are inappropriate in some cases when they are very ineffective – or even counterproductive! Still, cases where they are inappropriate are exceptional. The normal and central kind of case is one in which wrongness and blameworthiness are intimately connected. Forms of utilitarianism that deny this intimate connection are swimming in the wrong direction.

Not all forms of utilitarianism do deny the connection. Norcross mentions the view "WA2: An action is wrong if and only if it is optimific to punish the agent." But he makes two points against WA2.

One is that "it can sometimes be optimific to punish a utility-maximizer." That point is right. Its implication is that, on such occasions, according to WA2, the utility maximizer did wrong. Norcross clearly thinks it implausible that the utility-maximizer did wrong, even if punishing him would be optimific. So Norcross thinks this undermines WA2.

Norcross also attacks WA2 on the basis of the principle that correct moral judgments must be universalizable. This he construes as the principle that, if you did an act exactly like mine in intention and consequence and you were in exactly similar circumstances to mine, then if your action was wrong so was mine. He points out that, though you and I were in exactly similar circumstances and had the same intentions and our acts had the same results, it may be optimific to punish one of us but not the other. According to WA2, since it is optimific to punish one of us but not the other, one of us acted wrongly and the other didn't. But how could that be, given that our acts were in the same circumstances, had the same intentions, and produced the same consequences?

I think WA2 is implausible in the light of this objection of Norcross's, but we can modify WA2 to sidestep the objection. Consider WA3: an action is wrong if and only if it is optimific to punish (or at least blame) more or less any mentally competent adult who does the act. This is a rule-consequentialist theory of wrongness and its intimate connection with punishment. WA3 may be faulty, but it is a lot less obviously so than maximizing-act-consequentialism or scalar consequentialism.

There are interesting arguments in favor of scalar consequentialism. To my mind, the most powerful is that scalar consequentialism bypasses the notorious problem of drawing a line between permissible and wrong action. However, if a moral theory is justified to us only if it can explain why our more specific considered moral convictions are correct, if a moral theory is justified to us only if it can make sense of the moral convictions in which we have most confidence, then scalar consequentialism is just too radical.

I will later consider whether there are equally strong objections to rule-consequentialism, but first I will explain certain aspects of the formulation of rule-consequentialism.

The Focus on Internalization of Rules

There have been a variety of different formulations of rule-consequentialism. The one I currently favor is:

> Moral wrongness is determined by the code of rules whose internalization by the overwhelming majority of everyone everywhere in each new generation has maximum expected value in terms of well-being, with some priority for the worst off.

Why the reference to internalization? Indeed, rule-consequentialism was frequently formulated as holding that moral wrongness is determined by the code of rules the compliance with which would produce the best consequences.

Although compliance with rules is often the most important consequence of internalizing them, compliance isn't the only consequence of internalizing a rule. For example, internalizing a rule might make you happy, or sad, quite independently of any acts that rule leads you to perform. More importantly, remember the point above about the choice between a world where everyone cares strongly about some others but only weakly about the rest, and a world where everyone cares equally though weakly about everyone. Suppose the only way to get everyone to have internalized the rule "maximize the good, impartially considered" to the point where everyone would comply with this rule on every occasion is to make everyone completely and fully impartial. And suppose the only way to do that is to bring about the arrangement where everyone cares equally though weakly about everyone. The lack of strong feelings would drain the world of much (if not most) of its charm. It would be a world where everyone is mostly apathetic about everything. This would not be good. So a consequence of internalizing the rule "maximize the good, impartially considered" would be a degree of apathy that would not be good, though it would be compatible with everyone's complying with the rule "maximize the good, impartially considered."

If we do a cost–benefit analysis of the internalization of rules, we include the costs and benefits of any acts of compliance with those rules that result from the internalization of the rules. But, as we have seen, there can be other costs of rule-internalization. Intuitively, it seems that any cost or benefit of rule-internalization should be considered, not just whatever acts of compliance result. So rule-conse-quentialism is formulated in terms of internalization instead of more narrowly in terms of compliance.

The Majority of People in Each New Generation

The reason for not framing rule-consequentialism in terms of internalization of rules by the present generation is that the present generation has already inter-nalized a morality (or rather, one or another of many moralities). The present gen-eration may have already internalized distinctions and taboos that really are not justified. In any case, the cost–benefit analysis of rule internalization should not be skewed by moral attitudes people have already learned.

Let me illustrate why this is important. Suppose we run a cost–benefit analysis on a code of rules that requires religious toleration and forbids religious discrim-ination. Now suppose the people who will have to internalize this code have already been brought up to think that (e.g.) people of one religion are greatly superior to people not of that religion. Suppose they also believe that, in compe-titions for responsible or prestigious jobs, people of that religion should be given preference over people not of that religion. The costs of unlearning those atti-tudes and replacing them with a wholehearted commitment to religious tolera-tion and religious equality would be significantly higher than they would be if the religious toleration and equality were to be internalized by new generations, i.e. by humans who had not already been indoctrinated with religious discrimination and intolerance.

Of course, I am not denying that it is a good to try to get grown people to become more tolerant and accepting of others. Nor am I denying that the costs of doing so can be dwarfed by the benefits. What I am saying is that those costs of correcting people's moral beliefs should not be part of a cost–benefit analysis of the ideal moral code. Rather, we should think about a moral code's internal-ization by fairly young people, before they get indoctrinated into some alternative moral attitudes and beliefs. To be sure, there still will be considerable internaliza-tion costs. But they won't be skewed by having to correct past mistakes.

Expected rather than Actual Value of Rules

Above, I pointed to the rough match between rule-consequentialism's implica-tions and our considered convictions both about wrongness and about the inti-mate connection we take wrongness to have to blameworthiness. To the extent that we stress these points, we will need to formulate rule-consequentialism in terms of expected value rather than in terms of actual value.

Suppose that some change in social rules turns out to have much worse consequences impartially considered than people expected. For example, imagine a society where there are fairly pervasive prohibitions on sexual promiscuity. Suppose that at some point in time the sexual prohibitions are replaced by much more permissive rules about sex, and the reason for the change is precisely to permit more pleasure between consenting adults. However, let us suppose that, without anyone's predicting this, a terrible sexually transmitted disease spreads through the population via the new promiscuity. Here is an example where the actual value of a new set of rules is very different from its expected value.

Rule-consequentialists face a choice here. Should their theory claim that moral wrongness is whatever is forbidden by the rules that really would have the best consequences? Or should the theory be formulated in terms of the rules with the highest expected value?

Well, clearly it would be ridiculous to suggest that people should be blamed for failing to follow the rules that really would have the best consequences. The reason this would be ridiculous is that people cannot realistically be expected to know what those rules are. Far more plausible is the suggestion that people are blameworthy if they fail to follow the rules with the highest expected value.

So blameworthiness seems to be tied to expected value rather than to actual value. Wrongness is tied to blameworthiness. So, presumably, wrongness is also linked to expected value rather than to actual value.

There are many complexities about which perspective is appropriate for determining expected value. Is the right perspective merely the perspective of the agent? What if this agent is willfully ignorant of well-publicized information? So should we instead think of expected value as determined by the expectations of the average person in the society? Or by the publicized expectations of experts of the time? These difficult questions are unresolved amongst rule-consequentialists.

This much is clear, however. If rule-consequentialists want to maintain a tight connection between wrongness and blameworthiness, they need to specify wrongness by reference to prohibitions with high expected value, not to ones with high actual value.

Distribution

One of the main objections to utilitarianism has been that the greatest overall utility might be achieved by a distribution of benefits and burdens that leaves some very badly off and some very well off. In short, an equal distribution of utility might not maximize utility.

On careful reflection, however, not all increases in equality of outcome are good. To take the standard example of this, suppose the only way to equalize eyesight is to "level down" those with good eyes to the incapacity of the blind. Equality of outcome achieved through such leveling down is not in any way good.

So many who thought of themselves as attaching value to equality of outcome now favor giving priority to the worst off. Intuitively, it does seem very plausible that the worst off should have some degree of priority in our thinking. This idea has come to be called the principle of according priority to the worst off, or the principle of prioritarianism. (See Parfit 1997.)

Aggregate well-being combined with some priority for the worst off can be expressed mathematically as a weighted sum of well-being. This brings the priority toward the worst off into the calculation of the sum of well-being. For the sake of illustration, consider a comparison of two alternative possible moral codes, each of which could be internalized by a society containing only two groups of people. (See the illustration in tabular form, "Alternative possible moral codes." In this illustration, the people of group A are the worst off. When their welfare is given greater weight, the greater equality of well-being makes the Second Code preferable.) This example is highly abstract and artificially simplistic. But a more realistic example would bring in lots of detail and complexity that would be ultimately irrelevant to the point at issue here.

The first code would produce more well-being if well-being is calculated strictly impartially: 1,010,000 > 980,000. But if our calculation of total good gives twice the weight to the well-being of each of the worst off as it does to the well-being of each of the better off, then the calculation comes out favoring the more equal distribution: 1,060,000 > 1,020,000.

Rule-consequentialism can indeed be formulated so as to give extra weight to the well-being of the worse off. Often such kinds of rule-consequentialism are

Alternative Possible Moral Codes

FIRST CODE	Units of well-being		Total units of well-being for both groups	
	Per person	Per group	Impartially calculated	Weighted with worst off × 2 and others × 1
10,000 people in group A	1	10,000	1,010,000	1,020,000
100,000 people in group B	10	1,000,000		

SECOND CODE	Units of well-being		Total units of well-being for both groups	
	Per person	Per group	Impartially calculated	Weighted with worst off × 2 and others × 1
10,000 people in group A	8	80,000	980,000	1,060,000
100,000 people in group B	9	900,000		

called "distribution-sensitive rule-consequentialism." Alternatively, rule-consequentialism can be formulated so as to insist on giving equal weight to each individual's well-being, no matter how well off or badly off the person is. Rule-consequentialism of this second form is traditional rule-utilitarianism.

Rule-utilitarianism has on its side that it so clearly is an impartial moral theory. But the choice between the codes outlined in the tables above seems to many people to suggest that distribution-sensitive rule-consequentialism is more plausible than rule-utilitarianism. I think the matter is as yet unresolved. (See Hooker 2000.)

Old Objections

One old objection to rule-consequentialism is that it could lead to disaster. The objection supposes that rule-consequentialism is very strict about no exceptions to rules. For example, the objection imagines that the theory tells one not to take others' property without their permission, no matter what.

But suppose the only way for you to get to the nuclear power plant in time to turn off the switch and prevent nuclear disaster is to take my car without my permission. Would rule-consequentialism forbid you to take my car in this situation? No, for one rule whose general internalization would be optimific is a rule telling us to break other rules when necessary to prevent disaster. Note that the injunction to break other rules when necessary to prevent disaster is not an invitation to break other rules whenever this would produce merely a little more good. (This is because, if the difference in the amount of good between two possible outcomes between which you are choosing is only slight, then either both outcomes must be disasters or neither outcome is.)

Turn now to another objection to rule-consequentialism. According to its critics, rule-consequentialism faces a dilemma: either the theory is indistinct in that it collapses into extensional equivalence to act-consequentialism (i.e., it makes the same acts right and wrong, even if different criteria are used), or it is incoherent. The objection that rule-consequentialism collapses into extensional equivalence to act-consequentialism has different versions.

One version claims that rule-consequentialism would endorse just one rule: "maximize the good" (Smart 1973: 11–12). This objection assumes that, if each person successfully complies with a rule requiring each person to maximize good consequences, then good would be maximized. That good would be maximized under these conditions has been challenged. But whether or not everyone's complying with the act-consequentialist principle would maximize good, we should consider the wider costs and benefits of rule internalization. Would good in fact be maximized by the internalization of a rule requiring everyone always to do what will maximize good? It would not. To internalize just the one act-consequentialist rule is to become disposed to try to comply with it. Here we have act-consequentialism made into the agent's decision procedure. We've already seen why this is unlikely to be felicitous.

Another version of the collapse objection claims that, when some normally good rule calls for a sub-optimal action, rule-consequentialism must favor adding exception clauses to the rule so as to allow optimal action in these circumstances. And the same sort of reasoning will apply for all situations in which following some rule would not bring about the best consequences. Once all the exception clauses are added, rule-consequentialism requires the same actions as act-consequentialism.

This objection also won't work against the kind of rule-consequentialism that ranks systems of rules in terms of the expected consequences of their internalization. Consider, for example, widespread awareness of a ready willingness to make exceptions to rules. This widespread awareness could undermine people's ability to rely confidently on others to behave in agreed-upon ways. Furthermore, when comparing alternative rules, we must also consider the relative costs of teaching them. Clearly, the costs of teaching endlessly complicated and qualified rules to everyone would be too high. But once we admit that rule-consequentialism endorses rules that are limited in number and complexity, these rules would not be extensionally equivalent to act-consequentialism.

But critics of rule-consequentialism think this reply impales rule-consequentialism on the other horn of the dilemma. If the ultimate goal is the maximization of good, i.e. if rules are really merely a means to an end, isn't it incoherent to follow rules when one knows this won't maximize good?

Many rule-consequentialists try to answer this objection by showing how acceptance of rule-consequentialism would actually produce better consequences than acceptance of act-consequentialism. People in a society of rule-consequentialists would be better able to rely on each other to keep promises, tell the truth, and so on.

Whether or not that reply to the incoherence objection works, there is another – and I think better – reply. Remember that the best argument for rule-consequentialism is not the consequentialist one, and so not one founded on an overarching commitment to maximize the good. As I see it, the best argument for rule-consequentialism is that it does a better job than its rivals of matching and tying together and providing an impartial justification for our moral intuitions.

Could one really be a rule-consequentialist without having maximizing the good as one's ultimate moral goal? Yes. Here's how. Consider Sue, whose moral psychology is as follows:

- Her fundamental moral motivation is to do what is impartially defensible.
- She believes that acting on impartially justified rules is impartially defensible.
- She also believes that rule-consequentialism is on balance the best account of impartially justified rules.

Sue is motivated to comply with rule-consequentialism, but maximizing the good does not come into her motivation or her justification for it.

New Objections

As old objections are overcome, new ones come into prominence. However, since these new objections are very much topics of current debate, I will merely try to indicate what they are, rather than try to address them.

One of these new objections is that rule-consequentialism turns out to be far more demanding than its defenders have appreciated. (See Carson 1991; Hooker 2003.) Another is that, even if rule-consequentialism's implications are intuitively acceptable, its account of ultimate moral reasons is implausible. (See McNaughton and Rawling 1998; Gaut 1999; Montague 2000; Arneson forthcoming; Hooker forthcoming.) Another new objection is that that rule-consequentialism does not have a plausible story to tell about the situation in which new moral codes are taught. Rule-consequentialism needs a coherent description of those who are supposed to do the teaching of new generations. How could the teachers have already internalized the ideal code themselves? If these teachers have not already internalized the ideal code, then there will be costs associated with the conflict between the ideal code and whatever they have already internalized. (I owe this objection to John Andrews, Robert Ehman, and Andrew Moore.)

Whether rule-consequentialism can survive these or other objections remains to be seen. The theory is resourceful. But its critics are penetrating and persistent.

References

Arneson, Richard (forthcoming) "Sophisticated rule-consequentialism: some simple objections," *Philosophical Issues*.

Berkeley, George (1972) "Passive obedience, or the Christian doctrine of not resisting the supreme power, proved and vindicated upon the principles of the law of nature," in D. H. Monro (ed.) *A Guide to the British Moralists*. London: Fontana.

Carson, Thomas (1991) "A note on Hooker's 'Rule consequentialism'," *Mind* 100, pp. 117–21.

Cullity, Garrett (1995) "Moral character and the iteration problem," *Utilitas* 7, pp. 289–99.

Gaut, Berys (1999) "Ragbags, hard cases, and moral pluralism," *Utilitas* 11, pp. 37–48.

Hodgson, D. H. (1967) *The Consequences of Utilitarianism*. Oxford: Oxford University Press.

Hooker, Bradford W. (2000) *Ideal Code, Real World: a Rule-Consequentialist Theory of Morality*. Oxford: Oxford University Press.

——(2003) Review of Tim Mulgan, *Demands of Consequentialism*, *Philosophy* 78, pp. 289–96.

—— (forthcoming) Reply to Arneson and McIntyre, *Philosophical Issues*.

McNaughton, David, and Piers Rawling (1998) "On defending deontology," *Ratio* 11, pp. 37–59.

Montague, Philip (2000) "Why rule consequentialism is not superior to Ross-style pluralism," in Brad Hooker, Elinor Mason, and Dale Miller (eds.) *Morality, Rules, and Consequences* (pp. 203–11). Edinburgh: Edinburgh University Press.

Mulgan, Tim (2001) *The Demands of Consequentialism*. Oxford: Oxford University Press.

Parfit, Derek (1997) "Equality and priority," *Ratio* 10, pp. 202–21.

Rawls, John (1951) "Outline of a decision procedure in ethics," *Philosophical Review* 60, pp. 177–97.

—— (1971) *A Theory of Justice*. Cambridge, MA: Harvard University Press.

—— (1975) "The independence of moral theory," *Proceedings and Addresses of the American Philosophical Association* 48, pp. 5–22.

Scanlon, T. M. (1998) *What We Owe Each Other*. Cambridge, MA: Harvard University Press.

Slote, Michael (1984) "Satisficing consequentialism," *Proceedings of the Aristotelian Society*, suppl. vol. 58, pp. 139–63.

—— (1985) *Common-sense Morality and Consequentialism*. Oxford: Oxford University Press.

—— (1989) *Beyond Optimizing*. Cambridge, MA: Harvard University Press.

—— (1992) *From Morality to Virtue*. New York: Oxford University Press.

Smart, J. J. C. (1973) "An outline of a system of utilitarian ethics," in J. J. C. Smart and Bernard Williams, *Utilitarianism: For and Against* (pp. 1–74). Cambridge: Cambridge University Press.

Warnock, G. J. (1971) *The Object of Morality*. London: Methuen.

Chapter 12

Some Implications of Utilitarianism for Practical Ethics: the Case against the Military Response to Terrorism

Bart Gruzalski

Philosophers have applied utilitarianism with great success to ethical issues including animal liberation, tax policy, and the obligations of those who have more than they need to aid those who are dying from a lack of food, clothing, medicine, and shelter. In this essay I turn to an issue that is among the most pressing topics of the first years of the twenty-first century: the war on terrorism. What we should do about terrorism, as individuals and as nations, is politically contested as I write. I believe an ethical analysis can help to clarify some of the controversial issues at stake as well as broaden the framework of the conversation. In what follows I will take a systematic look, from a utilitarian perspective, at the US military response to terrorism. My main question is whether the US military response was morally permissible from a utilitarian perspective. Throughout much of the discussion, I will focus on a more chauvinistic question: given what people knew in the days and weeks following 9/11, was the US military response the best way to protect Americans? The answer to this chauvinistic question will provide a foundation for the answer to our main utilitarian question.

The Tragedy of 9/11

The context for this discussion began on September 11, 2001, when hijackers crashed two commercial airliners into the twin towers of the World Trade Center and a third into the Pentagon. A fourth hijacked airliner crashed in a field in

Pennsylvania. In response to this tragic attack, President George W. Bush launched what he called "the war on terrorism." The aims of this war, I assume, are two:

1   To bring to justice those still living who were responsible for the events of September11, 2001.
2   To bring about a more secure world with as little terrorism in it as possible.

I believe most people share these aims. We want to punish those who are still alive and who were responsible for these attacks. We also want to prevent terrorist acts in the future and to create a safer world with as little violence in it as possible. But not everyone would agree with aim (2). In place of (2), some would substitute the following:

2a   To bring about a more secure world for *Americans* with as little terrorism in it as possible.

(2a) is clearly a chauvinistic and not a utilitarian aim. But to jettison (2a) would be a mistake. First, since (2a) is a less complex aim than (2), it will be easier to ascertain whether the military invasions of Afghanistan and Iraq have succeeded in furthering this aim. Second, when we move to a utilitarian assessment involving (2), we will be able to use and build on our discoveries in assessing whether military invasions have advanced the goal of (2a).

In the war on terrorism, those articulating the goals quickly merged (1) into (2) or (2a). The logic of this is plausible. Unless those who caused the events of 9/11 are caught and held responsible, they could initiate further terrorist acts. Hence the aim of security includes bringing those responsible for 9/11 to justice. Following this line of thought, I too will focus on security and bring issues of punishment and responsibility into the discussion only when they impact on strategies for maximizing security from terrorism

Security

Although security of person and property is the foundation for a utilitarian theory of rights, security from *terrorism* is not a customary component of a utilitarian calculus. A secure world is, among other things, as free as possible from the physical and psychological effects of the violence brought about by terrorism. The physical effects of terrorism include killing, maiming, and the destruction of property. The psychological effects of terrorism fall into two different categories. The first category encompasses the psychological effects of being a victim of terrorism or being in a personal relationship with someone who is a victim of terrorism. This category includes shock, fear, stress, pain, horror, sympathy, grief, and more. The second category encompasses psychological effects in those who have not experienced a terrorist attack and are not in a personal relationship with someone who has been attacked. It includes the fear created by media presentations and government warnings about possible attacks on civilians and infrastructure. I will not include this second category in what follows, in part because such presentations and warnings cause fear and concern that, at least sometimes, have little to do with foreseeable threats based on available evidence. I will focus on the physical effects of terrorism and the psychological effects directly associated with these physical effects. They include, among others, pain, suffering, grief, and loss. These are all explicitly within the traditional scope of a utilitarian approach.

Terrorism

Although the above paragraphs refer to terrorism, what constitutes terrorism is not straightforward. The first question is about who can perform a terrorist action. Some want to limit terrorist actions to the actions of individuals or small groups. Others want to include the actions of nations and armies. A second question is whether, as the media and government often assert, violent acts against soldiers and military installations are acts of terrorism. A final issue is whether we can find any objective grounds for identifying a person (or group or state) as a terrorist. The idea is often expressed by the claim that one person's freedom fighter is another person's terrorist.

Two central features of terrorist acts cut through these contentious issues. First, a terrorist act is an act that is intended to inflict injury or death on civilians. However, not all acts that intentionally inflict harm on civilians are terrorist acts. A burglar may intentionally kill the civilian she is robbing but that does not make her act an act of terrorism or turn her into a terrorist. The second central feature of a terrorist act allows us to distinguish between the act of a murderous robber and the act of a terrorist. For an act to be an act of terrorism, the agent not only has to intend to injure or kill civilians, but her act has to be intended to serve a political agenda. Most robbers who commit violence are not doing so because they have a political agenda. On the other hand, those responsible for crashing the airplanes into the twin towers intended to injure and kill civilians and had a political agenda.

These two central features of terrorist acts provide criteria for clarifying the three issues above: who can be a terrorist, whether an attack against a military target can be an act of terrorism, and whether one person's freedom fighter is another person's terrorist. First, the two features of terrorism do not limit the agents of terrorism to individuals and groups but also allow for state terrorism. Second, an attack on a military installation is not an act of terrorism but a military act. Third, one person's freedom fighter is not necessarily another person's terrorist. A person is a terrorist only if she is trying to inflict injury or death on civilians. A freedom fighter might not do this but, instead, only attack military personnel and military installations. Such a freedom fighter would not be a terrorist. On the other hand, a person may be a freedom fighter who also tries to inflict injury and death on civilians as a way of obtaining freedom. Such a freedom fighter would be a terrorist. Freedom fighters sometimes are, and sometimes are not, terrorists.

Foreseeable Consequences versus Actual Consequences

When we assess actions on the basis of chauvinistic consequentialism or of utilitarianism, we are taking either a prudential or a moral perspective to assess what should be done or what should not be done. When we do this, we assess actions and policies on the basis of the evidence available at the time of action. The perspective of hindsight, although significantly better informed, is not the perspective to which people have access at the time of decision-making. Instead, those considering what they should do must make reasonable predictions on the basis of the best available evidence. For this reason, in making a utilitarian or a consequentialist assessment, we look to the foreseeable consequences of an action or policy, not its actual "hindsight" consequences. In addition, we need to be responsive to the fact that most acts and policies have several mutually exclusive foreseeable consequences that are of different values (e.g., rolling a die has six foreseeable consequences and we may value some more than others). In assessing an action or a policy, we take into account both the probability and the value of each of these relevant foreseeable consequences. An action, on this account, is right if and only if it is the best overall action a person can perform to avoid producing negative consequences and to bring about positive consequences. For example, even though the odds are very low that passing on a blind curve on a rural road will cause a horrific head-on collision, because the negative value of this highly improbable foreseeable consequence is so great, the overall assessment of the foreseeable consequences of passing another vehicle on a blind curve is negative. Hence, performing this act would typically be wrong on a utilitarian approach.

In applying both chauvinistic consequentialism and utilitarianism I use the following standard conception of consequences: an event is a consequence of an action only if there is some other action the agent could have performed that would have prevented the occurrence of the event in question. For example, my garden producing tomatoes in October is a consequence of my planting tomatoes in May, since, had I only planted other vegetables, there would be no October tomatoes. But not only did the tomatoes need to be planted, they needed watering. This example shows that an event may be among the consequences of several actions performed by several agents. Since these actions were performed on different occasions and could have been performed by different people, it is accurate to say that my October tomatoes are both a consequence of someone's watering them and a consequence of someone's planting them.

Chauvinistic Consequentialism

From a utilitarian point of view, (2a) is not a moral aim. Imagine, for example, there were two ways to achieve (2a): without killing anyone or by killing tens of thousands of innocent civilians. From a utilitarian perspective, achieving security for Americans by unnecessarily killing tens of thousands of innocent civilians would be morally repugnant. But not everyone would accept this critique of the chauvinistic perspective. Some might claim that their aim is to protect American citizens and any harm inflicted on others is irrelevant.

Rather than continuing this debate, I will adopt chauvinistic consequentialism (as specified in (2a)) and will return to a utilitarian perspective later. I take this approach for several reasons. I do not want to alienate those readers who adopt a chauvinistic perspective. There is much to discover within the parameters of the chauvinistic perspective regardless of whether the reader wishes, in the end, to adopt utilitarianism. And by initially limiting our investigation into the foreseeable consequences of the military war on terrorism to its impact on the security of Americans, we will be able to focus our attention without distraction on this limited range of foreseeable consequences. Later we will incorporate the foreseeable consequences on Americans into a full utilitarian assessment.

The Nonmilitary Context of the War against Terrorism

After 9/11, people around the world stood with America. The French newspaper *Le Monde*, immediately after 9/11, proclaimed: "Nous sommes tous Américains (We are all Americans)." As thousands of British people tearfully waved American flags, the band outside Buckingham Palace played "The Star-Spangled Banner" during a changing of the guard. The European leaders of NATO, for the first time in the organization's history, invoked Article 5 of its charter, calling on its 19 member nations to treat the attack on America as an attack on them all – a particularly impressive action, since Article 5 had been intended to guarantee American action to defend Europe from attack. These facts demonstrate that the world was in full sympathy with the United States and partly explain why most of the world's governments were collaborating in efforts to break up terrorist cells and to arrest terrorists. Governments around the world were shutting down flows of money that could support terrorism. Known terrorists could no longer move about freely. Security was tightened at border crossings, airports, and elsewhere to prevent the movement of terrorists and to thwart further attacks.

These aggressive actions to combat terrorism were part of the backdrop for the military effort but were not part of it. It is crucial to separate these nonmilitary actions from the military invasions to avoid trivializing the issues at stake by creating an imaginary straw man position. For example, Vice President Richard Cheney has claimed that those critical of post-9/11 military tactics would have done nothing. That is not true. Even those critical of military action would have embraced the worldwide clampdown on terrorists and their financing methods immediately after 9/11.

In what follows I am only assessing military actions. I assume that the efforts of arresting terrorists, impeding their movements across borders, breaking up terrorist cells, and blocking their funding would happen with or without the military actions of the US. The question is, given the backdrop of these *nonmilitary* actions, would the *military* invasions of Afghanistan and Iraq foreseeably make people safer? In the next few sections I will discuss these invasions from the chauvinistic consequential perspective.

The Invasion of Afghanistan

At 1 p.m. on October 7, 2001, President George W. Bush addressed the nation announcing the beginning of the war in Afghanistan. "On my orders," said the President, "the United States military has begun strikes against Al Qaeda terrorist training camps and military installations of the Taliban regime in Afghanistan." Bush said the point of these attacks was to "defend not only our precious freedoms, but also the freedom of people everywhere to live and raise their children free from fear." In addition, the attacks were intended to capture or kill Osama bin Laden, the person declared the mastermind of the 9/11 attacks.

In assessing whether the military invasion of Afghanistan was likely to make Americans safer, it is natural to ask the hindsight question: Are we safer because we invaded Afghanistan? The problem with this question and any answer is the implicit focus on actual consequences. Our interest here are the foreseeable chauvinistic consequences: were the foreseeable consequences of going to war positive for the safety and security of Americans?

Even this question is misleading. It suggests that we had only two options: invade or do nothing except the nonmilitary actions against terrorism cited above. We will assess a nonmilitary alternative below that included not only the background actions of breaking up terrorist cells, arresting terrorists, and cutting off funds from terrorists, but also other elements that plausibly would help undermine terrorism. Nonetheless, it is worth beginning with the non-comparative question: would the military invasion of Afghanistan foreseeably make Americans safer than they would have been had the US not invaded Afghanistan?

Those who planned and carried out the invasion saw that the invasion had at least three different categories of foreseeable consequences. The first was the defeat of Al Qaeda, the destruction of Al Qaeda camps and munitions, the capture or killing of many members of Al Qaeda, the possible capture or killing of Osama Bin Laden, as well as the injuries and deaths to US troops and their allies. The second was the harm that would be inflicted on civilians: directly with our weapons; indirectly through disruption of relief workers who were in Afghanistan to prevent starvation in the coming winter. The third was the foreseeable effect of these first two foreseeable consequences on the safety of Americans.

There was little doubt that eventually the US, with its allies, would destroy the training camps of Al Qaeda in Afghanistan and thereby severely disrupt the way Al Qaeda had traditionally functioned. Furthermore, it was foreseeable that the US and its allies would capture or kill many of the soldiers in Al Qaeda and many of their leaders, perhaps even Osama Bin Laden. What was not likely was that a military attack against the Taliban or Al Qaeda would defeat Al Qaeda. Al Qaeda was initially composed of experienced fighters from numerous countries including Afghanistan, Pakistan, Saudi Arabia, Iraq, Egypt, Iran, Syria, and the Yemen. These men, supported by the United States, fueled an insurgency in Afghanistan that led to a Vietnam-like quagmire for Russia. After this force defeated the Russians, it continued training new recruits, began supporting itself, and was able to move freely across the porous borders of the Middle East. It was foreseeable that, as the US military publicly prepared for an invasion of Afghanistan, Al Qaeda would mutate into a mobile and decentralized force with cells throughout the world. Many thousands of trained insurgents who were still in Afghanistan on September 12, 2001 would probably soon travel to other locations in the Middle East, including their own home countries, where they would continue recruiting and training more insurgents.

This posed the first difficulty with attacking Al Qaeda. A second difficulty was that an invasion of Afghanistan would kill, maim, widow, and orphan many innocent people. Although someone might think "so what?" the fact is that these foreseeable consequences would themselves create more hatred against the United States, especially since neither Afghanistan nor the Taliban had attacked the US. Should the escalation of hatred against the US provoke yet another "so what?" it needs to be pointed out that creating worldwide Islamic hatred of the US was foreseeably counterproductive to the aim of making Americans more secure. Provoking hatred of the United States throughout the Islamic world would likely lead to more attacks against Americans and so fail to satisfy the aim of security. The dynamics of retaliation guaranteed that the invasion of Afghanistan, given that many innocent people would be killed, would be counterproductive.

The most pertinent illustration of the dynamic of retaliation began on 9/11 in the United States. Within hours of the terrorist attacks on the World Trade Center and the Pentagon, *Time* magazine columnist Lance Morrow urged Americans to nourish rage and to celebrate hatred. "What's needed," he wrote, "is a unified, unifying Pearl Harbor soul of purple American fury – a ruthless indignation that doesn't leak away in a week or two." Morrow wanted the US to hit back hard, with a "policy of focused brutality." That call for vengeance was the outcome of the violence on 9/11. But just as the terrorist acts of 9/11 produced a Lance Morrow, it was foreseeable that acting out the hatred, ruthlessness, and retributory fury of US, Lance Morrows would create Islamic Lance Morrows who would celebrate hatred, ruthlessness, and retributory fury toward the US. When these Islamic Lance Morrows acted on their hatred and attacked Americans, their acts would foreseeably propagate more American Lance Morrows. These new Lance Morrows would urge yet more violence against those that they claimed were responsible for this new violence, and the foreseeable result would be more hatred of Americans and more violence against Americans. Few victims of violence, or their friends, or their progeny, will perceive the last blow against them as the blow that makes everything all right. These victims will feel that they have been wronged and will want to even up the score. When these victims retaliate, those who thought they were using violence to end violence will see the new retaliation as yet another wrong justifying yet more violence. This is the dynamics of retaliation and it leads only to more and more violence. Israel illustrates this dynamic, whichever side you think has a more just cause. Every suicide bomber motivates the Israeli government to further military action against Palestinians, and every additional Israeli military action motivates more Palestinian hatred, more hopelessness, and more revenge. Attacking the Taliban and Al Qaeda in Afghanistan would foreseeably further the cycle of violence.

It might be thought that the US was only responding to violence and so its military action would be seen as justified. There are three problems with this thought. First, neither Afghanistan nor the Taliban had attacked the United States. Second, the invasion would kill thousands of innocent civilian Muslims, inflicting many more civilian casualties per capita on Afghanistan than the attack on the Twin Towers inflicted on the United States. Finally and decisively, once the dynamics of retaliation has begun its cycle, the belief that your side's violence is justified, even if you are correct from some pie-in-the-sky perspective, does not protect your side from this cycle of retaliation. It is generally implausible to expect the most recent victim of violence to agree that the violence against her and her loved ones was justified. Maiming and killing innocent Afghan men, women and children would foreseeably only intensify hatred and encourage retaliation.

It might also be thought that the US was using "smart" weapons which foreseeably would cause very few civilian deaths and so avoid a cycle of retaliation. This response does not hold up under scrutiny. First, there is the targeting problem. "Smart" bombs are only as smart as those doing the targeting and, even then, a percentage of them go off course. Every technology has a failure rate. The personnel who target bombs also make mistakes. But the biggest problem with targeting was that information about targets was flimsy. The result was predictable: the US bombed farms and villages housing innocent civilians and even bombed wedding gatherings. A second and even more serious problem was that several of the weapons were known to inflict injury and death on innocent civilians. The best example is the cluster bomb. Human Rights Watch had called for a global moratorium on cluster bombs because they cause unacceptable civilian casualties. Each cluster bomb contains smaller bombs, called "bomblets," and these scatter, depending on the type of bomb used, over an area about the size of one or several football fields, producing a dispersal pattern that cannot be targeted precisely. The most commonly used cluster bomb contains 202 bomblets and there is a high initial failure rate (estimated at 20 percent in Afghanistan) of the bomblets to explode. The result is numerous unexploded soda-can-sized yellow "bomblets" that lie in wait for a curious child's touch or playful kick. A single bomblet can kill anyone within 150 feet (45 meters) and severely injure a person within 300 feet (90 meters). Used in the 1991 Persian Gulf War, these unexploded bomblets have later exploded, killing more than 1,500 Kuwaiti and Iraqi civilians since the war finished and injuring over 2,500 more civilians. When millions of bomblets are dropped on a country, even a small failure rate – a fraction of the 20 percent failure rate in Afghanistan – would foreseeably cause widespread civilian casualties, many of whom would be children.

The US military began using cluster bombs in the first week of bombing. Within three months of the start of the bombing in Afghanistan, US planes had dropped cluster bombs on more than a hundred cities in Afghanistan. The bombs foreseeably would kill and maim innocent civilians, many of whom would likely be children. The result was foreseeable: the US would make enemies throughout the Islamic world and create worldwide support for Al Qaeda.

Those defending the war may reply, again, that US security is worth the price of worldwide Islamic hatred. This rejoinder misses the point. It is not hatred which is the focus here, but the blowback in terms of further attacks that would make Americans less safe. To claim that the attempt to achieve security though this invasion was worth the price of hatred is, in this context, as nonsensical as claiming that this military attempt to achieve security was worth the price of making Americans less secure.

From a purely chauvinistic perspective, the invasion was wastefully counterproductive if the goal was to provide security for Americans. Mechanisms to protect Americans from further terrorist attacks were already in place. Heightened security, breaking up terrorist cells, arresting terrorists, and stopping the flow of terrorist financing was plausibly as good a defense as one could command to defend Americans. Although an intact Al Qaeda organization in Afghanistan would be a security threat, it would be less of a security threat than an Al Qaeda organization mutating across the globe and fully supported by growing worldwide Islamic hatred against the US. The invasion of Afghanistan foreseeably would create an even more dangerous enemy with worldwide support. Increased insecurity was the most likely foreseeable consequence of the US military invasion of Afghanistan.

The Invasion of Iraq

The administration wanted a short quick war in Iraq with few US casualties. "If asked to go into conflict in Iraq, what you'd like to do is have it be a short conflict," said General Myers, Chairman of the Joint Chiefs of Staff. "The best way to do that would be to have such a shock on the system that the Iraqi regime would have to assume early on the end was inevitable." The US planned to shock the Iraqi regime by dropping 3,000 bombs on targets in Iraq during the first two days. During the same 48 hours, 800 Tomahawk missiles would be fired into Baghdad – more than during the entire 1991 Gulf War. Baghdad is not an army base or a mountainous battlefield but a city full of civilians much like Chicago, San Francisco, or New York. The planned attack, called "Shock and Awe," was intended to shock Iraqis into surrender. General Myers and US Defense Secretary Donald Rumsfeld made it plain that there would be civilian casualties. The person who thought up the strategy, Harlan K. Ullman, boasted to CBS that it would have a sudden effect "rather like the nuclear weapons at Hiroshima." This was the planned murder of civilians and the foreseeable result was a surge of hatred against the United States.

Making the proposed invasion even more foreseeably counterproductive were two claims that were being undermined as quickly as they were being made: that Iraq had links with terrorists and that it had "weapons of mass destruction." Hans Blix and the UN inspection team that he led, for example, had found no evidence of these weapons. As a result, it appeared obvious to many observers that the planned invasion had nothing to do with terrorism or the alleged "weapons of mass destruction."

For these reasons, many nations and peoples of the world were passionately opposed to the invasion of Iraq as it was being planned. Millions of people demonstrated in the US and around the world. In London, up to 2 million people marched in protest against invading Iraq. Critics of the planned US invasion claimed it would be highly counterproductive. Career diplomat John Brown, who had served at the US embassies in London, Prague, Belgrade, and Moscow, resigned in protest. In his letter of resignation he warned Secretary of State General Colin Powell that "throughout the globe, the United States is becoming associated with the unjustified use of force" and that the President's unilateral actions were "giving birth to an anti-American century." Senator James M. Jeffords, Vermont's independent US senator, also dissented. He characterized US military policy as "heading us into a miserable cycle of waging wars that isolate our nation internationally and stir up greater hatred of America." The UN would not pass a second resolution on Iraq that would authorize the invasion. The hatred and disgust for the US that would result from killing and injuring Iraqis, all of whom were either innocent civilians or people defending their country from an invader, were fully foreseeable.

President H. W. Bush, George W. Bush's father, did not try to eliminate Saddam because of "incalculable human and political costs," as he called them. "We would have been forced to occupy Baghdad and, in effect, rule Iraq," he wrote. "The US could conceivably still [after seven years] be an occupying power in a bitterly hostile land" (Bush and Snowcroft 1998). It was foreseeable that the US military would get bogged down in Iraq. It was foreseeable that Iraq would become a recruitment poster for Al Qaeda. It was foreseeable that Iraq would become a shooting-gallery for those who wanted to attack US troops.

From a narrow chauvinistic foreseeable-consequence perspective, the US invasion of Iraq was a bad decision highly counterproductive to the safety of Americans. To better appreciate just how unnecessary this was, and to prepare the grounds for a utilitarian assessment, I will explore nonmilitary alternatives to the invasions of Afghanistan and Iraq.

An Alternative to the Invasion of Afghanistan

To appreciate more fully the wasteful counterproductive military invasion of Afghanistan, we need to examine at least one plausibly efficacious nonmilitary alternative. The initial US response to 9/11, and the response of the nations of the world, was nonmilitary. Governments followed up on terrorist leads, broke up terrorist cells, made arrests, and froze the funds of groups associated with Al Qaeda. Terrorists had no place to turn, no space in which to operate, and their funds were frozen. These strategies constituted the background for a more complete nonmilitary strategy.

A fuller nonmilitary response to terrorism would have included public trials. Public trials not only promote fairness, but they can create important precedents that have significant deterrence value. The Nuremberg Trials after World War II are a perfect example. The Nazis had committed horrible atrocities against humankind. Their crimes against humanity included genocide against Jews, gypsies, blacks, and others, as well as horror-show "medical" experiments on involuntary human subjects. The Allies captured many people who were responsible for these crimes and put them on trial. These defendants had full rights to defend themselves and their defense attorneys cross-examined witnesses. Nonetheless, twenty-two of the first twenty-four defendants were found guilty and sentenced, many to death. Importantly, the outcome of the Nuremberg Trials included much more than findings of guilt. These trials generated important precedents, known as the Nuremberg Code, that set strict ethical and legal guidelines for the treatment of war criminals, of prisoners, and of medical patients.

The US had the option of creating terrorist trials modeled on the Nuremberg Trials by using a world court. This would have insured fairness and openness, set important precedents, and had the foreseeable positive effect of keeping together a coalition against terrorism. Unfortunately, the US rejected the idea of a world court and, instead, insisted on putting members of Al Qaeda on trail in military courts. Many nations criticized these closed courts, raising the concern that the defendants would not have a fair trial. Some nations refused to send terrorist suspects to the US because of concerns about fairness and the ease with which these courts could impose the death penalty. A world terrorist court, modeled on the Nuremberg Trials, would have avoided this erosion of cooperation in the war against terrorism.

In addition to protecting Americans, the US wanted to bring those responsible for 9/11 to justice. Without a military invasion, the US could not arrest Osama bin Laden or bring him out of Afghanistan. However, the Taliban had offered to turn bin Laden over if the US would supply evidence that he was involved in 9/11. Instead of offering evidence and broadening the collaboration to fight terrorism, Bush rejected this offer and simply gave an ultimatum. The opportunity was missed to try to resolve the issue peacefully and to bring the person allegedly behind the attacks to justice. It might be objected that the nonmilitary alternative would not foreseeably have led to the capture of bin Laden. There were doubts that the Taliban could have turned him over even if they wanted to do so. But there were also doubts about whether the US military could capture or kill bin Laden. What was not in doubt was that by following the nonmilitary alternative the US would avoid killing thousands of innocent civilians and would isolate bin Laden and Al Qaeda by developing communications between the US and the Taliban. In contrast, the military invasion of Afghanistan began isolating the US and, by killing thousands of innocent Muslims, created support for Al Qaeda.

An Alternative to the Invasion of Iraq

When we turn to Iraq, a nonmilitary approach was an even more obvious strategy for protecting Americans. Instead of invading Iraq, one alternative approach would have let Hans Blix and the UN inspectors finish their job. As long as inspectors were on the ground, there was zero threat from Saddam Hussein. At the point the Bush administration decided to attack, Hans Blix was saying that the inspectors would fully verify the status of weapons in Iraq in less than two months.

In addition to letting the inspectors complete their job, the US could have insisted on overflights with high altitude surveillance planes to check for weapons and military activity. The US had adequate surveillance mechanisms at its disposal. Prior to the US invasion of Iraq, the BBC published nine leaflets that the US was dropping on Iraq. One of them states: "We can see everything." It showed a satellite beaming down toward the earth and a picture of a man rolling a green barrow. Another showed the picture of a missile. The text on the front, with the pictures, warned Iraqis that they were being closely watched and should not use nuclear, biological, or chemical weapons. On the back was written:

> The coalition has superior satellite technology which allows coalition forces to see the preparation and transportation of nuclear, biological, or chemical weapons. Unit commanders will be held accountable for non-compliance.

Given that satellites can transmit pictures of license plate numbers, U.S. surveillance was more than adequate to keep the U.S. fully informed about any potential treats originating in Iraq.

Since there was no military threat from Iraq, the US and the rest of the world could have lifted sanctions against Iraq and brought Iraq into the world trading community. That is the policy the US followed with China to persuade China to stop violating human rights. With Iraq, lifting sanctions would have permitted the middle class in Iraq to regain its status and begin exercising political pressure on Saddam Hussein from within Iraq. Instead of turning Iraq into a recruitment ground for Al Qaeda, the nonmilitary approach would have foreseeably undermined the support for terrorism in the Islamic world.

Further Nonmilitary Steps to Stop Terrorism

Breaking up terrorist cells, freezing the funds of terrorist organizations, putting terrorists on trial, and isolating Al Qaeda would have constituted the first step in an alternative strategy to protect Americans. The next stage would be to take meaures to stop the spread of terrorism. To appreciate fully the importance of taking these steps, we should take note of bin Laden's publicly stated justification of his attacks on Americans as a defense of Islam against US foreign policy. To stop the growing support for Al Qaeda in the Islamic world, we must realize why many Muslims believe that America is attacking Islam. The idea that Islam needs defending against American aggression has to be appreciated, because it is this idea that is sweeping the Islamic world.

In bin Laden's eyes, the US supports corrupt leaders in Islamic countries, has violated Islamic sovereignty by stationing its military on the Arabian peninsula, and unconditionally supports the brutal Israeli treatment of Palestinians. When we put these major complaints into a world context in which the US does not speak up for the autonomy of Islamic Kashmir and does not criticize the Russians for savagely suppressing an Islamic independence movement in Chechnya, bin Laden's interpretation of the situation, even if you do not agree with each detail, reflects US foreign policy sufficiently to be persuasive. Bin Laden has publicly stated he is fighting a war to defend Islam from US aggression and foreign policy and, as CIA analyst Michael Scheuer points out in *Imperial Hubris* (Anonymous 2004), the US invasion of two sovereign Islamic states could only justify this stance and make his point of view plausible throughout the Islamic world. A recent Defense Department publication points out:

Muslims do not "hate our freedom," but rather, they hate our policies. The overwhelming majority voice their objections to what they see as one-sided support in favor of Israel and against Palestinian rights, and the longstanding, even increasing support for what Muslims collectively see as tyrannies, most notably Egypt, Saudi Arabia, Jordan, Pakistan, and the Gulf states . . . Furthermore, *in the eyes of Muslims* [italicized in the original Defense Department publication], American occupation of Afghanistan and Iraq has not led to democracy there, but only more chaos and suffering. US actions appear in contrast to be motivated by ulterior motives, and deliberately controlled in order to best serve American national interests at the expense of truly Muslim self-determination. (Defense Science Board 2004)

This is a striking explanation, from within the US Defense Department, of why bin Laden sees himself and his fellow jihadi insurgents as defending Islam against American aggression. Given bin Laden's critiques of US foreign policy, the result of the invasions of Afghanistan and Iraq were foreseeable. The Defense Department document continues:

The dramatic narrative since 9/11 [two invasions of sovereign Islamic states] has essentially borne out the entire radical Islamist bill of particulars. American actions and the flow of events have elevated the authority of Jihadi insurgents and tended to ratify their legitimacy among Muslims. Fighting groups portray themselves as the true defenders of an Ummah (the entire Muslim community) invaded and under attack – to broad public support.

Since the military invasions of Afghanistan and Iraq, bin Laden and Al Qaeda have developed from a radical organization without widespread support to the perceived defenders of Islam. The Department of Defense document makes this explicit:

What was a marginal network is now an Ummah-wide movement of fighting groups. Not only has there been a proliferation of "terrorist" groups: the unifying context of a shared cause creates a sense of affiliation across the many cultural and sectarian boundaries that divide Islam.

The invasions of Afghanistan and Iraq have created anti-American sentiments around the globe. Again, quoting the Department of Defense:

Data from Zogby International in July 2004, for example, show that the US is viewed unfavorably by overwhelming majorities in Egypt (98%), Saudi Arabia (94%), Morocco (88%), and Jordan (78%). The war has increased mistrust of America in Europe, weakened support for the war on terrorism, and undermined US credibility worldwide . . . In a State Department (INR) survey of editorials and op-eds in 72 countries, 82.5% of the commentaries were negative, 17.5% positive. Negative attitudes and the conditions that create them are the underlying sources of threats to American's national security . . .

I have quoted from the Department of Defense document because these facts conflict with much of the media and government misinformation piped into US homes by Fox News, CNN, and talk radio. As the document states, US foreign policy is increasing the threat of terrorism by fueling anti-American hatred. To combat this anti-American sentiment the US would have had to undermine bin Laden's message that US foreign policy is anti-Islam. This would not have been possible simply with strategic advertising. The policies that Bin Laden and other Muslims were criticizing were undeniably harming Muslims; they had on-the-ground objective referents. So modifying the actions that were fueling hatred would have been the only way to prevent the growth of support for Al Qaeda.

One issue mentioned by the Department of Defense document is the US support of tyrannical regimes in Saudi Arabia, Egypt, and elsewhere. The only way to address this complaint would be to allow the will of the people within each of these countries to express itself, and not to prop up unpopular regimes just because they permit the US to establish military bases or obtain cheap oil. A second issue, raised by bin Laden on several occasions, is the presence of US troops in Saudi Arabia, the sacred homeland of Islam. Allegedly these troops were in Saudi Arabia to protect the Saudis from an attack by Iraq. There was no good reason not to withdraw these troops immediately in September 2001. Iraq posed no threat to Saudi Arabia. The third and final issue, widespread throughout the Islamic world, is the unconditional support of the US for Israel in its crushing policy towards Palestinians. This too could have a resolution: the US could have begun to pursue an even-handed policy. This would involve two policy adjustments. The first would be to put on the table the goals of a secure and economically viable Israeli state as well as a secure and economically viable Palestinian state. If these two goals were on the table, there were political arrangements that the two sides could have reached that would have honored UN resolutions. The second policy adjustment would be for the US to give as much aid and support to the Palestinians as it does to the Israelis. This even-handed approach would have shown the world that the US was not supporting aggression against Muslims.

Breaking up terrorist cells, arresting terrorists, putting terrorists on trial in a world court, negotiating with the Taliban, no longer propping up tyrannical Arab regimes, pulling US troops out of Saudi Arabia, and even-handedly dealing with the Palestinian–Israeli conflict would have been a successful strategy both to protect Americans and to stop the spread of anti-American insurgents. This non-military strategy would foreseeably have cost only a small fraction of the lives or the money that would be lost by taking the extraordinary step of invading a sovereign nation. These steps would foreseeably diminish hatred of the United States in the Islamic world by making it clear that the war against terrorism was not a war against Islam. These nonmilitary steps would have constituted a productive strategy for undermining terrorism and making Americans safer. Had these been the policies the US enacted after 9/11, Al Qaeda would still be a fringe group in the mountains of Afghanistan. All of this was foreseeable by late afternoon on September 11, 2001.

From Chauvinistic Consequentialism to Utilitarianism

When we move from a chauvinistic perspective to a utilitarian one, we must look equally at everyone the action or policy will foreseeably affect. This requires that we explore the foreseeable consequences of these acts not only as they impact on Americans, but also as they impact on the people of Afghanistan and Iraq. " 'Everybody is to count for one, nobody for more than one,' " John Stuart Mill wrote, "might be written under the principle of utility as an explanatory commentary" (Mill 1861, reprinted as Part II of this volume, Ch. V, para. 36).

Once we shed the narrow chauvinistic perspective, the horror and moral repugnance of the US military response reveals itself. To avenge the attacks of 9/11, the US military was willing to maim and kill thousands of innocent Afghans, many of them women and children, as well as tens of thousands of innocent Iraqis. It was fully foreseeable that the US invasion of Afghanistan and Iraq would kill pregnant women, old men, babies, young children, adolescents, adult women, and adult men. It was fully foreseeable that in these invasions people would be left dazed, watching their loved ones die from a US bomb or bullets fired by a nervous soldier. It was fully foreseeable that there would be people who would be injured but survive without arms, legs, or eyes. It was fully foreseeable that the survivors of these attacks, as well as their friends, neighbors, and extended families, would come to hate the US and that some would want to avenge what they saw as the unjustified murder of loved ones and the unjustified destruction of their cities, towns, and villages.

The US media have barely reported these horrible foreseeable consequences as they came to be actualized. To keep up the veil of illusion, the US government has often reported civilian casualties as if they were enemy combatants. The government has taken the extraordinary step of prohibiting journalists from taking photos of the flag-draped coffins of dead American soldiers as they are returned home, on the excuse that showing their coffins would be disrespectful to the dead (never mind that President Reagan's flag-draped coffin was publicly displayed for a week out of respect to his memory). The government has done much, with the complicity of the major US media sources, to disguise the costs of the military response to 9/11. Nonetheless, it was foreseeable that the invasion of Afghanistan would kill thousands of civilians, it was foreseeable that the invasion of Iraq would kill tens of thousands of innocents, and it was foreseeable that these two invasions would kill many hundreds of US solders and maim many thousands more. Since the US government had clear alternatives to these military invasions that would been more productive in achieving security for Americans and others, we must condemn on utilitarian grounds the military war against terrorism as morally wrong.

Another Foreseeable Consequence of the Invasions

In addition to the senseless loss of human life and undermining of the security of Americans, these military invasions have also been very costly financially. Estimates at the beginning of each war put the price tag at tens of billions of dollars per year (that figure, as we now know, is ridiculously low). These billions of dollars would go mainly to the manufacturers of equipment and munitions and to companies such as Halliburton for constructing bases and providing meals for troops. These billions would foreseeably drain the US Treasury and either force the administration to raise taxes or to cut services. Instead of raising taxes, the administration gave the wealthiest people in the nation a tax cut. The foreseeable result is that the government could no longer fund a number of security measures that were promised, including more police on the streets and adequate firefighters in firehouses, and, in addition, services would be cut nationwide.

The people whose services would be cut would primarily be the poor. For example, the federal government has cut back significantly on Section 8 housing subsidies. As a result of these cutbacks, entire families would foreseeably be in the streets unless they were lucky enough to squeeze in with friends and relatives. Likewise, federal dollars for education have dried up, poor students are receiving less support, and states cannot afford to pick up much of the slack. The disbursal of tax dollars now goes to large companies that are in various ways supporting military action. What is wrong with this from a utilitarian perspective is that putting these dollars into the coffers of large companies and their middle-class and wealthy owners, rather than putting them into the service of the poor, is not doing the best we can do to further the utilitarian ends of happiness and the reduction of suffering.

It might be thought that giving a dollar to a wealthy person is akin to giving a dollar to a poor person and so taking from the poor and giving to the rich balances out. This "reverse Robin Hood logic" does not hold up under analysis. Dollars are not intrinsically valuable. Giving dollars to a rich person and a poor person are not assessed as equal from a utilitarian perspective. What is equal are the intrinsic valuables: pain, suffering, happiness. The suffering of a rich person has the same value as the suffering of a poor person; the happiness of a rich person has the same value as the happiness of a poor person. But a thousand dollars provided to a poor person can alleviate suffering or provide goods that will make a significant difference in the poor person's degree of happiness. The same thousand dollars provided to a wealthy person does not have the same effect on the wealthy person's happiness. This is common sense, and is also supported by an economic principle referred to as the law of diminishing marginal utility. The marginal utility of an item is the ability of an additional unit of that item to produce positive intrinsic value. For example, in any given sitting, the first spoonful of ice-cream is more pleasurable than the hundredth spoonful. Likewise, for a poor person or family without a decent place to live, $1,000 a month alleviates suffering and stress and produces conditions for happiness to a much greater degree than it does for a wealthy person whose income is $200,000 a year. Yet the military war on terrorism, besides making Americans less safe, is moving money from the poor and middle-class to the wealthy, thereby causing suffering, for the poor at least, that is not compensated by the comparatively slight benefit to the wealthy. This leaves the poor suffering from a lack of basic services and even conflicts with a chauvinistic policy to make all Americans more secure and happier. All of this was foreseeable as these policies were chosen and so, from a utilitarian perspective, this shifting of resources from the poor to the rich is also morally wrong.

Haven't I Forgotten that the World is Better Off without Saddam Hussein?

In the case of the invasion of Iraq, it might be objected that I have overlooked the most important foreseeable consequence of the military invasion: removing Saddam Hussein from the presidency. Since there is a media and a political consensus that the world is better off without Saddam Hussein (as President of Iraq), this foreseeable result, of itself, may be thought to justify the invasion. After all, if the world is better off, then what caused the world to be better off would be justified, at least if the "better off" world was foreseeable. There is no question that it was foreseeable that the US invasion of Iraq would remove Saddam Hussein from the presidency of Iraq.

The claim that the world is better off without Saddam Hussein needs clarification. What the claim means is that the world, today, is better than it would be today, if Saddam Hussein were still the President of Iraq. I will more clearly state this comparison as follows:

(A) After the invasion of Iraq, the world is better off with Hussein out of power than it would be if, after the invasion, Hussein were still in power.

It is clear that (A) is a rather unrealistic statement. No one would plausibly think that the invasion of Iraq would not remove Hussein from power. More telling, I think, is that this is not what people mean when they say that the world is better off without Saddam Hussein. They are not comparing two different situations in a US-occupied Iraq. What is meant, I think, is more accurately expressed by the following:

(B) An Iraq, without the invasion and without Saddam Hussein, would be a better Iraq than an Iraq without an invasion and with Hussein still in power.

This, I think, is probably what people mean. They compare two pre-invasion Iraqs and imagine one with Hussein as President and one without Hussein as President. For this comparison to be accurate, we have to assume that whoever, or whatever group, were to replace Hussein would be an improvement. Let us assume that Hussein's replacement would be a benign, peace-loving, and compassionate leader. With this assumption, which is part of what people presuppose when they say or think (B), we can agree: the world would be better off without Hussein as President of a pre-invasion Iraq.

The problem with (B) is that this does not justify an invasion and the killing of tens of thousands of innocent Muslims. If it did, the following would be true:

(C) Because the US invaded Iraq, killed tens of thousands of innocent Muslims, and removed Hussein from power, the world is better off than it would be if Hussein were still President of Iraq with Hans Blix and his team of UN and US inspectors on the watch for any sign of weapons of mass destruction.

This statement is blatantly false. The world is not better off; Americans are not better off; Muslims are not better off. Al Qaeda is stronger and that organization is better off, but that is hardly an indication that (C) is true. (C) is false.

Why then is there this parrot-like repetition in the media and by politicians that the world is better off with Hussein gone? It is because those who believe this think of Iraq with this President and then without this President but exclude the military horrors of injury, killing, and destruction that was required to remove him from office by military force. Those who parrot this statement are not thinking realistically. What they say is like saying a city is better off without its corrupt mayor when the process of removing the mayor killed tens of thousands of the city's inhabitants, injured many tens of thousands more, and bombed the city into rubble. Such sloppy thinking is implicit in the claim that the invasion of Iraq is justified because the world is better without Hussein as its President.

The Purpose of this Assessment

What is the purpose of an analysis like the one above? As an intellectual exercise it perhaps has some merit. But from a moral perspective, that's not enough. The genuine merit of the above discussion is to open up ways of thinking about the morality and efficacy of militarism and its alternatives. The war on terrorism is hardly over, as events around the world make clear. Al Qaeda and sister organizations have launched more terrorist attacks since 9/11 than in a similar period prior to 9/11. Currently the US has over 100,000 troops mired in Iraq and many thousands stationed in Afghanistan. As I write this paragraph, George W. Bush has apparently (there are still some questioning about the vote) defeated John Kerry in the 2004 presidential race. Yet neither candidate was looking at nonmilitary solutions or acknowledging the fruitless counterproductive nature of military retaliation. Neither dared to mention an even-handed approach to try to solve the Palestinian–Israeli conflict. Bush is critical of a World Court; Kerry kept silent on the topic. Neither promised a complete withdrawal of US troops from the spiritual homeland of Islam.

If we want a safer world, whether for Americans or for everyone, we need to think critically about the war on terrorism and make our voices heard. Each of us has distinctive talents, unique opportunities, and can make different contributions to this effort. Each of us has an obligation to become informed, for without doing that we cannot assess the foreseeable consequences of the policies of our government. Media conglomerates like the New York Times or Fox News will not properly inform us. Both the New York Times and the Washington Post have publicly apologized for slanting their coverage before the invasion of Iraq in support of the administration's plan to invade. So how can we in the US become informed? Fortunately we do have an efficient tool for gathering information: the internet. It is important to check in with English language sites from outside the country: the websites of *The Guardian* and *The Independent*, both newspapers in the UK, are very useful for those seeking a broader picture. There are also helpful US sites such as "Common Dreams," "Truthout," and "Democracy Now!" that gather and share information from sources around the world. Those who researched these and similar sites before the Iraq invasion knew that there was no danger of Iraq using weapons of mass destruction against the United States.

Once a person becomes informed she can ask the question: "Given the alternatives available to me, what can I do to bring about a more sane and less military approach to the problem of terrorism?" We may feel our actions will not make a difference but, from the foreseeable consequence approach, that is shortsighted. There is usually a foreseeable possibility, even if small, that a thoughtful action, statement, or series of actions and statements can precipitate a large and significant change. We need to assess our talents, abilities, and opportunities to see what we can best do to make that difference. We need to assess how best we can inform others of the broader realities not being reported by the mainstream media. We need to assess how we can join together with those of like mind to begin nonviolently to force our leaders to adopt nonmilitary strategies to defeat terrorism. Our own security, the security of people around the world, and the possibility of a secure future for our children and grandchildren depends on us. Clearly the world leaders who currently are making decisions are not going to do this for us. We need nonviolently to force a change in US foreign policy.

As important as the issue of counterproductive militarism is for the security of people on the globe, utilitarianism does not require each of us to become active in this arena. First and foremost, from a utilitarian perspective, we are to be caring toward our loved ones, caring for those who depend on us, maintain our friendships, and take care that our own basic needs are met. Without doing all of this, we can plunge into political activism and then soon suffer burnout or, worse, be unable to care for our loved ones or even ourselves. Although some people are so positioned that they can move quickly into a life that is fully activist, for most people, at least at the beginning, activism replaces more frivolous activities while the person remains centered in a life of loved ones, family, and friends, in which basic needs are met. Second, not everyone is best suited for the struggle against militarism. As I stated in the opening paragraph, the war on terrorism is among the most pressing issues of the decade. There are other equally pressing issues including, for example, climate change. Still other issues, like starvation and factory farming, have attracted the attention of utilitarian thinkers and activists. Furthermore, the world needs doctors, hospice workers, nurses, teachers, all of whom will need to spend much of their energy in their professions. What is important, from a utilitarian perspective, is to begin becoming informed about issues and then begin weaving activism into one's life as far as possible. When one takes this perspective, the military war on terrorism is a pressing issue that will attract one's attention.

This essay is drawn from a book in progress on why nonviolence is ultimately the only way to defeat terrorism.

References

Anonymous (Michael Scheuer) (2004) *Imperial Hubris: Why the West is Losing the War on Terror.* Washington: Brasser's.

Bush, Sr., George, and Brent Scowcroft (1998) "Why we didn't remove Saddam," *Time,* March 2.

Defense Science Board (2004) *Report of the Defense Science Board Task Force on Strategic Communication.* Washington: Office of the Secretary of Defense, Department of Defense.

Mill, John Stuart (1861) *Utilitarianism.* Reprinted as Part II of this volume.

Index

CARMEL CLAY PUBLIC LIBRARY
55 4th Avenue SE
Carmel, IN 46032
(317) 844-3361
Renewal Line: (317) 814-3936
www.carmel.lib.in.us